*Introduction to*

*Stratificational Linguistics*

# Introduction to
# Stratificational
# Linguistics

**DAVID G. LOCKWOOD**

*Michigan State University*

HARCOURT BRACE JOVANOVICH, INC.

*New York   Chicago   San Francisco   Atlanta*

ISBN: 0-15-546213-X
Library of Congress Catalog Card Number: 72-76528

PRINTED IN THE UNITED STATES OF AMERICA

# *Preface*

This book is intended to fulfill the need for an introduction to the stratificational theory of language, particularly the version developed by Sydney M. Lamb of Yale University. It is not an introduction to linguistics as a whole, but rather presupposes an elementary familiarity with the concepts and background of modern linguistics. Such a minimum preparation might be achieved by thoroughly studying such a textbook as *Introduction to Descriptive Linguistics* by H. A. Gleason, Jr. (revised edition; Holt, Rinehart and Winston, 1961) or *Aspects of Language* by Dwight Bolinger (Harcourt Brace Jovanovich, 1968).

Since relatively few linguists are at present equipped to teach a course in stratificational linguistics even with the aid of such a textbook, this work is further intended to be adaptable for self-instruction by the linguistic scholar or advanced graduate student wishing to familiarize himself with the general principles and specific applications of stratificational linguistics.

The book is designed to provide a thorough introduction to the fundamental principles of the theory and its application to a considerable range of specific linguistic problems. Such specific treatments have been few in number, unfortunately, in the earlier stratificational literature.

I wish to take this opportunity to extend thanks to a number of persons who have aided me in the preparation of this text in one way or another. I am most indebted to Sydney M. Lamb. He provided my basic orientation to the theory, v beginning in a Linguistic Institute course at Ann Arbor in 1965 and continuing through a series of meetings and conversations over the years since that time. He encouraged me to develop and offer a course in stratificational theory here at Michigan State University, which was first given in the spring quarter of 1968, and further encouraged me to develop the materials used for this course into a textbook. He has also been of great assistance to me during the preparation of the book, through various briefings on the development of his theoretical ideas and through a thorough critical reading of the manuscript in its preliminary form, from which numerous valuable suggestions emerged.

I have also benefited from discussions of stratificational theory with the following persons: David C. Bennett (who also read and commented on parts of the manuscript), University of London; Ilah Fleming, Summer Institute of Linguistics; M. A. K. Halliday; Earl M. Herrick, Western Michigan University; Adam Makkai, University of Illinois, Chicago Circle; Peter A. Reich, University of Toronto; and William J. Sullivan, University of Florida. Special thanks are due to John Algeo of the University of Georgia, who provided a thorough review of the completed manuscript. The following exercises were contributed by Reich: 2 in Set 3B, 1–7 in Set 3D, and 1 in Set 4A. Exercise 8 in Set 3D and exercises 2 and 4 in Set 6A were contributed by Lamb. Exercise 2 in Set 4C is based on Arabic data contributed by Valerie Becker Makkai of the University of Illinois, Chicago Circle. All Answers to Exercises (Appendix II) are my own responsibility regardless of the source of the material. Errors and misinterpretations in any part of the text are, of course, my own.

I also wish to thank the College of Arts and Letters of Michigan State University for allowing me the necessary time for writing, and particularly Professor James P. Wang, Chairman of the Department of Linguistics and Oriental and African Languages, for his encouragement of the project. Finally, I am grateful to Mrs. Theresa Azzawi for helping to type and proofread the manuscript and for preparing the index and bibliography.

DAVID G. LOCKWOOD

# Contents

# 3

## *Notation Systems*

# 4

## *Grammatical Phenomena*

# 5

## *Semological Phenomena*

# 6

## *Phonological Phenomena*

# 7

## *Stratificational Theory and Other Views of Language*

# 8

## *Extensions and Future Developments*

*Introduction to*

*Stratificational Linguistics*

# 1

# *Language and Linguistics*

## 1.1  *Language and Communication*

In its daily use, language is a tool employed by human beings to achieve communication. This is not the sole function of language, but it is surely its most important function. Communication through the medium of spoken language is concerned with the conveying of concepts by means of vocal noises. Let us attempt to outline a simple view of what goes on when two individuals communicate using language. One participant in the communication process, let us label him A, goes from concepts inside his brain to muscle movements leading to the articulation of vocal sounds. A second participant, B, receives these vocal noises as they have been transmitted through the air. He perceives them by means of his auditory mechanism, which ultimately leads to a stimulation of his conceptual apparatus. If the attempt at communication has been successful, the conceptual stimulation produced in B's mind will correspond largely to that with which A began and will add some new information to B's store of knowledge, to which B may react as he feels appropriate. Figure 1.1 is a representation of this act of communication.

Obviously, the ordinary user of a language will have both the abilities of A in our scheme and those of B. He will be able to send messages as well as receive them. Many common kinds of human interaction involving language, in fact, require an individual to switch readily and repeatedly from one of these roles to the other. Let us label the role of A that of the **encoder**, and the role of B that of the **decoder**. The encoder's role thus involves going from concepts to 1

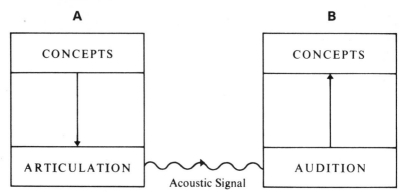

*Figure 1.1   A Simple Act of Communication*

articulation, while that of the decoder involves going from audition to concepts. In order to show that a single individual will have the ability to serve in both of these roles, we may attempt to superimpose the part of Figure 1.1 for A upon that for B. The upper boxes, labelled "concepts," will readily allow a superimposition, since for a single individual the concepts available at a given time will coincide regardless of his role. A greater problem exists for articulation and audition, since one is relevant for the role of the encoder, while the other is paramount for the decoder. Articulation and audition have in common, however, the fact that each deals with sound—the former with its production and the latter with its perception. Furthermore, the two are undoubtedly interrelated, despite the fact that one or the other will be predominant according to the role assumed. We associate in our brains the articulation of various sounds with the auditory impression our ears receive as a result of their articulation. We may therefore propose the term **phonic correlations** for the combination of articulation and audition, with the understanding that articulation will be of primary importance for encoding, while audition will be primary for decoding.

The term "correlation" may also be appropriate at the conceptual end of our schema. Concepts surely involve the correlation of many factors in our immediate and past experience. The concept "dog" for a speaker of English, for example, may involve visual impressions as to the appearance of various dogs in one's experience, auditory impressions as to the characteristic noises made by dogs, olfactory impressions as to the smell of a dog, tactile impressions as to the feel of a dog's nose and coat, and other, often idiosyncratic impressions based on individual experience, all of these combining and correlating to make up the total concept. We may therefore propose the term **conceptual correlations** as a more accurate substitute for what we termed "concepts" in Figure 1.1.

The superimposition of the roles of A and B with the indicated refinements of terminology lead us to the diagram of Figure 1.2, representing the potential activities of a single individual in the communication process. Here the activity

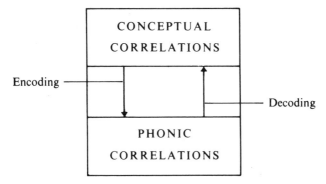

**Figure 1.2   The Individual's Activities in Communication**

of encoding is represented by the downward arrow, while decoding is represented by the upward arrow.

We have said nothing as yet about the box through which the arrows pass—the area lying between conceptual and phonic correlations, which is traversed in opposite directions in the processes of encoding and decoding. This area relating conceptual and phonic correlations, however, is an extremely important one for us, for it is what we will call the **linguistic system** or **language**. To be more precise, we will take language to be the code relating conceptual and phonic correlations. The knowledge of this code is what enables an individual to serve as an encoder and decoder for a particular language. The codes or languages of different individuals inevitably differ according to their experiences, but when these particular codes have enough in common, communication can still be achieved through their use. If the codes are sufficiently different, however, the individuals are said to have different languages, and direct communication by means of speech is not possible between them.

We have thus provided a preliminary definition of what we mean by language. It will be our task in the remainder of this book to elaborate upon this preliminary definition in terms of what has become known as stratificational theory. The first essential ingredient of this theory is the notion, presented here, that a language is a code known by its speakers, enabling them to serve as encoders and decoders in the communication process.

## 1.2   *Language and Relationships*

If we conceive of language as a code relating conceptual correlations to phonic correlations, it is a small step to the conclusion that a language is a system of relationships. It is a fundamental tenet of stratificational linguistics that relationships form the most appropriate characterization of a language. In order to understand why this characterization is insisted upon over other alternatives, we must take some additional factors into account.

If the linguistic code is a part of the knowledge of the speaker, it follows that like the rest of his knowledge it must be stored in his brain. The precise fashion in which this code, together with other parts of knowledge, is stored in the brain is not fully understood even by specialists in the field of neurophysiology. The details of the structures in the interior of the brain and their functioning are not accessible to direct observation.

But though we cannot observe the structure and operation of the linguistic portion of the brain, we can observe certain indirect manifestations resulting from this structure. These manifestations include linguistic behavior, which encompasses the sounds produced by the articulatory mechanism, and the association of these sounds with what we usually call meaning—the function of the sounds and their combinations in the culture or society. Sounds may be observed and measured by the procedures of the science of phonetics. Concepts as such may not be observed directly any more than the linguistic system can, but we can observe the reactions of members of a speech community to various linguistic events, thus gaining a picture of their function in the society. When one is studying his native language, introspection may also be of value in getting a picture of meanings, and when dealing with a different language, translation may serve a similar function. Both of these means are best used in conjunction with other observations, however.

The most fruitful approach to the study of a system which we can observe only through its indirect manifestations involves a procedure known as **modelling**. This procedure is implemented by constructing hypothetical systems known as **models**. In constructing these models, we try to make their behavior parallel the observable behavior of the unobservable system as closely as possible. Underlying this method of investigation is the assumption that the more closely the behavior of a model approximates that of the unobservable system under investigation, the closer the internal workings of the model can be expected to correspond to the internal structure of the actual system. The possibility of equally workable alternate models is not to be excluded, however.

An analogy may be drawn at this point from astronomy. One of the concerns of this science is the solar system and the motions of the various bodies within it. In order to observe the motions involved in a way that would make the internal structure and function of the solar system immediately obvious, it would be necessary to move outside the solar system and observe it from various points over a period of time. But man's ability to travel even within the solar system is still in its very beginning stages, and we seem far from the time when we will be able to go beyond our solar system, even with unmanned vehicles, to make such direct observations. Still, we have long been able to observe the apparent motions of the bodies of our solar system as they appear projected against the sky from earth. On the basis of these observations, astronomers have constructed models of the solar system and the motions of the bodies contained within it; moreover, they now feel that they have a highly accurate picture of how these motions would appear from a vantage point outside this system, though they are still limited to observations from earth or its immediate vicinity. When faced with two competing models accounting for the same observable facts, astronomers, and scientists in general, choose the one which provides the simpler account of these facts. Thus the Copernican system is preferred to the Ptolemaic.

In astronomy, our ability to make the direct observations we might desire is restricted by our present inability to travel beyond our solar system. In linguistics, we are limited by the lack of techniques (such as a powerful but harmless micro-X-ray) to allow us to observe the detailed workings of a brain in normal operation without damaging or destroying parts of its structure. Still the modelling technique gives us the possibility of studying the linguistic system in an indirect way.

In attempting to model the linguistic system, Sydney Lamb initially, in common with such Neo-Bloomfieldian linguists as Charles Hockett, conceived of it as a system of linguistic elements and relationships between them. Later Lamb was led to question whether both of these components were actually needed. It seemed quite clear that no adequate theory could be based on elements alone, so the relationships were apparently essential. He ultimately came to realize, furthermore, that the various kinds of elements within language are defined and distinguished wholly on the basis of their relationships to other elements. Once these relationships are adequately defined, in other words, the elements no longer have any content independent of them. Based on this observation, Lamb began to conceive of linguistic structure as consisting of relationships to relationships to relationships, intricately interweaving to form what could be called a **linguistic network**. He further noted that earlier linguists, such as Louis Hjelmslev and before him Ferdinand de Saussure, had advanced similar views.

Language need be seen as connecting to objects or elements, therefore, only on its periphery. These peripheral elements are what we have been terming conceptual and phonic correlations. Thus, independent of any extralinguistic considerations, Lamb arrived at a relational model of the linguistic system.

When he eventually came to inquire about the relation of his model of language to the brain, Lamb found that the linguistic networks he was working with had several points in common with the *networks of neural connections* which, it is agreed by specialists, exist in the brain. Neurophysiologists generally consider these neural interconnections to be somehow related to the storage of information. It is even conceivable that knowledge is actually stored in their connectivity as such, though such a view might be highly controversial, if not even startling, to many experts in this field. Although this is not the only view concerning the storage of knowledge, it is interesting to note that the stratificational view, arrived at independently of any consideration of neural structures, has turned out to bear a fairly close resemblance to what is known about them. In this way, stratificational theory may eventually be able to provide evidence on the relation of the neural networks to the storage of knowledge.

While it is one of the aims of stratificational theory to characterize language as it is represented in the brain, the theory is not yet in a position to claim to have attained this goal. But in view of its fundamental orientation, which insists that language consists of relationships, stratificational theory can claim to be closer to such a goal than any theory which does not make this assumption. How close it is with regard to particular details, however, remains a very much unanswered, and at present perhaps unanswerable, question.

## 1.3  *Stratification and Its Rationale*

The theory of language being presented in this book is called "stratificational," but from the basic principles presented up to now, it could just as well be termed "communicational" or "relational." It is now time to devote some discussion to the property of stratification, which has given the theory its commonly accepted name. It is no accident, however, that this principle is presented only following the discussion of other principles, for the notion of stratification is derived from those more basic principles and is therefore best understood in relation to them.

The basic justification for positing stratification in language is not difficult to understand within the context of the preceding discussion. We have established that it is in the nature of language to relate conceptual correlations to phonic correlations, the latter in turn relating to sound. The structures associated with the conceptual correlations and those proper to the phonic correlations must be vastly different. Phonic correlations must be adapted to the essentially linear nature of speech, for despite the simultaneous functioning of the vocal organs during speech, it is essentially limited by the time dimension. Conceptual correlations, on the other hand, must be adapted in their basic structure to the patterns of thought, which may conveniently be characterized as multidimensional and nonlinear. In view of the great structural diversity of the material which it is the task of language to relate, it seems reasonable to hypothesize that within language there exist several layers of structuring. One of these layers would relate fairly closely to the conceptual correlations, another quite closely to the phonic correlations, and it seems conceivable that one or more additional layers intervene between these two. Each of these layers will be called a **stratum**. On each stratum there may be assumed to be a **tactic pattern** or **tactics**—a pattern of relationships specifying the well-formed combinations of the "elements" of the stratum. Associated with the tactics are other patterns, which together with it form what may be termed a **stratal system**. The structure of stratal systems will be considered in greater detail in subsequent chapters.

When we undertake this subsequent study, we will see that each stratal system has a structure similar to that which some earlier linguists ascribed to language as a whole. The tactics, for example, is analogous to the traditional syntax, but instead of there being one tactics for the whole language, a separate tactics is believed to exist on each stratum.

The question of the number of strata necessary to account for a given language, or for language in general, is an empirical one, to be decided on the basis of the application of the general stratificational view to a variety of diverse languages. In Lamb's *Outline of Stratificational Grammar* (1966d),\* the maximum number of strata for any language was said to be six, but more recent research has suggested that this may have been an overestimate. In any case, it is essential that at least three strata be posited to account for any form of human language, and this number may be considered the minimum for any modern stratificational grammar.

A second part of the justification of a stratificational system has to do with what may be called "systematic nonsense." It is well known that two sequences of phonic elements equally unattested in a given language may provoke quite different reactions from the speakers of that language. Neither *dran* nor *dlan* is an actual word in English, for example, but English speakers would accept the former as a neologism under the appropriate circumstances and would invariably reject the latter as unpronounceable. The unpronounceability of this latter form is centered on the cluster *dl*, which never occurs in word-initial position in English. Other languages, such as Bulgarian, however, can perfectly well have such initial clusters. This particular one happens to occur, for example, in the Bulgarian word *dlan* 'palm of the hand.' In stratificational terms, this difference between English and Bulgarian can be localized in the **phonotactics**—the "syntax" of the phonology. If one's theory allows a phonotactics, as does stratificational theory, one can directly account for such distinctions, pointing out that while *dran* does not happen to have become associated with a particular meaning in English, it is perfectly allowable in English phonology, by analogy with such actual combinations as *dram, drain*, and *bran*.

Similarly, there are sentences which conform to the grammatical syntax of a language but fail to obey its semantic syntax or **semotactics**. For example the sentence *John will go yesterday* is, grammatically speaking, just as well formed as *John went yesterday* or *John will go tomorrow*, but it is semotactically ill formed in that it violates a restriction which we may informally characterize as a limitation on the tense of the verb phrase in the presence of certain temporal elements. The example *John will go yesterday* violates only the semotactics of English, while *Go John yesterday will* violates its grammatical tactics as well.

So we have seen two basic reasons for positing a stratificational organization in a linguistic system. First, such an organization provides gradual stages on

---

\*Detailed publishing information on sources cited by author and date appear in the Bibliography at the end of the book.

the way between the multidimensional conceptual organization and the essentially linear phonic organization. Second, the tactic patterns which form essential parts of the various stratal systems account for linguistic items which are deviant for a given language from some points of view, but not from others. On the basis of these factors, it would at least appear that a stratificational approach is a potentially fruitful means of exploring the systems which make linguistic communication possible.

## 1.4   *"Competence" and "Performance"*

Primary linguistic data consists of what we will term **texts**. This term refers not just to written material but to any internally coherent body of speech or writing, from a brief exclamation to a large encyclopedia. We have not yet referred explicitly to written language, but it should be clear that for languages with writing systems there exist **graphic correlations** pertaining to the encoding and decoding of marks on paper or other material, together with the phonic correlations we have already discussed. Like most books on linguistics, this one will deal primarily with the spoken aspect of language, but we can at least point out that written texts are not to be excluded from linguistic data.

More important than the inclusion of written language within our purview, however, is the fact that linguistic structure does not stop at the level of the sentence. This is not to say that producing an account of a language limited to sentence structures would not be an enormous task in itself, but there is no theoretical reason to limit our concern with language to the sentence and its constituents. There are many kinds of dependencies between the sentences in a text which should by no means be beyond the pale of linguistic science. Indeed, most sentences are in some way linguistically dependent on other sentences in their context, and a great many of these could not be used in the same form in isolation or in a significantly different context. Stratificational theory therefore assumes that the ultimate task of linguistics is to account for all texts in each language it considers.

It will turn out, however, that we will not wish to consider all the features of actual texts in the same light. Recordings of spoken texts uttered in informal circumstances, for example, are likely to contain a number of sentences which do not fully reflect the linguistic knowledge of the speaker, but rather violate his knowledge in one or more ways. Examples include false starts, slips of the tongue, and other errors which the very speaker who uttered them would immediately recognize as incoherent, whether or not he actually corrects himself on the spot. Such occurrences can be regarded as due to the malfunctioning of the linguistic system which the speaker has in his brain. It may ultimately be desirable for linguistics to account for these phenomena, but we surely do not wish to account for them in as direct a manner as we would account for texts without such deviations. For this reason, it is a common practice among linguists to edit such errors out of the texts used as data, with the aid of a native speaker of the language concerned.

These deviations are one way, then, in which a speaker's actual utterances do not reflect his knowledge of the language. In addition, what we can say is sometimes subject to limitations of a nonlinguistic nature. In our observations of data from any language, for example, we will inevitably find one or more longest texts (in terms of sentences or other units) and one or more longest sentences. But it is generally recognized that these limitations, even if extended to the longest text or sentence ever observed by anyone, do not reflect limitations which are part of the speaker's linguistic system, but only extralinguistic limitations based on such factors as the finiteness of breath, life, and memory. It has commonly been pointed out that given the longest attested sentence in any particular language, we can always make it longer in one or more ways. It is further recognized that there is no definite cut-off point in matters of this sort, a point at which a text or sentence ceases to be intelligible because of its length—no point at which we can say we have reached a definite limit. So by general agreement such limitations as these are not considered part of the speaker's linguistic knowledge and need not be accounted for by the linguist.

Observations of the sort we have been discussing have been used by Noam Chomsky as the basis for a distinction between theories of linguistic **competence** and theories of linguistic **performance**. In Chomsky's view, competence includes the properly linguistic knowledge of the native speaker, while performance is faced with the additional task of dealing with deviant utterances and extralinguistic limitations on speech. To the extent that this distinction flows from the observations related above, and others along the same line, its appropriateness cannot be disputed. We surely would not expect linguistics to treat deviant linguistic behavior in the same fashion as nondeviant, nor would we want to consider nonlinguistic limitations on linguistic performance a prime part of linguistic data.

In practice, however, this distinction has been misapplied. Specifically, it has allowed some linguists to lose sight of the fundamental fact that the speaker makes use of his linguistic competence when he encodes or decodes messages. As a result, we have been presented with purported competence models with an organization which could not conceivably bear the slightest resemblance to the system the speaker has in his brain. The implausibility of such models has been admitted by their proponents, but the competence-performance distinction has been evoked as an excuse for this failure.

In order to clarify this situation and explain the reaction of stratificationalists to it, it is useful to recognize a division of performance into two different aspects. One of these aspects may be termed **ideal performance**. It includes conventions for the activation of a plausible competence model to account for an idealized performance, subject neither to the malfunctions nor to the extralinguistic limitations reflected in real data. A model of ideal performance may be taken to consist of a model of competence, plus conventions for its activation. The second aspect, which may be termed **actual performance**, adds to the ideal performance model an account of deviant linguistic behavior and (as far as possible) of extralinguistic limitations.

It is perfectly possible to keep the three domains of competence, ideal performance, and actual performance apart in the course of linguistic description. In setting up a viable model of competence, however, it is necessary to take ideal performance into account to the extent that it must turn out to be possible to add conventions of activation to the competence model to produce an ideal performance model with a degree of plausibility. It should further be expected that advances in the account of ideal performance will exercise an influence on the competence model in view of the interdependence between them.

In short, a basically valid distinction between competence and performance should not lead to the establishment of hermetically sealed disciplines incapable of influencing each other. In particular, the building of competence models must not be allowed to proceed in isolation from work on models of ideal performance. To ignore this caution is to run the risk of placing competence models in the realm of purely mathematical systems which have no connection with the actual linguistic system which the speakers of a language know and use.

Claims that stratificational theory seeks "only a model of performance" are therefore untrue. The theory recognizes a place for the competence-performance distinction. At the same time, it insists that a plausible model of competence must be incorporable without modifications into a performance model, which in its ideal aspect includes only the conventions necessary to allow the model to operate.

## 1.5   *Linguistic Theory and Its Goals*

The goals of the science of linguistics have varied considerably over the past fifty years. We may broadly sketch the changing emphases of linguistic study in the following terms.

Under the strong influence of Boas, Sapir, Bloomfield, and their immediate followers, linguistics in the United States was primarily a **descriptive** science. Its main concern was the description of linguistic data, particularly the data of spoken texts, and the emphasis was on descriptions arrived at by the segmentation and classification of this data. The dominant view held that linguistic units such as phonemes and morphemes were to be found in the data, and it was seen as the linguist's task to discover them by scientific procedures. A description of a given set of data was required, above all, to be as complete and accurate as possible, though it was always expected to project beyond the actual data examined. The analytical procedures used at this time often led to nonunique solutions—competing descriptions of the same data in considerably different terms. Bernard Bloch, for example, analyzed English *sang* as consisting of an allomorph /sæŋ/ of the morpheme {sing} and an allomorph ∅ of the suffixal morpheme {Past Tense}. Hockett suggested that the same data might better be treated in terms of a portmanteau morph /sæŋ/ realizing {sing} and {Past Tense} simultaneously. Finally, H. A. Gleason, Jr., preferred to view *sang* as encompassing /siŋ/ plus a replacive allomorph of {Past Tense} of the form æ ← (i) '/æ/ replaces /i/.' Though various arguments were advanced in favor of one solution or another, prevailing opinion saw the choice among them as a matter of personal preference, and the differences were commonly considered inconsequential as long as the solutions were interconvertible.

Out of this situation emerged Noam Chomsky, who developed ideas of Zellig Harris into an approach which moved the focus of linguistics from the items discovered in the data to a system of rules to account for, or generate, the data. With the rise of Chomsky to preeminence, **generative linguistics** came to replace the descriptive approach. In this trend, the goal has been to discover general principles governing the data and to formulate them in terms of a precise mathematical formalism of rules. At the same time, the procedures by which principles are discovered, which had been greatly emphasized by the descriptivists, were divorced from matters of linguistic theory. In place of the goal of a precise discovery procedure for linguistic structure Chomsky substituted the goal of an **evaluation procedure**, a means of deciding between competing solutions of the same facts by measuring the relative simplicity and generality of rule formulations.

The generative approach has clearly been fruitful in stimulating research in areas of language study which had been neglected by the descriptivists. Its demand for a rigorous precision of formulation, furthermore, has brought into the open a number of matters which earlier views left implicit. Also, the freeing of linguistic theory from adherence to discovery procedures has marked a clear advance. On these grounds, generative linguistics should be viewed as a definite forward step for the science as a whole.

At the same time, the mere adoption of a formalism and liberation of theory from a procedural orientation do not guarantee that one will be able to provide an account of the linguistic system which is realistic from the point of view of the function of language in communication, much less the relation of language to the brain. In these areas the generative approach has failed. The chief reason for its failure is, in the opinion of stratificationalists, connected with its insistence on a formalism which is basically inappropriate for the characterization of the structure of human language. This formalism originated in the fields of mathematics, formal logic, and automata theory, but its adequacy in these fields does not assure its appropriateness in other applications. It may be adequate to summarize general principles concerning linguistic data, but the assumption that it has any but the most tenuous and oblique resemblance to the actual linguistic system would be disastrous.

Generative linguistics has also failed in practice in one of the areas in which it initially seemed so promising. It has failed to devise a workable evaluation measure for competing solutions. Again the fault seems to lie in the formalism used, which provides basically different kinds of systems for phonology, syntax, and semantics, as well as a lexical component, so that solutions resulting in complications in one component at the expense of simplifications in another cannot be compared.

Thus the time has come for another change of focus in linguistics, which is in some ways a greater departure from generativism than the latter was from descriptivism. This new focus may be called **cognitive linguistics,** and stratificational theory is attempting to provide the basis for a move in this direction. As the focus of descriptive linguistics was on items in the data, and that of generative linguistics has been on rules reflecting generalizations pertaining to the data, that of cognitive linguistics must be on relationships representing the information in the speaker's brain.

It should be understood that the labels "descriptive" and "generative" refer to the prime thrust of the periods to which they are applied. Precursors of more advanced views are to be found as a distinct minority in each of these periods. Thus in the descriptive period there were precursors of the generative view, who sought more abstract treatments suggestive of those which later came into more general favor. There were also those whose appeal to measures of simplicity remind us of a later time.

Likewise, in both the descriptive and generative periods, there have been linguists who have advocated moving linguistics in a cognitive direction. In the descriptive period, Hjelmslev expressed the point of view that "a totality does not consist of things but of relationships." In the generative period, Chomsky himself has expressed interest in the goal of relating language to the brain in such works as *Language and Mind* (1968). His actual discussion in that work, however, addressed itself far too little to the genuine problems in this area.

It is also the case that each more sophisticated view along this scale takes over the essential goals of its predecessors. The generativists have certainly sought to describe linguistic data, but their descriptions have been incorporated into rules rather than being expressed in the more direct item-and-arrangement statements used by the descriptivists. Likewise, the cognitive approach seeks to account for the data and like the generative approach seeks to do so in a precise and formal way. Each step along this scale can be seen as adding a further goal to those of its predecessors, with certain adjustments such as the abandonment of discovery procedure as a goal of linguistic theory.

It may also be useful to view the progression of these views as a scale on which one can move in actually dealing with data. In the early stage of one's analysis of a language, one is likely to be limited to making descriptive statements. As more of the system becomes clear, one can advance to the stage of writing generative rules (of which those advocated by Chomsky are just one possible sort), and at the most advanced stage, one can begin to work with systems of relationships which incorporate the principles earlier stated in rules and in turn account for the data concerning which the initial descriptive statements were made.

Hjelmslev's distinction of form, substance, and purport should also be brought into the discussion of these three points of view. **Form** is essentially the abstract system of relationships connecting conceptual correlations to the phonic (or graphic) correlations, to which we have given the name language. A zone of **purport** is an amorphous area of the real world upon which the form imposes an organization, and this organization is the **substance**. An example of a zone of purport on the phonic (or expression) side of language is the vowel zone, with its continuous gradations along several phonetic dimensions. The form of each language, however, imposes a particular organization on that vowel zone, which is a part of the expression substance. Similarly, on the semantic or content side we may have such zones of purport as the color spectrum, which is continuous in nature but is given an organization into particular color categories by each linguistic system.

Hjelmslev (1961, p. 57) provided a very useful analogy:

> . . . by virtue of the content-form and the expression-form, and only by virtue of them, exist respectively the content substance and the expression substance, which appear by the form's being projected on to the purport, just as an open net casts its shadow down on an undivided surface.

Thus the form corresponds to the net, the purport to the undivided surface, and the substance to the shadow.

Descriptive linguistics was oriented almost entirely to substance, as may be seen in its strong propensity for the segmentation and classification of data in its analysis. At the other end, cognitive linguistics is concerned primarily with form, as was its predecessor Hjelmslev. Generative linguistics occupies an intermediate ground. It has been concerned with abstract systems, but the nature of these systems has been such that it remains dependent on substantive items, which have had to be projected to the deepest layers of its structure. It has worked with an elaboration of the model which Hockett dubbed **item-and-process**, and the fact that items are essential in such a system has prevented generative linguistics from freeing itself from a dependence on substance. In a stratificational grammar, however, no items are needed within the linguistic system, which may be conceived as a series of purely relational connections between conceptual and phonic correlations.

# 2

# A Preliminary Sketch
# of Linguistic Structure

## 2.1  Relations and Strata

If we take a language to be a system of relations intervening between conceptual correlations and phonic correlations, in accordance with the view set forth in the preceding chapter, our next task is to develop a general outline of the nature of these relationships. Section 1.3 presented a preliminary consideration of the basis for a stratificational view, but here the evidence will be developed in greater detail.

The simplest hypothesis we might entertain about the relationship of conceptual and phonic correlations is that there exists a direct connection between the two—in other words, a one-to-one connection between sounds and meanings. This would be the case, for example, if a regular meaning-sound correlation could be established between the semantic components of a term and its phonetic makeup. In analyzing *boy*, for instance, we might hypothesize a connection of the meaningful element "human" to [b], "male" to [o], and "young" to [y]. This correlation would be significant if it could be shown to be valid for the language as a whole. We need not be detained long by such a hypothesis, however, for any serious consideration of linguistic data in any reasonable quantity will make it clear that the relationship involved is certainly more complicated than this. If such were the case with human language, in fact, linguists would have no object for their study, for to say that the conceptual-phonic connections are all direct is to say that a language, as we have defined it, has no structure. Apparently, some systems of animal communication do have this property, so that one distinct cry will be associated with danger,

14

another with the search for a mate, and a third with the discovery of a food supply. Such a fact is evidence that the term "language" is not appropriate for this kind of communication system.

A somewhat less naïve hypothesis is one which sees certain combinations of sounds associated as a group with certain meanings, accompanied by a recognition that the sounds in question will recur in different meaningful groups. We could view [boy], for example, as a combination of sounds associated with the concept "boy" = "human" + "male" + "young," recognizing that the sound [b] recurs in the phonic representation of the concepts "bird," "bush," "rib," and many others. Further, [o] recurs in the representations of such concepts as "law," and "ball," and [y] recurs in "yeast," "pie," "foil," and so on. This hypothesis, which might be termed the "word theory," has at least the virtue of giving language a nonvacuous form, for one has to recognize the relationship between each meaningful unit (or **sign**) and its phonic components, and further the relationship between the [b] in *boy* and that in *bush, rib*, and so on—the fact that the "same" sound can function as a part of different combinations. This "word theory" is close to the idea that many monolingual speakers of various languages must have when they suppose that differences between languages are almost entirely a matter of vocabulary, and that one can therefore make accurate translations from one language to another with the aid of an adequate bilingual dictionary.

One does not have to look too far, however, to find that the "word theory" is not adequate for the treatment of languages. We find, for example, that the arrangements of corresponding words show considerable differences from one language to another. To give a simple example, in English we say *the long river*, but while the Spanish words corresponding to these are *el, largo*, and *río*, the Spanish speaker will regularly say *el río largo*, placing the words for 'long' and 'river' in the opposite order from the English speaker. Furthermore, if one wants to say in Spanish 'the long table,' given the above pattern and the Spanish word *mesa* 'table,' it will turn out to be incorrect to say *\*el mesa largo*—one must say *la mesa larga*, with a different gender agreement. Thus, the "word theory" is fundamentally inaccurate because it makes no provision for syntactic and morphological relations, a basic part of all languages.

To provide for these kinds of phenomena, we must add to our theory a recognition that the patterns by which words, or more accurately morphemes, can combine together are also a part of language. So we amend the "word theory" to provide in addition to a vocabulary a syntax which specifies how the morphemes may combine together to form words, phrases, sentences, and potentially even whole texts. With this theory, we come to a recognition that there are two basic types of relationships in a language. Those concerned with the connection of conceptual correlations to the phonic correlations may be termed **realizational**. Those concerned with combinatory possibilities may be termed **tactical**. These relationships may be schematically diagrammed as in Figure 2.1. If the conceptual correlations are conventionally represented as being at the top, and the phonic correlations at the bottom, then realizational

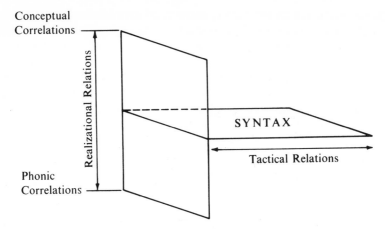

**Figure 2.1   Tactical and Realizational Relationships**

relationships may be thought of as arranged vertically, and the tactical relationships may be placed horizontally, connecting with the vertical plane at just the point where the morphemes are taken to occur, since morphemes have upward connections to their meanings and downward connections to their pronunciations, as well as tactical connections governing their distribution.

Further considerations of linguistic data lead us to conclude that there are other language-specific patterns pertaining to the sound system. It may be recognized, that is, that the particular phonic entities which make up our morphemes are not sounds as such, but are themselves abstractions which are commonly known as phonemes. Phonemes may be realized by sounds, but they are often realized by different sounds in different environments, as linguists have known for a long time. If this is taken to be the case, it would appear that morphemes bear the same type of relationship to phonemes that larger tactical units bear to the morphemes, namely, one of composition.

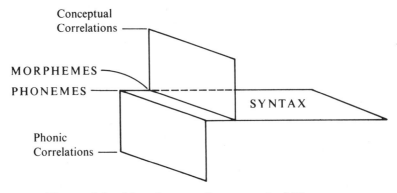

**Figure 2.2   Morphemes Composed of Phonemes**

In such a model, the morpheme-to-phoneme relationships would be handled in the same plane as the tactics, while those of the phonemes to the sounds which realize them would belong in the realizational plane. A scheme of this sort is represented in Figure 2.2.

Such a scheme is appropriate if the relationship between morphemes and phonemes is one of composition. But we must now examine whether this is actually the case. In his book *Language* (1933), Leonard Bloomfield wrote that "morphemes . . . are composed . . . of phonemes." But this position turns out not to be compatible with another which he expressed in the same chapter of the book, namely, the notion that morphemes can have alternate forms. Such forms have since come to be termed "allomorphs." Since allomorphs are themselves composed of phonemes, it must be that allomorphs are phoneme combinations which realize morphemes and are on a lower level than morphemes. It is on this lower level that the compositional relationship between allomorph and phoneme is dealt with. It may be the case, of course, that a given morpheme, such as *boy*, will have only one allomorph, but the frequent occurrence of phonemically different shapes of morphemes, such as /pæθ/ and /pæð/ (in *paths*), /gow/ and /went/, or /t/ as in *ripped*, /d/ as in *fibbed*, and /əd/ as in *rented*, makes it necessary to posit a distinction. The only alternative is to consider such examples as those cited as different morphemes in view of the phonemic differences between them, despite the identity of both their connections to meaning and their syntactic function. If we reject this alternative, we are left with the morpheme-allomorph model, which is essentially the one which developed in Neo-Bloomfieldian descriptive linguistics, though some linguists of this school have equivocated on the relation of morphemes to phonemes. This sort of model is diagrammed in Figure 2.3.

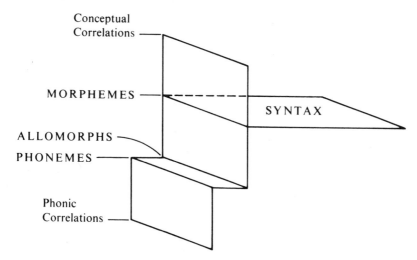

**Figure 2.3  Morphemes Realized by Allomorphs**

A further refinement comes with the recognition that phonemes have patterns of combination independent of the morphology and syntax—the recognition of a tactics of phonemes as well as a tactics of morphemes. This provision allows us to account for the fact that particular phoneme combinations may be.considered acceptable for a given language despite the fact that no actual word in the language contains them. Evidence from English for this point of view has already been cited in Section 1.3 in connection with our discussion of the examples *dran* (/dræn/) and *dlan* (/dlæn/), the first of which would be an acceptable neologism for English speakers, while the second would not. We can account for this fact if we assume that the English phonotactics allows the initial cluster /dr/—which it must to deal with such forms as *dram*, *drug*, and *drain*—but does not allow initial /dl/.

With the recognition of a phonotactics, we have arrived for the first time in the present survey at a model with two full strata. The tactics of morphemes, or morphotactics, operates on the morphemic stratum, while the phonotactics operates on the phonemic stratum. This model is diagrammed in Figure 2.4.

Our view of the phonemic stratum may be augmented by the recognition that phonemes are not simple, but are rather composed of simultaneous, partly independent properties, each with an individual relation to the phonic correlations. Such properties may conveniently be termed **components**. The English phoneme /m/, for example, might be described as having a component of labial articulation and a component of nasality. The latter component would be shared by the English phonemes /n/ and /ŋ/, and the former would recur in such phonemes as /p/, /b/, /f/, /v/, and /w/. In some termin-

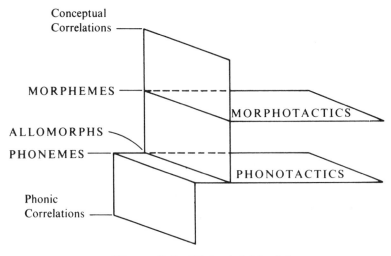

*Figure 2.4   Bistratal Model*

ologies, we find the terms "feature" or "distinctive feature" used for something analogous to a component. When phonology is discussed in detail (Chapter 6), however, we will find some important differences which make the analogy only a rough one.

Even if we add components to the two-stratum model of Figure 2.4, it is still not without its difficulties. A literal interpretation of this model requires the postulation of separate allomorphs to account for all possible differences in the phonemic realizations of morphemes. If all such differences were as random and unsystematic as those exhibited in the English examples *go/went*, *good/better*, and *bad/worse*, this type of account would be quite acceptable. In many languages, however, a great percentage of the phonemic variation in the realization of morphemes follows recurrent patterns which are exceedingly general for the linguistic system as a whole. In Russian, for example, literally hundreds of morphemes show a regular alternation between /o/ and /a/, conditioned by stress. A few examples are shown here:

| | |
|---|---|
| /dóm/ 'house' | /damá/ 'houses' |
| /pór/ 'of the times' | /pará/ 'time' |
| /mór, a/ 'sea' | /mar, á/ 'seas' |

Since such minimal pairs as /dóm/ 'house' and /dám/ 'of the ladies' show /o/ and /a/ to be separate phonemes in Russian, the allomorph method of description would require us to list each of the allomorphs separately for each individual morpheme exhibiting this alternation. Yet it becomes clear without deep study that this alternation is purely conditioned by stress: when stressed /o/ occurs in a given morpheme, we get a corresponding /a/ when the syllable is unstressed in another morphological form. In order to allow us to handle such exceedingly common recurrent alternations, an alternative model of the relation between morphemes and phonemes has been proposed. Instead of positing units of morpheme size on the phonemic stratum, as does the allomorph method, this alternative posits phoneme-sized units on the morphemic stratum, which are then realized by phonemes. These phoneme-sized units, of which morphemes can be said to be composed, have most frequently been termed **morphophonemes**. For the Russian data, this approach would set up morphemes with the morphophonemic shapes **dom**, **por**, and **mor,**; it would then provide for the alternate phonemic realizations of **o**: /o/ when stressed and /a/ elsewhere. This alternative to the model of Figure 2.4 is diagrammed in Figure 2.5.

Many alternations in the phonemic shapes of morphemes are sufficiently systematic to warrant their treatment by the use of morphophonemes, which yields a more general treatment than does the use of allomorphs. Other alternations, such as those of *good/better*, *go/went*, and *bad/worse*, however, can be treated only very awkwardly within the morphophonemic model. To handle the alternation /gow/ ~ /wen/, for example, we might try to posit a

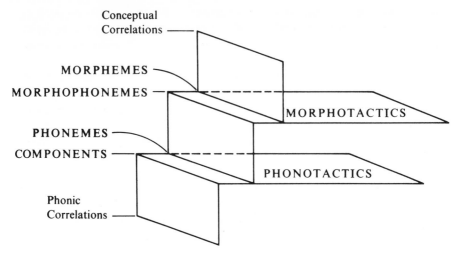

**Figure 2.5  Morphemes Composed of Morphophonemes**

morphophoneme **g**$^{\text{w}}$, realized alternatively by /g/ or /w/, followed by a morphophoneme **œ**, realized alternatively by /o/ or /e/, and finally a morphophoneme **w̃**, with the realization /w/ or /n/. It would turn out, however, that all
these morphophonemes would be needed only for this single pair of alternate
forms. They would not recur and would be completely *ad hoc* devices for this
one alternation, so it would be simpler to use the allomorph method in this
instance.

One might at first suppose that the conflict of these two methods of description can be solved only by deciding which of the two is the better. In this case,
however, there is an alternative which incorporates the advantages of both
methods with none of their drawbacks. It posits BOTH lower-level morphemes
analogous to allomorphs AND upper-level phonemes analogous to morphophonemes. Unlike their counterparts in the models of Figures 2.4 and 2.5,
however, these entities may be thought of as standing in a compositional
relationship to each other, on their own level, between the separate levels of
phonemes and morphemes. To avoid confusion, these units are called **allo-
morphs$_2$** and **morphophonemes$_2$** in the scheme diagrammed in Figure 2.6.

This approach allows us to account in an economical way for four separate
situations. First, there is the situation in which a morpheme has only one
allomorph. English *fish*, for example, has only the allomorph /fiš/. This
situation would be handled in this model by a single allomorph$_2$ composed of
three morphophonemes$_2$ which do not have alternate phonemic realizations
in any of the environments in which they occur. Second, there is the situation
in which a morpheme has morphologically conditioned allomorphs, and only
these. If we consider a nonstandard dialect of English which has *go* and *went*

but not *gone* (using *I have went*, and so on), we would find such a case; the morpheme has different allomorphs₂ in different environments, but the morphophonemes₂ composing each of these are not subject to further alternation. In the the third situation, we have only morphophonemic alternation. An example of this is the third-person singular verb ending in English, whose alternate forms are all phonologically conditioned: /s/, /z/, and /əz/. This morpheme would have only one allomorph₂, consisting of the morphophoneme₂ z, which would be subject to alternate realizations in different environments. Finally, there is the situation in which there are both morphologically and phonologically conditioned alternations in the realization of the same morpheme. The past-participle morpheme in English is an example of this type. It has an allomorph₂ **d** with the phonologically conditioned phonemic realizations /d/, /t/, and /əd/, and an allomorph₂ **n** with the alternate realizations /n/ (as in *drawn*—following a vowel nucleus) and /ən/ (as in *taken*).

Let us now consider further the structure of the morphemic stratum. Up to this point we have assumed that the morphemes connect directly upward toward the conceptual correlations as well as downward toward their allomorphs. But there is evidence that this is not the case. Consider the English examples *understand, undergo, withstand, withdraw, undertake*. From the point

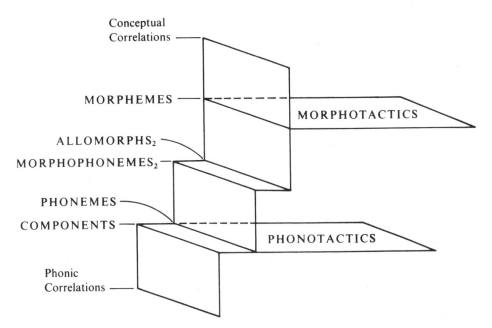

**Figure 2.6  *Allomorphs₂ Composed of Morphophonemes₂***

of view of upward connections toward the conceptual correlations, these elements are indivisible. None of them can be broken down into separate parts with an individual connection to meaning. Yet formally each of them is divisible into two elements, the first of which is one of *under* or *with*, and the second of which is one of *stand, go, draw,* or *take.* Each of these elements also happens to occur as a separate word, but its meaning in this function has no direction connection with that of the meaningful compounds in which it occurs. We may further note that these compounds show the same morphological peculiarities as the counterparts corresponding to their second elements. Compare the past-tense forms: *stood, understood, withstood; went, underwent; drew, withdrew; took, undertook.* This evidence leads us to the conclusion that the verbs under consideration are unitary with respect to their connections in the direction of conceptual correlations, as well as with respect to their syntactic behavior, but at the same time compound with respect to their allomorphs. This peculiarity may readily be accounted for by positing a unit larger than a morpheme, which may be composed of one or more morphemes. A simple unit of this type would be *stand,* while *understand* would be compound. The difference is analogous to that between the simple allomorph **z** for the third-person singular of verbs and the compound allomorph **fiš**. Let us term this larger grammatical unit having connections to conceptual correlations and to the grammatical tactics a **lexeme**.

It will also turn out that the intermediate stratum on which we have posited the allomorph$_2$ with its constituent morphophonemes$_2$ can be considered to have its own tactics, which makes it a full stratum with a structure analogous to that of the other two. We may assume this at this point, leaving the discussion of detailed evidence for it until a later chapter.

We now have a model of three strata with a very parallel structure: on each there are units which connect upward toward the conceptual correlations as well as functioning in a tactics, and these are composed of one or more units which connect downward toward the phonic correlations. This parallelism can be more readily highlighted if we modify our terminology at this point. Following Lamb, we will keep the terms "phoneme" and "lexeme" and introduce neologisms with the suffix **-on**, which is used in physics for elementary particles, to designate the smaller units of which the -emes are composed. Thus a lexeme is composed of one or more **lexons**, and a phoneme of one or more **phonons**. The term "morpheme" is no longer needed for its more or less traditional referent, now the lexon, so we may use it for the allomorph$_2$, naming its constituent morphophonemes$_2$ **morphons**. Thus *go* (the traditional morpheme) is a lexon with *go* and *wen* as alternate morphemic realizations. Each of these morphemes in turn consists of morphons. So given the roots *lex-, morph-,* and *phon-* for the three strata under consideration, with X standing for any of them, we may make the general statement that the Xotactics operates on the Xemic stratum determining well-formed combinations of Xemes, which are composed of Xons. And the -on of any stratum is realized by an -eme on the

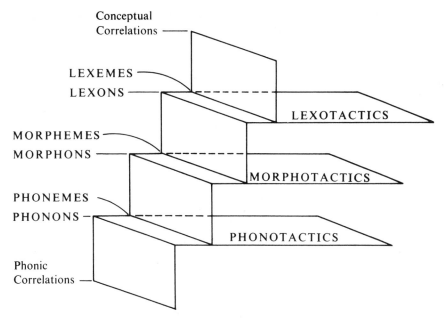

**Figure 2.7   Tristratal Model with Revised Terms**

stratum below (or by alternate -emes). All these considerations lead us to the tristratal model diagrammed in Figure 2.7.

Not even lexemes, however, can be said to relate directly to conceptual correlations. There is at least one more stratum between the lexemic and the conceptual systems. In order to justify this distinction in a preliminary way, let us examine a few of the phenomena which point to the existence of such a higher stratum, called **sememic**.

One of the facts which help to establish this stratal difference is the existence of alternation above the level of lexemes. Consider *big* and *large*, which are two lexemes in English. It might seem on first consideration that these two are complete synonyms, always connecting to the same conceptual correlations. But if this were the case, it would be possible to substitute one for the other in any example where either occurs without affecting the meaning. This test works in such examples as *It's a big stone* and *There's a big building*, where the substitution of *large* for *big* makes no difference. But suppose we try the same test with the sentence *She's my big sister*. For the usual meaning of *big* in this context, we cannot substitute *large* without making a difference. We can handle this situation, however, if we posit two sememic entities: "$big_1$," realized indifferently by the lexeme *big* or the lexeme *large*, and "$big_2$," realized only by *big*. There would also be a definite difference in the connections of "$big_1$" and "$big_2$" to the conceptual correlations, in that those of one would involve size, while those of the other would refer to age.

There is also a definite tactic difference between "big₁" and "big₂" which is not expressable in terms of their lexemic realizations. "Big₁," namely, can be applied to any kind of object, concrete or abstract: *big horse, big stone, large doubt*. But "big₂" is restricted to occurrence with a few kinship terms, mainly "brother" and "sister." This is part of the evidence for a separate **semotactics**. Note further that the lexemic combination *big sister* is potentially ambiguous. The meaning associated with "big₂" is most usual for it, but it can have the other meaning in such a context as the following: *My sister Mary is two years younger than I am, but I can say she's my big sister because she weighs 250 pounds*. Finally, note the additional tactic difference between "big₁" and "big₂" with regard to their occurrence with the comparative and superlative sememic units: "big₂" cannot be compared—*bigger sister* or *biggest brother* can be understood only in the sense of "big₁."

Further evidence for the existence of a separate sememic stratum comes from the consideration of meaningful relationships among lexemes, which can best be explained if we view the sememic entities they realize as multiple. Compare the examples shown in Table 2.1. Each of the items in the first column of this table is a generic term for a type of animal, while the terms in the other three columns are more specific. Those of the second column refer specifically to male animals, those of the third to female animals, and those of the fourth to young animals. We can readily account for the relatedness of these lexemes by considering those of the last three columns complex on the sememic stratum, so that lexemic *stallion* is the realization of sememic "horse" AND "male," *hen* the realization of "chicken" AND female," *fawn* the realization of "deer" AND "young," and so on. Note further that if one does not know or recall the proper monolexemic designation, it is possible to realize each of these sememic components as a separate lexeme—one may say *mare* OR *female horse, rooster* OR *male chicken, lamb* OR *young sheep*.

### Table 2.1   Related Lexemes

| | | | |
|---|---|---|---|
| 1. horse | stallion | mare | colt |
| 2. chicken | rooster | hen | chick |
| 3. deer | buck | doe | fawn |
| 4. sheep | ram | ewe | lamb |

This is just a sample of the phenomena which justify the establishment of a sememic stratum. Further consideration of its structure will be provided later. Suffice it for the present to point out that on this stratum there will be sememes, semons, and a semotactics, as indicated in Figure 2.8.

Certain versions of the stratificational model, particularly the one used as the basis of Lamb's *Outline of Stratificational Grammar*, have proposed additional strata. We will initially deal with only these four, however, and defer consideration of the possibility of additional ones until later chapters.

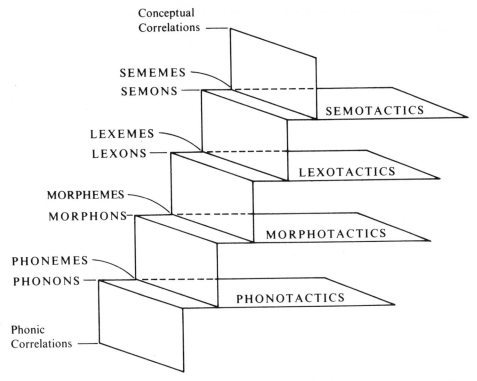

*Figure 2.8   Four-Stratum Model*

Having seen a certain amount of the evidence which has led to the postulation of the four strata already set up, we may naturally ask how one knows on which of these to deal with a given phenomenon. The general answer is that a phenomenon is best handled at the point where it can be most simply fitted into the total system of relationships. The specific answer for any given phenomenon can be provided only as the result of experimentation and is always subject to alteration when further facts are taken into account. This situation results from the fact that language is a highly interdependent system, each portion of which is ultimately linked to each of the other portions.

## 2.2   Entities and Their Symbolization

In the course of the preceding section a series of "entities," namely, the various -emes and -ons, have been introduced. In view of the insistence in Chapter 1 that language is a system of relationships and that the items necessary in both "item-and-arrangement" and "item-and-process' models have hampered these theories, one may ask what the status of these entities will be in stratificational theory. Are they "items," making it a grammar of items and relationships rather than one of just relationships?

The answer is that the entities discussed here are points in the total network of relationships, and their labels are assigned as a matter of convenience, having no status in the theory whatsoever. In the stratificational system of relationships to be detailed in later chapters, these labels are simply added at various points in the total network of relationships as reference points to aid the linguist in discussing this system. When all necessary relationships are properly represented, the internal structure of the language will be resolved into these relationships, as only they have a status in the theory. The only "entities" which are not just points in the linguistic network are the conceptual and phonic correlations, which connect to the linguistic system but lie outside it. Labels placed within such a system make no contribution to its content, but they do contribute to its readability, and this is their primary justification.

Since these entities will be talked about and used repeatedly in the discussion of a stratificational treatment of linguistic phenomena, it will be convenient to have a uniform system for their symbolization. It has become a common practice in linguistics to distinguish entities on different levels with different bracketings. In this book we will make use of the system of bracketings introduced by Lamb in his *Outline of Stratificational Grammar*. In this system slashes labelled by a one- or two-letter abbreviation with mnemonic reference to the name of the unit involved are used. For the -emes of each stratum, the label is a single letter—S, L, M, P. For the -ons, the same letter followed by N is used—thus, SN, LN, MN, PN. This system is exemplified by the following selection from the entities discussed in the preceding section.

| | | |
|---|---|---|
| The sememe "horse" | : | $^{\text{S}}$/horse/ |
| The semon "mare"* | : | $^{\text{SN}}$/mare/ |
| The lexeme *undergo* | : | $^{\text{L}}$/undergo/ |
| The lexon *go* | : | $^{\text{LN}}$/go/ |
| The morpheme *good* | : | $^{\text{M}}$/g u d/ |
| The morphon o (Russian): | | $^{\text{MN}}$/o/ |
| The phoneme /p/ | : | $^{\text{P}}$/p/ |
| The phonon of labiality | : | $^{\text{PN}}$/Lb/ |

Inside the bracketing, any symbol which keeps the different entities apart may be used in theory, but in practice symbols with mnemonic value are obviously better suited to the purpose of aiding the reader of a description. On the upper two strata, it is usually convenient to use a word or word-combination in conventional orthography, if the language has one. Phonemes

---

* This semon is realized by the lexeme $^{\text{L}}$/mare/ referred to in the above discussion. It realizes the sememes $^{\text{S}}$/horse/ and $^{\text{S}}$/female/ taken together.

and morphons are usually symbolized by single letters, and phonons by a two-letter abbreviation. A morpheme may conveniently be represented either orthographically or by the symbols for the sequence of morphons which make it up.

## 2.3   *Types of Interstratal Discrepancy*

In the course of relating some of the evidence which points to the establishment of different strata, we have had the occasion to refer to various kinds of differences between corresponding units on adjacent strata. We may now survey the types of relationships which can exist between such units, introducing appropriate terms for the situations which we find.

In general, the relationship between the entities of different strata is termed **realization.** An entity of a lower stratum is said to **realize** a corresponding entity of a higher stratum, and to be its **realization**. The entity of the higher stratum which it realizes is the **realizate.**

The most elementary kind of realization which may exist over a full stratum of difference (from -eme to -eme or from -on to -on) may be termed **simple realization**. This refers to the case in which an entity of one stratum corresponds always and only to an entity of the adjacent stratum. Over a full stratum of difference, this will seldom turn out to be the case, though the possibility of its occurring should not be excluded.

More usual than simple realization is the occurrence of some kind of deviance from a strict one-to-one correspondence across a full stratum. In such cases an interstratal **discrepancy** is said to exist.

One important type of discrepancy is **diversification**, which occurs when a unit of the upper stratum has alternate realizations on the lower stratum. The English lexeme $^L$/go/, for example, is realized by $^{LN}$/go/, which in turn is realized by the morpheme $^M$/go/ in some environments and by the morpheme $^M$/wen/ in others. This diversification may be termed **conditioned**, since the environment must be taken into consideration to determine the proper realization. We have also seen the diversification in which $^S$/big$_1$/ is alternately realized as $^L$/big/ or $^L$/large/. This diversification is **unconditioned**, corresponding to free variation.

The opposite of diversification is **neutralization**—the situation in which two or more distinct elements of the upper stratum are realized indifferently by a single lower-stratum element. The lexeme $^L$/big/ provides an example, as it may realize either $^S$/big$_1$/, as in *big stone*, or $^S$/big$_2$/, as in *big sister*.

The last two examples show an interlocking of neutralization and diversification: $^L$/big/ may realize either $^S$/big$_2$/ or $^S$/big$_1$/, but the latter has the alternate realization $^L$/large/.

Another important type of realizational discrepancy is **composite realization**. This occurs when a single indivisible unit of one stratum is realized by a combination of units on the stratum below. This very frequent situation is illustrated by $^{LN}$/fish/, realized as $^{MN}$/f/ followed by $^{MN}$/i/ followed by $^{MN}$/š/.

The opposite situation, termed **portmanteau realization**, is less frequent. It occurs when a combination of upper-stratum units is realized by a single unit on the lower stratum. An example would be the realization of $^{S}$/horse/ and $^{S}$/female/ as $^{L}$/mare/. The classic example of this discrepancy is French $^{P}$/o/ (*au*), the realization of $^{M}$/à/ 'to' followed by $^{M}$/le/ 'the (masculine).' Hockett introduced the term "portmanteau morph" for this situation, and Lamb has generalized this to portmanteau realization, allowing it to apply between any two strata.

Portmanteau and composite realization may also interlock. In Latin, for example, the sequence of morphons $^{MN}$/:rum/ is the composite portmanteau realization of the lexons $^{LN}$/Genitive Case/ and $^{LN}$/Plural/, occurring in such examples as *deārum* 'of the goddesses' and *oppidōrum* 'of the towns.'

Another type of discrepancy is **zero realization**, which occurs when an element of the upper stratum is realized by nothing on the lower stratum. This situation is illustrated by the English lexon $^{LN}$/Plural/, which has the realization zero in *sheep* (*are in the fields*).

**Empty realization** is the opposite of zero realization: no element occurs on the upper stratum, but one occurs on the lower, determined by the pattern of elements which does occur as a result of the realization of upper-stratum elements. The element which occurs as an empty realization may be called a **determined element**. Some of the uses of *do* in English illustrate this situation, since $^{M}$/do/ is determined for certain kinds of questions as well as for negative statements, as in *Do you speak English?* and *I do not know.* Empty realization is a generalization of what Hockett called the "empty morph." Research based on stratificational theory has shown empty realization to be a much more frequent phenomenon than was once thought.

The final type of realizational discrepancy between strata is most appropriately termed **anatactic realization** or **anataxis**. This Greek term may be glossed 'difference of ordering,' and it refers to the situation in which two elements on the upper stratum occur in one order, while their realizations on the lower stratum occur in the opposite order. In Korean, for example, the morphonic sequence $^{MN}$/a l h k o/ (with a morpheme boundary between $^{MN}$/h/ and $^{MN}$/k/) is realized on the phonemic stratum as $^{P}$/a l k h o/ 'ailing.' (Carried a full stratum to the phononic level, composite realization will also be involved if it turns out to be desirable to analyze Korean $^{P}$/k/ and $^{P}$/h/ as consisting of two or more phonons each.) The term "metathesis" is frequently used for this phenomenon, but since this term refers to a process rather than a relationship, it is better reserved for diachronic linguistics, where processes of change are actually involved. Synchronically no process is involved, only a difference of order between realizates and their realizations.

All of these discrepancies may, of course, interlock in various complex ways. Take, for example, the English lexon $^{LN}$/Plural/, which has various realizations (diversification)—some of them simple, like $^{MN}$/Z/ in *rags*; others complex, like $^{MN}$/tə/ in *stomata* and *syntagmata*; and another zero (*sheep*). Its realization $^{MN}$/n/ in *oxen* shows neutralization with one of the realizations of $^{LN}$/Past Participle/, as in *taken*.

## EXERCISE FOR CHAPTER 2

### Interstratal Discrepancies

Each item below includes a list of one or more entities of one stratum, to the left of the double slash, and one or more entities of the next lower stratum, to the right of the double slash. Each such set enters into a realizational relationship. On the basis of previous examples and your knowledge of English, determine the type of discrepancy or discrepancies (there may be more than one) involved in each item and describe it using the terms introduced in Section 2.3.

*Examples*

**A.** $^{LN}$/cat/ // $^{MN}$/k/ $^{MN}$/æ/ $^{MN}$/t/

   *Answer:* Composite realization

**B.** $^{S}$/big$_1$/ $^{S}$/big$_2$/ // $^{L}$/big/

   *Answer:* Neutralization

**1.** $^{LN}$/Past Participle/ // $^{MN}$/d/ $^{MN}$/n/

**2.** $^{SN}$/undertake/ // $^{LN}$/under/ $^{LN}$/take/

**3.** $^{M}$/cell/ $^{M}$/sell/ // $^{P}$/s/ $^{P}$/e/ $^{P}$/l/

**4.** $^{S}$/sibling/ $^{S}$/male/ // $^{L}$/brother/

**5.** $^{MN}$/d/ // $^{PN}$/V(oice)d/ $^{PN}$/Ap(ical)/ $^{PN}$Cl(osed)/

**6.** $^{SN}$/red-headed woodpecker/ // $^{LN}$/red/ $^{LN}$/head/ $^{LN}$/Past Participle/ $^{LN}$/wood/ $^{LN}$/peck/ $^{LN}$/-er/

**7.** $^{L}$/two/ $^{L}$/Ordinal/ // $^{M}$/second/

**8.** $^{SN}$/can/ // $^{LN}$/be/ $^{LN}$/able/ $^{LN}$/to/ $^{LN}$/can/

**9.** $^{LN}$/good/ $^{LN}$/bet/ // $^{MN}$/b/ $^{MN}$/e/ $^{MN}$/t/

**10.** $^{SN}$/Negative/ $^{SN}$/wide/ // $^{LN}$/narrow/

# 3

## Notation Systems

### 3.1  *The Need for a Precise Notation System*

Any theory about the structure of language needs a precise system of notation in order to represent its ideas concerning the treatment of linguistic phenomena in a straightforward manner. Some may insist that the most direct means of conveying and representing linguistic analyses is in words, since it is easier to learn the new terms or senses of terms which might be needed than to learn a whole new system of notation. Prose statements may be easier to understand and just as accurate for the representation of some of the very elementary facts about linguistic structure, but a complete and precise treatment of more complex facts will not be possible without recourse to a notation system appropriate to this task. Once such a system is learned, it can be more easily applied and manipulated in the treatment of intricate data.

A useful analogy is that of the road map. If our route is simple, involving only a few changes of direction, we can just as well represent our instructions in spoken or written words. But the more intricate this route may be, the more useful it becomes to have a map, either printed or drawn, to serve as a guide. The notational conventions used in drawing and reading maps are not always immediately apparent without special study, and those who have occasion to use maps are forced to learn them. Though some people claim to be confused by these conventions, the individual of normal intelligence will be able to learn them if necessary. Similarly, the linguist who is going to deal with intricate phenomena, which he wants to treat in as precise and complete a manner as possible, will need to learn the conventions of a precise system of notation which is appropriate to the representation of these phenomena. The effort expended in learning such a system will have its rewards in permitting the linguist to treat these more complex phenomena fully, as well as to follow the proposals of others concerning their treatment.

The primary notation system used in stratificational linguistics is a graphic notation which represents linguistic relationships by various kinds of nodes which are interconnected by lines. As we have seen, the theory emphasizes the relational nature of linguistic structure, and the graphic notation provides as direct a representation of the relationships involved as any practicable system known. Algebraic notations, though interconvertible with the graphic, are less direct and precise.

It is important, however, not to confuse the notation system with the theory itself. It is not correct, for example, to say that the theory asserts that language is made up of lines and nodes. Rather the theory maintains that language is analyzable into interconnecting relationships, which are conventionally represented by nodes connected by lines in the graphic notation system. One should therefore not be confused by the fact that in the ensuing presentation, the basic relationships are set forth together with the node-shapes which are used to represent them.

## 3.2   *Fundamental Types of Nodes*

One very important relationship in linguistic structure is that of a combination to its components. This is called an AND relation. In phonology, for example, we may say that the syllable *dib* consists of the phonemes P/d/, P/i/, and P/b/. Or the English lexeme L/withdraw/ may be described as consisting of the lexons LN/with/ and LN/draw/. The particular relationship illustrated by these examples is the **downward AND**, which is graphically represented by a triangular node with an upward line from the top and two or more downward lines from the bottom, as in Figures 3.1a and 3.1b. The upward line from this node symbolizes the constitute or combination, and the downward lines, its constituents or components. The examples mentioned above are diagrammed in Figures 3.1c and 3.1d.

Further examples are seen in morphology, where the morpheme M/big/ consists of the morphons MN/b/, MN/i/, and MN/g/, and in semology, where one of the realizations of the sememe S/goodbye/ is *I'll see you later*, which may be broken into the semons SN/I/, SN/Future/, SN/see/, SN/you/, SN/late/, SN/Comparative/. These analyses are represented by the diagrams of Figures 3.1e and 3.1f.

In all of the cited examples, the order of constituents is significant, so that P/bid/ and P/ibd/ are different from P/dib/, though all three have the same constituents. Similarly, the sequence of lexons LN/draw/ LN/with/ is not at all

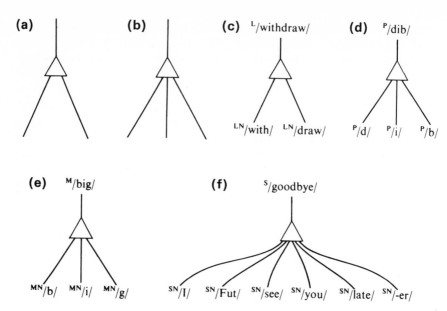

**Figure 3.1  Downward Ordered ANDS**

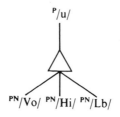

**Figure 3.2  Downward Unordered AND**

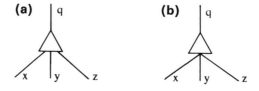

**Figure 3.3  Downward ANDS**

the same as the sequence $^{LN}$/with/ $^{LN}$/draw/. In some instances, however, the order of elements is insignificant, as when we say that the phoneme $^{P}$/u/ has the simultaneous components (phonons) vocalic, high, and labial. To distinguish this latter situation from the one in which the order of elements is significant, we use an **unordered** AND. In the graphic representation of this relationship, the downward lines come from a single point along the bottom of the triangle, as in Figure 3.2, in contrast to the ordered ANDs of Figure 3.1.

So in general, the diagram of Figure 3.3a indicates that $q$ consists of $x$ followed by $y$ followed by $z$, while 3.3b indicates that $q$ consists of $x$, $y$, and $z$ simultaneously or in no specified order.

Downward ANDs in combination may be used to represent the constituent structure of various linguistic constructions. For example, the English sentence *The little boy attentively watched the fast train* may be interpreted as having the constituent structure shown in Figure 3.4a (among other alternatives). Hockett's sentence *England uses the foot-pound-second system* may be thought of as having the constituent structure diagrammed in 3.4b.

Any of the various conceptions of constituent structure may be presented by the use of a hierarchically ordered series of downward ANDs. Each line may be given a label, as in Figure 3.5a, or alternatively, the labels may be applied to the AND nodes themselves and to the terminals, as in 3.5b.

Labels within such a representation have no theoretical significance; they are merely a convenience to make the diagrams easier to read. Labels at the bottom or the top of such a sequence of nodes indicate to what else a configuration of nodes connects. In a complete diagram of structure, the labels at the top refer to conceptual correlations, and those at the bottom refer to phonic correlations. Since one commonly wishes to focus on a more narrow selection from the total structure, the terminal labels are a substitute for draw-

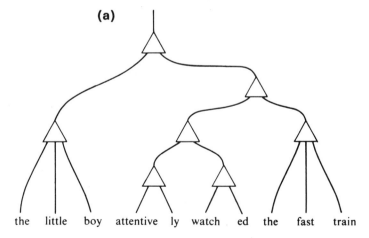

**(a)**

the    little    boy    attentive    ly    watch    ed    the    fast    train

*Figure 3.4   Representation of Constituent Structure*

**(b)**

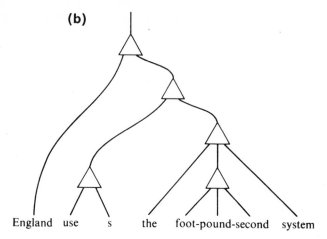

England   use   s   the   foot-pound-second   system

*Figure 3.4   Representation of Constituent Structure (continued)*

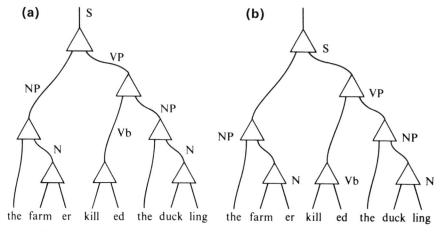

*Figure 3.5   Labelling Diagrams of Constituent Structure*

ing lines and nodes which are likely to be irrelevant for the treatment of the phenomena being focussed upon.

The same means of representing constituent structure may be used to indicate the structure of a single word, as in Figure 3.6a, and to show phonological constituent structure, as in 3.6b.

Another fundamental linguistic relationship is that which a class bears to its members. In stratificational terminology, this is called an OR relationship. The class of intransitive verbs in English, for example, includes the members *come, go, work, die, live,* and so on. Such a relationship is symbolized graphically by a node resembling a bracket lying on its side. A **downward OR**, as in Figures 3.7a and 3.7b, has one upward line and two or more downward lines, the same as a downward AND. The relationship of the class of intransitive verbs to its members may therefore be symbolized as in Figure 3.7c. Any other class needed in linguistic description may be graphically represented in a similar manner. The class of English consonants occurring after $^P$/g/ in a syllable onset, for instance, includes /r, l, w, y/, as in *grow, glen, Gwen, gules*. This class is represented in Figure 3.7d.

Another use of the downward OR comes when a single entity has alternate realizations, as when the sememe $^S$/big$_1$/ is described as having either $^L$/big/ or $^L$/large/ as its realization, diagrammed in Figure 3.8a. Or the morphon $^{MN}$/F/ may be said to have the alternate realizations $^P$/f/ and $^P$/v/, as in the English forms *life* and *lives*, as shown in 3.8b.

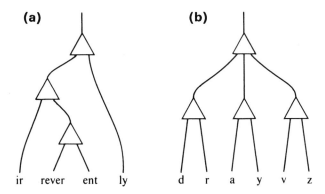

**Figure 3.6  Other Types of Constituent Structure**

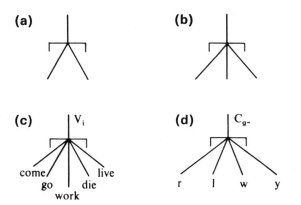

**Figure 3.7  Downward Unordered ORS**

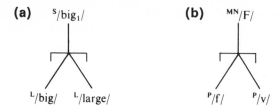

**(a)** $^S$/big$_1$/

**(b)** $^{MN}$/F/

$^L$/big/   $^L$/large/

$^P$/f/   $^P$/v/

**Figure 3.8   Alternate Realizations**

Suppose we wish to represent the constituent structures of the sentences

  a. Bill sees John.
  b. Mary sees John.
  c. Tom sees John.

Their individual structures are diagrammed in Figure 3.9. If we want to account for all three sentences in a single diagram, we may connect the three individual diagrams with a downward OR at the top, as in Figure 3.10a. But the same facts may also be represented as in 3.10b, since the three choices differ only in their first constituent.

The diagram of Figure 3.10b is obviously simpler, and for this reason it seems preferable to that of 3.10a, which essentially corresponds to a mere listing of the different sentences with their respective constituent structures.

To investigate further possibilities, let us add to our corpus of data the following sentences:

|  |  |  |
|---|---|---|
| d. Bill sees June. | l. Mary sees June. | t. Tom sees June. |
| e. Bill sees Art. | m. Mary sees Art. | u. Tom sees Art. |
| f. Bill kills John. | n. Mary kills John. | v. Tom kills John. |
| g. Bill kills June. | o. Mary kills June. | w. Tom kills June. |
| h. Bill kills Art. | p. Mary kills Art. | x. Tom kills Art. |
| i. Bill takes John. | q. Mary takes John. | y. Tom takes John. |
| j. Bill takes June. | r. Mary takes June. | z. Tom takes June. |
| k. Bill takes Art. | s. Mary takes Art. | aa. Tom takes Art. |

All these options are represented in the diagram of Figure 3.11, which could readily be extended to handle further options by simply adding more choices to the ORs. (For example, the possibility of a past-tense form has been suggested in this diagram by the inclusion of the suffix *-ed* as an alternative to the *-s* shown in the above forms.)

The use of ORs in combination with ANDs allows a great many different constituent structure graphs to be collapsed into a single one. How can we determine exactly how many such diagrams are recoverable from that of Figure 3.11 or any other? The following procedure will allow this number to be determined without actually producing each distinct diagram.

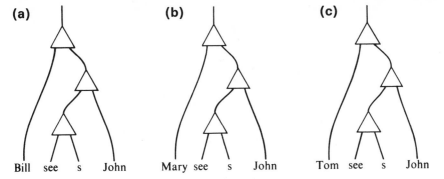

**Figure 3.9 Individual Constituent Structures**

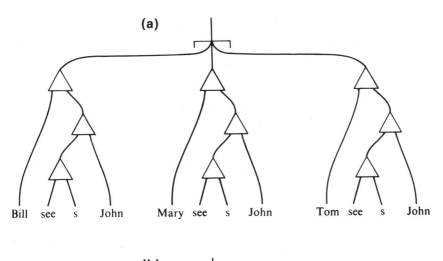

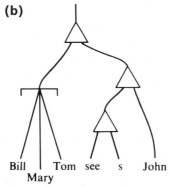

**Figure 3.10 Use of ORS with ANDS**

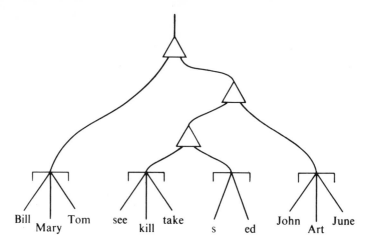

***Figure 3.11    Extended Diagram***

1. A line at the bottom of the diagram is assigned a value *1*.

2. The line above any node immediately dominating lines whose value has been determined may be assigned a value as follows:

   a. At an OR, the values of the dominated lines are *added* to determine the value of the dominating line.

   b. At an AND, the values of the dominated lines are *multiplied* to determine the value of the dominating line.

3. At all higher nodes, repeat Procedure 2 until the line at the top of the diagram receives a value. This value will correspond to the total number of different combinations of terminal elements of distinct structure for which the graph provides.

Figure 3.12 shows the application of Procedures 1, 2, and 3 to a diagram like that of Figure 3.11.

In addition to the downward OR already introduced, we may have **upward unordered ORs**, as shown in Figure 3.13. This configuration is used to indicate the occurrence of neutralization. For example, there are two English morphemes corresponding to the sequence of morphons $^{MN}$/w e l/. One occurs in *It's a deep well*, the other in *They work well together*. The lines leading to each of these morphemes, which are quite different in their morphological and syntactic behavior, may be joined at an upward OR, with the downward line from this node leading to the corresponding sequence of morphons. This avoids the necessity of listing the identical sequence twice. This example is illustrated in Figure 3.14a.

Among the lexemes of English are the intransitive verb $^{L}$/come/, the preposition-adverb $^{L}$/across/, and the transitive verb $^{L}$/come across/. With the aid

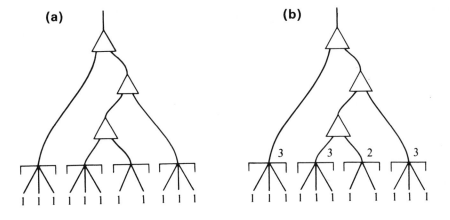

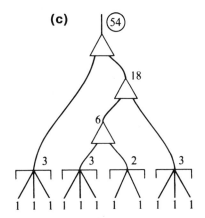

**Figure 3.12   Determining the Number of Outputs
Provided for in a Diagram**

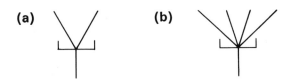

**Figure 3.13   Upward Unordered ORS**

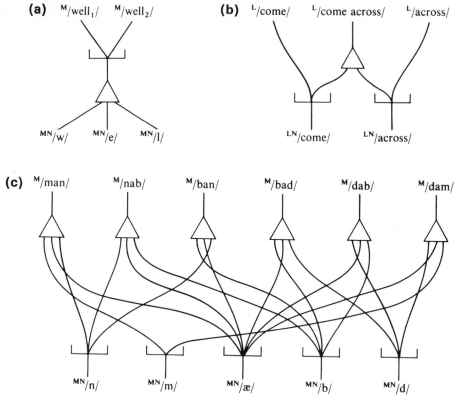

**Figure 3.14   Uses of Upward ORS**

of upward ORs, we may show that the lexons under consideration function either as part of this complex lexeme or as separate lexemes. This is illustrated in Figure 3.14b. This diagram could be expanded to show the recurrence of $^{LN}$/come/ in such combinations as $^{L}$/come down with/ 'contract (a disease),' and that of $^{LN}$/across/ in $^{L}$/put across/ 'explicate.'

Various morphemes also share morphons, and the multiple function of such morphons can be shown at upward ORs on the morphemic stratum, as illustrated in Figure 3.14c.

In general, there is a smaller number of -ons in the system of a given stratum than of -emes, because many -emes consist of a combination of -ons. Each recurrent -on will be represented by the downward line from an upward OR.

We may also find uses for upward ORs in dealing with constituent structures. In the earlier example in Figure 3.11, we provided for *Bill*, *Mary*, or *Tom* as a possible subject and *John*, *Art*, or *June* as a possible object. Actually, we could extend our data so that any of these six could serve in either of these functions. This would lead to the diagram of Figure 3.15a. This repetition of the same information can be avoided by the use of an upward OR allowing the same class to occur in two different functions. The downward line from the OR node

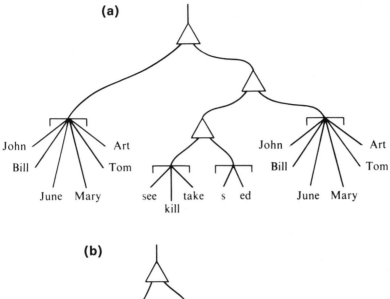

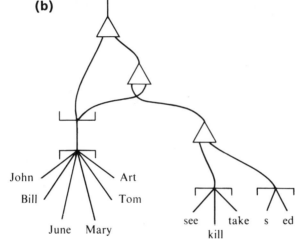

**Figure 3.15   Another Use of the Upward OR**

may be thought of as representing the class, while the upward nodes represent its different functions in the syntax. This simpler alternative is shown in Figure 3.15b.

It should be noted at this point that only the connections of a line to nodes are important in this notation. The length of a line and the particular configuration it assumes are irrelevant. The fact that one line crosses another is likewise of no importance.

In following the above procedure for determining the number of different constituent structure diagrams recoverable from a single graph, all of the lines above an upward OR are assigned the same value as the single line below it.

(The exercises of Set 3A at the end of this chapter may be done at this point.)

## 3.3   *Simplification of Tactic Diagrams*

Diagrams such as Figure 3.15b, combining downward ANDs, downward ORs, and upward ORs to provide accounts of a number of distinct constituent structures, are called **tactic diagrams,** since their configurations are typical of the tactic portions of a stratificational grammar. A constituent structure diagram such as those of Figure 3.9, which are some of the many derivable from 3.15b, is termed a **trace.** A trace is read from a tactic diagram by taking all paths from an AND, making a choice at each downward OR, and simply passing through an upward OR. Since the trace represents the structure of only one example, it contains no ORs, only ANDs.

In the preceding discussion we have had occasion to make reference to the relative simplicity of various tactic representations. We selected 3.10b over 3.10a and 3.15b over 3.15a, for example, on the grounds of the greater simplicity of the preferred alternative. These two situations are illustrative of a number of general principles which allow tentative tactic diagrams to be simplified. A series of such principles will now be set forth and illustrated.

### *Principle 1*

When a downward OR dominates two or more ANDs which share one or more constituents, the diagram may be simplified by making the AND dominant, and using ORs to dominate only those parts which are actually different.

The simplification of Figure 3.10a to 3.10b has already illustrated this principle, which captures the notion of factoring out the common characteristics and representing them only once. The simplification of Figure 3.16a to 3.16b provides an abstract illustration of this principle.

### *Principle 2*

Whenever the same option or the same combination is needed at two or more points in a tactic system, the system will be more simply

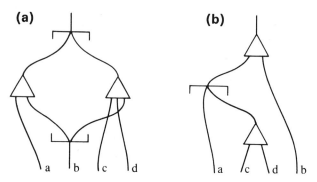

**Figure 3.16   Principle 1: Shared Constituents**

represented if the option or combination is described only once and connected via an upward OR to the various points where it is needed.

This principle has been illustrated with respect to options (downward ORs) in the simplification of Figure 3.15a to 3.15b. It is easy to see that the same principle would apply to a combination (downward AND). Suppose that instead of the various proper names shown in Figure 3.15, our possible subjects and objects are *the man, a man, the woman, a woman, the janitor, a janitor*. Then by the same principle as was applied in the case of Figure 3.15, the representation of Figure 3.17a would simplify to that of 3.17b.

Abstract illustrations of this principle are provided by the simplification of Figure 3.18a to 3.18b, and 3.18c to 3.18d.

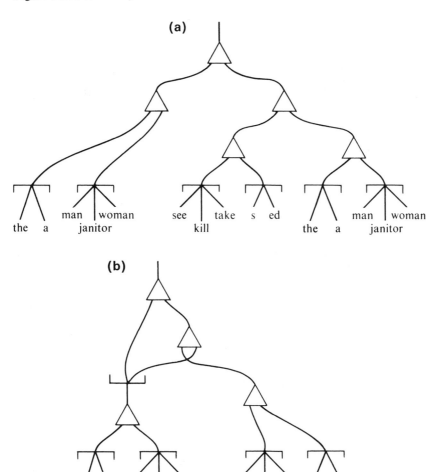

**Figure 3.17  Identical Combinations**

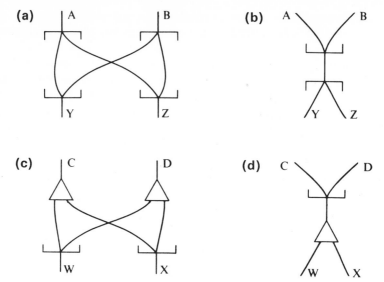

**Figure 3.18   Principle 2: Identical Choices or Combinations**

## Principle 3

Two successive nodes of identical configuration are not allowed in a diagram of the linguistic system. Two or more such identical nodes may be collapsed into a single node with an increased number of branches.

This principle is an affirmation of the notion that the classes and constructions relevant to a tactic system must be established on a nonarbitrary basis, justifiable in terms of that system. Suppose, for example, that we want to divide the class of intransitive verbs into three subclasses, one including *come* and *go*, another including *live* and *die*, and a third including *work*. Such a classification is represented by the diagram of Figure 3.19a. But by Principle 3 such an *a priori* classification is not justifiable unless it can be shown that these

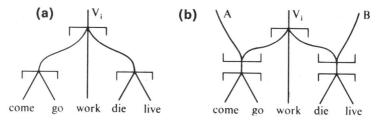

**Figure 3.19   Establishment of Subclasses**

putative classes actually have distinct syntactic functions. If this turns out to be the case, the subclassification could be justified. For example, suppose the class *come, go* is found to have a set of syntactic functions, A, in which other members of the class of intransitive verbs do not participate, while the class *die, live* is found to have a similarly distinct set of functions, B. This evidence would provide a justification for the subclassification shown in Figure 3.19a, by demonstrating the need for upward ORs with branches leading upward to these additional functions, as well as to those which all intransitive verbs share in common. These upward ORs would separate the downward ORs, thereby precluding their collapse by Principle 3. If this kind of evidence were not found, the subclassification would be arbitrary. This justification of the subclasses is shown in Figure 3.19b.

A similar line of reasoning applies to constituent analysis: we do not set up constructions in a tactic diagram unless our data provides a justification for them. By this principle, in fact, Figure 3.17b should reduce to 3.20a, considering only the data for which it was originally set up to account. In earlier examples such as 3.17b, however, the constituency divisions were represented in anticipation of the consideration of further factors which would ultimately justify them. For example, if we consider intransitive clauses such as *A man works* and *The janitor came*, the subject-predicate distinction will be justified, since an additional downward OR will be needed to show the choice between a transitive and an intransitive predicate, as shown in 3.20b (where $V_t$ and $V_i$ represent the classes of transitive and intransitive verbs, respectively). Further considerations may ultimately justify the separation of the constituent containing the verb stem followed by the ending as well. If we wish to leave

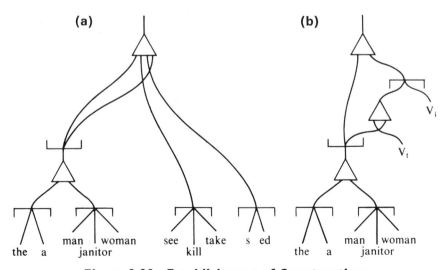

*Figure 3.20  Establishment of Constructions*

**(c)**

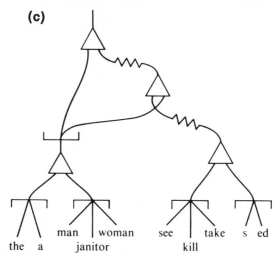

**Figure 3.20  Establishment of Constructions** *(continued)*

successive nodes uncollapsed in a tactic diagram in anticipation of their ultimate justification by such evidence, we may use wavy lines to indicate the omission of one or more nodes. Figure 3.20c shows this convention applied to Figure 3.17b.

Abstract examples of the application of Principle 3 are provided in Figure 3.21, where 3.21a reduces to 3.21b, and 3.21c reduces to 3.21d.

It should be noted that this principle is applicable only to tactic diagrams

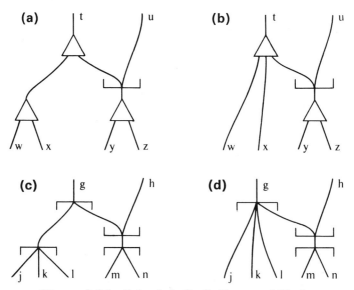

**Figure 3.21  Principle 3: Collapse of Nodes**

**Figure 3.22   Optionality of A**

and not to traces, since the intervening ORs are not represented in a trace. The use of successive downward ANDs in traces is therefore legitimate as long as these ANDs are justifiable in the tactic system from which the trace derives.

### Principle 4

When a downward OR dominates a single element and an AND dominating that same element and something else (in either order), the diagram may be simplified by making the AND dominant and considering the noncommon element optional. The optionality of a line may be treated with a downward OR leading to that line or to zero. Such an option may be represented graphically as in Figure 3.22, for the optional element A.

Consider, for example, the data *stay, stay here, stay there, live, live here, live there, work, work here, work there.* The simplest account of this corpus which does not take optionality into account is represented in Figure 3.23a, but by this principle it may be simplified to 3.23b.

It may be shown that once the zero element is introduced, Principle 4 can be considered only a special case of Principle 1. This is true because A alone is the same as A plus zero. So the diagram of Figure 3.23c (which makes an unusual use of the zero element that would never occur in a diagram of the

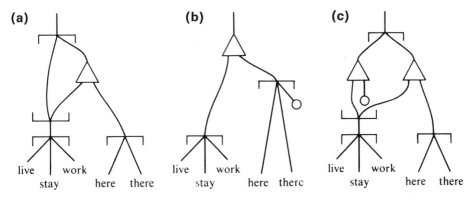

**Figure 3.23   Illustration of Optionality**

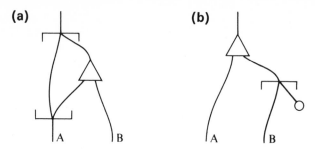

**Figure 3.24   Principle 4: Optionality**

linguistic system) is essentially equivalent to that of 3.23a, and the application of Principle 1 to 3.23c will yield 3.23b.

An abstract example of the application of Principle 4 is provided by the simplification of Figure 3.24a to 3.24b.

### Principle 5

Multiple options or combinations which show partial similarities may be factored to allow simplifications by Principle 2.

This principle is actually a reversal of Principle 3, as may be seen by examining the diagrams of Figure 3.25, representing an abstract example. Here 3.25b would simplify to 3.25a by Principle 3, but using Principle 5 we may reverse this and then apply Principle 2 to get the representation given in 3.25c. The latter captures the generalization that there exists a class B, D which is a subclass of the classes 1, 2, and 3.

As a corollary to Principle 5, it may be stated that given a figure with the properties of 3.25b, which can be simplified either by Principle 3 (to 3.25a) or by Principle 2 (to 3.25c), Principle 2 takes precedence over Principle 3.

We see, then, that of our five principles the first three are basic, while the other two are special cases of the basic ones.

(The exercises of Set 3B at the end of this chapter may be done at this point.)

## 3.4   Environmental Conditioning

None of the tactic diagrams considered up to now has allowed a choice to be conditioned by another factor provided for in another part of the diagram. All of the choices at downward ORs have been treated as if they were completely free ones. But it is obvious that a great many of the options found in actual language are conditioned ones. Options in one part of the system condition other options elsewhere. To allow the representation of such situations, it is

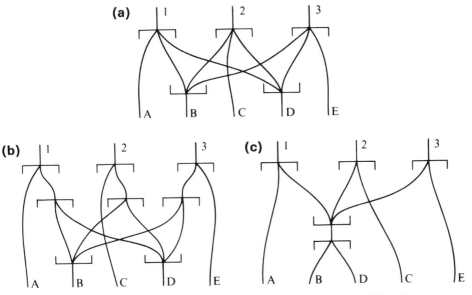

**Figure 3.25** **Principle 5: Factoring and Resimplification**

useful to have a means of introducing the property of **context sensitivity** into our diagrams, that is, the property by which some options are conditioned by surrounding elements.

The introduction of this concept requires some additional nodes. One of these is the **downward ordered OR**, which differs in shape from the other, unordered OR in exactly the same way that an ordered AND differs from an unordered one. Examples of this node are shown in Figure 3.26.

The meaning of ordering for an OR is a matter of the priority of choices. Suppose that we want to represent the fact that *a* will lead down to *p* under certain conditions, otherwise to *q* under other conditions, or otherwise to *r*. Figure 3.27a shows such a conditioned choice, with the priority of *p* over *q* and *q* over *r* represented by the ordering of the lines. But the environmental conditions still have to be explicitly provided for. Suppose that the condition for

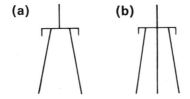

**Figure 3.26** **Downward Ordered ORS**

**(a)** 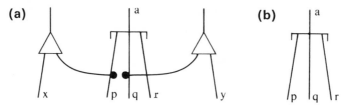 **(b)**

*Figure 3.27   A Conditioned Choice*

the occurrence of *p* is the occurrence of a preceding *x*, while that for *q* is the occurrence of a following *y*. This situation is represented in Figure 3.27b.

This diagram introduces another new node, the **enabler**—so called because it enables the particular option which it governs to be taken when a condition is satisfied, provided an option with higher priority is not also allowed. This node is represented by a solid bump drawn on one side of the line leading down to the conditioned element. It is joined from the opposite side by a conditioning line, which leads upward to a downward AND, whose other branch leads to the conditioning element. If the conditioning element will precede the conditioned choice, the conditioning line will come from the last branch of a downward ordered AND, as in the case of *x*; if the conditioning element will follow the choice, the conditioning line will come from the first branch of a downward ordered AND, as in the case of *y*. The conditioning element may also be simultaneous with the conditioned, in which case the AND will be unordered, as shown in Figure 3.28.

In any case, the conditioning line will always be identifiable as the one leading to the enabler, which is conventionally placed on the opposite side of the conditioned line to which it is joined. A conditioning line will have no effect, of course, if the OR it helps to govern is not pertinent, or if a choice with higher priority is possible.

In order to see a comparison of a context-sensitive treatment using ordered ORs and enablers with a **context-free** treatment not allowing these connections, let us consider the following hypothetical data, where the individual letters may be thought of as representing phonemes, morphemes, words, and so on.

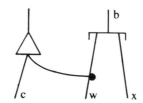

*Figure 3.28   Simultaneous Conditioning*

| | | | |
|-----|-----|-----|-----|
| ADP | ADS | MEP | MFS |
| ADQ | ADT | MEQ | MFT |
| ADR | BDS | MER | NFS |
| BDP | BDT | NEP | NFT |
| BDQ | CDS | NEQ | |
| BDR | CDT | NER | |
| CDP | | | |
| CDQ | | | |
| CDR | | | |

The context-free tactics of Figure 3.29 provides for all of these combinations by positing two alternative constructions: one with D in the central position, accounting for all combinations in the first two columns; a second with E or F in the central position, accounting for all combinations in the third and fourth columns.

In preparation for providing an alternative context-sensitive solution for the same problem, it may be observed that the data incorporates the following restrictions:

1. In position I, A, B, C, M, N may occur.
2. In position II, D, E, F may occur.
3. In position III, P, Q, R, S, T may occur.
4. If A, B, or C occurs in position I, D must occur in position II.
5. If P, Q, or R occurs in position III, E must occur in position II, unless A, B, or C occurs in position I.
6. If neither of the conditions described in 4 and 5 is fulfilled, F must occur in position II.

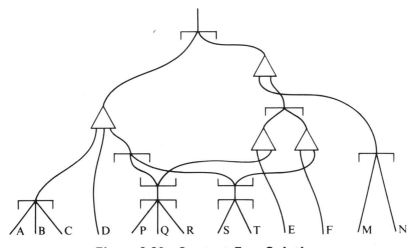

**Figure 3.29   Context-Free Solution**

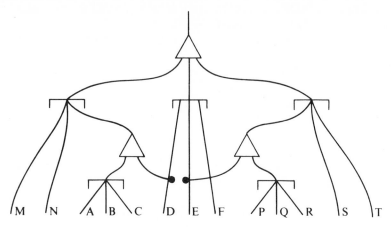

*Figure 3.30   Context-Sensitive Solution*

The restrictions expressed in 4, 5, and 6 represent instances in which the choice in position II is controlled by what is selected in other positions. Disregarding for the moment the possibility of other interpretations, we may incorporate these restrictions into a diagram which handles all the combinations in our data with a single construction, as shown in Figure 3.30.

(The exercises of Set 3C at the end of this chapter may be done at this point.)

## 3.5   *Additional Nodes and Configurations*

At times there may be no theoretical limit to the number of times a part of a tactic pattern may be used in succession. This property, known as **recursion**, may be indicated by the use of an optional recursive loop in the pattern, such as that shown in Figure 3.31. This figure provides for the combinations AB, ABAB, ABABAB, ABABABAB, and so on, up to an indefinitely large

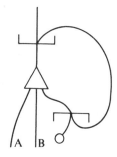

*Figure 3.31   Recursive Loop*

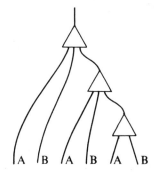

*Figure 3.32    Trace for* **ABABAB**

number of combinations of AB's. It should be clear that the generative power of a graph containing such a loop is not countable by the measuring procedure outlined in Section 3.2, since it is infinite.

It may be argued that recursive loops of this sort have the effect of assigning excess structure. The trace from Figure 3.31 for ABABAB, for example, is given in Figure 3.32.

For cases where the assignment of this amount of structure does not seem to be justified, Lamb proposed in the *Outline of Stratificational Grammar* a special **coordination element**, symbolized by a closed semicircle. This node allows the single line which it dominates to be taken an indefinite number of times without producing excess structure. In place of the recursive structure of Figure 3.31, therefore, we may use the coordination element as in Figure 3.33a, and in place of the trace represented in Figure 3.32, we will have that of 3.33b. This may be reinterpreted as 3.33c if we introduce the convention that the coordination symbol may be replaced by a downward ordered AND in a trace. Like the loop, this element makes the generative power of a tactic diagram infinite.

In many languages, reduplication is a very frequent phenomenon, and it is not readily statable in terms of the nodes we have been considering. In order to handle this phenomenon, Lamb in his *Outline* introduced the **reduplication**

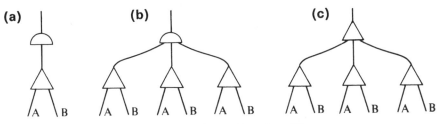

*Figure 3.33    Coordination Element*

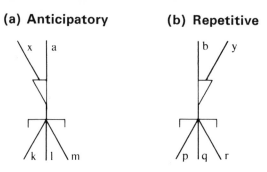

**(a) Anticipatory**      **(b) Repetitive**

**Figure 3.34   Reduplication Elements**

**element**. This element defines a special kind of context sensitivity in which one option is taken repeatedly in a tactic system. This element is symbolized by a wedge lying alongside a line immediately above a downward OR. It specifies that the reduplicating line, which attaches to this wedge, will take the same path at the OR that is used for the main line to which the wedge attaches. If the following use of the main line is the controlling factor, we use the **anticipatory** reduplication element, shown in Figure 3.34a; if the preceding use controls, we have a **repetitive** reduplication element, as shown in 3.34b. In these examples, the lines from *a* and *b* are main lines, while those from *x* and *y* are reduplicating lines.

To see an example of the use of these nodes, we may consider a language in which the articulator ("point of articulation") for a nasal is the same as that for the following stop. Suppose the nasals and stops of this language are as follows:

$$m = \Big/ \!\! \begin{matrix} \text{Ns} \\ \text{Lb} \end{matrix} \!\! \Big/, \quad n = \Big/ \!\! \begin{matrix} \text{Ns} \\ \text{Ap} \end{matrix} \!\! \Big/, \quad \tilde{n} = \Big/ \!\! \begin{matrix} \text{Ns} \\ \text{Fr} \end{matrix} \!\! \Big/, \quad \eta = \Big/ \!\! \begin{matrix} \text{Ns} \\ \text{Do} \end{matrix} \!\! \Big/, \quad p = \Big/ \!\! \begin{matrix} \text{Cl} \\ \text{Lb} \end{matrix} \!\! \Big/,$$

$$t = \Big/ \!\! \begin{matrix} \text{Cl} \\ \text{Ap} \end{matrix} \!\! \Big/, \quad \check{c} = \Big/ \!\! \begin{matrix} \text{Cl} \\ \text{Fr} \end{matrix} \!\! \Big/, \quad k = \Big/ \!\! \begin{matrix} \text{Cl} \\ \text{Do} \end{matrix} \!\! \Big/$$

The situation described may now be symbolized as in Figure 3.35a, using the anticipatory reduplication element, since the articulator for the stop plays the controlling role. If, in some other language, the articulator for the nasal is found to play the controlling role, the repetitive reduplication element is used, as in Figure 3.35b.

Research to date has not yet established whether the coordination and reduplication elements are properly treated as independent linguistic relationships or as shorthand abbreviations for more complex configurations of some of the other relationships.

To handle portmanteau realization, we also need a pair of upward AND nodes, one ordered and one unordered. The **upward ordered** AND will be

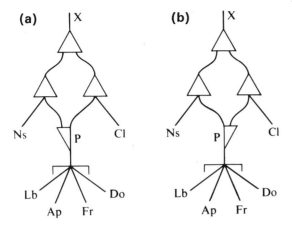

**Figure 3.35** *Phonological Reduplication*

needed, for example, to represent the French portmanteau realization of $^M$/à/ 'to' and $^M$/le/ 'the' as $^P$/o/, as shown in Figure 3.36a, since the order of the two realizates is readily establishable by comparing other forms such as the feminine *à la* 'to the.' In cases such as the portmanteau realization of $^S$/sheep/ and $^S$/male/ as $^{SN}$/ram/, however, no such evidence establishing an order exists; therefore an **upward unordered AND** is used, as in Figure 3.36b.

## 3.6 *Interstratal Connections*

We must now consider the means of connecting the various strata. According to the conception presented in Chapter 2, the various tactic systems may be conveniently visualized as a series of horizontal planes, intersected by vertical connections perpendicular to the tactics.

A special node is used to indicate the intersections of tactic and realizational portions. It can have from two to four connections and has come to be represented by a diamond shape, selected because of its four sides. In view of this

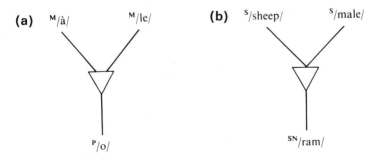

**Figure 3.36** *Upward* **ANDS**

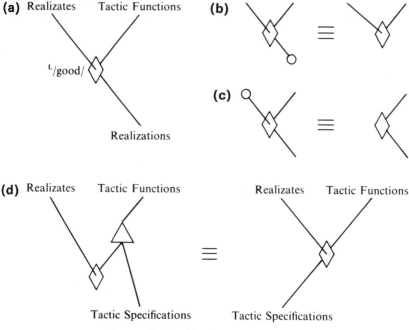

**Figure 3.37   Varieties of Diamonds**

shape, the node has become known as the **diamond node**. The most common variety of diamond has the three connections defining an ordinary -eme: an upward connection toward the conceptual correlations, a downward connection toward the phonic correlations, and a lateral connection toward its function in the tactics of its stratum. Such a diamond may be thought of as representing the -eme itself. A typical example is seen in the portrayal of the lexeme <sup>L</sup>/good/ in Figure 3.37a.

When the realization of an -eme is always zero, we might assume that the realizational line simply leads down to the zero element, but as shown in Figure 3.37b, this fact may be represented more simply by a diamond with only two connections, one upward toward the realizates and the other toward the tactic functions. Similar considerations lead to the equivalence depicted in 3.37c, creating another two-way diamond for use in cases of empty realization.

We may sometimes encounter an -eme with no realization in terms of the -emes of the next stratum down, but with a definite effect on the choices made in the tactics of that lower stratum. Using conventions developed so far, this would be given the preliminary representation shown in the first part of 3.37d. But the lower left side of the diamond is precisely for such tactically lower connections, so this configuration can be rewritten as shown in the second part of 3.37d. An example of the use of this device may be shown if we consider one of a number of languages, French for example, where interrogation (Q)

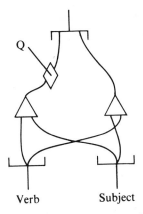

**Figure 3.38  Diamond for Tactic Specification**

is realized as a specification to realize subject and verb in the order verb+sub-
ject rather than the usual subject+verb. This situation may be represented
tentatively as in Figure 3.38.

The situation in which both an overt realization and a tactic specification
are involved can be represented with a four-way diamond. The general schema
for a diamond node is shown in Figure 3.39. This figure shows that the lines
running along the northwest-to-southeast axis belong to the realizational
portion, while those running along the northeast-to-southwest axis belong to
the tactics.

The fact that diamonds may intersect the tactic pattern at points other than
at its bottom means that the term "realizational plane" is inappropriate.
Realizational lines are simply perpendicular to the tactics and intersect a given

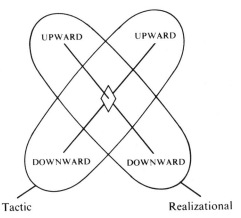

**Figure 3.39  Diamond Node**

tactic pattern at the most appropriate point, not necessarily arranging themselves in a plane. The term "tactic plane" is likewise inappropriate because tactic lines can readily cross one another, so the tactics itself must be three-dimensional.

## 3.7   *The General Measure of Simplicity*

All the principles for simplification of diagrams discussed in Section 3.3 were based on a more fundamental principle which allows us to compare alternate diagrams and determine their relative simplicity. In order to understand this principle, it is necessary to consider the distinction between surface information and effective information.

**Surface information** has to do with the number and complexity of the relationships expressed within a diagram. Two diagrams connecting identical lines at identical nodes are identical in surface information, regardless of the actual placement of the nodes and the length of the lines. The set of possible outputs accounted for by such a pair of diagrams will necessarily be the same, as will the traces representing the internal structure of these combinations. But two diagrams may provide an account for the same set of actual outputs and yet differ in surface information. In such a case, the diagrams are said to have the same **effective information**. All the pairs of diagrams cited in Section 3.3 to illustrate the principles of simplification differ in surface information but convey the same effective information.

For purposes of comparison, it is convenient to have a method for measuring the surface information of a given graph. It is not immediately obvious what such a measure should be, except that it must have some relation to the number and complexity of the relationships represented in the graph. In such a case, the proper method to use in evolving a procedure is one of trial and error. A hypothesis is made concerning a possible measure, and it is tested on cases where it is clear that one solution incorporates more generalization than another and should therefore be considered simpler. A hypothesis that gives positive results for a wide variety of such clear cases may then be considered more likely to be generally applicable, so that it will also give results in cases where the relative simplicity of two possibilities is not intuitively obvious.

Using such an approach, the following measure of surface information has evolved. This method was devised as a result of research by Peter Reich, reported in his paper "Symbols, relations, and structural complexity" (1968b).

Step 1.   Count the number of nodes in a diagram ($N$), disregarding diamonds with only two connections.

Step 2.   Count the number of connections above three at any node ("extra lines") ($L$).

Step 3.   Add $N$ and $L$ for the preliminary measure of surface information.

Step 4. Among diagrams with identical effective information, that which receives the lowest number by Step 3 is judged to be simpler and therefore preferable. If this step does not provide a decision, also consider the figure $N$. The graph with the smaller number of nodes will be considered simpler.

*Example* If two alternative diagrams have 5 nodes and 3 extra lines in one case, and 4 nodes and 4 extra lines in the other, $N+L = 8$ in both cases, but the second diagram is judged to be simpler by virtue of having fewer nodes.

In some instances, the simplification of linguistic diagrams will involve a trial-and-error process using this measure of simplicity as a tool. This will be the case, for example, when it is clear that the application of the principles of simplification described in Section 3.3 will achieve greater economy, but there appear to be alternate possibilities for applying these principles, resulting in more than one solution. The use of this method is also indicated when no direct simplification using the principles is possible, but a reorganization resulting from a different strategy may lead to an alternative solution differing in complexity. In either of these cases, the procedure to follow is to graph all alternate solutions which seem possible and apply the measure of surface information to each one to find out which seems preferable.

This procedure is, of course, only a means of judging the relative simplicity of proposed solutions. It can never guarantee that a still simpler alternative does not exist for a given set of data. Furthermore, the approach which seems simplest for a certain limited corpus may not continue to be the simplest when the corpus is expanded. In other words, the measure of surface information must apply ultimately to the total description, the graph of the entire linguistic system. This fact must be borne in mind when the procedure is used. An approach which counts out as simpler for one part of the linguistic system may so complicate some other part of that system that its net effect is a greater amount of surface information, which would mean that it is actually less desirable than its alternative.

Although this procedure has been found to be the most generally useful measure of surface information yet proposed, further research may result in its refinement.

(The exercises of Set 3D at the end of this chapter may be done at this point.)

## 3.8 *Algebraic Notation*

The graphic notation with which we have been working is extremely useful for many purposes. It portrays the relationships of which stratificational theory assumes the linguistic system to be composed in a much more direct manner than other types of notation, such as the algebraic notation commonly used

### Table 3.1   *Algebraic Representation of* ANDs *and* ORs

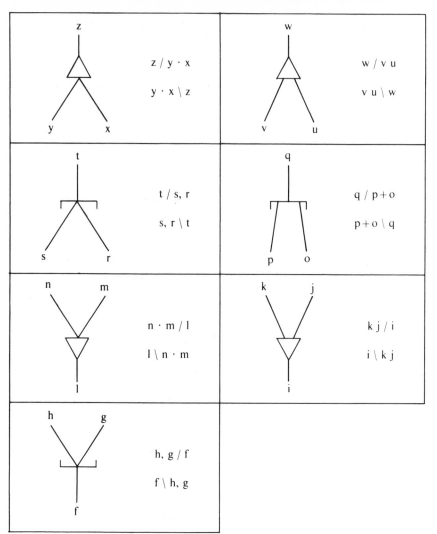

|  |  |
|---|---|
| z / y · x | w / v u |
| y · x \ z | v u \ w |
| t / s, r | q / p+o |
| s, r \ t | p+o \ q |
| n · m / l | k j / i |
| l \ n · m | i \ k j |
| h, g / f |  |
| f \ h, g |  |

in connection with other linguistic theories. On the other hand, it is obvious that in dealing with large amounts of data the graphs become cumbersome from a practical point of view. For this reason, it is necessary to use an algebraic notation for some purposes in stratificational linguistics. The graphic notation is still considered the primary one, however, and the simplicity measure is based on it. It is taken to represent the linguistic system more directly, while an algebraic description is simply an indirect way of describing a graph.

The algebraic system used by stratificationalists to represent the AND and OR relationships has the following properties. Algebraic formulas, like nodes in a graphic description, have two or more elements on one side, and only one on the other. The two sides of a formula are separated by a diagonal line. If the multiple elements are on the right side of this diagonal, the formula represents a downward relationship; if they are on the left side, it represents an upward relationship. The further nature of the formula is indicated by the symbols which occur between the elements of the multiple side: unordered AND $= \cdot$ $(a \cdot b)$; ordered AND $=$ no symbol $(a\ b)$; unordered OR $=$ , $(a, b)$; ordered OR $= +$ $(a+b)$. Formulas may alternatively be written with the downward element(s) on the left if a reverse diagonal is used, so $a\ b\ /\ x$, for example, is equal to $x \setminus a\ b$. The representation of the ordinary AND and OR nodes in this system is summarized in Table 3.1.

Given a graph consisting entirely of AND and OR nodes, one may convert it into algebraic form by writing a formula for every node in the graph. In this case, each line in the graphic representation will have to be assigned a label, which may be either mnemonic or arbitrary, and this label will be used to symbolize the line in the algebraic representation. We may also apply such labels when we are working with graphic notation, but as we have seen, they are merely aids to the reader and have no status except at the top and bottom of a portion of the graph.

This kind of algebraic description, with a one-to-one correspondence of formulas to nodes, can be measured for simplicity as readily as its graphic equivalent: $N$ will correspond to the number of formulas, while $L$ will correspond to the number of elements above two on the multiple sides of the formulas.

Depending on one's purpose, however, it is possible to write algebraic formulas in quite different ways, while still adhering to the same general set of notational conventions. Figure 3.40, for example, shows two different labellings of the same diagram: 3.40a labelling lines and 3.40b labelling nodes and terminals. Different algebraic descriptions on the basis of these different

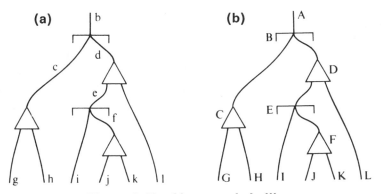

*Figure 3.40  Alternate Labellings*

labellings are then possible. The description based on the line labelling is as follows:

$$b / c, d$$
$$c / g \ h$$
$$d / e \ l$$
$$e / i, f$$
$$f / j \ k$$

On the basis of the node labelling, we may describe the effects of each node *B* through *F* in terms of its connections to other nodes or terminals, as follows:

$$B = A / C, D$$
$$C = B / G \ H$$
$$D = B / E \ L$$
$$E = D / I, F$$
$$F = E / J \ K$$

An algebraic description may often be further simplified if certain additional conventions are introduced. We may, for example, group the members of constituents or options by the use of parentheses as in ordinary algebra, allowing a number of separate formulas to be collapsed into one. As an alternative to the five formulas based on the line labelling, the following single formula may be used:

$$b / g \ h, \ (i, j \ k) \ l$$

This system avoids the need for many of the intermediate labels.

A special convention for representing optionality may also be introduced: optional constituents may be enclosed in brackets instead of being shown in an OR formula with zero as one choice. So the formula $x / a \ [b] \ c$ will be equivalent to the two formulas $x / a \ d \ c$ and $d / b, \ \varnothing$.

Although this use of collapsing conventions involving parentheses and brackets reduces the number of algebraic formulas and symbols needed to represent the same effective information, it is the contention of the theory that these differences are devoid of linguistic significance, because they are not matched by any corresponding simplifications of the graph. Such differences applying only to algebraic representation with no effect on the number and complexity of nodes in a graph are matters of **superficial information**. The same graph may be described by algebraic representations differing in superficial information, but the choice between such representations can be made only on practical or esthetic grounds and is without theoretical significance. The difference between linguistically significant surface information and the irrelevant superficial information must be recognized before any workable evaluation procedure can be evolved, a fact which renders this task more difficult for theories which use algebraic representations primarily or exclusively.

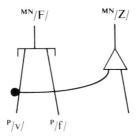

*Figure 3.41   Realization of* $^{MN}$/F/

For the algebraic representation of conditioned options such as would be graphically represented by a downward ordered OR controlled via enablers, a somewhat different form of algebraic formulation is used. This **realization formula** incorporates the conditioning environments expressed via the enablers with the alternate realizations. Let us consider, for example, the algebraic representation of the specification that $^{MN}$/F/, as in *life, knife,* and *leaf,* has the realization $^{P}$/v/ when followed by the $^{MN}$/Z/ of the plural suffix, and elsewhere the realization $^{P}$/f/. This is graphically represented in Figure 3.41.

Algebraically, the downward ordered OR would of course be represented by the formula $^{MN}$/F/ / $^{P}$/v/ + $^{P}$/f/, but to represent the conditioning environments we can refine this formula to (bracketings omitted)

$$F \parallel \underline{\quad} Z / v \quad + \parallel --- / f$$

This may be read as "$^{MN}$/F/ in the environment of following $^{MN}$/Z/ is realized as $^{P}$/v/, and in other environments it is realized as $^{P}$/f/." The double vertical bar therefore marks the environment specification (in terms of upper-stratum units). The line shows the position of the realizate with respect to the conditioning factor; a broken dash in the environment position indicates "everywhere else." It may be convenient to write such formulas in two or more lines, one for each realization with its environment, as

$$F \parallel \underline{\quad} Z / v$$
$$+ \parallel --- / f$$

Each such line of a formula may be termed a **subformula,** with the realizate being stated only once for the whole series of subformulas.

Finally, algebraic conventions for the representation of the coordination and reduplication elements may be suggested.

The coordination element may be indicated by following the label for the element to which it applies by an asterisk (*). So Figure 3.33a may be represented algebraically as

$$X / (A\ B)*$$

The reduplication element may be symbolized by an equals sign (=) accompanying the label for the (main) line to which the reduplication element attaches. The equals sign precedes the symbol in the case of anticipatory reduplication and follows it in the case of repetitive reduplication. Following this convention, Figure 3.35a may be represented by the algebraic formulas

$$X \,/\, (Ns \cdot \,= P) \,(Cl \cdot P)$$
$$P \,/\, Lb, Ap, Fr, Do$$

In the case of Figure 3.35b, the first formula would be instead

$$X \,/\, (Ns \cdot P) \,(Cl \cdot P =)$$

Algebraic conventions for the representation of diamonds have not been devised, since it is seldom necessary or convenient to represent them in an algebraic system.

(The exercises of Set 3E may be done at this point.)

## EXERCISES FOR CHAPTER 3

### Set 3A: Counts of Generative Power

Following the procedures outlined in Section 3.2, determine the number of outputs possible from each of the following tactic diagrams.

**1.**

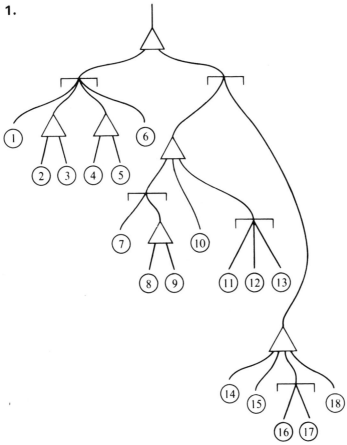

**2.**

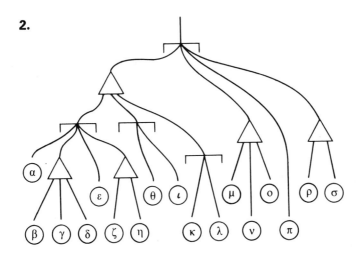

**3.**

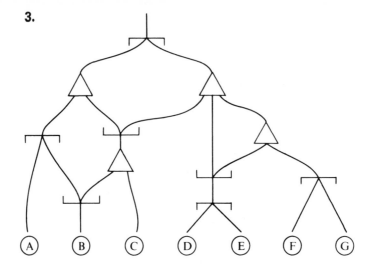

**4.**

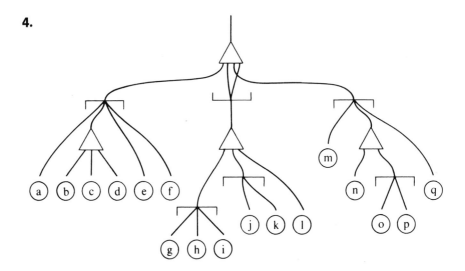

**5.**

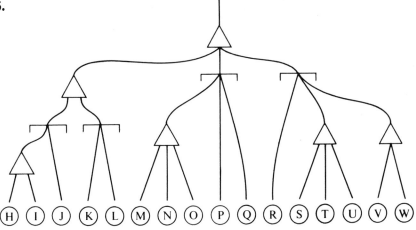

**6.**

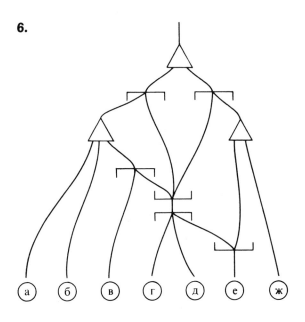

## Set 3B: Simplification

Simplify the following diagrams in accordance with Principles 1–5 as outlined in Section 3.3.

**1.**

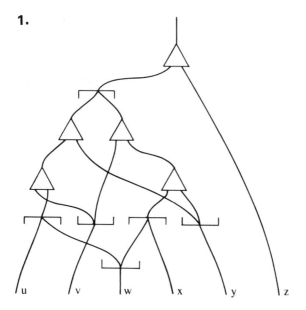

**2.**

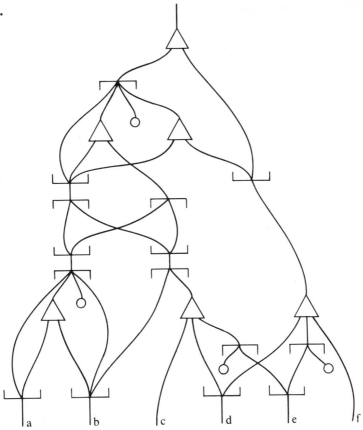

**3.**

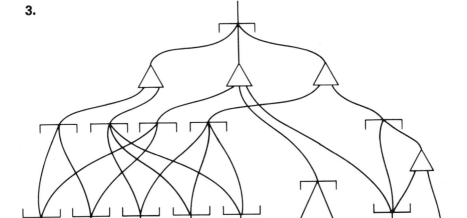

## Set 3C: Reading Diagrams

Indicate five possible sequences of symbols accounted for by each diagram below.

**1.**

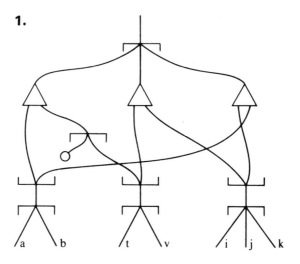

**2.**

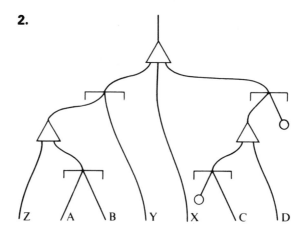

**3.**

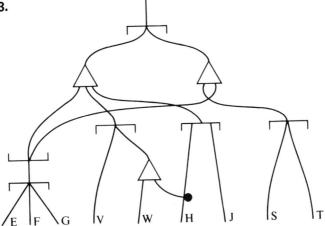

E  F  G  V  W  H  J  S  T

**4.**

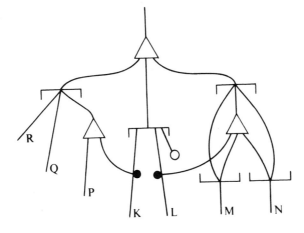

R  Q  P  K  L  M  N

**5.** For each of the symbol sequences listed below, indicate whether or not it is permitted by the accompanying tactic diagram. Your answers may be indicated by the use of + for "permitted" and − for "not permitted."

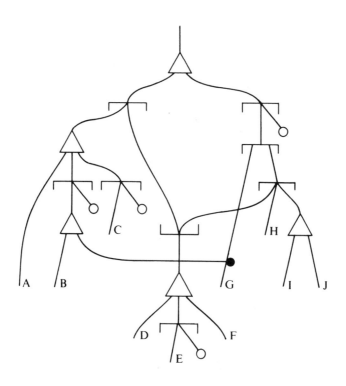

|       |          |          |
|-------|----------|----------|
| **a.** ABCG | **f.** AJ | **k.** ABGDE |
| **b.** DE | **g.** AC | **l.** DEFG |
| **c.** DF | **h.** DFDE | **m.** DEIJ |
| **d.** ABIJ | **i.** ADEF | **n.** ACIJDF |
| **e.** ABCHIJ | **j.** DFDFDF | **o.** ABC |

## Set 3D: Writing Diagrams

For each item below, draw the simplest possible diagram such that what is on the left of the double slash leads down to what is on the right. Consider only context-free solutions.

*Examples*

**A.** z // a

**B.** a // a b

**C.** z // a b, b c

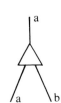

**1.** a // s t, t r, r s

**2.** b // p p

**3.** c // m x, m y

**4.** d // h j, h v j, h w j

**5.** e // talt, marm, talm, malt, tart, tarm, malm, mart

**6.** z // a b, a b c, a b c f, a b d g, a b e f, a b e g

**7.** (one diagram)

   x // a, a c

   y // b, b a c

   z // c, a c b

**8.** (one diagram)

   r w // a

   r w // b

   r y // c

   r z // d

## Set 3E: Notational Conversion

For problems 1 and 2, assign labels as necessary and convert the graph indicated from this chapter into algebraic form. Use one formula for each node.

**1.** Figure 3.17b.                    **2.** Figure 3.29

For problems 3 and 4, convert each graph indicated into a *single* algebraic formula. Why is the single formula a less than ideal way of algebraically representing these two graphs?

**3.** Figure 3.15b                    **4.** Figure 3.29

For problems 5, 6, and 7, draw the graph corresponding to the set of algebraic formulas given. Apply labels to the lines corresponding to the symbols in the formulas.

**5.** t / h p

p / ([g] (y, z)), b [d]

**6.** s / A B [c]

A / x, y, z, w, t

B ‖ (z, w, t)—/ f

+ ‖ --- / g, h

**7.** X / D E [X]

D / (t o [p]), r [s] Q

E / [w [y]] r D

Q ‖ s—/ t

+ ‖ --- / ∅ (zero)

# 4

# *Grammatical Phenomena*

## 4.1 *Morphological Classes and Constructions*

According to a long tradition, grammatical phenomena are commonly divided into **morphology** and **syntax**. This distinction, separating phenomena internal to and external to the grammatical word, is extremely useful in dealing with many languages, particularly highly inflected ones. It will be adopted here for the purpose of organizing our discussion.

To begin our consideration of morphology, let us examine the inflectional data presented in Table 4.1. This table shows four paradigms from standard Czech. They are given in traditional orthography, which is fairly close to a morphonic transcription of this language.

### Table 4.1   Czech Noun Paradigms

|  | *'woman'* | *'winter'* | *'city'* | *'word'* |
|---|---|---|---|---|
| N(ominative Sg) | žena | zima | město | slovo |
| A(ccusative Sg) | ženu | zimu | město | slovo |
| G(enitive Sg) | ženy | zimy | města | slova |
| L(ocative Sg) | ženě | zimě | městě | slově |
| D(ative Sg) | ženě | zimě | městu | slovu |
| I(nstrumental Sg) | ženou | zimou | městem | slovem |

### Table 4.1   Czech Noun Paradigms (continued)

|          | 'woman'  | 'winter' | 'city'   | 'word'   |
|----------|----------|----------|----------|----------|
| NP(lural)| ženy     | zimy     | města    | slova    |
| AP       | ženy     | zimy     | města    | slova    |
| GP       | žen      | zim      | měst     | slov     |
| LP       | ženách   | zimách   | městech  | slovech  |
| DP       | ženám    | zimám    | městům   | slovům   |
| IP       | ženami   | zimami   | městy    | slovy    |

An examination of this data leads us to recognize the following four classes of morphemes:

A class $(S_1)$ containing the stems *žen-* and *zim-*.
A class $(S_2)$ containing the stems *měst-* and *slov-*.
A class $(E_1)$ containing the endings a, u, y, ě, ě, ou, y, y, $\varnothing$, ách, ám, ami.
A class $(E_2)$ containing the endings o, o, a, ě, u, em, a, a, $\varnothing$, ech, ům, y.

Given these classes, we can account for the data exhaustively by setting up two constructions, one consisting of $S_1$ followed by $E_1$, the other of $S_2$ followed by $E_2$. This information may be presented in algebraic notation as follows:

W(ord) / $N_1$, $N_2$
$N_1$ / $S_1$ $E_1$
$N_2$ / $S_2$ $E_2$
$S_1$ / žen, zim
$S_2$ / měst, slov
$E_1$ / a, u, y, ě, ě, ou, y, y, $\varnothing$, ách, ám, ami
$E_2$ / o, o, a, ě, u, em, a, a, $\varnothing$, ech, ům, y

The same information may be presented graphically as in Figure 4.1. In such tactic diagrams, as we have already seen, classes are represented by downward unordered ORs, and constructions are represented by downward ordered ANDs.

Subscript letters have been used in this treatment to mnemonically suggest the case-number association involved, since some endings for different case-number associations have the same shape. There are only two full endings which function in both $E_1$ and $E_2$, however—namely, ě for L and $\varnothing$ for GP. The fact that these two endings recur in the expression of the same case-number can be explicitly handled by connecting them to a single downward OR below an upward OR leading to their separate functions in the tactics, as suggested by the inset to the figure.

In order to see the extent of this kind of overlap in the membership of ending classes, let us consider four more Czech paradigms, each representing a different class from those already considered. This data is displayed in Table 4.2.

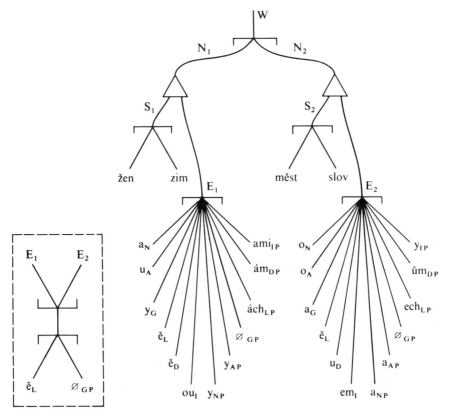

**Figure 4.1 Graphic Representation of Czech Paradigms**

**Table 4.2 Additional Czech Noun Paradigms**

|     | 'barrel' | 'flower' | 'guest' | 'son'  |
|-----|----------|----------|---------|--------|
| N   | sud      | květ     | host    | syn    |
| A   | sud      | květ     | hosta   | syna   |
| G   | sudu     | květu    | hosta   | syna   |
| L   | sudě     | květu    | hostu   | synu   |
| D   | sudu     | květu    | hostu   | synu   |
| I   | sudem    | květem   | hostem  | synem  |
| NP  | sudy     | květy    | hosté   | synové |
| AP  | sudy     | květy    | hosty   | syny   |
| GP  | sudů     | květů    | hostů   | synů   |
| LP  | sudech   | květech  | hostech | synech |
| DP  | sudům    | květům   | hostům  | synům  |
| IP  | sudy     | květy    | hosty   | syny   |

Combining the data of this table with that of Table 4.1, we see evidence for six classes with a great deal more overlap of the ending classes than was found in the initial data. Table 4.3 highlights this overlap.

### Table 4.3   Common Endings in Czech Noun Paradigms

|   | ① | ② | ③ | ④ | ⑤ | ⑥ |
|---|---|---|---|---|---|---|
|   | žen-<br>zim- | měst-<br>slov- | sud- | květ- | host- | syn- |
| N | a | o | ∅ | ∅ | ∅ | ∅ |
| A | u | o | ∅ | ∅ | a | a |
| G | y | a | u | u | a | a |
| L | ě | ě | ě | u | u | u |
| D | ě | u | u | u | u | u |
| I | ou | em | em | em | em | em |
| NP | y | a | y | y | é | ové |
| AP | y | a | y | y | y | y |
| GP | ∅ | ∅ | ů | ů | ů | ů |
| LP | ách | ech | ech | ech | ech | ech |
| DP | ám | ům | ům | ům | ům | ům |
| IP | ami | y | y | y | y | y |

If we follow the same procedures that were used in treating the data of Table 4.1, we will have six separate constructions associating stem and ending classes. But though each ending class is in some way distinct from every other one, there will be a great deal in common among the various ending classes. On the basis of the display in Table 4.3, we can set up the following **macro-classes** among the ending classes $E_1$ through $E_6$, defined by the existence of one or more endings of the same form and realizational function serving in two or more ending classes.

(a) 1, 2          :   Ending $\varnothing_{GP}$

(b) 3, 4          :   Endings $\varnothing_A$, $u_G$

(c) 5, 6          :   Ending $a_A$

(d) 1, 2, 3       :   Ending $\check{e}_L$

(e) 4, 5, 6       :   Ending $u_L$

(f) 1, 3, 4       :   Ending $y_{NP}$

(g) 2, 5, 6       :   Ending $a_G$

(h) 3, 4, 5, 6    :   Endings $\varnothing_N$, $\mathring{u}_{GP}$

(i) 1, 3, 4, 5, 6 :   Ending $y_{AP}$

(j) 2, 3, 4, 5, 6 :   Endings $u_D$, $em_I$, $ech_{LP}$, $\mathring{u}m_{DP}$, $y_{IP}$

In each of these cases, and only in these, we find two or more of the six stem classes represented here taking the same endings for the particular case-number combinations involved. These cases of overlap represent generalizations which will have to be captured in our treatment of these morphological facts. Obviously, a mere extension of the principles applied in Figure 4.1 will not do for this purpose. The relevant generalizations can be dealt with, however, if we treat these classes in the fashion suggested in Figure 4.2. Here we recognize six constructions, as represented by the downward ANDs labelled (1)-(6). The downward unordered ORs $E_1$-$E_6$ represent the ending classes, but rather than having twelve branches each, these ORs connect to further structures which give explicit recognition to the macroclasses (a)-(j). Each macroclass is, in fact, represented by an upward OR, each of which has been given its appropriate label in the figure. So, while each downward OR $E_1$-$E_6$ leads down ultimately to twelve endings, it does so through a series of upward and downward ORs to capture these generalizations. Furthermore, the diagram has been organized so as to reflect the inclusion of macroclasses one within the other, allowing as simple an organization as possible. The macroclass (j), for example, is shown to include (h) and $E_2$, while (h) includes (b) and (c). In this diagram, a convention is introduced to avoid downward ORs with numerous branches. This involves using representation of the downward OR node with a list appended to it. Each item in the list would be represented by a separate branch in the fuller form of the diagram.

The method of analysis reflected in this diagram follows ultimately from the simplicity principle, for it will turn out that the analysis represents the simplest organization of classes and constructions possible for this data.

In addition, the solution to this problem bears on a much more general principle, applying to all types of tactic classification. With the aid of an abstract example, we can now state this principle more explicitly. Suppose

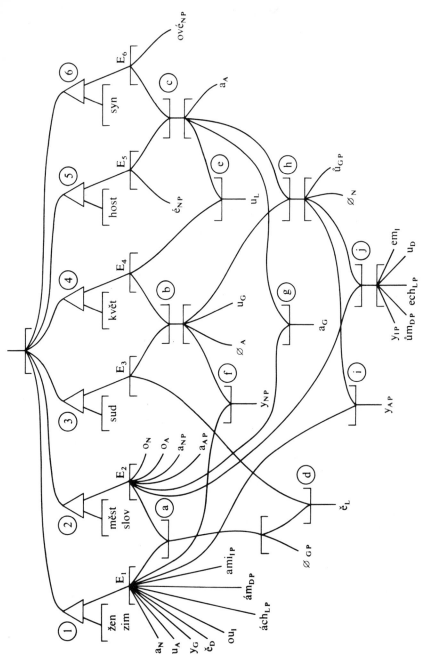

***Figure 4.2   Analysis of Six Czech Noun Classes***

we have the entities A–J of any stratum, with tactic considerations justifying the following classes among them:

$$1 \,/\, A, B, C$$
$$2 \,/\, A, B, C, D, E$$
$$3 \,/\, D, E$$
$$4 \,/\, D, E, F, G$$
$$5 \,/\, F, G$$
$$6 \,/\, F, G, H, I, J$$
$$7 \,/\, H, I, J$$

One approach to the treatment of these phenomena would establish only the seven downward classes shown in the series of formulas. Overlapping class memberships would then be individually represented by an upward OR for each entity belonging to more than one class. This approach would result in the diagram shown in Figure 4.3a.

A second approach would establish the first-level classes A, B, C; D, E; F, G; and H, I, J and then lead up from them to their separate functions 1–7. In this way classes 2, 4, and 6 would be shown to be composites of other classes.

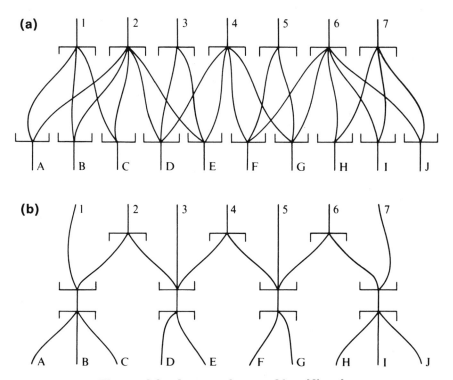

**Figure 4.3  Approaches to Classification**

This approach, diagrammed in Figure 4.3b, is clearly simpler, a fact which is confirmed by the simplicity measure, in that $N + L$ for 4.3a is $17 + 14 = 31$, while for 4.3b it is $11 + 4 = 15$. Extended to other cases, this principle means that we follow the simplicity measure and establish as many levels of classes as necessary to deal with generalizations.

This principle finds application, among other places, in the establishment of parts of speech. Some linguists in the past have established only one level of such classes, including NOUN, VERB, and ADJECTIVE, for example. Morphemes such as *fancy* (which can be any of the three), *fish* (noun or verb), and *clear* (verb or adjective) would be dealt with as individual cases, as in the approach of Figure 4.3a. An alternate approach would set up one level of classes based on total range, thereby differentiating *fancy*, *fish*, and *penetrate* into three separate classes at the beginning. Then a second level of classes would gather the items with identical individual functions, which would bring the above three into the class VERB, though *fancy* and *fish* would belong to other second-level classes as well. This second approach corresponds to that of Figure 4.3b and is preferable by the simplicity principle.

(The exercises of Set 4A at the end of this chapter may be done at this point.)

## 4.2  *Morphological Alternation*

In addition to providing for classes and constructions, any treatment of morphology must deal with alternation phenomena. Much of the traditional allomorphic alternation, of course, is more properly relegated to the phonology. Certain kinds of alternation, however, must still be considered morphological in nature.

A number of examples of morphological alternation are provided by the Czech data discussed in the previous section. Let us begin our discussion of this phenomenon, however, with the somewhat less complex situation provided by the English data of Table 4.4.

### Table 4.4  Some English Alternations

|  | | $^{LN}$/Comp/ | $^{LN}$/Sup/ |
|---|---|---|---|
| $^{LN}$/good/ | gud | beT r | beT st |
| $^{LN}$/bad/ | bæd | wər s | wər st |
| $^{LN}$/soft/ | soft | soft r | soft st |

This table shows the lexons involved as labels for its rows and columns, adjectives being used for the rows, and suffixes for the comparative and superlative (and the unsuffixed positive) in the columns. The results of the combinations are provided at the intersections of these rows and columns, in a tentative morphonic transcription. Note that $^{MN}$/T/ is a morphon with alternate realizations $^{P}$/t/ and ⌀—it recurs in *latter, last*. The vowel preceding *r* or *st* in the ultimate forms of *better, softer, softest* will be provided by the phonology.

If we look at the facts in this way, we see three alternations: $^{LN}$/good/ has the alternate realizations $^{MN}$/gud/ and $^{MN}$/beT/; $^{LN}$/bad/ has the alternate realizations $^{MN}$/bæd/ and $^{MN}$/wər/; and $^{LN}$/Comp/ has the alternate realizations $^{MN}$/r/ and $^{MN}$/s/.

Two different ways of treating such alternations stratificationally have been proposed. The one suggested by the *Outline of Stratificational Grammar* defines the alternants shown here as morphemes, in terms of which the tactics is stated. This places the alternation between the lexons and the morphemes. Figure 4.4 shows this treatment of the data at hand (updated from the *Outline* by the use of diamonds).

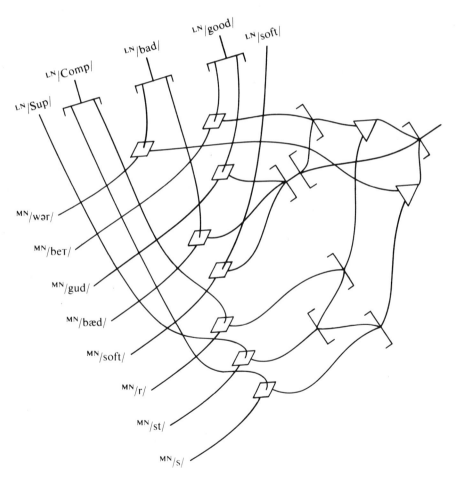

**Figure 4.4  English Comparison with Lexonic Alternation**

Here the alternations are depicted by downward ordered ORs above the tactics, and there are eight diamonds, one for each alternant. According to the idea behind this conception, the conditioning environments for alternate realizations are provided by the tactics in the following manner: considering the tactic environment of each possible alternant, one selects the alternant which the tactics permits, using the precedence provided by the ordered ORs in case more than one fits. Each of the alternations in the English data will therefore be handled as follows:

1. $^{LN}$/Comp/—The tactics allows $^{MN}$/s/ only if preceded by $^{MN}$/wər/, so it will occur there, and elsewhere $^{MN}$/r/ will occur.
2. $^{LN}$/good/—The tactics allows the preferred alternant $^{MN}$/beT/ only when followed by one of the suffixes $^{MN}$/r/ or $^{MN}$/st/, so it will occur in these environments and $^{MN}$/gud/ will occur elsewhere.
3. $^{LN}$/bad/—The tactics allows the preferred alternant $^{MN}$/wər/ only before $^{MN}$/s/ or $^{MN}$/st/, so it will occur in these environments and $^{MN}$/bæd/ will occur elsewhere.

Note that the tactics, operating by itself, will allow the combinations $^{MN}$/gud r/, $^{MN}$/gud st/, $^{MN}$/bæd r/, $^{MN}$/bæd st/. These results are ruled out, however, by the precedence of the ordered ORs. These tactic possibilities, nevertheless, allow English speakers to decode the regularized forms of children or nonnative speakers, and they provide the basis for an explanation of such overgeneralizing errors. Note further that this tactic pattern would have to be made more complicated if these possibilities were to be completely excluded.

The basic difficulty with the idea of allowing the tactics to condition alternations without additional apparatus is that it has proven unworkable as the basis for a model of performance. It has not been possible to give performance-oriented definitions of the nodes so that they will operate in the desired way that we have verbally described.

This brings us back to a point made earlier: work on a model of ideal performance should be allowed to influence work on the model of competence. According to this principle, we should consider alternate possibilities which may prove more workable.

The alternate approach we will consider was suggested in its essence in Lamb's paper "Kinship terminology and linguistic structure" in 1965, though it has been formalized only more recently. It is diagrammed in Figure 4.5, which differs from Figure 4.4 most significantly in that the ordered ORs showing the alternations are *below* instead of above the tactics. This means that the tactics works at a higher level of abstraction than that of Figure 4.4 and is, as a result, considerably simpler in this case. (It also works out better if all downward ORs with zero as one alternative are considered ordered. This practice will be followed here and in all subsequent tactic diagrams.)

subclasses in our data, followed by the realization formulas for $^M$/Pt/ and $^M$/PP/.

## CLASSES

    ①     rig, pik (but for the whole language the most general class)

    ②     sel

    ③a    siŋ

    ③b    sit

    ③c    šayn

    ③d    howld

    ③e    baynd

    ③f    θiŋk, tiyč, kæč, siyk, fayt, bay

    ④a    grow

    ④b    teyk

    ④c    giv

    ⑤     friyz, breyk, čuwz

## REALIZATION FORMULAS

| | |
|---|---|
| $^M$/Pt/ ‖ ③a — /æ$^+$ | $^M$/PP/ ‖ ③a — /ə$^+$ |
| , ‖ ④a — /uw$^+$ | , ‖ ④a , ④b , ④c , ⑤— /n |
| , ‖ ④b — /u$^+$ | + ‖ --- /(the same as for $^M$/Pt/) |
| , ‖ ④c — /ey$^+$ | |
| , ‖ ⑤— /ow$^+$ | |
| + ‖ ③b — /æ$^+$ | |
| , ‖ ③c — /ow$^+$ | |
| , ‖ ③d — /e$^+$ | |
| , ‖ ③e — /aw$^+$ | |
| , ‖ ③f— /o$^+$t$^+$ | |
| + ‖ --- /d | |

The note on the last subformula indicates that the two morphemes $^M$/Pt/ and $^M$/PP/ share certain subformulas in the description of their realizations.

The second important difference, of course, is that enablers and conditioning lines are used to indicate conditioning environments for the alternations. To highlight their status, conditioning lines have been drawn as broken lines. We can also note from this example that conditioning lines are not required to follow either the tactic or the realizational "planes," but may run from one to the other. In particular, as shown here in the case of the conditions permitting <sup>MN</sup>/beT/ and <sup>MN</sup>/wər/, a conditioning line running to an enabler in the realizational pattern may originate at an appropriate point in the tactics. The conditioning line providing for <sup>MN</sup>/s/ as the realization of <sup>LN</sup>/Comp/, however, originates from a different point in the realizational pattern because this realization is specific to the environment after <sup>MN</sup>/wər/ and does not apply after other realizations of <sup>LN</sup>/bad/, as can be seen if one recalls that English speakers can decode *badder* as a deviant comparative but would never expect \**badse*, which would result if the occurrence of <sup>MN</sup>/s/ for the comparative were conditioned by *bad* in general.

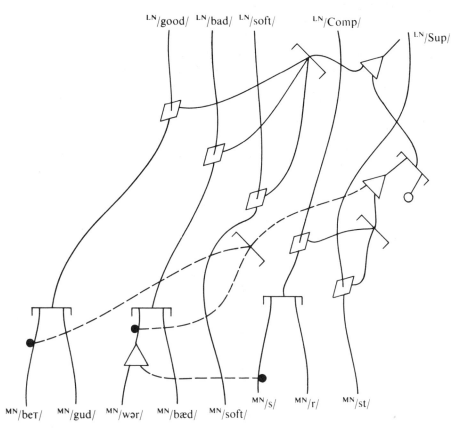

**Figure 4.5  *English Comparison with Morphemic Alternation***

It is interesting to note that this treatment in fact provides a simpler account of the situation than that of Figure 4.4, even if we disregard the operational difficulties occasioned by the latter. The simplicity measure $N + L$ reveals a count of $20 + 2 = 22$ for Figure 4.4, while for 4.5 it is $18 + 1 = 19$.

The adoption of this conception makes it necessary to establish a terminological difference to distinguish the undifferentiated entities represented by the diamonds of Figure 4.5 from the combinations of morphons which realize them. We will term the diamonds morphemes as before, and establish the term **morphemic sign** for their realizations. Thus a morpheme is the realization of a lexon, and it participates in the tactics. Such a morpheme is realized by one or more alternate morphemic signs, each consisting of one or more morphons. The term "morphemic sign" was originally introduced in the *Outline*, but it was not used in earlier chapters of this book because we have spoken loosely up to now of morphemes consisting of morphons. The configuration intervening between morphemes and morphemic signs, characterized especially by the downward ordered ORs and enablers, may be termed the **morphemic alternation pattern**.

In view of this conception of the treatment of alternation, we may now consider anew some of the Czech data treated in preliminary form in Section 4.1. For simplicity of illustration, we will deal only with the formation of accusative and genitive cases, singular and plural, for the six classes illustrated there. This limited amount of data does not by itself suffice to distinguish all six classes, but in view of the evidence already at hand requiring their separation, all six will still be recognized.

In terms of these six classes, the realization of the case-number combinations being considered may be stated by the following realization formulas:

$$A \parallel \text{①}\underline{\quad}/u$$
$$, \parallel \text{②}\underline{\quad}/o$$
$$, \parallel \text{⑤}, \text{⑥}\underline{\quad}/a$$
$$+ \parallel \text{---}/\varnothing$$

$$AP \parallel \text{②}\underline{\quad}/a$$
$$+ \parallel \text{---}/y$$

$$G \parallel \text{①}\underline{\quad}/y$$
$$, \parallel \text{③}, \text{④}\underline{\quad}/u$$
$$+ \parallel \text{---}/a$$

$$GP \parallel \text{①}, \text{②}\underline{\quad}/\varnothing$$
$$+ \parallel \text{---}/\mathring{u}$$

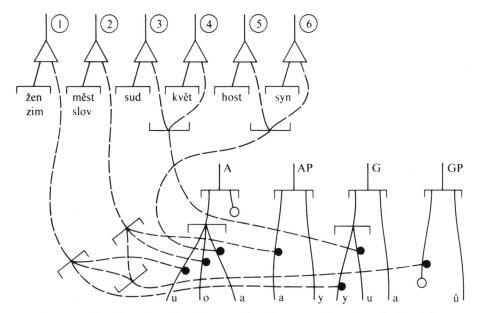

*Figure 4.6 Morphemic Alternation Pattern for Czech Genitive and Accusative*

In these formulas a new convention is introduced to distinguish subformulas which are significantly ordered with respect to each other from those which are only arbitrarily ordered: the comma (for an unordered OR relationship) is used at the beginning of a subformula which is unordered with respect to the preceding one, while the plus (ordered OR) is used when the order is significant.

The same information is represented graphically in Figure 4.6. In this kind of system, it should be noted, conditioning environments need to be pointed out explicitly only for the less common, more restricted realizations. The most usual one may be left as the unconditioned alternate from the last branch of the OR. The simplicity principle will of course be decisive in case of any doubt as to which alternant to treat as unconditioned.

Here the tactics provides the division of the stems into the classes necessary to provide the conditioning environments, while the endings involve only abstract categories: the numbers and cases as such. In this sense, AP and GP may be considered portmanteau realizations of the plural morpheme with the accusative and genitive morphemes, respectively. Singular, however, can be regarded as merely the absence of the specification of plurality, and as such, as the unmarked number. Therefore A and G would be the realizations of the accusative and genitive morphemes alone. It may be expedient to recognize an unmarked case as well, in which instance nominative seems the most likely candidate. Evidence for this position includes, among other things, the fact that in many languages with case systems, including Czech, speakers use the

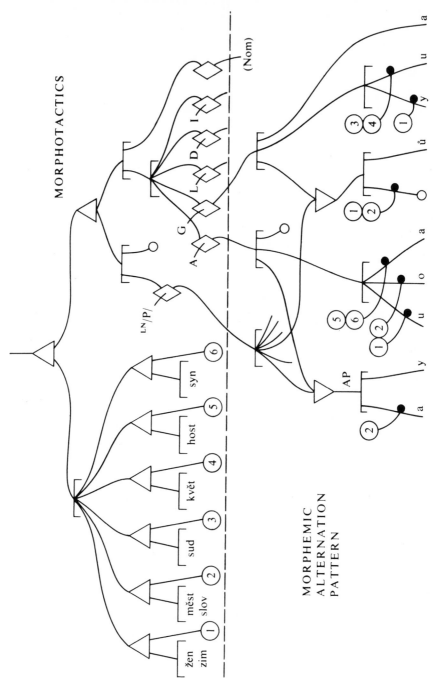

*Figure 4.7   Czech Morphotactics and Alternations*

nominative when the occasion requires the use of a noun without any grammatical context, as in calling out the names of objects or phenomena. The tactics of Figure 4.7 is based on this assumption, so that it treats nominative plural as the morpheme $^M/P/$ alone and nominative singular as the absence of any lexonic suffix specification. Case and number morphemes are joined at a downward unordered AND, since there is no basis for establishing an order between them. The part of the morphemic alternation pattern represented explicitly in Figure 4.6 is shown here in a form which, while less explicit, is easier to read. Instead of full conditioning lines, it uses reference numbers at both the enablers and the conditioning points in the tactics. The user of such a diagram may mentally draw in a specific line as he needs it without creating the tangle of intersecting lines which can be a practical problem in this notation. Of course, the algebraic notation is also very useful for representing morphemic alternation patterns in the form of realization formulas. In practical work, the two notations can complement and supplement each other in various ways.

(The exercises of Set 4B at the end of this chapter may be done at this point.)

## 4.3 *Morphological Simultaneity*

In the example of Czech cases and numbers, we stipulated that the morphemes representing these categories would be regarded as coming from a downward unordered AND. The fact that $^M/P/$ is always realized as a portmanteau with any case which occurs makes it impossible to establish any order between these two morpheme classes, though the portmanteaus realizing them always occur following the stem. There are some further uses for downward unordered ANDs in the morphology of certain languages, and the evidence for this will be discussed in this section.

Let us consider first the English verb forms listed in Table 4.5. In many traditional treatments, the patterns exhibited by this data have been described in terms of a process of replacement of the vocalic nucleus of the simple form shown in the first column with another nucleus in the formation of the past-tense and past-participial forms in the other two columns. Stratificational theory, however, is forced by its fundamental principles to look for the pattern of relationships underlying these supposed processes.

#### Table 4.5   English Verb Forms

| | | | |
|---|---|---|---|
| 1. | siŋ | sæŋ | səŋ |
| 2. | kliŋ | kləŋ | kləŋ |
| 3. | baynd | bawnd | bawnd |
| 4. | šayn | šown | šown |
| 5. | howld | held | held |
| 6. | sit | sæt | sæt |
| 7. | strayk | strək | strək |

Let us therefore put forward the hypothesis that the realization of $^{LN}$/Pt/ in *sang* is a morpheme which occurs simultaneously with the stem $^{M}$/siŋ/. It is realized by the morphon $^{MN}$/æ$^{+}$/, which has the special property that its phonemic realization takes precedence over that of any ordinary vowel morphon, such as the $^{MN}$/i/ in $^{M}$/siŋ/. In cases where two vowels are signalled simultaneously to the phonology, the conflict will be resolved in favor of the vowel having this precedence. Morphons with this special property may be termed **preemptives**, and may be conveniently marked by a superscript $^{+}$ in their symbolizations. If we extend this assumption to all the data of Table 4.5, we come up with the morphonic representations given in Table 4.6. These representations are based rather directly on the classical phonemic forms given in the initial data, so the details of their representation should not be taken as the final ones which might be arrived at after further consideration.

### Table 4.6  Morphonic Representations of English Verb Forms

| | | | |
|---|---|---|---|
| 1. | siŋ | (siŋ) · æ$^{+}$ | (siŋ) · ə$^{+}$ |
| 2. | kliŋ | (kliŋ) · ə$^{+}$ | (kliŋ) · ə$^{+}$ |
| 3. | baynd | (baynd) · aw$^{+}$ | (baynd) · aw$^{+}$ |
| 4. | šayn | (šayn) · ow$^{+}$ | (šayn) · ow$^{+}$ |
| 5. | howld | (howld) · e$^{+}$ | (howld) · e$^{+}$ |
| 6. | sit | (sit) · æ$^{+}$ | (sit) · æ$^{+}$ |
| 7. | strayk | (strayk) · ə$^{+}$ | (strayk) · ə$^{+}$ |

The details of how the phonology will be able to handle this preemptive phenomenon will be taken up in Chapter 6. If we make the assumption for the moment that we will be able to deal readily with the phonological aspects of this treatment, it seems clear that it provides a more general account of the facts involved than other alternatives which might suggest themselves. The treatment of *sang*, *sung* and the others as portmanteaus, for example, would obscure the fact that the only difference between *sing*, *sang*, and *sung* is in the vowel. This fact would also be left inexplicit if *sing*, *sang*, and *sung* were to be treated as alternate realizations of a single morpheme, as others have suggested.

All the verb forms in this material can be said to exemplify a single basic construction covering verbs having preemptive realizations of the lexons $^{LN}$/Pt/ and $^{LN}$/PP/. The alternate realizations of these, including the neutralization occurring between the two for a good portion of the data, may be handled in the morphemic alternation pattern. In order to provide the necessary conditioning, of course, various stem subclasses will need to be recognized in the tactics. A graphic treatment of this data along the general lines suggested in Section 4.2 is shown in Figure 4.8. The labels for the alternate realizations of the morphemes $^{M}$/Pt/ and $^{M}$/PP/ are given the superscript $^{MS}$ for morphemic sign, though some also happen to be single morphons as well. (The significance of the (x) label in the diagram will be explained later.)

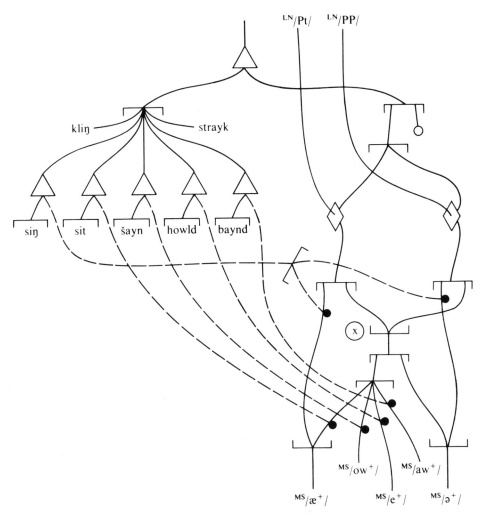

**Figure 4.8   English Verbs with Preemptives**

We may now augment this data with the additional English verb material given in Table 4.7. These fifteen verbs give a representative sample of the additional phenomena found in English verb morphology. Examples 1 and 2, of course, represent regular verbs with a suffix having the morphonic form $^{MN}$/d/. Its alternate realizations are easily handled by the phonology. Example 3 has the regular suffix with a preemptive as well. This preemptive may be considered a determined element. Examples 4–9 all involve verbs with a preemptive past and a past participle formed with the suffix $^{MN}$/n/ (the /ə/ in some forms will be provided by the phonology). Examples 7–9 additionally have a determined preemptive which happens to be the same as the significant

### Table 4.7    Additional English Verb Forms

|     |        |        |         |
| --- | ------ | ------ | ------- |
| 1.  | rig    | rigd   | rigd    |
| 2.  | pik    | pikt   | pikt    |
| 3.  | sel    | sowld  | sowld   |
| 4.  | grow   | gruw   | grown   |
| 5.  | teyk   | tuk    | teykən  |
| 6.  | giv    | geyv   | givən   |
| 7   | friyz  | frowz  | frowzən |
| 8   | breyk  | browk  | browkən |
| 9.  | čuwz   | čowz   | čowzən  |
| 10. | θiŋk   | θot    | θot     |
| 11. | tiyč   | tot    | tot     |
| 12. | kæč    | kot    | kot     |
| 13. | siyk   | sot    | sot     |
| 14. | fayt   | fot    | fot     |
| 15. | bay    | bot    | bot     |

one occurring in their respective past forms. The series 10–15 shows an interesting preemptive phenomenon—the realization of both $^{LN}$/Pt/ and $^{LN}$/PP/ contains a preemptive vowel $^{MN}$/o$^+$/ followed by a preemptive consonant $^{MN}$/t$^+$/. The phonology can easily be arranged to provide that the realization of this consonant morphon will have precedence over any other consonant or consonant cluster in the coda (the final portion of a closed syllable, following the vowel nucleus), just as preemptive vowels have precedence in the syllable nucleus. Examples 14 and 15 may seem somewhat different from the others, in that the same consonant occurs at the end of all the forms in 14 and no coda consonant occurs at all in the simple form of 15. No special provisions are needed, however, to treat these as cases of the same general phenomenon: $^{MN}$/t$^+$/ will take precedence over $^{MN}$/t/ in 14 and over the lack of final consonant in 15.

Considering the data of Tables 4.5 and 4.7 together, we see the following tactic situations:

(1) Suffixal realizations of $^{LN}$/Pt/ and $^{LN}$/PP/ (1 and 2 of Table 4.7)

(2) Suffixal realizations of $^{LN}$/Pt/ and $^{LN}$/PP/ with a determined preemptive (3 of Table 4.7)

(3) Preemptive realizations of $^{LN}$/Pt/ and $^{LN}$/PP/ (10–15 of Table 4.7 and all of Table 4.5)

(4) Preemptive realization of $^{LN}$/Pt/ and suffixal realization of $^{LN}$/PP/ (4–6 of Table 4.7)

(5) Preemptive realization of $^{LN}$/Pt/ and suffixal realization of $^{LN}$/PP/ with a determined preemptive (7–9 of Table 4.7)

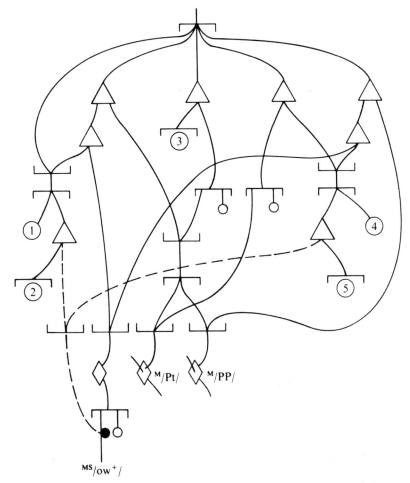

**Figure 4.9  Tactics for Some English Verb Classes**

A tactic pattern handling this situation is shown in Figure 4.9. We still have only one past and one past-participle morpheme, but they are shown by the tactics to function as suffixes in some cases and as simultaneous preemptives in others. The circled reference numbers show the points at which the corresponding classes of the above list will fit into the tactics. Note that this treatment initially combines classes ① and ② on the one hand, and ④ and ⑤ on the other. They are then differentiated according to whether the potential determined preemptive $^{MS}$/ow$^+$/ is allowed to occur or not, with ② and ⑤ conditioning its occurrence, as shown.

Some of these classes, of course, will need to be divided into subclasses to allow the conditioning of alternate realizations of $^M$/Pt/ and $^M$/PP/. Rather than providing the full graphic treatment of this structure, we will list the subclasses in our data, followed by the realization formulas for $^M$/Pt/ and $^M$/PP/.

## CLASSES

①  rig, pik (but for the whole language the most general class)

②  sel

③ⓐ  siŋ

③ⓑ  sit

③ⓒ  šayn

③ⓓ  howld

③ⓔ  baynd

③ⓕ  θiŋk, tiyč, kæč, siyk, fayt, bay

④ⓐ  grow

④ⓑ  teyk

④ⓒ  giv

⑤  friyz, breyk, čuwz

## REALIZATION FORMULAS

$^M$/Pt/ ‖ ③ⓐ — /æ$^+$

, ‖ ④ⓐ — /uw$^+$

, ‖ ④ⓑ — /u$^+$

, ‖ ④ⓒ — /ey$^+$

, ‖ ⑤ — /ow$^+$

+ ‖ ③ⓑ — /æ$^+$

, ‖ ③ⓒ — /ow$^+$

, ‖ ③ⓓ — /e$^+$

, ‖ ③ⓔ — /aw$^+$

, ‖ ③ⓕ — /o$^+$t$^+$

+ ‖ --- /d

$^M$/PP/ ‖ ③ⓐ — /ə$^+$

, ‖ ④ⓐ , ④ⓑ , ④ⓒ , ⑤ — /n

+ ‖ --- /(the same as for $^M$/Pt/)

The note on the last subformula indicates that the two morphemes $^M$/Pt/ and $^M$/PP/ share certain subformulas in the description of their realizations.

The shared subformulas are those after the first + in the formula for $^M/Pt/$. In the graphic notation, this fact will be indicated by the use of an upward OR such as that marked with $\text{(x)}$ in Figure 4.8.

Another morphological phenomenon outside the realm of simple prefixes and suffixes is infixation. For an example of this phenomenon, let us examine the Latin data in Table 4.8.

### Table 4.8  Infixation in Latin

1. **rump**ō 'I break'       **rup**tum 'broken'
2. **vinc**ō 'I conquer'     **vic**tum 'conquered'
3. **jung**ō 'I join'        **jug**um 'yoke'
4. **relinqu**ō 'I leave'    **relic**tum 'left'
5. **tang**ō 'I touch'       tetigī 'I touched'

In each of these examples, the first-person singular present form of the first column shows a root with a nasal infix before its final consonant. In the forms of the second column, the same root occurs without the infix. In some of these cases, there are additional vocalic or consonantal alternations for which the phonology of Latin will be called upon to account. But putting these aside, we can see that the nasal infix to the root is common to the present stems of all these verbs.

Such infixes may readily be viewed as preemptives of a special type—consonants which preempt the absence of a consonant in a particular position. We have already seen one case of the preemption of zero in the example *bought*, where general considerations make it worthwhile to treat this as morphonically (bay) $\cdot$ $(o^+t^+)$ with the $^{MN}/t^+/$ preempting the absence of final coda. In the case of the Latin infixes, $^{MN}/n^+/$ is phonologically realized in the position before the final consonant of the root, where otherwise no consonant at all would occur. The accommodation of its realization to the point of articulation of the following consonant is another general phonological phenomenon which is of no concern to the morphology.

By analogy with our treatment of the more usual preemptives, we may surmise that the morphology of Latin provides $^{MN}/n^+/$ simultaneous with the root in the forms of the first column, while the phonology handles its positioning as well as other aspects of its realization. Thus the stems of the first column are morphonically (rup) $\cdot$ $n^+$, (wik) $\cdot$ $n^+$, (jug) $\cdot$ $n^+$, (lik$^W$) $\cdot$ $n^+$, and (tag) $\cdot$ $n^+$. While it may be slightly awkward to term the infixes "preemptives," the two phenomena involve the same kind of morphological structure, one of simultaneous morphemes, and the difference between them is purely a matter of their phonological realization. The term **simulfix** may be provided to cover all affixes which occur simultaneous with a root morpheme. Preemptives and infixes are two types of simulfixes distinguishable in terms of the phonology.

A third kind of simulfixing is frequent in Semitic languages such as Hebrew or Arabic. Let us consider the data from Amharic presented in Table 4.9.

### Table 4.9  Amharic Verb Forms

|   | 3Sg Past | 3Sg Present | Imperative Sg | Infinitive | Gloss |
|---|----------|-------------|---------------|------------|-------|
| 1. | wəsədə | yiwəsidal | wisəd | məwsəd | 'take' |
| 2. | məsələ | yiməsilal | misəl | məmsəl | 'resemble' |
| 3. | gət'əmə | yigət'imal | git'əm | məgt'əm | 'join' |
| 4. | dəgəmə | yidəgimal | digəm | mədgəm | 'repeat' |
| 5. | nəgədə | yinəgidal | nigəd | məngəd | 'trade' |
| 6. | wərədə | yiwəridal | wirəd | məwrəd | 'get down' |

Adapted from Problem 8 of Merrifield et al., *Laboratory Manual for Morphology and Syntax* (Santa Ana, Calif.: Summer Institute of Linguistics, 1967), p. 3.

As we may see, the third-person singular past is characterized by the suffix *-ə*, the third singular present by the prefix *yi-* and the suffix *-al*, the imperative singular by no prefixes or suffixes, and the infinitive by the prefix *mə-*. If these affixes are stripped off, however, we still find variation in the stems which are left. In row 1, for example, we get *wəsəd-*, *-wəsid-*, *wisəd*, and *-wsəd*, and the other rows show analogous variation. What is constant for all these different stems, across the four columns of any one row, are the three consonants which form the roots *w-s-d* 'take,' *m-s-l* 'resemble,' *g-t'-m* 'join,' *d-g-m* 'repeat,' *n-g-d* 'trade,' and *w-r-d* 'get down.' And down the various rows in any one column we find the constant vowel pattern *ə-ə*, *ə-i*, *i-ə*, and *∅-ə*. The symbol *∅* is used in representing the final pattern to indicate that the *ə* will go between the second two consonants of the root rather than the first two.

A fairly traditional way of treating this situation is with discontinuous morphemes. The triconsonantal roots occur with vocalic sequences which could be called interfixes. From a stratificational point of view, however, interfixes can be considered just another variety of the simulfixing phenomenon seen in our previous examples. The phonology could then be set up so as to realize the consonants of the root and the vowels of the interfix in their proper order, by means which will be detailed in Chapter 6.

The morphological tactics providing for the data of Table 4.9 is shown in Figure 4.10.

Note that a special zero vowel morphon $^{MN}/∅/$ must be recognized as a part of the simulfix occurring in the infinitive. In the phonology the realization of this morphon will have the effect of satisfying the first vowel position, but it will have no phonetic realization.

We have in this section provided evidence that morphological affixes may be divided into three types: prefixes, suffixes, and simulfixes. The last class includes the more traditional replacives (preemptives), infixes, and interfixes, which are distinguished according to their phonological realizations.

(The exercises of Set 4C at the end of this chapter may be done at this point.)

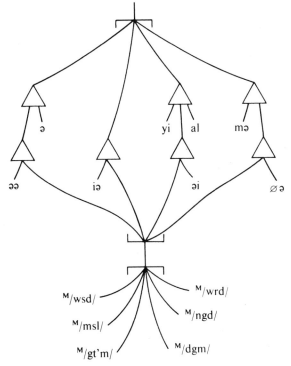

*Figure 4.10  Tactics for Amharic Verb Forms*

## 4.4  Constituent Structure

The analysis of constructions into their constituents presents problems for both morphology and syntax. The view which became known as "immediate constituent theory," stemming from the work of Bloomfield, maintained that constructions are in principle to be broken down in purely binary steps (Wells 1947, Nida 1949). An alternative view, known as "string constituent analysis," insisted that constituent cuts should be in principle multiple, corresponding to a relatively small number of "levels" (ranks) of syntactic structure (Longacre 1960).

In stratificational theory, the ultimate validity of any constituent analysis is based on the simplicity principle. We can demonstrate this with the English forms *unclearly* and *unevenly*. Their constituent structure depends on the trace from the tactics which accounts for them, as well as related forms involving some of the same morphemes. For these particular items there are three possible traces, as represented for *unclearly* in Figure 4.11. The tactics from which these structures would be traces would be required to account also for such related forms as *clear, even, unclear, uneven, clearly, evenly*. It would also need to take

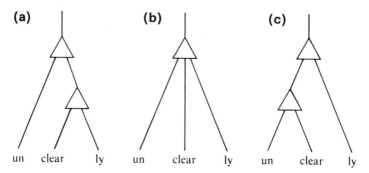

**Figure 4.11    Alternative Constituent Structures**

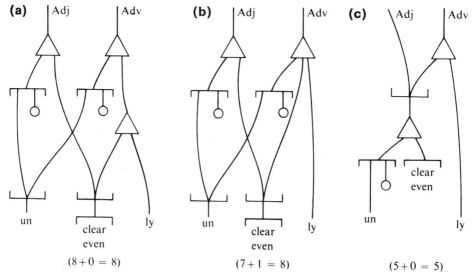

$$(8+0 = 8) \qquad (7+1 = 8) \qquad (5+0 = 5)$$

**Figure 4.12    Tactics Assigning Alternative Constituent Structures**

Reprinted from *Outline of Stratificational Grammar* by Sydney M. Lamb, Georgetown University Press, Washington, D.C., 1966, p. 53.

into account the fact that *clearly, unclearly, evenly, unevenly,* as adverbs, have a different distribution from the other forms (all adjectives). Three diagrams which provide for these additional facts are shown in Figure 4.12. They assign the constituent structures represented by the corresponding traces of Figure 4.11.

The simplicity counts show that Figure 4.12c, assigning the structure of

4.11c, is by far the simplest. The same procedure can be applied to any other dubious cases of constituent structure in morphology or syntax, reducing the question of constituent structure analysis to a matter of the simplicity of the tactic structures which define the traces, considered in terms of the total structure of the language. Various criteria and procedures which have been proposed for making constituency cuts are valid, therefore, only to the extent that they lead to the same results as the simplicity principle.

It has long been recognized that the same sequence of units may be assigned alternate constituent structures by different possible traces. This situation may be termed **tactic ambiguity.** Two of the classic examples of this phenomenon are shown in the traces of Figure 4.13.

The ambiguities which are handled in this way are essentially the same ones that were handled by classical immediate constituent theory. Other sorts of ambiguities are handled as matters of interstratal relationship, or neutralization within a stratal system.

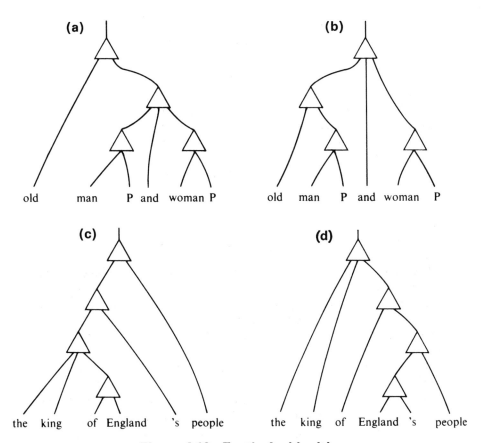

**Figure 4.13 Tactic Ambiguities**

### 4.5   *Further Syntactic Principles*

In order to see the application of the principles of stratificational theory to syntactic data, let us consider the hypothetical corpus presented in Table 4.10.

### *Table 4.10   Hypothetical Syntactic Data*

|  |  |
|---|---|
| 1. Lama uza zomat. | 'The butcher sees the tailor.' |
| 2. Lama uza ve zomat. | 'The butcher does not see the tailor.' |
| 3. Uza lama zomat? | 'Does the butcher see the tailor?' |
| 4. Uza lama ve zomat? | 'Doesn't the butcher see the tailor?' |
| 5. Voni goro lamat. | 'The lawyer hits the butcher.' |
| 6. Voni goro ve lamat. | 'The lawyer does not hit the butcher.' |
| 7. Goro voni lamat? | 'Does the lawyer hit the butcher?' |
| 8. Goro voni ve lamat? | 'Doesn't the lawyer hit the butcher?' |
| 9. Zoma duri vonit. | 'The tailor admires the lawyer.' |
| 10. Zoma duri ve vonit. | 'The tailor does not admire the lawyer.' |
| 11. Duri zoma vonit? | 'Does the tailor admire the lawyer?' |
| 12. Duri zoma ve vonit? | 'Doesn't the tailor admire the lawyer?' |
| 13. Voni duriba zenot. | 'The lawyer admired the judge.' |
| 14. Zeno uzalo gadut. | 'The judge has seen the man.' |
| 15. Gadu goroba ve zomat. | 'The man did not hit the tailor.' |
| 16. Durime zeno bizet? | 'Will the judge admire the woman?' |
| 17. Bize subu uzaba voni vilot. | 'The beautiful woman saw the old lawyer.' |
| 18. Voni subu gorolo zomalet. | 'The handsome lawyer has hit the tailors.' |
| 19. Zeno uzaba vonile gozet. | 'The judge saw the good lawyers.' |
| 20. Uzalo bizele vilo ve lamalet? | 'Haven't the old women seen the butchers?' |

If we were given this data as a syntactic problem, our task would be to account for it in a tactic diagram. In many such syntactic problems, however, we are expected to account not just for the given data but also for reasonable projections from it—further forms which we are led to expect from the data even though they do not actually occur in it. It would be possible, of course, to account only for the twenty sentences given, but to do so would likely involve additional complications introduced for the sole purpose of excluding forms whose absence from the corpus is accidental. So here we are given a form meaning 'the butcher sees the tailor,' but not 'the butcher will see the tailor,' or 'the butcher saw the tailor.' It is altogether reasonable to expect that there will be a way to say these things as well, and since some of the examples which do occur provide a means of hypothesizing how they might be said, it is not unreasonable to provide for them. Needless to say, our preliminary generalizations may be incorrect for an actual language, as the real forms may exhibit variations not predictable from the data examined; but since our ultimate hope is to account for an infinity of sentences in our syntax (not to mention texts), we will always have to predict unobserved forms on the basis of those we have observed, and mistakes in our preliminary estimates can be ironed out on further investigation. Keeping this projection principle in mind, therefore, let us examine this data in a preliminary fashion to see what general observations we can make about it.

We may first note that the order of statements is subject + verb + object, while that of a yes-no question is verb + subject + object. The object, it will be noted, always carries the final suffix -*t*. The plural of nouns is formed with the suffix -*le* (18, 19, 20), and nouns may have postposed modifiers such as *vilo* 'old,' *subu* 'beautiful/handsome,' or *goze* 'good.' The verb has an unsuffixed present, a past formed by the suffix -*ba* (13), a future with -*me* (16), and what we may tentatively term a "perfect" in -*lo* (18, 20). There is also a negative element *ve* which comes after the verb in a statement (2, 6, 10, 15), but after the subject in a question (4, 8, 12, 20). In other words, it comes after the subject-verb complex, whatever its internal order, and before the object.

In attempting to provide a tactics incorporating these and other possible observations, it might prove convenient to begin with separate diagrams for statements (Figure 4.14a) and questions (Figure 4.14b).

In comparing these two diagrams, we see that the only difference between them has to do with the occurrence of the subject (S) before or after the verb with its tense suffix, reflecting the observed structural differences between

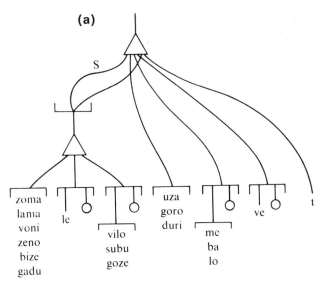

**Figure 4.14  Tactics of Statements and Questions from the Data of Table 4.10**

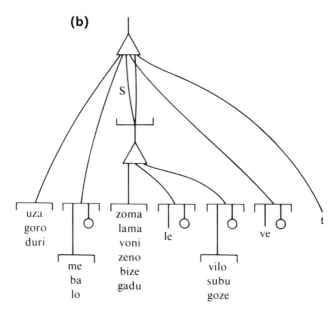

**Figure 4.14    Tactics of Statements and Questions from the Data of Table 4.10 (continued)**

statements and questions. To deal with this situation, we may resort to a device discussed earlier (Section 3.6). We may postulate an upper-stratum element Q whose realization on the stratum on which the syntax operates is to select the order V S as opposed to the more neutral order S V which occurs in statements. This hypothesis is reflected in Figure 4.15, which integrates the separate diagrams of Figure 4.14.

It may be noted that the total number of distinct outputs from this diagram, calculated by the procedure described in Section 3.2, is 110,592, or a projection of 110,572 over the original twenty sentences. This is fairly remarkable considering the limited vocabulary and syntactic repertoire represented, and the lack of recursion in the diagram.

This diagram shows that the element Q, signalled from the upper stratum, requires the selection of the order V S, while its absence requires the order S V. The selection of Q as the marked element illustrates a further aspect of a principle touched upon earlier in the discussion of the Czech declension. This principle, known as **markedness**, is founded on the notion that some elements and constructional selections are conveniently and insightfully analyzed as the absence of some element. When the element is present, the situation is termed **marked**, and when it is absent, the situation is termed **unmarked**. A situation may be unmarked in contrast to one or more marked situations. Some aspects of markedness are undoubtedly universal—this is likely true of the marked status of questions as opposed to the corresponding statements—while other aspects may vary from one language to another.

It should be pointed out that markedness is not inexorably bound up with the matter of overt versus zero expression. The two factors are partly related, however. We may use the Czech noun data considered earlier as an illustration of this point. In Czech, the combination of the unmarked case and the unmarked number—the nominative singular—is often expressed by zero, but this is not always the situation. On the other hand, certain other case-number combinations, such as the singly marked accusative singular or the doubly marked genitive plural, sometimes have zero realization. There may be a general rule, however, that (1) if any category of a set ever has zero expression, the unmarked one will, and (2) a marked category may never have zero as its sole means of expression. At least this position is not incompatible with the Czech data on either count.

The ultimate justification for the selection of a marked or unmarked status for a given category is the principle of simplicity, which must take external connections to the conceptual correlations and the phonic correlations into account. In this regard, unmarked categories are often capable of being neutral

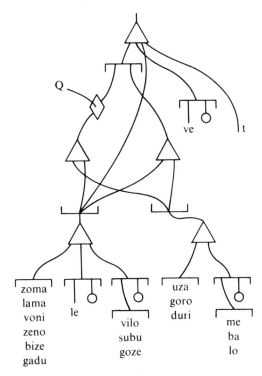

**Figure 4.15   Solution to the Data of Table 4.10**

as to the contrast under consideration. Present tense, for example, can express past or future actions in many languages, either or both of which provide evidence for its unmarked status among the tenses. In some languages, the expression of plurality is optional, allowing the so-called singular form to be used in either singular or plural situations. In Slavic languages such as Russian, the perfective aspect focusses specifically on the completion of the event, while the unmarked imperfective does not signal this focus, but may refer to an event which is completed or to be completed if this fact is not to be focussed upon. We can tentatively rely on such criteria as these in assigning marked or unmarked status, but they are ultimately dependable only to the extent that they are confirmed by the principle of simplicity.

Consideration of this sample problem has permitted us to discuss in connection with syntactic data the basic principle of classes and constructions already applied in morphology. It has also allowed discussion of the realization of elements as syntactic selections and the notion of markedness.

(The problems of Set 4D at the end of this chapter may be done at this point.)

### 4.6   Concord and Government

Two important grammatical phenomena whose treatment must be approached by any theory of language are concord and government. We may view **concord** as basically that situation in which different grammatical items in a single phrase or clause must agree in the selection of particular grammati-

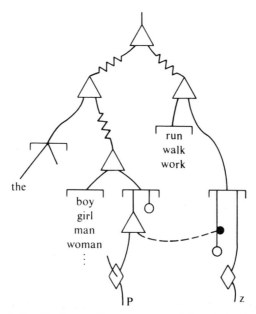

**Figure 4.16   A Preliminary Treatment of English Verbal Concord**

cal categories. A simple example is provided by the English forms *The boy runs* and *The boys run*, where the form of the verb varies according to the number of the noun serving as its subject: a singular subject is accompanied by a singular verb, such as *runs*, a plural subject by a plural verb, such as *run*. It appears that we can characterize this situation by a conditioning line running from the selection of plural for the subject to the verbal suffix position, where it has the effect of blocking the occurrence of a suffix *-s*, which would otherwise occur. This treatment is diagrammed in Figure 4.16.

In Figure 4.17 we revise this preliminary treatment to account for the

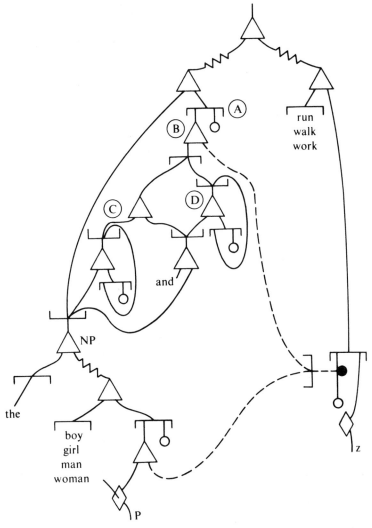

**Figure 4.17   A Refined Treatment of English Verbal Concord**

further complication introduced when we consider such sentences as *The boy and the girl run.* Here the plural form of the verb is determined when the subject of the sentence is coordinate, regardless of whether any of the coordinated phrases happens to be plural. This means, in fact, that we must build a conditioning line for plural verbs into our treatment of coordination as well as one depending on the selection of the plural morpheme.

This diagram incorporates a fairly elaborate structure for specifying coordinate noun phrases without the aid of the less explicit coordination element (Section 3.5). This structure is shown to be optional by the downward ordered OR marked (A). The AND marked (B) shows the origin of the second conditioning line for plural verbs. Below this point, we get two alternative structures. That under the AND marked (C) allows one or more noun phrases followed by *and* and another noun phrase, providing for such examples as *the boy, the man, and the girls.* The structure under the AND marked (D) allows an indefinite number of NP's all preceded by *and*, thus providing for *the boy and the girl, the boys and the men and women,* and so on. The diagram shows that the selection of either of these coordinating structures, or of a plural noun, or both, in the subject results in a plural verb.

Let us now consider a somewhat different concord situation, that of number and case in the Russian noun phrase. The data illustrating this phenomenon is presented in Table 4.11, which gives the various singular and plural case forms of the phrase 'my beautiful table.' All these forms are presented in transliteration from Russian orthography.

### Table 4.11    Russian Number and Case Concord

|   | *Singular* | *Plural* |
|---|---|---|
| N | moj krasivyj stol | moi krasivye stoly |
| A | moj krasivyj stol | moi krasivye stoly |
| G | moego krasivogo stola | moix krasivyx stolov |
| L | moëm krasivom stole | moix krasivyx stolax |
| D | moemu krasivomu stolu | moim krasivym stolam |
| I | moim krasivym stolom | moimi krasivymi stolami |

We can characterize such grammatical situations as this in terms of the relevance of the number and case selection for the entire noun phrase. Number selection depends primarily on semantic factors, while that of case is related to syntactic function. These selections then affect the morphological form of every word in the phrase which is capable of being inflected for number and case, essentially nouns and adjectives. This basic property of simultaneity of number and case with the whole phrase is shown in Figure 4.18.

The morphology, however, will require a potentially multiple realization of number and case specification, one realization on each noun and adjective. What is needed to provide for such a situation is a means of specifying that a

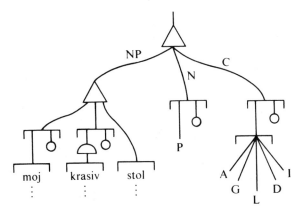

***Figure 4.18   Simultaneity of Number and Case with* NP**

given marked case or number selection will be capable of occurring as many times as necessary in the course of the phrase with which it is associated. Since there is no theoretical limit to the number of adjectives that may occur in such a phrase, this means an indefinitely large number of times.

In order to allow this, we may assume that when an ordered AND is dominated in a tactic pattern by an unordered AND, the lines from the unordered AND other than that to the ordered AND lead to specifications which are "switched on" for the entire duration of the sequence from the ordered AND and are thus available as many times as needed. By this convention the lines C and N in Figure 4.18 will lead to specifications active for the entire duration of NP.

So, taking into account that (1) case and number will be separately realized on each noun or adjective of the phrase, and (2) case is ultimately dependent on syntactic functions (and is occasionally a direct realization of a specification originating in the semology), we arrive at the diagram of Figure 4.19. The upward ORs at the top of this diagram lead to various syntactic functions requiring particular marked cases, or to semantic connections such as "Possession," one of the realizates of the genitive. Each of the ANDs below these ORs leads to the specification of a case morpheme, and further connects to another upward OR, which also gathers lines for the unmarked nominative. Since the case is already simultaneous with the whole phrase, only the number is specified from the downward unordered AND below this point. It will provide for the plural morpheme $^M$/P/ where required. In this treatment, morphological and syntactic phenomena are covered in a single diagram. A full discussion of morphological and syntactic phenomena and their treatment is provided in Section 4.7.

To allow for the suffixation which ultimately carries the concording elements, a determined "concord" suffix is provided for each adjective and noun.

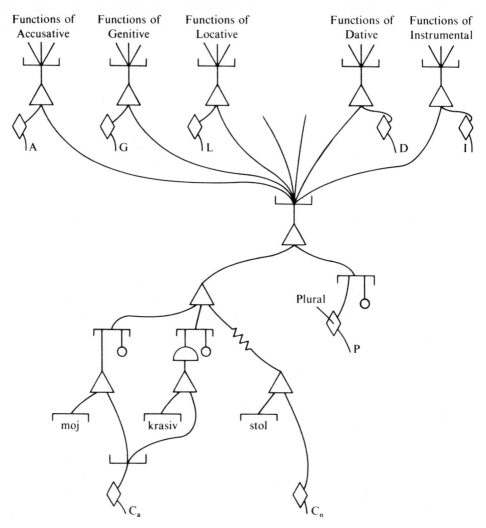

**Figure 4.19   Russian Case and Number Concord**

Let us assume two separate elements ($C_a$, $C_n$) due to the considerable difference in realization between adjectival and nominal suffixes. This hypothesis is, of course, subject to verification by the simplicity principle. These concording suffixes will be realized portmanteau with any marked case or number specifications, and they will be subject to further conditions according to classes shown in the tactics. All of this may be provided for in the alternation pattern below the tactics.

A somewhat different type of concord is the gender agreement found in many languages, including Russian. The nominative singular *moj krasivyj stol* 'my beautiful table,' for example, is headed by the masculine noun *stol*, but with the feminine noun *kniga* 'book' and the neuter noun *pero* 'pen,' we get *moja krasivaja kniga* 'my beautiful book' and *moë krasivoe pero* 'my beautiful pen.' Although these distinctions are completely neutralized in the plural (as far as adjectives are concerned), there is a further distinction among the masculine and feminine nouns which is relevant for the accusative of both singular and plural for the masculine, though only of the plural for the feminine. Compare, for example, the masculine accusative plurals *moi krasivye stoly* 'my beautiful tables' (like the nominative) and *moix krasivyx mal'čikov* 'my handsome boys' (like the genitive), and likewise the feminines *moi krasivye knigi* 'my beautiful books' and *moix krasivyx devoček* 'my beautiful girls.' *Stol* and *kniga* are inanimate nouns, while *mal'čik* and *devočka* (the nominative singulars of the above) are animate.

Figure 4.20 shows additional details needed to account for the specification

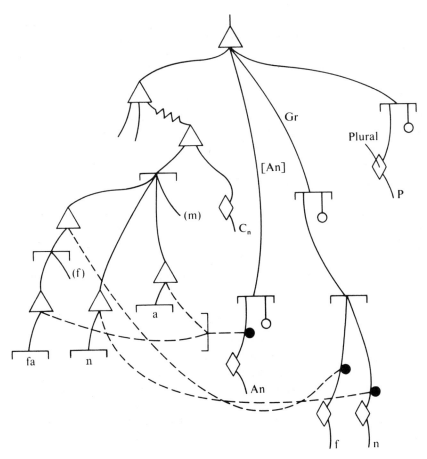

**Figure 4.20  Russian Gender Concord**

of gender (Gr) and animateness (An). It shows that these specifications, like those for number and case, are relevant for the entire noun phrase. Their conditioning, however, is from within the phrase rather than from outside it, as provided by the enablers connected to the noun classes (*f*, *n*, *a*, and *fa*) which have been added to the tactics for noun stems.

It is assumed here, subject to ultimate verification based on the simplicity principle, that the neuter and feminine genders are marked in contrast to the masculine. Animate is also assumed to be marked as opposed to inanimate. This tentative assignment is based on a number of considerations, including realizational neutralizations.

Gender, including animateness, will then be realized as portmanteaus with the concord suffixes within the noun phrase, in the same way as case and number specifications. There is reason to question, however, whether the gender specification is relevant for the nouns themselves, or just for the accompanying adjectives. In Russian, declensional classes of nouns happen to correlate to a considerable extent with genders, but this correlation is not complete. The exceptions, however, can be handled as special subclasses, and the gender information can be used in the considerable number of cases where it will predict the declensional endings correctly. In other languages, of course, gender may have little or no correlation with the inflection of nouns, in which case it can be disregarded.

Another kind of grammatical restriction which plays an important part in many languages is known in traditional grammar as **government**. This relation is said to pertain, basically, when a particular grammatical class affects the selection of a grammatical category, such as a case, on an element accompanying it in a construction. In Russian, for example, verbs are said to govern particular cases in their objects. A large class of verbs—including *videt'* 'to see,' *znat'* 'to know'—governs the accusative. Another class of verbs, including *pomogat'* 'to help,' governs the dative; another, including *komandovat'* 'to command,' the instrumental; and one including *izbegat'* 'to avoid,' the genitive.

This situation can be handled by a fairly simple elaboration of what we have already shown in Figure 4.19: among the lines coming into the upward ORs at the top of this diagram are lines coming from constructions involving verbs with possible objects in each of the appropriate cases, accompanied by the appropriate NP, one with accusative, another with genitive, and so on. This elaboration is sketched in Figure 4.21.

A similar situation may exist for prepositions, which in languages like Russian govern nominal phrases in particular cases, in a way similar to the verbs illustrated above. Russian, as it turns out, has a class of prepositions associated with each of its marked cases. Their treatment would involve downward ordered ANDs representing each type of prepositional phrase, with the first branch leading to the class of prepositions, the second to the NP of the appropriate case.

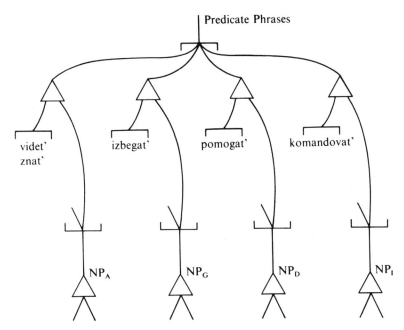

**Figure 4.21 Russian Verbal Government**

A further problem of interest in the treatment of concord arises when one nominal phrase occurs within another. Any of the types of Russian noun phrases we have outlined, for example, may be followed by a qualifying phrase, which may be a genitive noun phrase of possession, or any of various prepositional phrases. Take, for instance, the expanded phrases *bol'šoj avtomobil' našego professora*, literally 'big automobile our-of professor-of' with genitive qualification, and *bol'šoj avtomobil' iz Ameriki* '. . . from America,' where *našego professora* is a genitive noun phrase and *iz Ameriki* a prepositional phrase including a genitive noun phrase governed by *iz* 'from,' each with a qualifying function. Furthermore, the phrase fulfilling this function can be further qualified, which suggests the existence of an unlimited looping structure.

Figure 4.22 shows a suggested means of handling such possessive genitive and prepositional qualifiers. Inserted between the upward ORs and the downward unordered ANDs specifying cases is a downward ordered AND whose second branch leads to the optional looping construction. Both of the examples of the latter shown here loop into the genitive, but others in the language will lead to other cases. The disturbing thing about this representation is that a separate downward ordered AND is needed for each type of NP. It would seem

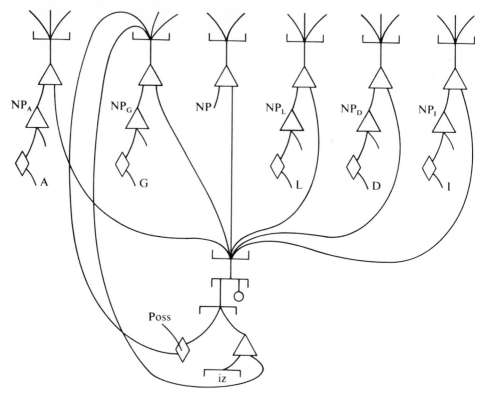

**Figure 4.22   Optional Qualifying Loops to NP's**

preferable if we could use only one such AND applying to all these phrases, and thus capture the generalization that any NP may be expanded in this way. But it is necessary to place this AND above the point of specification of the simultaneous cases in order to insure that no more than one marked case will be specified for any given stretch of morphemes. Otherwise, embedded noun phrases would, by the conventions governing simultaneity that we have already elaborated, receive more than one case specification. If this were allowed, it would be necessary to introduce special mechanisms to sort these out in the realizational portion. It is possible that further consideration of the structure of Russian and similar languages may ultimately lead to a solution to this problem. This more detailed consideration, however, is beyond the scope of this introductory work.

In any event, this section has provided suggestions for the stratificational treatment of a number of types of concord and government. Government, it has been proposed, is best provided for by distinguishing types of constructions in the tactics, as the types of predicate phrases and prepositional phrases mentioned for Russian. Concord in noun phrases is treated as involving specifications simultaneous with the entire phrase, either controlled from within it, as with gender, or from without, as with number and case. Concord between subject and predicate, however, seems more easily handled by context sensitivity.

(The exercises of Set 4E at the end of this chapter may be done at this point.)

## 4.7 The Stratal Status of Morphology and Syntax

In this chapter we have been considering a wide variety of phenomena in the grammars of various languages which have traditionally been treated under the rubrics of "morphology" and "syntax." However, we have yet to outline the overall model for the grammatical portion of a language in general and define the place of morphological and syntactic phenomena within this model.

One model of these relationships was presented in the *Outline of Stratificational Grammar* (Lamb 1966d). It has a morphology-syntax division which corresponds essentially to the stratal difference between the morphemic stratal system and the lexemic stratal system. Thus the lexotactics, taking primary responsibility for clause structures, corresponds closely to the traditional syntax ("surface syntax" in transformational terms). The morphotactics, dealing primarily with grammatical words, handles the same things as the traditional morphology. Lexotactic classes include those defining government and concord, while morphotactic classes are based on inflectional and derivational patterns.

This model supports, therefore, the notion that the morphology-syntax distinction is more than just a matter of rank (size-level), but rather a stratal distinction. This basic grammatical model is represented in Figure 4.23. The function of each of the patterns shown may be outlined as follows.

The **semonic alternation pattern** accounts for the relation between semons and the lexemes which realize them, providing for diversification, neutralization, and other discrepancies, as well as for simple realization between them.

The **lexotactics** specifies what combinations of lexemes are well formed, particularly in clause structure and below. As we have said, it covers the principal domain of traditional syntax.

The **lexemic knot pattern** was originally a series of upward AND nodes, which were later replaced by the diamonds introduced in Section 3.6. It allows the semology, through the semonic alternation pattern, to control the operation of the lexotactics, thus ensuring that in the normal operation of the language the output of this stratal system will be well formed according to the specifications of higher strata as well as according to the specification of this stratal system. The lexemic knot pattern further allows the lexotactics to condition alternate realizations of semons.

The **lexemic sign pattern** is in a sense the vocabulary of the lexemic stratal

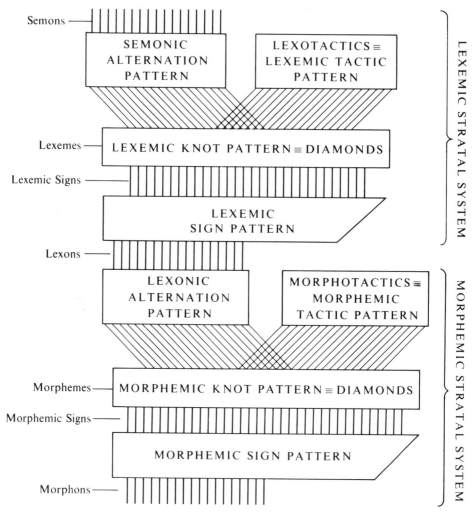

**Figure 4.23   Model of Grammar, Outline Version**

system. It specifies the lexonic composition of each lexemic sign. Many lexemes lead down to just one lexemic sign, but the *Outline* allowed neutralization and portmanteau realization to be treated as discrepancies between lexemes and lexemic signs.

The **lexonic alternation pattern**, the uppermost portion of the morphemic stratal system, deals with realizational relationships connecting lexons with the morphemes which realize them.

The **morphotactics** deals with the specifically morphological tactic features of the language, accounting for inflectional and productive derivational patterns. It has the grammatical word as its basic domain.

The **morphemic knot pattern**, more recently the morphemic diamonds, allows the interaction of the lexonic alternation pattern and the morphotactics in a way similar to that in which the lexemic knot pattern allows the interaction of its tactic and alternation patterns.

The **morphemic sign pattern** spells out each morphemic sign in terms of morphons, which serve as the inputs to the phonology in the encoding process. It is thus the vocabulary of its stratal system.

Several revisions have caused this model to be superseded by a more recent one. Much of the available stratificational literature on grammatical structure, however, was written with a version of the *Outline* model in mind. Therefore it is necessary for anyone seeking to read this literature to be acquainted with the earlier model as well as with the revised one.

For purposes of comparing these two models, let us consider a set of data which includes both morphological and syntactic phenomena. We can present the solution to it according to the earlier model, and later also present it according to the revised model to allow comparison. For this discussion, let us use the Latin data listed in Table 4.12.

In attempting to cast this data into the model of the *Outline*, let us consider the morphological facts it exemplifies. It illustrates two classes of inflected stems, which we may, following the usual conventions, call "nouns" and "verbs." Nouns in this data show inflection in three cases—nominative, accusative, and ablative—with singular and plural forms of each. They exhibit three inflectional patterns for these case forms, exemplified by *puella*, *ami:cus*, and *pater*. A morphotactic treatment of these nouns is provided in Figure 4.24.

It must be admitted that this treatment takes a rather overly simplistic view of the stem-ending separation in Latin. A greater degree of morphophonemic abstraction could significantly reduce the total number of morphemes, and thereby the number of diamonds for endings. We are not yet prepared to justify such an analysis, however, so no harm will be done if we follow this analysis in both of the accounts we set out to compare. The only morphophonemic abstraction which has been made at this point involves the stems of the third class, which are assumed to end in $^{MN}$/r/. It may be assumed that the phonology will provide for the realization of this morphon as $^{P}$/er/ in final position.

The ordered ORs are built into this ending system in anticipation that the nominative singular will be found to be the unmarked case form in Latin, as it is in Czech and Russian. Thus its ending, when it has one, will be a determined element inserted by the morphotactics in the absence of a marked form connecting from the lexology.

Next we consider the verb morphology, where we find a somewhat simpler situation than with the nouns. The personal endings -*t* and -*nt* occur in both of the tenses represented. The past tense (actually the Latin imperfect) is consistently signalled by -*:ba*, and there are two further verb classes for which

### Table 4.12   Latin Grammatical Data

| | |
|---|---|
| 1. puella patrem amat | 'the girl loves the father' |
| 2. pater fi:lium amat | 'the father loves the son' |
| 3. ma:ter cum amiti:s ambulat | 'the mother is walking with the aunts' |
| 4. fi:lius cum puella: labo:rat | 'the son is working with the girl' |
| 5. ami:cus puellam monet | 'the friend warns the girl' |
| 6. amita cum patre ambulat | 'the aunt is walking with the father' |
| 7. agricola cum amita: labo:rat | 'the farmer is working with the aunt' |
| 8. fe:mina fi:lium timet | 'the woman fears the son' |
| 9. fi:lius ma:trem portat | 'the son is carrying the mother' |
| 10. amitai fe:minam uident | 'the aunts see the woman' |
| 11. patre:s amitam monent | 'the fathers warn the aunt' |
| 12. fi:lii: ami:cum amant | 'the sons love the friend' |
| 13. ami:ci: cum ma:tre ambulant | 'the friends are walking with the mother' |
| 14. agricolai patre:s timent | 'the farmers fear the fathers' |
| 15. amitai agricola:s porta:bant | 'the aunts were carrying the farmers' |
| 16. ma:tre:s fi:lio:s uident | 'the mothers see the sons' |
| 17. puellai cum ami:co: labo:rant | 'the girls are working with the friend' |
| 18. fe:minai amita:s portant | 'the women are carrying the aunts' |
| 19. ami:cus sine puelli:s ambulat | 'the friend is walking without the girls' |
| 20. fe:minai cum patribus labo:rant | 'the women are working with the fathers' |
| 21. ma:ter ami:co:s ama:bat | 'the mother loved the friends' |
| 22. patre:s cum ma:tribus ambulant | 'the fathers are walking with the mothers' |
| 23. fi:lii: cum amiti:s labo:ra:bant | 'the sons were working with the aunts' |
| 24. fra:tre:s agricolam uide:bant | 'the brothers saw the farmer' |
| 25. fi:lius puella:s uide:bat | 'the son saw the girls' |
| 26. fra:tre:s fe:mina:s time:bant | 'the brothers feared the women' |
| 27. puella sine fe:mina: labo:ra:bat | 'the girl was working without the woman' |
| 28. fra:ter cum fe:mini:s ambula:bat | 'the brother was walking with the women' |
| 29. amitai sine fra:tre ambula:bant | 'the aunts were walking without the brother' |
| 30. patre:s cum agricola: cla:mant | 'the fathers are shouting with the farmer' |
| 31. fi:lii: sine agricoli:s ambulant | 'the sons are walking without the farmers' |
| 32. fra:ter ma:tre:s mone:bat | 'the brother warned the mothers' |
| 33. agricolai fra:tre:s mone:bant | 'the farmers warned the brothers' |
| 34. ami:ci: sine fi:lio: cla:ma:bant | 'the friends were shouting without the son' |
| 35. pater fra:trem time:bat | 'the father feared the brother' |
| 36. ma:ter cum fi:lii:s cla:mat | 'the mother is shouting with the sons' |
| 37. fe:minai sine ami:ci:s labo:ra:bant | 'the women were working without the friends' |
| 38. ma:tre:s cum fra:tribus cla:ma:bant | 'the mothers were shouting with the brothers' |
| 39. ami:cus agricola:s porta:bat | 'the friend was carrying the farmers' |
| 40. patre:s fi:lio:s ama:bant | 'the fathers loved the sons' |

the vowels *-e* and *-a* may be regarded as determined suffixes. This analysis of the verb forms is represented in Figure 4.25.

The OR at the top of this diagram is actually the same OR that occurs at the top of Figure 4.24. It is shown here to have additional branches, suggesting the consolidation of Figures 4.24 and 4.25, which will not actually be shown here.

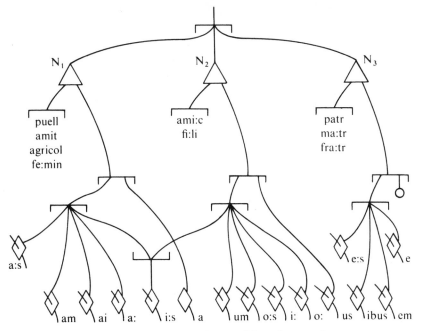

**Figure 4.24   Latin Noun Morphotactics**

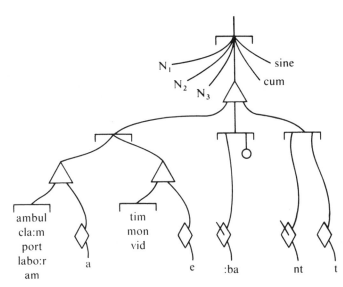

**Figure 4.25   Latin Verb Morphotactics**

Now we will proceed to the lexotactics, which must handle the syntactic phenomena according to this conception. Here case and number will be treated as abstract categories, with nominative and singular unmarked. The syntactic phenomena involved include the function of nominative nouns as subjects, accusative nouns as objects, and ablative nouns as the objects of the prepositions *cum* and *sine*. We must also deal with the concord between subject and verb, and the fact that the verbs of one class must be accompanied by objects, while those of the other class are accompanied (in this data) by prepositional phrases. A tactic diagram accounting for this situation, including appropriate projections beyond the actual data, is shown in Figure 4.26.

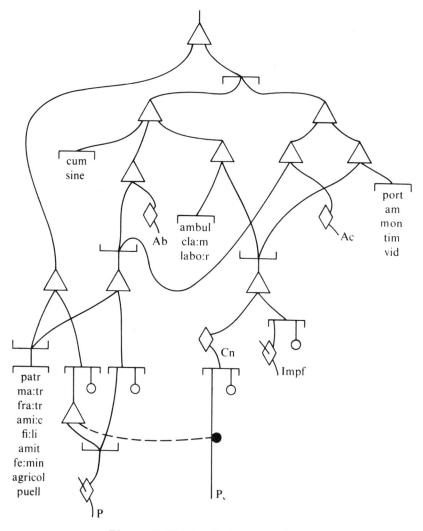

**Figure 4.26   Latin Lexotactics**

In this representation, all grammatical categories are shown simultaneous with the stem, since the order of their realizations will be indicated by the morphotactics. In stratificational theory, it is generally postulated that the lower tactic order will take precedence during the encoding process. This diagram treats the two marked cases as determined elements on this level. In actuality, however, $^L$/Ac/ may be a realization of the semon $^{SN}$/Goal/, but this will not affect the comparison being made as long as the interpretation is kept consistent. Number in the verb is also a determined element, realized as $^{LS}$/P$_v$/ (verbal plurality) in the appropriate environment, and otherwise as zero. The diamonds and enabler shown in this diagram are actually features introduced subsequent to the *Outline*, but the intention here is to apply the relations now available using two different conceptions of the grammatical model to allow their comparison.

Since not all the lexemes and lexemic signs provided by this diagram are in one-to-one correspondence with morphemes in the morphotactics of Figures 4.24 and 4.25, we will need to consider some additional nodes in the intervening patterns. The discrepancies that must be treated here include portmanteau realization, diversification, and neutralization, and all of them involve a total of only three lexemes: $^L$/P/, $^L$/Ac/, and $^L$/Ab/. The portmanteau realization involving these three lexemes is diagrammed in Figure 4.27, which represents the upper part of the lexemic sign pattern.

Below the bottom of this diagram will come the lower part of the lexemic sign pattern, dividing each lexemic sign into its constituent lexons. In our data, however, there is no evidence for any complex lexemes, so each of the lines will pass through this portion without encountering any nodes.

Each of the lines at the bottom of Figure 4.27, however, will be subject to alternate realizations in the morphology, and these alternatives must be shown in the lexonic alternations. The only significant part of this pattern is shown in Figure 4.28; the lines for other lexemes will pass through the pattern without

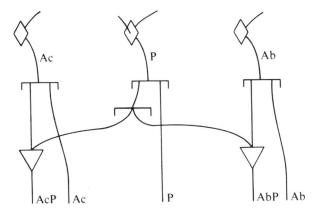

*Figure 4.27 Portmanteau Realization of Case and Number*

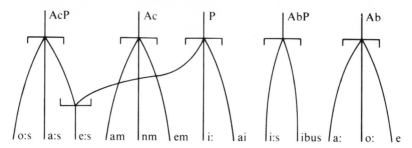

**Figure 4.28   Lexonic Alternation Pattern for Case and Number**

encountering any nodes, since they are in one-to-one correspondence with morphemes.

The combination of Figures 4.27 and 4.28, therefore, represents the only significant part of the realizational portion in the solution to this problem according to the *Outline* model.

Let us now enumerate the major revisions in the grammatical model which have occurred since the *Outline* and show how they affect the treatment of the same Latin data.

Diamonds, of course, have already been represented in the diagrams shown, replacing the upward unordered ANDs of the *Outline*'s knot patterns. The essential differences represented by the introduction of diamonds, it turns out, cannot be illustrated by this data, since they involve diamonds with two or four connections, or those which enter into the middle of the tactics when a tactic selection rather than an overt -eme is the realization of the -on of the upper stratum to which the diamond connects. All of these situations have been discussed and illustrated in previous sections of the book.

Together with the introduction of the diamonds, it also proves convenient to regard the tactic pattern of each stratal system as belonging in a horizontal orientation, intersecting with the vertically arranged patterns of the realizational portion. Each point of intersection, of course, is marked by a diamond.

The second major revision of the model has involved the introduction of a second alternation pattern into each stratal system. The *Outline* model, as shown in Figure 4.23, has only one alternation pattern in each stratal system, and this is placed above and conditioned by the tactics. Each such pattern is named according to the realizates involved in its alternations, which will be the -ons of the stratum above. Thus the alternation patterns in the lexemic and morphemic stratal systems were called the semonic and lexonic alternation patterns, respectively. The revised model incorporates, in addition to these, a second alternation pattern within each stratal system, which is located below the tactics. Naming these also according to their realizates, they will be the **lexemic alternation pattern** (in the lexemic stratal system) and the **morphemic alternation pattern** (in the morphemic stratal system).

Concomitant with this introduction of subtactic alternation patterns has come the introduction of conditioning lines and enablers to condition alternatives. The conditioning lines for the alternation patterns of any stratal system will all originate within that system, and normally in its tactic pattern. From the morphotactics, for example, conditioning lines will go to enablers in both the lexonic alternation pattern and the morphemic alternation pattern. This means that those alternations assigned to the -onic alternation pattern of a given stratal system will be conditioned in terms of the outputs, while those assigned to the -emic alternation pattern will be conditioned in terms of their inputs. A lexonic alternation, for example, will occur when a lexon is realized by alternate morphemes, with a conditioning environment stated in terms of morphemes. A morphemic alternation, on the other hand, will occur when a morpheme is realized by alternate morphemic signs, with its conditioning environment likewise stated in terms of morphemes. We may thus speak of -onic alternations as output-conditioned, and of -emic alternations as input-conditioned. The most essential determining factor in assigning an alternation to one or the other of these alternation patterns within a stratal system will be whether its treatment can be fitted in most simply and efficiently as an output-conditioned and therefore -onic alternation, or as an input-conditioned and therefore -emic one. This point follows, of course, from the more general principle of simplicity.

This contrasts with the *Outline* model, where all alternations had to be treated as -onic and therefore output-conditioned. This requirement sometimes forced otherwise unneeded distinctions to be made in the tactics, causing the tactic pattern to be more complicated than would otherwise be necessary. In a still earlier version of stratificational theory, as reflected most clearly in Lamb's article "On alternation, transformation, realization, and stratification" (1964b), all alternations were treated as input-conditioned. The revised model, however, allows both input-conditioned and output-conditioned alternations, and it further allows two levels of alternation within a single stratal system, while the earlier models provided for only one such level.

This revised model is summarized in Figure 4.29, which may profitably be compared with the sketch of the earlier model presented in Figure 4.23.

The sign patterns of this revised model have essentially the same form and function described for the corresponding patterns of the *Outline* model. The tactic patterns differ in that they define combinations of elements at a somewhat higher level of abstraction from the phonic correlations than do the corresponding patterns of the earlier model. This greater abstraction is a direct result of the introduction of the -emic alternation patterns. As already explained, the alternations dealt with in the alternation patterns are conditioned by enablers connected via conditioning lines, generally to classes defined in the tactics.

Let us now examine in detail the consequences of the enumerated revisions for the treatment of our Latin data. In the case of the lexotactics shown in

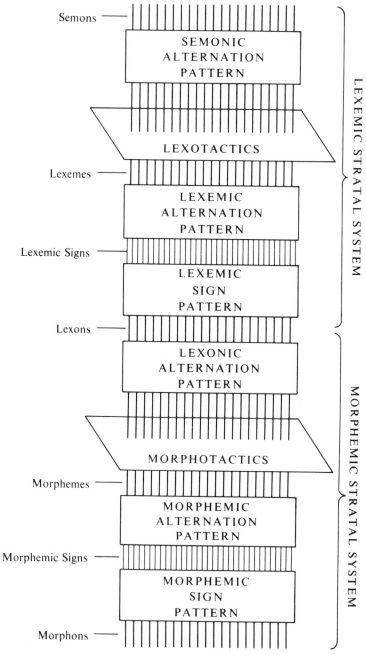

*Figure 4.29   Revised Model of Grammar*

Figure 4.26, no changes will be required. It should be pointed out, however, that the alternate realizations of $^L$/N/, as conditioned via the enabler and conditioning line, will be part of the lexemic alternation pattern.

For the morphotactics, in contrast, considerable change will be necessitated by the introduction of the morphemic alternation pattern. Figure 4.30 shows these changes in a morphotactics for the nouns, together with the accompanying morphemic alternation pattern.

Since no alternations are required in the treatment of verb morphology, this treatment will remain unchanged in the new version, as shown in Figure 4.25. As for the remaining realizational patterns, the portmanteau realization shown in Figure 4.27 will remain, as a part of the lexemic alternation pattern. (In the *Outline*, this treatment was regarded as a part of the lexemic sign pattern.) The alternations shown in Figure 4.28, however, are now treated in the morphemic alternation pattern of Figure 4.30. Therefore the lexonic alternation pattern will be vacuous for this particular data. For languages in general, of course, there will still be some alternations which are more conveniently handled in the -onic alternations than in the -emic ones, but the -onic alternations will generally be much fewer in number than the -emic ones of the same stratal system.

In summary, the treatment of the Latin data according to the *Outline* model involves Figures 4.24 through 4.28. That according to the revised model involves Figures 4.25, 4.26, 4.27, and 4.30.

Finally, some considerations for the practical representation of grammatical analyses based on this model may be mentioned. Tactic patterns are most conveniently represented by the use of graphic notation, though large portions of tactics may need to be broken down into more manageable segments for presentation. Compare, for example, the separation seen in Figures 4.24 and 4.25. Within such diagrams, downward ORs with a large number of branches may conventionally be reduced to simply a representation of the node over a list of lexeme or morpheme labels, as exemplified in a number of tactic diagrams in this chapter.

The algebraic realization formula notation is often the most convenient way of representing lexemic and morphemic alternation patterns, though the graphic form of Figure 4.30, with reference numbers or letters in place of fully explicit conditioning lines, is often not objectionable.

Semonic and lexonic alternation patterns are usually not too extensive to be represented graphically, often with the relevant part of the associated tactic pattern.

It is seldom convenient to represent the sign patterns graphically. Examples of such graphic representations are provided by Figure 4.31, showing a part of the lexemic sign pattern for English (4.31a), and part of the morphemic sign pattern for the Latin data considered in this chapter (4.31b). It is possible to avoid the explicit representation of such patterns by labelling each lexemic

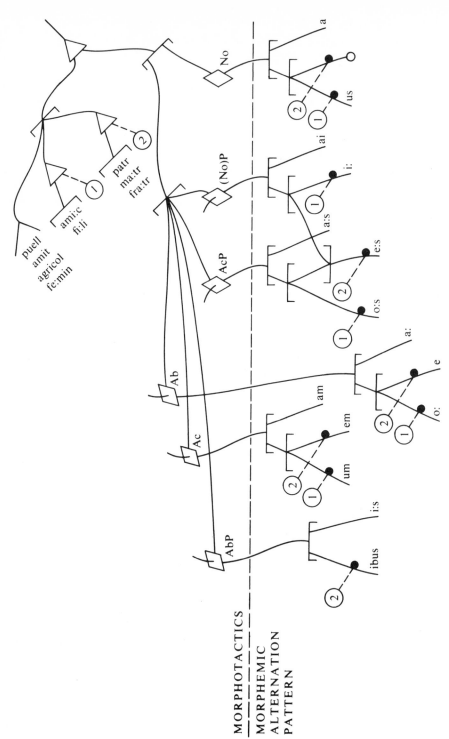

*Figure 4.30  Revised Treatment of Latin Noun Morphology*

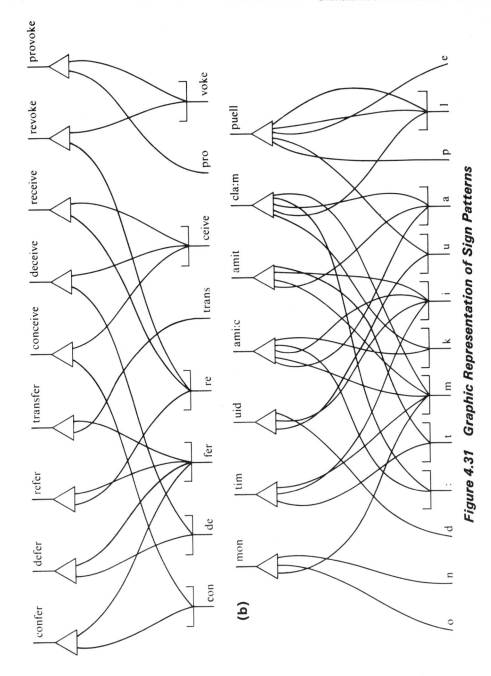

*Figure 4.31   Graphic Representation of Sign Patterns*

sign and morphemic sign with a sequence of symbols corresponding to those assigned to the lexons or morphons which make them up. Thus the lexemic sign $^{LS}$/transfer/ may be symbolized rather $^{LS}$/trans fer/, with the break showing where the constituent lexons are separated and therefore implying the lexonic composition $^{LN}$/trans/ and $^{LN}$/fer/. Morphemic signs may similarly be given in what amounts to a morphonic transcription, so $^{MS}$/ami:c/ can be taken to imply the composition $^{MN}$/a/ and $^{MN}$/m/ and $^{MN}$/i/ and $^{MN}$/:/ and $^{MN}$/c/.

(The exercises of Set 4F may be done at this point.)

## EXERCISES FOR CHAPTER 4

### Set 4A: Morphological Tactics

In producing the diagrams of Set 4A, you may find it desirable to use two shorthand devices in the representations of downward unordered ORs. As was explained in Section 4.1, a downward OR with a list appended underneath it is used to avoid drawing in a separate line for each branch. Sometimes it is convenient to encompass only some of the branches within such a listing, since others may lead down to further nodes which are to be shown. This is the case in several places in the answer to problem 2 below, for example. The subset of branches so listed may be placed under a pair of branches to group them. You will find these shorthand devices used where appropriate in the answers to the exercises for Chapter 4. Only context-free solutions should be considered in this section.

1. Draw a diagram of the portion of English morphotactics for which the following data furnishes evidence. The forms in the column at the far right are plural nouns. Ignore the graphic allomorphs in *y/i*.

| coward | cowardly | uncowardly | cowardliness | uncowardliness | cowards |
|--------|----------|------------|--------------|----------------|---------|
| friend | friendly | unfriendly | friendliness | unfriendliness | friends |
| sand | sandy | unsandy | sandiness | unsandiness | sands |
| milk | milky | unmilky | milkiness | unmilkiness | milks |
| ink | inky | uninky | inkiness | uninkiness | inks |

2. Draw a tactic diagram generating the numerals one through nine hundred ninety-nine in spoken English.

3. The following Spanish verb paradigms are given in conventional orthography. Account for them in a morphological tactic diagram. Where they are not consistently written, accent marks may be ignored for the purposes of this problem.

'plow'

| | Present | Imperfect | Preterite | Future | Conditional |
|---|---|---|---|---|---|
| 1Sg | aro | araba | aré | araré | araría |
| 2Sg | aras | arabas | araste | ararás | ararías |
| 3Sg | ara | araba | aró | arará | araría |
| 1Pl | aramos | arábamos | aramos | araremos | araríamos |
| 2Pl | aráis | arabais | arasteis | araréis | araríais |
| 3Pl | aran | araban | araron | ararán | ararían |

On the same pattern: *dudo* 'I doubt,' *robo* 'I steal'

'drink'

| | Present | Imperfect | Preterite | Future | Conditional |
|---|---|---|---|---|---|
| 1Sg | bebo | bebía | bebí | beberé | bebería |
| 2Sg | bebes | bebías | bebiste | beberás | beberías |
| 3Sg | bebe | bebía | bebió | beberá | bebería |
| 1Pl | bebemos | bebíamos | bebimos | beberemos | beberíamos |
| 2Pl | bebéis | bebíais | bebisteis | beberéis | beberíais |
| 3Pl | beben | bebían | bebieron | beberán | beberían |

On the same pattern: *barro* 'I sweep,' *como* 'I eat'

'write'

| | Present | Imperfect | Preterite | Future | Conditional |
|---|---|---|---|---|---|
| 1Sg | escribo | escribía | escribí | escribiré | escribiría |
| 2Sg | escribes | escribías | escribiste | escribirás | escribirías |
| 3Sg | escribe | escribía | escribió | escribirá | escribiría |
| 1Pl | escribimos | escribíamos | escribimos | escribiremos | escribiríamos |
| 2Pl | escribís | escribíais | escribisteis | escribiréis | escribiríais |
| 3Pl | escriben | escribían | escribieron | escribirán | escribirían |

On the same pattern: *vivo* 'I live,' *admito* 'I admit'

NOTE: Consider all alternations in this problem morphologically determined. Do not attempt to establish a phonological conditioning for them.

## Set 4B: Alternation

1.  Reconsider your solution to problem 2 in Set 4A. How can the tactics be simplified by relegating some of the alternation to the alternation pattern?

2.  Account for the following Latin forms using a morphological tactics with conditioned alternations. Consider the positive forms to consist of two morphemes each, the others of three each.

|  | | | |
|---|---|---|---|
| 1. | ve:rus 'true' | ve:rior 'truer' | ve:rissimus 'truest' |
| 2. | bonus 'good' | melior 'better' | optimus 'best' |
| 3. | magnus 'large' | maior 'larger' | maximus 'largest' |
| 4. | stultus 'stupid' | stultior 'stupider' | stultissimus 'stupidest' |
| 5. | bellus 'pretty' | bellior 'prettier' | bellissimus 'prettiest' |
| 6. | parvus 'small' | minor 'smaller' | minimus 'smallest' |
| 7. | altus 'deep' | altior 'deeper' | altissimus 'deepest' |
| 8. | la:tus 'wide' | la:tior 'wider' | la:tissimus 'widest' |

9.  malus 'bad'          peior 'worse'          pessimus 'worst'
10. longus 'long'        longior 'longer'       longissimus 'longest'
11. ca:rus 'dear'        ca:rior 'dearer'       ca:rissimus 'dearest'
12. superus 'high'       superior 'higher'      summus 'highest'

## Set 4C: Simulfixing

**1.** On the model provided by the treatment of English verbs presented in Section 4.3, account for the morphology of the following English forms. Regard the regular plural forms as containing the morphemic sign $^{MS}/Z/$.

| | | | | | |
|---|---|---|---|---|---|
| 1. | baks | baksəz | 8. | guws | giys |
| 2. | hæt | hæts | 9. | maws | mays |
| 3. | dog | dogz | 10. | laws | lays |
| 4. | aks | aksən | 11. | mæn | men |
| 5. | čayld | čildrən | 12. | wumən | wimən |
| 6. | fut | fiyt | 13. | šiyp | šiyp |
| 7. | tuwθ | tiyθ | 14. | dir | dir |

**2.** Use a context-free morphological tactics to account for the following data from Modern Literary Arabic in the simplest possible form. (The symbols ḥ and 9 are used for the voiceless and voiced pharyngeal spirants, respectively. The symbol ḍ represents a pharyngealized voiced dental stop.)

1.  katabtu   'I wrote'                          1a.  ʔaktubu    'I am writing'
2.  katabta   'you (masculine) wrote'            2a.  taktubu    'you (m.) are writing'
3.  katabti   'you (feminine) wrote'             3a.  taktubi:na 'you (f.) are writing'
4.  kataba    'he wrote'                         4a.  yaktubu    'he is writing'
5.  katabat   'she wrote'                        5a.  taktubu    'she is writing'

6.  ḍarabtu   'I hit'                            6a.  ʔaḍribu    'I am hitting'
7.  ḍarabta   'you (m.) hit'                     7a.  taḍribu    'you (m.) are hitting'
8.  ḍarabti   'you (f.) hit'                     8a.  taḍribi:na 'you (f.) are hitting'
9.  ḍaraba    'he hit'                           9a.  yaḍribu    'he is hitting'
10. ḍarabat   'she hit'                          10a. taḍribu    'she is hitting'

11. fahimtu   'I understood'                     11a. ʔafhamu    'I am understanding'
12. fahimta   'you (m.) understood'              12a. tafhamu    'you (m.) are understanding'
13. fahimti   'you (f.) understood'              13a. tafhami:na  'you (f.) are understanding'
14. fahima    'he understood'                    14a. yafhamu    'he is understanding'
15. fahimat   'she understood'                   15a. tafhamu    'she is understanding'

16. fataḥtu   'I opened'                         16a. ʔaftaḥu    'I am opening'
17. fataḥta   'you (m). opened'                  17a. taftaḥu    'you (m.) are opening'
18. fataḥti   'you (f.) opened'                  18a. taftaḥi:na 'you (f.) are opening'
19. fataḥa    'he opened'                        19a. yaftaḥu    'he is opening'
20. fataḥat   'she opened'                       20a. taftaḥu    'she is opening'

21. lama9tu   'I shone'                          21a. ʔalma9u    'I am shining'
22. lama9ta   'you (m.) shone'                   22a. talma9u    'you (m.) are shining'
23. lama9ti   'you (f.) shone'                   23a. talma9i:na 'you (f.) are shining'
24. lama9a    'he shone'                         24a. yalma9u    'he is shining'
25. lama9at   'she shone'                        25a. talma9u    'she is shining'

| | | | |
|---|---|---|---|
| 26. jalastu | 'I sat' | 26a. ʔajlisu | 'I am sitting' |
| 27. jalasta | 'you (m.) sat' | 27a. tajlisu | 'you (m.) are sitting' |
| 28. jalasti | 'you (f.) sat' | 28a. tajlisi:na | 'you (f.) are sitting' |
| 29. jalasa | 'he sat' | 29a. yajlisu | 'he is sitting' |
| 30. jalasat | 'she sat' | 30a. tajlisu | 'she is sitting' |
| | | | |
| 31. qataltu | 'I killed' | 31a. ʔaqtulu | 'I am killing' |
| 32. qatalta | 'you (m.) killed' | 32a. taqtulu | 'you (m.) are killing' |
| 33. qatalti | 'you (f). killed' | 33a. taqtuli:na | 'you (f.) are killing' |
| 34. qatala | 'he killed' | 34a. yaqtulu | 'he is killing' |
| 35. qatalat | 'she killed' | 35a. taqtulu | 'she is killing' |
| | | | |
| 36. 9alimtu | 'I knew' | 36a. ʔa9lamu | 'I am knowing' |
| 37. 9alimta | 'you (m.) knew' | 37a. ta9lamu | 'you (m.) are knowing' |
| 38. 9alimti | 'you (f.) knew' | 38a. ta9lami:na | 'you (f.) are knowing' |
| 39. 9alima | 'he knew' | 39a. ya9lamu | 'he is knowing' |
| 40. 9alimat | 'she knew' | 40a. ta9lamu | 'she is knowing' |

**3.** Account for the morphological phenomena exhibited by the following artificial language data by means of a morphological tactics and alternation pattern. Use simulfixing where necessary. Assume that the lexons being realized by morphemes include one for each stem and also $^{LN}$/Acc/ (accusative) and $^{LN}$/P/ (plural).

| | Nom Sg | Nom Pl | Acc Sg | Acc Pl | Gloss |
|---|---|---|---|---|---|
| 1. | sugo | sugora | sugot | sugorat | 'sky' |
| 2. | man | mun | mant | munt | 'grass' |
| 3. | nilo | tonilo | nilot | tonilot | 'pond' |
| 4. | mel | melra | melt | melrat | 'bear' |
| 5. | fol | ful | folt | fult | 'deer' |
| 6. | rifa | rifara | rifat | rifarat | 'meadow' |
| 7. | fode | tofode | fodet | tofodet | 'ear' |
| 8. | pir | pur | pirt | purt | 'knife' |
| 9. | more | morera | moret | morerat | 'campfire' |
| 10. | gafi | togafi | gafit | togafit | 'beaver' |
| 11. | idi | idira | idit | idirat | 'tree' |
| 12. | bek | buk | bekt | bukt | 'pot' |
| 13. | mot | met | mott | mett | 'uncle' |
| 14. | son | toson | sont | tosont | 'aunt' |
| 15. | bolu | tobolu | bolut | tobolut | 'foot' |
| 16. | lar | ler | lart | lert | 'eye' |
| 17. | xabu | xabura | xabut | xaburat | 'dog' |
| 18. | fode | fodera | fodet | foderat | 'stream' |
| 19. | fik | fek | fikt | fekt | 'stone' |
| 20. | ema | toema | emat | toemat | 'star' |

**Set 4D: Syntax**

1. Use the following data as the basis for a diagram of a fragment of English syntax. Use your knowledge of English to provide for further projections beyond the data, within the same vocabulary and syntactic patterns.

   1. He knows John.
   2. He knows that John lives here.
   3. Mary lives there.
   4. Mary knows Mark.
   5. Mary knows that Mark works here.
   6. John sees Mark.
   7. John sees that Mark knows Jim.
   8. Mark sees that Tom knows that Jane sees Mary.
   9. She likes Mark.
   10. Tom understands Mark.
   11. Tom understands that Mark likes Jim.
   12. Jim knows that Sue lives there.
   13. Sue works here.
   14. Alice likes Mary.
   15. Mary knows that John likes Alice.
   16. Jim detests Mary.
   17. Alice understands that Mary detests Sue.
   18. He understands John.
   19. Mark sees that Mary knows that he works there.
   20. Sue sees Mary.

2. The Roman numeral system is a language-like system with a syntax of its own. Write a tactic diagram accounting for all well-formed combinations of Roman numerals from 1 (I) through 899 (DCCCXCIX). Consider only the most usual form of Roman numerals, that which does not allow four successive occurrences of the same element, so that 4 = IV (not IIII), 9 = IX, 40 = XL, and so on. The diagram should be so organized that it will not provide more than one way to generate the same sequence of elements, nor should it allow a null output.

3. Use the following data from Russian as the basis for a syntactic diagram. Include reasonable projections, but do not attempt to provide for the various subject nouns as objects, as they will have case forms which are not shown in this data. All data is given in a transliteration of the Cyrillic orthography.

   | | | |
   |---|---|---|
   | 1. | Tanja sidit tam. | 'Tanya sits there.' |
   | 2. | Sidit li Tanja tam? | 'Does Tanya sit there?' |
   | 3. | Miša stoit zdes'. | 'Mike stands here.' |
   | 4. | Stoit li Miša zdes'? | 'Does Mike stand here?' |
   | 5. | Vanja rabotaet naprotiv. | 'Johnny works across the way.' |
   | 6. | Rabotaet li Vanja naprotiv? | 'Does Johnny work across the way?' |

| | | |
|---|---|---|
| 7. | Maša čitaet knigu. | 'Masha reads a book.' |
| 8. | Čitaet li Maša knigu? | 'Does Masha read a book?' |
| 9. | Professor pišet pis'mo. | 'The professor writes a letter.' |
| 10. | Pišet li professor pis'mo? | 'Does the professor write a letter?' |
| 11. | Vanja nosit doklad. | 'Johnny carries the report.' |
| 12. | Nosit li Vanja doklad? | 'Does Johnny carry the report?' |
| 13. | Predsedatel' čitaet pis'mo. | 'The chairman reads a letter.' |
| 14. | Čitaet li doktor gazetu? | 'Does the doctor read the newspaper?' |
| 15. | Vidit li Miša knigu? | 'Does Mike see the book?' |
| 16. | Igraet li Tanja zdes'? | 'Does Tanya play here?' |
| 17. | Vanja igraet na dvore. | 'Johnny plays outside.' |
| 18. | Rabotaet li doktor na dvore? | 'Does the doctor work outside?' |
| 19. | Sidit li predsedatel' zdes'? | 'Does the chairman sit here?' |
| 20. | Stoit li Maša naprotiv? | 'Does Masha stand across the way?' |

## Set 4E: Concord

1. Account for the following Spanish noun phrases in a tactic and realizational diagram. Include reasonable projections from this data, namely, combinations of nouns with all the other adjectives. The odd-numbered nouns are feminine, the even-numbered ones masculine.

| | | |
|---|---|---|
| 1. | la kasa | 'the house' |
| 1a. | las kasas | 'the houses' |
| 1b. | la kasa linda | 'the pretty house' |
| 1c. | las kasas lindas | 'the pretty houses' |
| 2. | el lapis | 'the pencil' |
| 2a. | los lapises | 'the pencils' |
| 2b. | el lapis lindo | 'the pretty pencil' |
| 2c. | los lapises lindos | 'the pretty pencils' |
| 3. | la muxer | 'the woman' |
| 3a. | las muxeres | 'the women' |
| 3b. | la muxer biexa | 'the old woman' |
| 3c. | las muxeres biexas | 'the old women' |
| 4. | el profesor | 'the professor' |
| 4a. | los profesores | 'the professors' |
| 4b. | el profesor alto | 'the tall professor' |
| 4c. | los profesores altos | 'the tall professors' |
| 5. | la nasion | 'the nation' |
| 5a. | las nasiones | 'the nations' |
| 5b. | la nasion interesante | 'the interesting nation' |
| 5c. | las nasiones interesantes | 'the interesting nations' |
| 6. | el libro | 'the book' |
| 6a. | los libros | 'the books' |
| 6b. | el libro roxo | 'the red book' |
| 6c. | los libros roxos | 'the red books' |

|       |                        |                      |
|-------|------------------------|----------------------|
| 7.    | la mano                | 'the hand'           |
| 7a.   | las manos              | 'the hands'          |
| 7b.   | la mano limpia         | 'the clean hand'     |
| 7c.   | las manos limpias      | 'the clean hands'    |
| 8.    | el ermano              | 'the brother'        |
| 8a.   | los ermanos            | 'the brothers'       |
| 8b.   | el ermano biexo        | 'the old brother'    |
| 8c.   | los ermanos biexos     | 'the old brothers'   |
| 9.    | la karta               | 'the letter'         |
| 9a.   | las kartas             | 'the letters'        |
| 9b.   | la karta roxa          | 'the red letter'     |
| 9c.   | las kartas roxas       | 'the red letters'    |
| 10.   | el pie                 | 'the foot'           |
| 10a.  | los pies               | 'the feet'           |
| 10b.  | el pie limpio          | 'the clean foot'     |
| 10c.  | los pies limpios       | 'the clean feet'     |
| 11.   | la tierra              | 'the land'           |
| 11a.  | las tierras            | 'the lands'          |
| 11b.  | la tierra alta         | 'the high land'      |
| 11c.  | las tierras altas      | 'the high lands'     |
| 12.   | el ombre               | 'the man'            |
| 12a.  | los ombres             | 'the men'            |
| 12b.  | el ombre interesante   | 'the interesting man'|
| 12c.  | los ombres interesantes| 'the interesting men'|

**2.** Account in a tactic diagram for the following Old Church Slavic data, including reasonable projections. Note that it incorporates both concord (between subject and verb) and two types of government: between verb and prepositional phrase-type and between preposition and object.

|     |                      |                               |
|-----|----------------------|-------------------------------|
| 1.  | mǫži živetŭ vŭ gradæ | 'the man lives in the city'   |
| 2.  | mǫži idetŭ vŭ gradŭ  | 'the man goes into the city'  |
| 3.  | mǫži živǫtŭ vŭ gradæ | 'the men live in the city'    |
| 4.  | mǫži idǫtŭ vŭ gradŭ  | 'the men go into the city'    |
| 5.  | rabŭ živetŭ vŭ gradæ | 'the slave lives in the city' |
| 6.  | rabŭ živetŭ blizŭ grada | 'the slave lives near the city' |
| 7.  | rabi živǫtŭ blizŭ grada | 'the slaves live near the city' |
| 8.  | rabi idǫtŭ kŭ gradu  | 'the slaves go toward the city' |
| 9.  | mǫži žive vŭ gradæ   | 'the man lived in the city'   |
| 10. | žena ide vŭ gradŭ    | 'the woman went into the city'|
| 11. | ženy živǫ vŭ xramæ   | 'the women lived in the house'|
| 12. | rabi idǫ kŭ xramu    | 'the slaves went toward the house'|

13. dæva ide vŭ xramŭ      'the maiden went into the house'
14. dævy živǫtŭ vŭ xramæ      'the maidens live in the house'
15. cæsarjĭ žive vŭ gradæ      'the king lived in the city'
16. cæsarji idǫ vŭ grobŭ      'the kings went into the tomb'
17. rabŭ živetŭ vŭ grobæ      'the slave lives in the tomb'
18. dæva živetŭ blizŭ groba      'the maiden lives near the tomb'
19. dævy idǫ kŭ grobu      'the maidens went toward the tomb'
20. ženy živǫtŭ blizŭ xrama      'the women live near the house'

NOTE: The alternation between the endings *-ĭ* and *-ŭ* for singular subject nouns of one type is phonologically conditioned and need not be accounted for in your diagram. Use the ending *-ŭ* to subsume both subclasses.

## Set 4F: Morphology-Syntax Problems

1. Consider the following phrasal data from a hypothetical language. Distinguish the syntactic phenomena involving concord classes from the morphological phenomena involving the inflectional classes of nouns.
   a. Draw a diagram of the lexotactics and lexemic alternation pattern to account for the concord classes and all phenomena other than specific shapes of affixes.
   b. Draw a second diagram of the morphotactics of nouns and adjectives to account for the forms of these that can occur. Assume that the concord of nouns and adjectives will be controlled from the lexemic stratal system of 1a above.

| | | | |
|---|---|---|---|
| 1. gumada guzori | 'a big lion' | 1b. lamada lazori | 'big lions' |
| 1a. gumadan guzori | 'the big lion' | 1c. lamadan lazori | 'the big lions' |
| 2. dobu zizori | 'a big beetle' | 2b. midobu mizori | 'big beetles' |
| 2a. dobun zizori | 'the big beetle' | 2c. midobun mizori | 'the big beetles' |
| 3. karobi kazori | 'a big ear' | 3b. harobi hazori | 'big ears' |
| 3a. karobin kazori | 'the big ear' | 3c. harobin hazori | 'the big ears' |
| 4. kabiti kazori | 'a big cow' | 4b. labiti lazori | 'big cows' |
| 4a. kabitin kazori | 'the big cow' | 4c. labitin lazori | 'the big cows' |
| 5. guruto guzori | 'a big tree' | 5b. laruto lazori | 'big trees' |
| 5a. guruton guzori | 'the big tree' | 5c. laruton lazori | 'the big trees' |
| 6. soga dozori | 'a big monkey' | 6b. disoga hazori | 'big monkeys' |
| 6a. sogan dozori | 'the big monkey' | 6c. disogan hazori | 'the big monkeys' |
| 7. ŋukara zizori | 'a big dog' | 7b. mikara mizori | 'big dogs' |
| 7a. ŋukaran zizori | 'the big dog' | 7c. mikaran mizori | 'the big dogs' |
| 8. dogandu dozori | 'a big leaf' | 8b. hagandu hazori | 'big leaves' |
| 8a. dogandun dozori | 'the big leaf' | 8c. hagandun hazori | 'the big leaves' |
| 9. kanambo kazori | 'a big book' | 9b. lanambo lazori | 'big books' |
| 9a. kanambon kazori | 'the big book' | 9c. lanambon lazori | 'the big books' |

|   |   |   |   |
|---|---|---|---|
| 10. kaŋagu kazori | 'a big robe' | 10b. haŋagu hazori | 'big robes' |
| 10a. kaŋagun kazori | 'the big robe' | 10c. haŋagun hazori | 'the big robes' |
| 11. lunoŋka mizori | 'a big canoe' | 11b. noŋka duzori | 'big canoes' |
| 11a. lunoŋkan mizori | 'the big canoe' | 11c. noŋkan duzori | 'the big canoes' |
| 12. lusito mizori | 'a big river' | 12b. sito duzori | 'big rivers' |
| 12a. lusiton mizori | 'the big river' | 12c. siton duzori | 'the big rivers' |

**2.** Add the following Old Church Slavic data to that given for problem 2 in Set 4E. Produce a bistratal description of the lexotactics and morphotactics for which the corpus provides evidence, along with the associated alternation patterns. Your account should provide for reasonable projections from this data, but note the supplementary information which follows the list below.

| | | |
|---|---|---|
| 21. | mǫžĭ sæditŭ vŭ gradæ | 'the man sits in the city' |
| 22. | žena ležitŭ vŭ xramæ | 'the woman lies in the house' |
| 23. | rabŭ bæžitŭ vŭ grobŭ | 'the slave flees into the tomb' |
| 24. | dæva sædæ vŭ grobæ | 'the maiden sat in the tomb' |
| 25. | cæsarjĭ leža blizŭ xrama | 'the king lay near the house' |
| 26. | žena bæža kŭ gradu | 'the woman fled toward the city' |
| 27. | rabŭ viditŭ ženǫ | 'the slave sees the woman' |
| 28. | žena udaritŭ mǫža | 'the woman strikes the man' |
| 29. | mǫžĭ prætitŭ rabu | 'the man warns the slave' |
| 30. | ženy prætętŭ cæsarju | 'the women warn the king' |
| 31. | mǫži udarętŭ dævǫ | 'the men strike the maiden' |
| 32. | dævy vidętŭ raba | 'the maidens see the slave' |
| 33. | rabi udarętŭ cæsarja | 'the slaves strike the king' |
| 34. | ženy prætętŭ mǫžu | 'the women warn the man' |
| 35. | mǫži vladǫtŭ rabomĭ | 'the men rule the slave' |
| 36. | ženy vladǫ mǫžemĭ | 'the women ruled the man' |
| 37. | dæva vladetŭ cæsarjemĭ | 'the maiden rules the king' |
| 38. | rabŭ vlade dævojǫ | 'the slave ruled the maiden' |
| 39. | cæsarji vladǫ ženojǫ | 'the kings ruled the woman' |
| 40. | mǫžĭ præti ženæ | 'the man warned the woman' |
| 41. | rabi prætišę dævæ | 'the slaves warned the maiden' |
| 42. | voždĭ vidæ dævǫ | 'the leader saw the maiden' |
| 43. | voždi bæžašę kŭ xramu | 'the leaders fled toward the house' |
| 44. | dæva stoja blizŭ raba | 'the maiden stood near the slave' |
| 45. | rabi sædæšę blizŭ mǫža | 'the slaves sat near the man' |
| 46. | mǫži ležašę blizŭ ženy | 'the men lay near the woman' |
| 47. | rabŭ sædæ blizŭ cæsarja | 'the slave sat near the king' |
| 48. | cæsarjĭ stojitŭ blizŭ dævy | 'the king stands near the maiden' |
| 49. | voždĭ udari cæsarja | 'the leader struck the king' |
| 50. | rabi udarišę ženy | 'the slaves struck the women' |
| 51. | voždi vidæšę raby | 'the leaders saw the slaves' |

| 52. | cæsarjĭ vidæ dævy | 'the king saw the maidens' |
|-----|-------------------|---------------------------|
| 53. | dævy vidętŭ mǫžę | 'the maidens see the men' |
| 54. | cæsarjĭ præti dævamŭ | 'the king warned the maidens' |
| 55. | voždĭ vlade ženami | 'the leader ruled the women' |
| 56. | ženy prætišę mǫžemŭ | 'the women warned the men' |
| 57. | cæsarjĭ vladetŭ voždi | 'the king rules the leaders' |
| 58. | mǫžĭ prætitŭ rabu | 'the man warns the slave' |
| 59. | žena præti rabomŭ | 'the woman warned the slaves' |
| 60. | voždĭ vladetŭ raby | 'the leader rules the slaves' |

SUPPLEMENTARY INFORMATION:

1. The traditional names of the cases represented in the data may be used as a basis for labels for the lexemes and morphemes concerned. They are as follows:

   Nominative: Subjects
   Accusative: Objects of 'see,' 'strike,' 'into'
   Genitive: Object of 'near'
   Locative: Object of 'in'
   Dative: Objects of 'warn,' 'toward'
   Instrumental: Object of 'rule'

2. The prepositions can have plural as well as singular objects. This fact should be provided for in the lexotactics, but the data is insufficient to allow the full morphological specification of their form. The plurals of these cases for the inanimate nouns found, however, are the same as those of 'slave.'
3. The verbs 'flee,' 'stand,' 'lie' belong to the same class as 'sit,' 'see,' but some of their endings differ due to morphophonemic alternation. Such endings involve a morphon [MN]/æ/.
4. The nouns 'king,' 'man,' 'leader' belong to the same class as 'slave.' The endings are morphonically transcribed with the same alphabetic symbols as those of the latter, except for the accusative plural, which is [MN]/y/.

# 5

## Semological Phenomena

### 5.1  Fundamental Supragrammatical Phenomena

Among Neo-Bloomfieldian linguists it was a common assumption that no linguistic structure more abstract from the speech signal than the morphology and syntax existed. More recent linguists, however, have come to the conclusion that there are indeed structures representing a greater abstraction from the phonic correlations than the morphemic and lexemic strata. Such structures, the study of which may be broadly termed **semology,** are at the same time less abstract from the conceptual correlations than is phonological and morphological structure. From a point of view that sees language as connecting conceptual and phonic correlations, the most abstract sort of structure is actually that of the morphemic and lexemic stratal systems, as characterized in Chapter 4. The phonology represents a greater degree of abstraction from the conceptual correlations, but a lesser degree from the phonic correlations. The semology, on the other hand, shows the greatest abstraction from the phonic correlations, but a lesser amount from the conceptual.

Two of the basic phenomena which traditional semanticists have treated are synonymy and polysemy. By **synonymy** we mean the situation in which two forms of expression mean the same. An example would be the terms *little* and *small* in English. Neo-Bloomfieldian linguists commonly considered there to be no true synonyms, since they defined synonymy as the situation in which two expressions could be completely substitutable for each other in all con-

texts. Using this strict definition, the cited example would be ruled out by such a phrase as *my little sister*, in which the substitution of *small* for *little* would change the meaning. The traditional notion of synonymy can be salvaged, however, if we recognize that it has actually been used to indicate not complete substitutability in all contexts without change of sense but PARTIAL substitutability, that is, complete substitutability in some contexts. Thus *small* and *little* would be synonyms in view of the fact that they are mutually substitutable in a subset of their occurrences without affecting the meaning of the utterances in question. In stratificational terms, this situation would be represented by the occurrence of a downward OR somewhere in the linguistic system between the conceptual correlations and the morphemes.

The refusal of the Neo-Bloomfieldians to admit synonymy is connected with the widespread belief, stemming from the writings of Bloomfield himself, that the morpheme is a meaningful unit. Bloomfield conceived of each morpheme as being paired with a single unit of meaning which he termed a **sememe.** This term had been used still earlier by the Swedish linguist Adolf Noreen. Bloomfield provided the general definition of the sememe—"the meaning of a morpheme"—but he refrained from any attempt to define the individual sememes associated with particular morphemes, relegating this task to other sciences. Stratificational linguists, on the other hand, recognize that the morpheme is not properly a meaningful unit, so that morphemes may interconnect with meanings in various ways, one of which is the synonymy relationship just defined.

Another type of relationship between morphemes and their meanings is **polysemy.** This is the converse of synonymy, the situation in which a single expression can have more than one meaning. The above case of *little* can serve as an example here, since it can mean 'small' as in *little book* and 'younger' as in *little sister*. In terms of stratificational relations, polysemy involves an upward OR intervening between a morpheme and the conceptual correlations to which it connects. The interlocking of synonymy and polysemy is shown in Figure 5.1.

Traditional scholars have made a distinction between polysemy and homonymy. The former is usually said to involve one expression (word) with different meanings, while the latter involves two words which just fortuitously

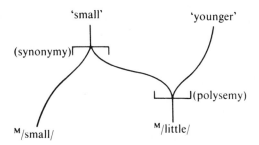

***Figure 5.1   Interlocking of Synonymy and Polysemy***

happen to sound the same. In practice, etymology and spelling are frequently taken into consideration in distinguishing the two, and this consideration hardly seems appropriate in a synchronic study based primarily on spoken texts. The term **homonymy** could be applied, however, to instances of neutralization below the morphemic stratum, particularly in the morphemic alternation pattern. An example would be the noun *wright*, the adjective *right*, and the verb *write*, whose difference in morphosyntactic behavior as well as connection to meaning would result in their being considered different morphemes, while they would neutralize into a single morphemic sign. The term "polysemy" could then be applied to neutralizations above the morphemic stratum. This usage would correspond partly, but not completely, to the traditional one. The pair *sale/sail*, for instance, would be a case of polysemy by this criterion, since both words are nouns with the same morphological and syntactic occurrence privileges. Traditionally, however, they would be considered homonyms in view of their distinct spelling and etymology.

It was mentioned earlier (Section 2.1) that the meanings of some terms may be divided into meaningful components. This property, known as **componency,** may be illustrated by the data originally shown in Table 2.1. It may be reinterpreted in the graphic form shown in Figure 5.2.

Another important fact which indicates that the relation of morphemes to meaning is not a simple one is the existence in every language of combinations of morphemes which have a meaning either completely unrelated to the meanings of their individual parts or including something more than the

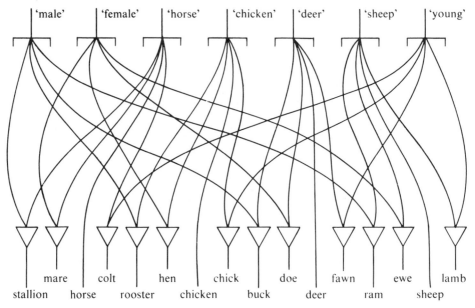

*Figure 5.2  **Componency in Animal Names***

simple sum of these meanings. Such expressions may be called **idioms,** and the phenomenon may be called **idiomaticity.** Most idioms are complex lexemic signs, being composed of more than one lexon. A few examples from English follow.

1. *Red herring* could refer to a particular kind of fish having a ruddy color, but as an idiom it means 'a phony issue raised to distract attention' and thus is treated by speakers as a unit having no relation to the individual meaning of its parts.
2. *Come down with,* as in *Eustace came down with smallpox,* has the meaning 'contract (a disease).' It contrasts with its literal counterpart, seen in *Algernon came down with the crayons.*
3. *Kick the bucket* as an idiom means 'die,' in contrast to the literal 'strike the pail with one's foot.' Note that *The cow kicked the bucket* could be ambiguous, in that it could have either the literal or the idiomatic meaning.
4. *Woodpecker* is an idiom despite the fact that woodpeckers do indeed peck wood. The idiom refers not to just any bird or other animal which happens to peck wood at one time or another but to a specific group of species. Furthermore baby woodpeckers do not peck wood until they have learned to do so, but they are nevertheless woodpeckers.
5. *Madison Square Garden* is an example of a name which may have originally been descriptive but has now become institutionalized. The present *garden* is not at Madison Square, nor is it a garden in the usual sense. Even if we admit the sense 'athletic arena of a certain kind' for *garden,* and the term were used to refer to such a garden at Madison Square, it would still be an idiom if it were an institutionalized proper name rather than a mere description. *Madison Square,* incidentally, is itself an idiom, like most complex geographic names.

As a complex lexemic sign, each of the idioms mentioned so far is represented by a downward ordered AND in the lexemic sign pattern. There are also some idioms which are a whole clause in length and may be considered complex sememic signs whose components are known as **semons.** Examples include various proverbs and sayings, such as *Don't put all your eggs in one basket, A rolling stone gathers no moss, He has two strikes against him already,* and *Strike while the iron is hot.* Each of these has a literal counterpart, of course, and the two have the same structure on the lexemic stratum and below but differ on the sememic stratum.

Another semological property which has long been recognized in traditional semantics is **antonymy,** or oppositeness of meaning. True antonyms may be regarded as pairs of terms whose lexemic structure is X and un-X. Examples include *large* and *small* ($^{L}$/un large/), *deep* and *shallow* ($^{L}$/un deep/), and *old* and *young* ($^{L}$/un old/). The analysis of these terms has as its basis the fact that *large*, *deep*, and *old* are unmarked, as evidenced by their use in questions about the quality in general. When we say *How large is it?*, *How deep is it?*, *How old is it?*, we leave no implication that we think the object involved is necessarily large, or deep, or old. When we ask *How small is it?*, *How shallow is it?*, *How young is it?*, on the other hand, we imply that we know or think that the thing is small rather than large, shallow rather than deep, or young rather than old. In the nominalized forms referring to the quality in general, furthermore, we find the same morpheme as in the unmarked form, or else a form unrelated to either morphologically. We get *depth*, and also *length*, *height*, *width*, referring to the whole range of the property, while *shallowness*, *shortness*, *lowness*, and *narrowness* refer only to degrees of the negated quality. We may also get portmanteaus such as *size* (for the range large/small) and *age* (young/old), which may be analyzed as the realizations of $^L$/large/ and $^L$/old/, respectively, with the lexeme $^L$/th/, realized elsewhere as a suffix such as *-th* or *-ness*. Figure 5.3 diagrams some of these nominal relations.

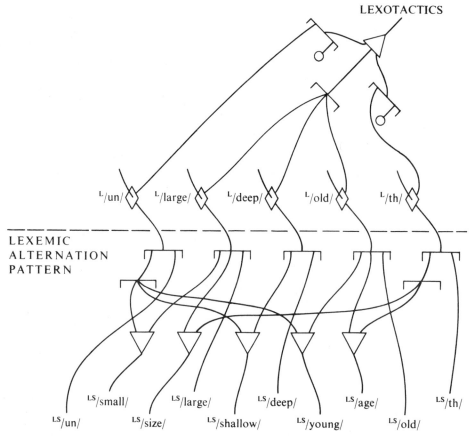

**Figure 5.3  Antonyms and Their Nominalizations**

Some other examples which have traditionally been considered antonyms are actually quite different from these. *Male* and *female* are not true antonyms, but are rather members of a semological class which has only two members. *Female* would not be properly analyzed as *un* + *male*, nor would *male* be analyzable as *un* + *female*. Such pairs as *come* and *go* and *bring* and *take* are likewise not susceptible to the same analysis as true antonyms. Like the true antonyms, however, their relationship involves markedness, but not by $^L$/un/. Rather *go* and *take* are unmarked, while their counterparts *come* and *bring* carry the additional component of 'direction toward the speaker (or his displaced point of reference).'

A further linguistic property which the semology will be called upon to account for is the relation of such sentences as

Myron dropped the rock.
The rock was dropped by Myron.

These active/passive pairs, as well as further types such as *It was Myron that dropped the rock*, *The one that dropped the rock was Myron*, *It was the rock that Myron dropped*, and *Myron's dropping of the rock*, have received increasing attention from linguists during the past decade. Gleason has suggested the term **agnation** to distinguish this relation from other ways in which constructions may be related. It should be noted that agnation is not the same as synonymy, which we have defined as alternate realization represented by a downward OR between the conceptual correlations and the morphemes. Though an active sentence and its corresponding passive may describe the same basic event, they differ in other semantic factors—in this case the participant upon which a certain kind of focus is placed.

Agnate forms such as those cited do, however, share a common structure—a basic core denoting the event and its participants, which is realized in different ways depending on other elements which may be present in the same configuration. The core structure in the realizates of the agnate forms cited above involves the association of an action of *dropping* with *Past*, with two accompanying participants—an agent *Myron* and a goal *rock*. The difference between the simple active and passive forms in the semology depends on the selection of a **focus** within this configuration. If the agent is in focus, the realization will be active; if the goal is in focus, it will be passive. In addition, either the agent or the goal, independent of the status of either as focussed, may be selected as **topic**. In combination with agent focus, an agent topic would result in *It was Myron that dropped the rock*, while a goal topic would produce *It was the rock that Myron dropped*. With a goal focus, agent topic selection results in *It was by Myron that the rock was dropped*, and goal topic produces *It was the rock that was dropped by Myron*.

Subsequent sections of this chapter will treat this and other forms of agnation in greater detail.

## 5.2   *Predication Structure*

In traditional syntax, the clause is one of the most fundamental units. The simple sentence contains a single clause, and the so-called compound and complex sentences involve coordinate and subordinate clauses. The clause as such is a particular rank in the lexotactics in the model arrived at in Section 4.7, but the most essential control for clause structure originates in the semotactics. The basic semotactic structure serving as the realizate of the clause may be termed the **predication.** A predication may also be realized as certain types of phrases, as in *Myron's dropping of the rock.* The basic structure of a predication includes an event sememe accompanied by one or more participants in that event. In *Myron dropped the rock* and its agnate forms, for instance, the event is $^S$/drop/. One participant is the agent $^S$/Myron/, and the other is the goal $^S$/rock/. The total core structure of this predication is represented in Figure 5.4. In this figure only unordered ANDs are used, and the role of each participant is shown by the role sememes $^S$/Ag/ for agent and $^S$/Gl/ for goal. Additional sememes in this figure are $^S$/Def/, realized as the definite article, and $^S$/Past/, realized as the past-tense lexeme.

Event sememes are divided into classes according to the number and type of participants which may accompany them. Among the participant types which a predication may contain, each marked with an identifying sememe of its own, are **agent, goal, recipient, instrument, causer,** and **beneficiary.** Also, there are various circumstantial attributes to the predication, such as **time, location,** and **manner.**

Various researchers are today investigating what we are calling predication structure, both within stratificational theory and with other approaches. It is not our intention here to present a definitive treatment of this problem,

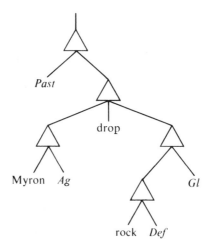

**Figure 5.4   A Predication Structure**

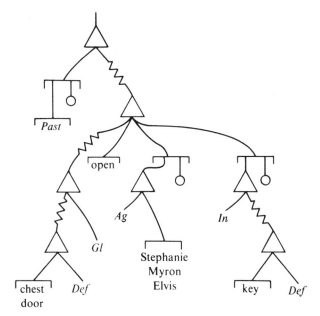

**Figure 5.5 Some Participants with $^S$/open/**

but only to suggest how the general phenomenon will fit into a stratificational grammar. The concrete analyses which follow should therefore be regarded as highly tentative. The reader who has other ideas on the handling of the phenomena involved in predication structure is invited to cast his own ideas into the stratificational framework, using the general notions presented in this book.

The event sememe $^S$/open/ belongs to a class which may occur with varying combinations of major participants. It may occur with agent and goal, as in *Stephanie opened the chest*; with instrument and goal, as in *The key opened the chest*; with all three of these, as in *Stephanie opened the chest with the key*; or with goal only, as in *The chest opened*. These facts are represented in the tactic diagram of Figure 5.5, which shows the optionality of agent and instrument and the obligatory nature of the goal for this event sememe and others of the same class. It provides exactly the possible choices enumerated above, as well as indicating some different possible choices of participant sememes.

Many other options are of course possible, including the very important one of focus. As we have said, focus controls the lexotactic selection of subject and that of a passive verb form as opposed to an active one. In order to see what choices of focus we have with just the participants now under discussion, let us consider the set of agnate forms differing in focus related to the event *Stephanie opened the door with a key*.

open · Gl · Ag · In
Stephanie opened the door with a key.                 (agent focus)
The door was opened by Stephanie with a key.    (goal focus)

open · Gl · Ag
Stephanie opened the door.                            (agent focus)
The door was opened by Stephanie.                  (goal focus)

open · Gl · In
A key opened the door.                                 (instrument focus)
The door was opened with a key.                     (goal focus)
The door opened with a key.                           (?)

open · Gl
The door was opened.                                    (goal focus)
The door opened.                                         (?)

The first two basic types, with an agent present, exhibit a quite straight-forward situation. Either agent or goal may be in focus, but not instrument, with goal focus determining passive voice. In the other two types, where no agent is present, there is the possibility of goal focus resulting in a passive, of instrument focus where this participant is present, and of an additional form in which the goal serves as subject but the verb is active. These last-mentioned forms, unexpected on the basis of our preliminary account, may be handled if we adopt a modification of our treatment of focus. One of the possible focus types for each combination can be considered unmarked, so that no focus element will be present in the structure. When an agent is present, what we have been calling "agent focus" can be considered the unmarked form. In the other cases, the unmarked focus will account for the third possibility, indicated by the question marks above. Thus goal focus will always determine a passive, while absence of focus or instrument focus will leave the verb in its active (unmarked) form. The subject will be the participant in focus; and if there is no focus, the agent; or if there is no agent, the goal. If we add these focus possibilities to what we have in Figure 5.5, we get the tactic diagram of Figure 5.6.

This structure shows that focus may be on the goal, or if no agent is present, on instrument. The unordered AND at the top of the diagram helps to specify that only one focus may occur within a predication: it dominates one con-ditioning line, and once this is used it cannot be used again until another predi-cation is selected. The ordered OR immediately above *Fc* indicates that focus is optional in that predications may occur with unmarked focus. For any given vocabulary selection, we get precisely the nine traces we need to corres-pond to the nine combinations of participants and focus.

Now let us consider a different event sememe and its possible participants and focus situations, namely, $^{S}$/give/. With this sememe a goal is again obliga-tory, and there are two optional participants, agent and recipient, as in

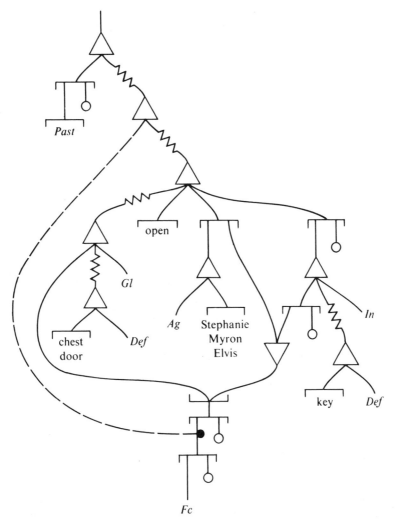

**Figure 5.6 Focus with Major Participants Accompanying**
**ˢ/open/**

*Elvira gave Eustace the book.* We may get the following combinations of participants and focus.

give · Gl · Ag · Rc
Elvira gave Eustace the book.
Elvira gave the book to Eustace.          (unmarked focus)
The book was given to Eustace by Elvira.  (goal focus)
Eustace was given the book by Elvira.     (recipient focus)

give · Gl · Ag
Elvira gave the book.                          (unmarked focus)
The book was given by Elvira.                  (goal focus)

give · Gl · Rc
The book was given to Eustace.                 (goal focus)
Eustace was given the book.                    (recipient focus)

give · Gl
The book was given.                            (goal focus)

In this data, we see several differences from the situation in which instrument is a participant, as in the examples with $^S$/open/. In the first place, recipient, unlike instrument, may be in focus regardless of whether agent is present, accounting for the three focus types shown in the three-participant combinations above. Second, recipient focus requires a passive verb, unlike instrument focus but like goal focus. Third, there appears to be no option of an unmarked focus in the absence of agent—we get no such possibilities as *The book gave* or *The book gave to Eustace*, parallel to *The door opened* and *The door opened with a key*.

The second fact is a matter of the lexotactic realization of semotactic structures, while the other two must be accounted for by restrictions on focus selections in the semotactics. Basically, we need to provide that focus, occurring on either goal or recipient, is optional when an agent is present but obligatory when it is absent. This provision is made in the diagram of Figure 5.7, which parallels Figure 5.6 for this type of event sememe.

This diagram provides for only one occurrence of focus within a predication, as does Figure 5.6. But in the presence of an agent, it allows focus to be optional, while otherwise it provides for an obligatory focus. This specification is provided by the series of downward ordered ORs controlled by enablers, shown at the bottom of the diagram. The first enabler connects to the top of the construction and provides for only one focus per predication, since once it has been used, a conditioning signal will not be available again until another predication is selected. The second enabler, connected to the agent construction, provides for the optionality of focus in the presence of agent. Otherwise, the structure is set up so that it cannot be satisfied without a focus selection.

For each type of predication, there are also several additional optional elements which cannot be in focus and are not generally subject to restrictions according to the type of event sememe. These optional elements are listed below, with examples.

*Time*        Myron gave Stephanie the wallet YESTERDAY.
              Hilda will open the chest NEXT WEEK.
*Location*    Elvira works IN WAPAKONETA.
              Simon and Leslie are vacationing IN IDAHO.
*Beneficiary*  Stephanie watered the lawn FOR HILDA.
              Elvis washed the car FOR EUSTACE.

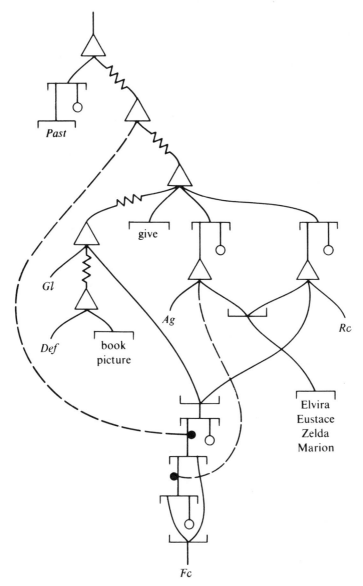

**Figure 5.7  Focus with Major Participants Accompanying**
**ˢ/give/**

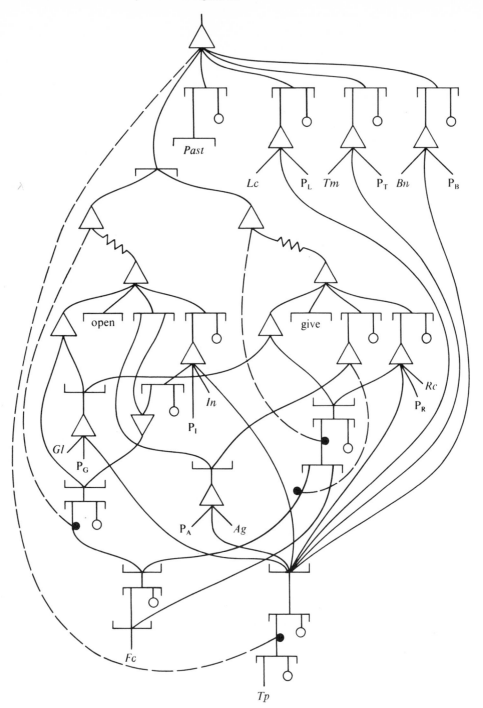

**Figure 5.8  Focus and Topic for Two Predication Types**

Though these elements cannot be in focus in English, the language does have a way of placing a special kind of emphasis upon them. This technique also applies to the elements which may be in focus, independently of the occurrence of this focus. This phenomenon, alluded to earlier, may be called **topic.** The sentence *Eustace gave Stephanie the key yesterday* has unmarked focus and no topic, according to our analysis. Any of the participants in its sememic structure, however, may optionally be accompanied by the sememe $^S$/Tp/ (topic), resulting in the following variations, all keeping the unmarked focus:

It was Eustace that gave Stephanie the key yesterday.      (agent topic)
It was to Stephanie that Eustace gave the key yesterday.   (recipient topic)
It was the key that Eustace gave Stephanie yesterday.      (goal topic)
It was yesterday that Eustace gave Stephanie the key.      (time topic)

The variation of focus would, of course, result in still further varieties of the same core predication.

This situation can be handled if, in addition to focus, we provide in our semotactics for an optional topic as a part of each predication, to be associated with any of the various possible participants or circumstantials (time, location, manner). Figure 5.8 integrates Figures 5.6 and 5.7, adding the three optional elements and provisions for a single optional topic in each predication. This will result in the realization of the topicalized element in the *It was . . . that* phrase at the beginning of the lexotactic clause which realizes this predication. Details of these realizational matters will be provided in Section 5.3.

(The exercises of Set 5A at the end of this chapter may be done at this point.)

## 5.3   *Realization of Focus and Topic*

Our account of agnate clauses differing in focus and topic is still not complete. We have described the semotactic structures which provide for the realizates of these agnate types, but our description of the lexotactic realization of these structures has thus far been only an informal one. It will be our task in this section to see how this informal account can be translated into the more formal terms of a network of relationships.

For purposes of this illustration, let us take an event sememe defining a third type of predication, namely, $^S$/chase/. We will first treat it semotactically, as we did $^S$/give/ and $^S$/open/ in the preceding section. We will then go beyond this to give a full account of the lexotactic realizations of these structures. We may first observe that $^S$/chase/ occurs in predications with two major participants, agent and goal. It may have either the unmarked agent focus

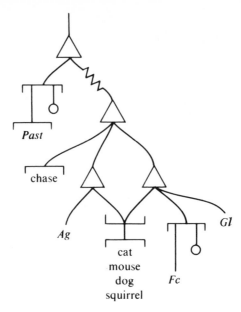

**Figure 5.9   Participants and Focus Accompanying ˢ/chase/**

or goal focus. With *cat* as agent and *mouse* as goal, for example, we get *The cat chased the mouse* with unmarked focus, and *The mouse was chased by the cat* with goal focus. Figure 5.9 shows a semotactic description of these alternatives.

This diagram is analogous to those of Figures 5.6 and 5.7 in providing for the occurrence of major participants and focus only. Since only goal, of the two major participants, may take a marked focus, there is no need for the specification of only one focus per predication here. A detail which has been omitted is the possibility of the absence of agent, resulting in an obligatory focus on the goal, in the *The mouse was chased*. This detail could easily be accounted for in the same way as for the similar situation in Figure 5.7, but has been ignored here in order to simplify the explanation as much as possible.

This semotactics will be connected through a series of realizational patterns to a lexotactics providing the necessary structures to realize its output. A lexotactics containing the needed active and passive structures is shown in Figure 5.10. The first line from the downward ordered AND at the top of the diagram leads to the noun phrase which serves as subject. The middle line leads to the verbal structure, which if passive will begin with a form of *be*. Following this, the main verb will occur with its proper suffix. This verb will be the only verbal form to occur in an active clause. From the third line there are two options—either a noun phrase preceded by ᴸ/by/ (as in the passive *The cat was chased by the dog*) or a noun phrase followed by ᴸ/m/ (as in *The dog chased the cat*). The lexeme ᴸ/m/ will be realized as a suffix on such pro-

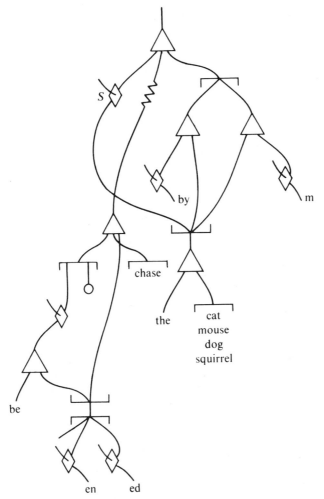

**Figure 5.10 Lexotactics for Some Active and Passive Clauses**

nominal forms as *him, them, whom*; it will enter into portmanteau realization to give *me, us, her*; elsewhere it will be realized as zero.

In this tactics, there is no control to prevent the generation of such impossible forms as *The cat chased by the dog* (where *chased* is past, not past participle) or *The mouse was chased the cat*. This control, however, will be provided from the sememic stratum, as we shall see presently. It is a general principle in stratificational theory that restrictions dealt with on a higher stratum do not need to be repeated on a lower one.

In each case where a diamond has been overtly shown in Figure 5.10, its connection to the upper stratum will be significant for the treatment of focus.

We will now enumerate the sememes of Figure 5.9 to which each of these connects.

$$
\begin{array}{ll}
^L/\text{by}/ & \backslash \quad ^S/\text{Ag}/ \\
^L/\text{m}/ & \backslash \quad ^S/\text{Gl}/ \\
^L/\text{ed}/ & \backslash \quad ^S/\text{Past}/ \\
^L/\text{be}/ \ldots {}^L/\text{en}/ & \backslash \quad ^S/\text{Gl}/ \cdot {}^S/\text{Fc}/ \\
\text{S (subject)} & \backslash \quad ^S/\text{Ag}/, ({}^S/\text{Gl}/ \cdot {}^S/\text{Fc}/)
\end{array}
$$

Looking at the total of this information, we see that there is a pattern of alternate and portmanteau realization which is depicted graphically in Figure 5.11, along with the tactics of Figure 5.10.

This graph specifies that $^S/\text{Fc}/$, in all occurrences shown here, is realized portmanteau with $^S/\text{Gl}/$. This portmanteau has a triple realization: subject specification (S) followed by specification of a form of $^L/\text{be}/$, followed by the verbal suffix $^L/\text{en}/$ (past participle). If $^S/\text{Fc}/$ does not accompany $^S/\text{Gl}/$, the latter is realized as $^L/\text{m}/$, since the clause will then be active. $^S/\text{Ag}/$ has the alternate realizations $^L/\text{by}/$ and subject specification (S). The former occurs when the passive $^L/\text{be}/$ is specified, as shown by the conditioning line running to the enabler that controls the ordered OR for the realization of this sememe.

The fact that the realization of this portmanteau, which may be termed $^{SS}/\text{Ps}/$ (passive), is partly discontinuous is specified by the lexotactics. To demonstrate this, we will survey the realization of $^L/\text{be ed chase en}/$ (*was chased*) in detail. The line leading to S is specified first in the realization of $^{SS}/\text{Ps}/$, but it may be ignored for the moment. The next part to be specified is the form of *be*, including stem and affix. At this point $^S/\text{Past}/$ will have been signalled simultaneously with the whole predication, or at least with its event sememe and modifiers, and it will be realized on $^L/\text{be}/$. The other possible affix $^L/\text{en}/$ will not be specified from the sememic sign pattern until the form of *be* has been realized, due to the ordering of the AND in this pattern. When the form of *be* has been realized, the diamond leading to $^L/\text{en}/$ will be activated, and it will be realized the next time the tactics permits it, which in this case will be following the main verb $^L/\text{chase}/$. Thus the lexotactics will put out in sequence $^L/\text{be}/$ $^L/\text{ed}/$ $^L/\text{chase}/$ $^L/\text{en}/$.

A further point which needs some explanation is the realization of $^S/\text{Ag}/$ and $^S/\text{Gl}/$ in the various positions. It is assumed here that when one of these sememes is realized in the lexotactics, its accompanying participant sememes will be realized as a part of the same construction. Thus if we realize $^S/\text{Ag}/ \cdot {}^S/\text{cat}/ \cdot {}^S/\text{Def}/$ in subject position, we will get $^L/\text{the}/$ $^L/\text{cat}/$ in that position, and if we have $^S/\text{Gl}/ \cdot {}^S/\text{dog}/ \cdot {}^S/\text{Def}/$ in the same predication, we will get the realization $^L/\text{the}/$ $^L/\text{dog}/$ $^L/\text{m}/$. A problem arises in the performance aspect of such a specification. If we interpret all the downward unordered ANDs in the semotactics as defining strict simultaneity, it would appear that the participant-role marking sememes and the participant sememes with their

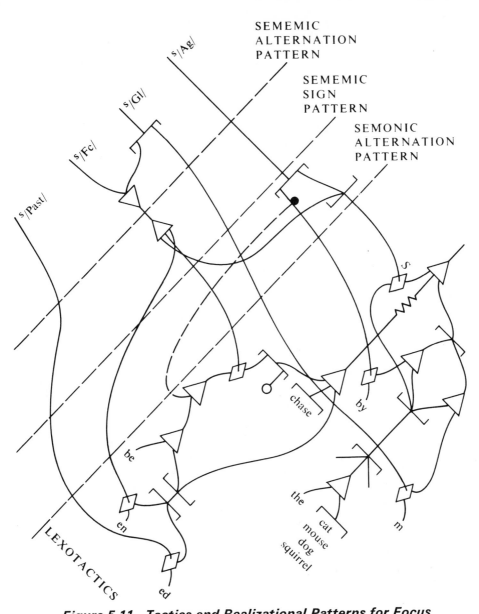

*Figure 5.11  Tactics and Realizational Patterns for Focus*

modifiers will all be available at the same time, regardless of the particulars of their association—thus $^S$/Gl/ · $^S$/Ag/ · $^S$/Def/ · $^S$/dog/ · $^S$/cat/ · $^S$/Def/ in no particular order. If this were to be the case, of course, there would be no control on the lexotactics to distinguish *The dog chased the cat* from *The cat chased the dog*, or *The dog was chased by the cat* from *The cat was chased by the dog*.

This would seem to mean that we cannot interpret all the downward unordered ANDs shown in the semotactics of Figures 5.6, 5.7, and 5.9 as indicating absolute simultaneity. At least two alternate solutions suggest themselves. Each involves the ANDs grouping the event sememe with the accompanying participants and circumstantials.

The first alternative is to replace the unordered nodes in these positions by ordered ones, their order being established on the basis of some sort of structural evidence rather than arbitrarily. (See Reich 1970 for a suggestion about such evidence.)

A second possibility is to define these specific ANDs as *arbitrarily sequential*. This would mean that the lines from such an AND would be activated one at a time, but in no established order. This order could be thought of, in fact, as being established by the lexotactics, which could bring down a group of signals at the point at which it was ready for them. In any case, the participant sememe associated with any role sememe, as well as any modifying elements such as $^S$/Def/, would be realized as a part of the same immediate construction which embodies the realization of its role sememe. This provision would guarantee that the association of roles with participants defined by the semotactics would be preserved and not arbitrarily muddled.

Now that the discontinuous realization of $^{SS}$/Ps/ has been handled, we have the basis for considering the more complex structure of the English core verb phrase, which will require further discontinuous realization in the lexotactics. One of the fuller expansions of this construction is *had been being taken*, a past, perfect, progressive, passive verb phrase. Figure 5.12 shows the lexemic analysis of this construction and the association of each lexeme with a corresponding sememic sign. Using the same principles already outlined above for the realization of $^{SS}$/Ps/, we may now treat the fuller phrase with the lexotactics shown in Figure 5.13. This structure works for a repeated series of discontinuous constituents in the same way as Figure 5.11 handles the realization of $^{SS}$/Ps/. The first finite verb realized takes the general tense suffix, in

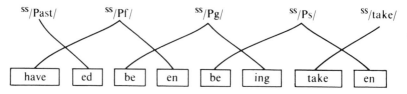

*Figure 5.12  Discontinuous Constituents*

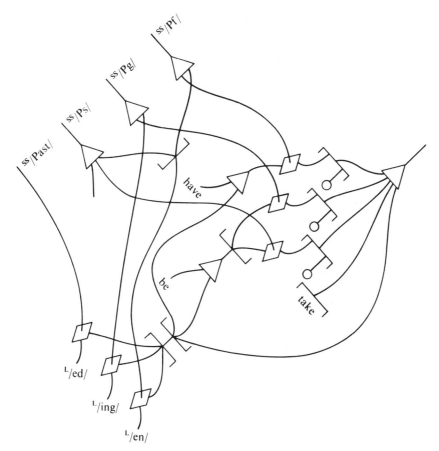

**Figure 5.13** *Discontinuous Realization in the Lexotactics*

this case ᴸ/ed/, and the suffixation of additional verbs in the phrase is determined by the order in which the suffixes are made available, defined by the interaction of the lexotactics with the realizational pattern above it.

Next we must consider how ˢ/Tp/ will be realized lexologically. For purposes of this illustration, let us take the topicalized variations related to *The cat chased the mouse*. With unmarked focus, we will have the possibility of

| | |
|---|---|
| It was the cat that chased the mouse. | (agent topic) |
| It was the mouse that the cat chased. | (goal topic) |

and with goal focus, we may get

| | |
|---|---|
| It was by the cat that the mouse was chased. | (agent topic) |
| It was the mouse that was chased by the cat. | (goal topic) |

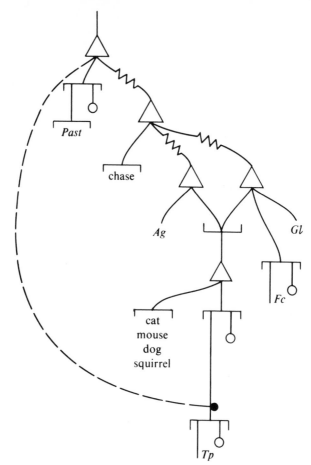

**Figure 5.14   Topic in a Predication with** $^S$/**chase**/

Of course, various circumstantials such as time and location could also be topicalized if they were present, but for simplicity of explanation we will leave them aside here.

To provide for the occurrence of $^S$/Tp/ we need to make some additions to the semotactics of Figure 5.9. These additions, as in Figure 5.14, show the potentiality of topic with either agent or goal and include the previously introduced device assuring the selection of only one topic per predication.

Next we need to consider a lexotactics which will provide the indicated realizations of $^S$/Tp/, as well as those of focus already considered. This will have to be an expansion and modification of Figure 5.10. The major thing which needs to be added is the *It was . . . that* construction, which serves as the characteristic realization of $^S$/Tp/. This and other necessary modifications are shown in Figure 5.15. If we keep in mind that other sememes grouped with

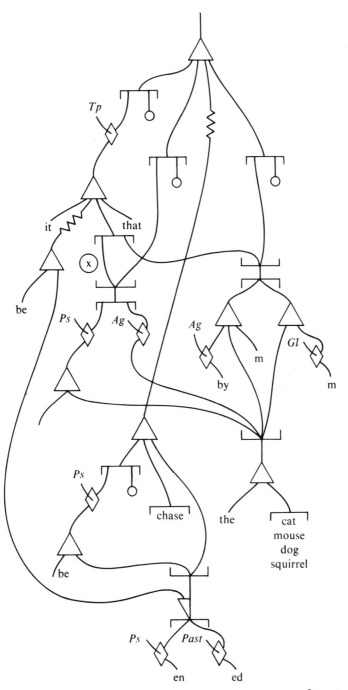

**Figure 5.15   Lexotactics for the Realization of ˢ/Tp/**

$^S$/Tp/ in the semotactics will be realized as a part of the same construction with it (all other things being equal), the diagram is not particularly difficult to interpret. The clause construction is shown to begin with the optional topic construction, controlled by a diamond leading upward directly to $^S$/Tp/. In this construction *it*, *be*, and *that* are determined elements. *Be* takes as its suffix a reduplication of the tense of the core verb phrase element. In the position between the form of *be* and the *that*, the participant which is topicalized will be realized. It will therefore occur here rather than in the usual position which it would occupy in the agnate form without topic. It is for this reason that the subject and object/agent phrase lines are shown as optional in this diagram, in contrast to Figure 5.10.

One detail not treated here, partly because it is variable according to dialect, is the regularization of the form of the topicalized element. With pronominal realization of agent, this diagram would provide for *It was he that chased the mouse*, but if the goal were pronominal and in focus, the result would be *It was him that the cat chased*. Most dialects of English presumably do not have this situation, but rather have generalized one pronominal form or the other. Colloquial language favors the objective forms, which we have analyzed as containing $^L$/m/, while more formal language would favor the simple forms, which we have analyzed as not containing this suffix. To account for the colloquial variety, we need only provide within the topic construction a downward ordered AND with its second branch leading to a determined occurrence of $^L$/m/ at the point marked (x) in Figure 5.15 (a bit above the "subject" diamond). For the more formal variant, we need a device to block the realization of $^S$/Gl/ as $^L$/m/, which could easily be provided. Note in Figure 5.15 the addition of a determined occurrence of $^L$/m/ after the noun phrase in the agent construction, since we will, of course, get *by me*, *by them*, *by her*, and so on.

Whatever further modifications may be necessary to provide for additional data and to incorporate other varieties of focus and topic, such as those discussed informally in Section 5.2, this discussion has served an important purpose. It has demonstrated the general way in which stratificational theory seeks to account with its networks of relationships for the data which was formerly thought to require transformations. In place of transformations, a stratificational grammar operates with tactic patterns on various strata, which are connected to one another. Each tactic pattern defines an infinite set of well-formed combinations of its basic elements or -emes. These elements are not actual entities, of course, but points in the network having connections upward and downward as well as to their tactic functions. The arrangement of elements on one stratum, as we have seen, may differ in various ways from the arrangements of their realizates or realizations on other strata. In the performance model, the lower-stratum arrangements will prevail in the process of encoding, as each lower stratum represents a successively closer approximation to the arrangements of the substantive phonic correlations which manifest the language. In decoding, on the other hand, the priority will be reversed, since in this process each higher stratum encountered represents a successively closer approximation to the arrangements of the conceptual correlations. The ability of a stratified system of relationships to get along without transformations is enhanced, incidentally, by the fact that certain elements of a given stratum may be realized in whole or in part as the choice of a construction in the tactics of the stratum below. Examples include ${}^S$/Tp/, parts of ${}^{SS}$/Ps/, and the element Q discussed in Chapter 4.

## 5.4 *Subordinate Predications*

We have not yet considered the semological structure of sentences containing attributes. A number of problems connected with the phenomenon of attribution will be discussed in this section.

Let us first consider phrases containing adjectives in their realized form, such as *the green pencil*. Linguists have observed for some time that such a phrase is agnate to *the pencil that is green*, and further to the full sentence *The pencil is green*. All of these realized structures have in common the fact that they attribute a quality, in this case greenness, to an object—namely, the pencil. We can therefore postulate for the phrase *the green pencil* a sememic structure somewhat like that shown in Figure 5.16. Here *Attr* is an element indicating that *green* designates an attributed property, while the subordination of this to the AND also dominating the structure of *the pencil* indicates that it is to this object that the property is being attributed.

Such a sememic combination may function as an independent declaration, in which case ${}^S$/Attr/ will be realized lexically as *be*, giving the configuration shown in Figure 5.17a. The element *Decl* indicates that a declaration is being made. In this case, the interrogative element *Int* could occur in the position occupied by *Decl*, resulting in a question ultimately realized as *Is the pencil green?*

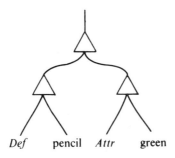

*Def*    pencil    *Attr*    green

**Figure 5.16 Sememic Structure of the green pencil**

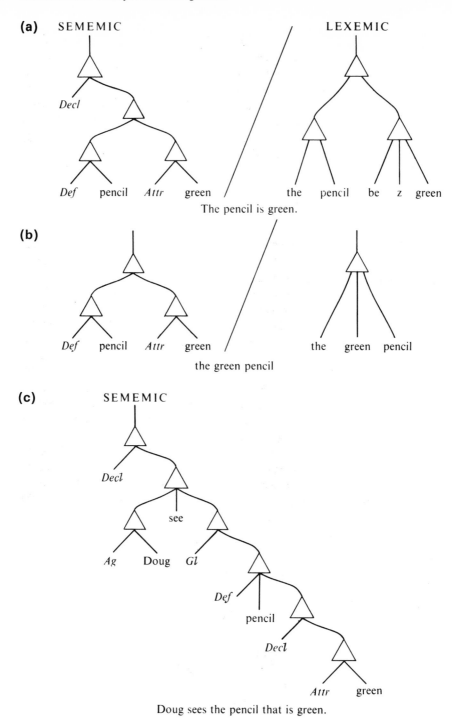

**Figure 5.17  Attributive Structures and Their Realizations**

If it is not a declaration, but simply a part of another predication, a similar combination will have the realization *the green pencil*, with $^S$/Attr/ being realized as zero, as shown in Figure 5.17b.

Finally, there is the realization *the pencil that is green*. This involves a subordinate declaration. An appropriate sememic structure for this is given in Figure 5.17c, the sememic realizate of the sentence *Doug sees the pencil that is green*.

This tentative hypothesis about the sememic relations accounting for the agnate nature of the examples shows three ways in which an attribution may fit into the sememic structure. We may now examine some subordinate clauses of other types to see how these ideas will apply to further attributions.

Let us take the sentence *Tom saw the cat that the dog chased*. Here *that the dog chased* is, of course, a subordinate clause, attributive to *cat*. Its basic function is therefore similar to that of the attributions already considered. In this case, however, a type of predication involving agent and goal is involved, one which indicates that the cat is the goal of the action of chasing by a dog. We may also note the contrasting form *Tom saw the cat that was chased by the dog*, which shows that the focus of the subordinate predication serving as an attribute may vary in a similar way to that of a main predication.

Figure 5.18 shows a possible way of accounting for this material, consistent with what has already been said about attribution. Here $^S$/Attr/ is shown to co-occur with a predication in which one of the roles lacks an associated participant. This has the effect of indicating that the role in question is being attributed to the object to which the predication is subordinate, in this case *cat*. The two diagrams, of course, indicate the distinction of agent and goal focus, accounting for the differences of voice in the ultimate realization.

It must be emphasized that this particular hypothesis is by no means offered as a definitive solution to the problem. It is given merely as a suggestion, subject to modification on the basis of more complete empirical research into the form of the semotactics and a fuller consideration of the data for which it must account. At the present state of research in these areas, it is a major undertaking merely to suggest in more than vague terms what the nature of the evidence necessary for the confirmation or disconfirmation of such a hypothesis might be.

In accordance with the above outline, we will assume for present purposes that attributives of various sorts have in their semotactic trace an element $^S$/Attr/ co-occurring with the attributed structure, this structure being subordinated to the element being qualified. Attributive elements will include not only those realized as adjectives and subordinate clauses but also those realized as adverbs, which are distinguished in the semology by being attributed to sememes other than those designating things. The sememic elements usually realized as adjectives or adverbs may be given the name **descriptives.**

Another type of subordinate predication is not attributive, but rather fulfills a more direct role in the predication structure. Consider the following sentences.

**(a)**

**(b)**

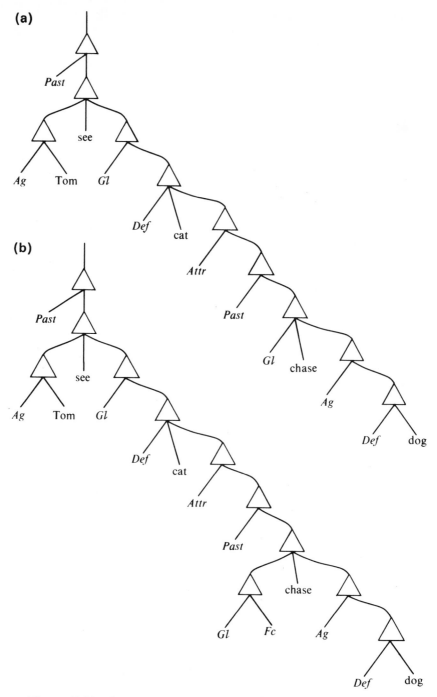

**Figure 5.18   Subordinate Predications with Agent and Goal**

Bruno saw Sammy eat anchovies.
Penelope knows (that) Sammy eats anchovies.

These examples illustrate two different varieties of subordinate nonattributive clause. The first, usable with such verbs as *see*, *hear*, and *feel*, shows no tense variation but only that of voice, representable as focus on the sememic stratum. This contrast is illustrated by *Bruno saw anchovies eaten by Sammy*, which is agnate to the first example.

The second type can be used with a wider variety of verbs, including *know*, *think*, and *believe*, as well as *see*, *hear*, and *feel*. It is characterized by an optional *that*, a determined lexemic element, and also by the possibility of tense distinctions. In place of *eats* in the second example above, we may get *ate*, *will eat*, *can eat*, and so on. This is in addition to the usual distinctions of voice, as in *Penelope knows that anchovies will be eaten by Sammy*.

It seems clear that these constructions can contrast, since certain verbs can occur with either of them, as in

Penelope will see Sammy eat anchovies.
Penelope will see that Sammy eats anchovies.

This contrast, furthermore, is not a matter of diversification, since the two sentences are not completely synonymous. The *that* type can be described as a fact-oriented construction: what is perceived is the truth of some fact indicated by the clause. The tenseless type is action-oriented: what is perceived is not just the truth of the event but the action itself, in progress. In this case, the action of the subordinate clause will necessarily be simultaneous with that of the main verb, which serves to explain why no tense distinctions are possible within the construction. As a very clear example of a case in which one version may be true while the other is false, we may consider

Elmira sees that John is losing weight.
Elmira sees John lose weight.

We will treat the more general fact (*that*) type as unmarked sememically, involving simply the sememic occurrence of a predication as goal, as shown in Figure 5.19a. The action type will be treated as marked by the occurrence of a sememe $^S$/Act/ simultaneous with the goal, leading to the difference of realization. This is shown in Figure 5.19b. Some event sememes, like *see*, *hear*, and *feel*, will be able to take either construction, while others may take only the fact type. As an example of an event sememe taking only the action type, we may cite *watch*, since we can say *Penelope watches Sammy eat anchovies*, but not \**Penelope watches that Sammy eats anchovies*. Many event sememes, of course, will not be able to take either type of subordinate predication.

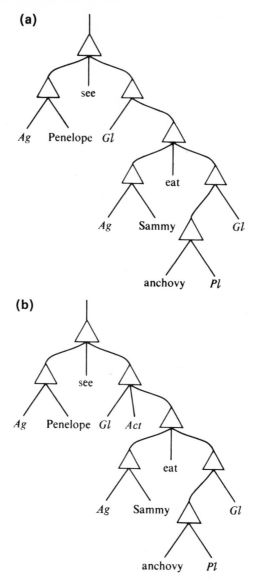

**Figure 5.19   *Semmic Structure of Contrasting Subordinate Predications***

We have thus surveyed some of the more important types of subordination, including various kinds of attribution, treated as one of its subtypes. In this connection, we have discussed sememic structures containing an attribution element, and others which contain an "action" element. At this point, the lexemic realization of these elements is left unformalized. We need to know a great deal more about these matters before a full formalization will be profitable.

(The exercises of Set 5B at the end of this chapter may be done at this point.)

## 5.5   *The Two Strata of Semology*

The preceding discussion has been confined to the structure of the sememic stratal system. Other treatments of stratificational semology, such as that in Lamb's *Outline*, however, have referred to a second semological stratal system above the sememic. This stratal system was originally called the hypersememic. More recently, Lamb has begun to use the term **gnostemic** for this highest stratal system, since it has to do with the organization of knowledge. There is some question as to whether this stratal system is properly a part of language or just an auxiliary to language, for it will clearly have to include a good many phenomena which have not traditionally been viewed as a part of language. The answer to this question is perhaps more than anything a matter of how we want to define language. The essential point is that between the sememic stratal system and the conceptual correlations there is another stratal system which may be called the gnostemic. The structure of this stratal system appears to differ from that of other strata in a number of ways, while having other points in common with the others. It can be thought of as occupying a sort of middle ground between language and nonlanguage. Whether we choose to draw a major boundary above or below the gnostemics, or whether we dismiss the question as irrelevant, may be substantially arbitrary. The purpose of this section is to indicate some of the structural differences we can expect to find between the sememic and gnostemic stratal systems, and to make some general remarks about the structure of the gnostemic.

To begin in more general terms, we could say that the gnostemic stratal system, being the closest to the conceptual correlations, represents as nearly as possible the natural way of thinking about things, while the sememic provides the first degree of accommodation of this to what will ultimately emerge as speech or writing.

We have seen that the morphemic and lexemic stratal systems will account in a rather detailed way for the structure of words, phrases, and (less fully) clauses. The sememic stratal system, and its tactics in particular, will be called upon to account in greatest detail for the structures corresponding to the traditional clauses and sentences, though it will contain elements realized as smaller units as well. On the gnostemic stratum, finally, we will be called upon to extend our account to the still higher ranks of paragraph and text. We know that the theory maintains that texts and their subdivisions have a linguistic well-formedness. It turns out that this well-formedness can best be accounted for in terms of that layer of structure showing the least degree of abstraction from the conceptual correlations, the gnostemic stratal system. We can therefore cite as one difference between the sememic and gnostemic stratal systems the distinction in the scope of the basic generative cycle for each stratal tactics. For the semotactics, this scope goes up to the level corresponding to the sentence, which may be called the **proposition.** The term "sentence" is more appropriately applied, in accordance with traditional usage, to the lexemic realization of the proposition. Factors controlling the external compatibility of propositions, however, originate in the gnostotactics, whose basic cycle must extend all the way to the text.

Let us now survey a series of examples of discrepancy between these two strata which have been suggested by a number of stratificational writers. We may begin with some examples of diversification. The sememes $^S$/before/ and $^S$/in-front-of/ can be considered alternate realizations of a single gnoston, which can be labelled $^{GN}$/anteriority/. On the sememic stratum, the two must be shown to differ in their combinability: $^S$/before/ can be used either in a temporal sense (as in *before the service*) or in a spatial one (as in *before the altar*). On the other hand, $^S$/in-front-of/ is restricted to the spatial sense. Bennett (1968) has suggested that this spatial versus temporal conditioning is provided by the semotactics, corresponding to a difference between the class of participant sememes and the class of event sememes.

A second example of diversification is provided by the realizations of the gnoston $^{GN}$/die/, as diagrammed in Figure 5.20. This unit, itself likely a portmanteau realization of the gnostemes $^G$/Cess(ative)/ and $^G$/live/ has (among others) the three realizations $^{SS}$/die/, $^{SS}$/pass-away/, and $^{SS}$/kick-the-bucket/. The latter two, besides being complex in their ultimate realizations, are more restricted in their distribution. Ignoring the jocular connotations of $^{SS}$/kick-the-bucket/, we note that it can be used in reference to humans or animals but not plants, which can nevertheless be said to die:

My aunt died/kicked the bucket.
Our dog died/kicked the bucket.
Their philodendron died/*kicked the bucket.

Ignoring its euphemistic connotations, $^{SS}$/pass-away/ is even more restricted, in that it may be used only in reference to humans:

My aunt passed away.
*Our dog passed away.
*Their philodendron passed away.

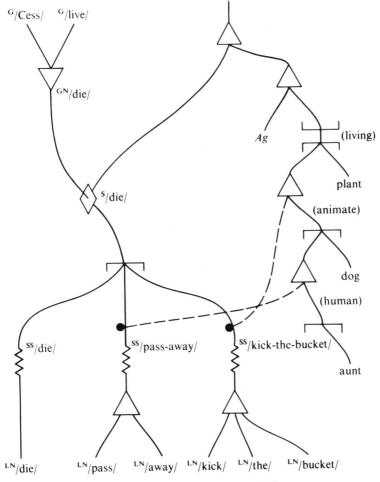

**Figure 5.20   Realizations of** <sup>GN</sup>**/die/**

In the diagram, these facts are indicated by the enablers, which allow these selections to be made only under the appropriate conditions. Because the OR node representing the diversification is unordered, <sup>SS</sup>/die/ may be taken under any circumstances. The sememic signs <sup>SS</sup>/kick-the-bucket/ and <sup>SS</sup>/pass-away/ will connect ultimately to lexemic signs whose breakdown into their constituent lexons will be indicated in the lexemic sign pattern.

There may also be cases of neutralization between the two strata. This occurs in particular in connection with the identification of participants in an event. A separate gnosteme may be thought of as existing for each individual in the experience of the language user (including fictional or imaginary persons as well as real ones). On the sememic stratum, two or more such individuals may be realized by the same sememe. When we hear such a sentence as *Bill phoned Bill*, for instance, we understand that two different individuals with the same name are involved. We can think of two separate gnostemes $^G$/Bill$_1$/ and $^G$/Bill$_2$/, each connecting to particular conceptual correlations representing one's knowledge of that individual. Many of these gnostemes may be neutralized on the sememic stratum. The same gnostemes are also subject to diversification, as $^G$/Bill$_1$/ may, under the appropriate circumstances, be realized as *Bill, my friend, Bill Jones, he*, and so on.

This consideration introduces the complicated question of pronominalization. In accounting for this phenomenon, we may assume in general that pronouns do not exist on the gnostemic stratum but come in as the sememic realizations of various elements. For a simple first-person pronoun form such as *I*, the gnostemic realizate is that individual gnosteme identified (by its association with another gnosteme) as "speaker." For a second-person pronoun such as *you*, it is that individual (or individuals in English) identified as "addressee." Third-person pronouns are used for persons and things not identified as serving in either of these roles, but whose identification is clear from the context of the discourse or situation. Matters of referential identity further distinguish ordinary and reflexive forms of pronouns, the reflexive form being chosen when the pronoun realizes the same gnosteme as the grammatical subject. Since the notion of subject seems best represented in terms of lexotactic structure, the reflexive/nonreflexive distinction is likely to be more appropriately handled on the lexemic stratum. In any case, pronouns provide an important example of neutralization and diversification between the gnostemic and sememic stratal systems.

Related to the question of pronominalization is the notion that the traces from the gnostotactics representing a text or subpart of one have a structure which is not only to a great extent nonlinear but also multiply connected, such that these traces may contain closed loops instead of the purely tree-like structures characteristic of the lower strata. We have so far used only tree-like traces, but for the gnostemic stratum it may be assumed that traces for the structure of a text may have a multiple connectedness, giving these traces a form which Gleason (1968) has termed a **reticulum.** The term "network" has also been used for such structures, but in view of the networks of relationships into which modern stratificational theory sees the entire language organized, it is better to use a less confusing term.

The major property leading to the multiple connectedness of gnostemic traces is the fact that the gnosteme representing a particular individual will occur only once in the gnostemic structure of a text, regardless of how many different roles this individual may play in the different events in the text. This single gnosteme will be connected to as many separate events as necessary. As a sample of the consequences of this assumption, let us consider the following simple English narrative.

John came into the room and hung up his coat. He sat down and greeted Mary. She brought him his pipe and newspaper. They discussed trivia all evening.

A rough sketch of the gnostemic structure which might correspond to this narrative is presented in Figure 5.21. Let us survey some of the properties of this representation. The ordered AND at the top of the diagram orders the events in their logico-temporal sequence. In this simple case, this order corresponds to that of the realized forms, but in another instance, certain events might be realized in another order. The first two events, for example, could be reported in the form *John hung up his coat after he came into the room.* Each individual event is separated in this representation, even though some may be reported in the same sentence, such as (1) and (2), and also (3) and (4). This would be another discrepancy between the gnostemic and sememic strata, since on the latter the groupings will correspond more closely to the realized sentence structure. The upward ANDs at the bottom make the structure reticular. They show all the roles which may be associated with the gnosteme in the different events of the narrative. In the case of *John*, these include agent, recipient, and possessor, some of which occur more than once. And *Mary* is twice the agent and once the goal. Some of the events are broken down into components: *come = go · directional, bring = take · directional.* Other elements may ultimately be broken down as well but are left unanalyzed in this representation. Doubtless the configurations in Figure 5.21 do not in general show the degree of difference from the corresponding sememic ones that actually exists. This is true because our knowledge of gnostemic structures is so extremely limited, a situation due both to their inherent complexity and to the fact that so little study has been devoted to them.

Another important property of the gnostotactics is the inclusion within it of the **taxonomic hierarchies** characteristic of the language. These comprise a part of our cognitive knowledge about the classification of things and other phenomena. Such a hierarchy provides a representation of the fact that the meanings of some terms are included within those of others, as well as other kinds of relationships in meaning. As examples of the first, we may note that the meaning of *oak* includes that of *tree*, which includes that of *plant*; or the meaning of *tiger* includes that of *cat*, which includes that of *carnivore*, which includes that of *mammal*, which includes that of *animal*. A sample of a taxonomic hierarchy accounting for these facts as well as some others is shown in Figure 5.22.

The classification of plants and animals is one of the easier portions of the total taxonomy to represent, but the concept of the taxonomic hierarchy includes the classification of a much wider variety of phenomena. This part of one's knowledge is, of course, subject to much wider variation from one individual to the next than are the essentials of the lower strata. The knowledge

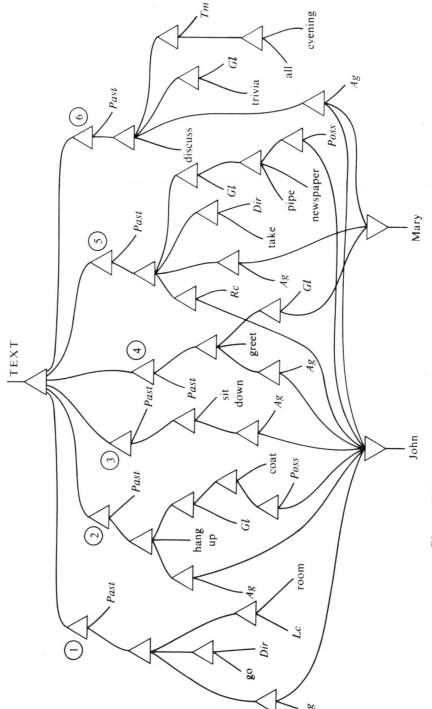

*Figure 5.21   Gnostemic Structure of a Simple Narrative*

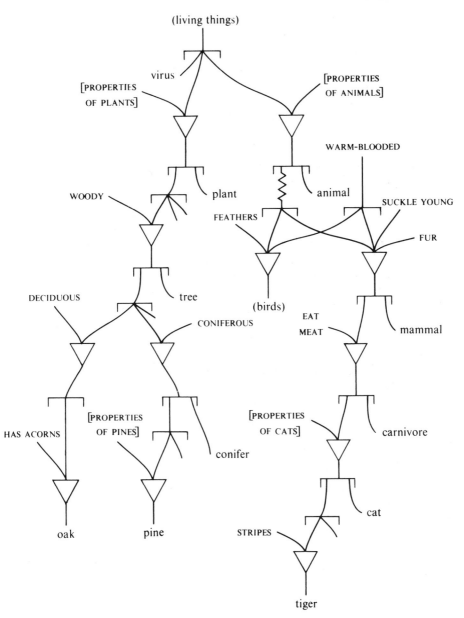

**Figure 5.22   Sample Taxonomic Hierarchy**

stored in such hierarchies is also subject to being altered and added to as long as one remains short of senility. An important part of learning in general, in fact, may be characterized as the building of new portions of network.

Despite the taxonomic hierarchies' being based on certain universals of human experience and powers of observation, we know that there is no universal taxonomic hierarchy drawn upon by all languages, because different cultures characteristically impose different classifications on the same objects or phenomena.

These hierarchies are represented, then, as a part of the gnostotactics, whose duty it is to distinguish sensical texts from nonsensical ones. Connections leading upward to the properties designated in capital letters in the diagram go to other points in the gnostotactics.

There has been some discussion among linguists as to whether semantic well-formedness is within the proper domain of linguistics, in view of the fact that many utterances which might be ruled out as nonsensical in isolation can be understood and accepted if sufficient context has been built up for them. This fact is easily explained, however, if we bear in mind that this portion of the network is subject to change as new facts are learned. The context needed to provide for what would offhand seem a deviant utterance leads to the learning of new material—whether fact or fantasy—which does change this network to allow for such utterances. Therefore the fact that we would generally expect the gnostotactics of English to rule out such a sentence as *Yesterday the sleeping table married its jumping lake* (Lamb 1969) on a number of grounds does not mean that a speaker's actual network could not be changed in one way or another so as to give it an interpretation.

This survey may be concluded with an overview of the structure of the sememic and gnostemic stratal systems. Figure 5.23 shows the general structure of the sememic stratal system, which has an interconnection of patterns similar to those of the lower strata. The functions of these patterns may now be summarized.

The **gnostonic alternation pattern** provides for those alternate sememic realizations of gnostons which are conditioned, via enablers, by sememes and sememe classes from the semotactics.

The **semotactics** provides for well-formed propositions, the realizates of sentences. A single proposition may realize more than one gnostemic event, each event generally being realized by a predication or as part of a compound predication. The sequences of propositions provided by the semotactics are well formed only by virtue of the control exercised by the gnostemic stratal system. Pronouns are introduced on this stratum, partly as a result of the fact that closed loops are not allowed in its tactic traces. This stratal system includes designations of focus and topic, which originate in the gnostemic stratal system.

The **sememic alternation pattern** provides for alternate sememic signs as realizations of the same sememe, under conditions provided via enablers from

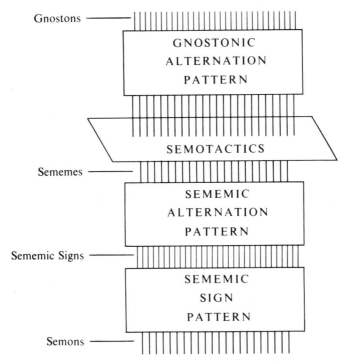

**Figure 5.23   The Sememic Stratal System**

sememe classes in the semotactics. It also accounts for such portmanteau realizations as $^S$/Gl/ · $^S$/Fc/ = $^{SS}$/Ps/.

The **sememic sign pattern** relates sememic signs to semons, providing for complex sememic signs, which will be entities realizing single sememes but realized by a combination of lexemes. An example is $^{SS}$/Ps/, discussed earlier.

Because so little research has been carried out, we can say much less about the structure of the gnostemic stratal system. It does appear certain that an important part of this stratal system will be the **gnostotactics,** whose task it will be to account for all and only the sensical texts of the language, and significant subparts of these. It operates under the control of the wholly extralinguistic conceptual correlations, and sets out events in their logico-temporal order. This tactic pattern contains as one of its important features the taxonomic hierarchies providing for the classificatory interrelations of objects and other phenomena which any speaker assimilates from his culture. Also, each real or imagined individual in the particular speaker's experience is represented by a single gnosteme. Because such a gnosteme of individual identity is given only once in a text, traces from the gnostotactics have the form of a reticulum rather than that of a tree.

By analogy with other strata, it could be hypothesized that the gnostemic stratal system also contains sign and alternation patterns, but such a conclusion remains highly speculative. Therefore no diagram of the gnostemic stratal system analogous to that of the sememic system will be attempted. Even what we have stated regarding the assignment of properties to the various patterns is, of course, based on the current state of research and is therefore likely to be changed as our understanding progresses.

It cannot be overemphasized how vast and relatively unexplored the field of semology is, despite increasing interest in it by linguists of various persuasions. The gnostotactics of a language, though necessarily finite, is so vast and complex that the goal of a complete gnostotactics for even a single language is unrealistic and impractical. All that one can do, for now and the foreseeable future, is to deal with what turn out to be tiny bits and pieces of this structure. This approach will produce accounts which, due to the nature of language as an interconnected system, are subject to significant modification as further bits are studied and interrelated.

Even the much more modest goal of a complete semotactics seems too much to ask at the present. One of the greatest adventures of current linguistic research lies, however, in moving closer to such a goal, even though progress toward it may be slow and scarcely perceptible. The author feels that the basic framework provided by stratificational theory gives, by its very nature, a more fruitful basis for the ultimate pursuit of these inevitably remote goals than alternate frameworks based on fundamentally different assumptions.

## EXERCISES FOR CHAPTER 5

### Set 5A: Basic Predication Structure

1. Interpret the following semotactic traces as English sentences in accordance with the principles outlined in Section 5.2. The elements *Decl* and *Int* are used to distinguish declarative and interrogative clauses.

**a.**

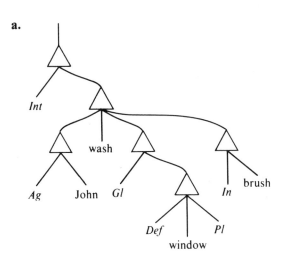

**b.**

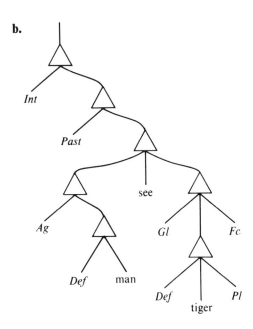

**c.**

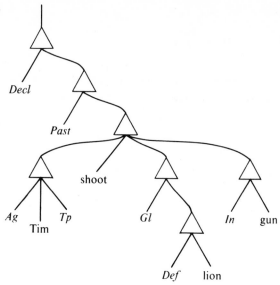

**d.**

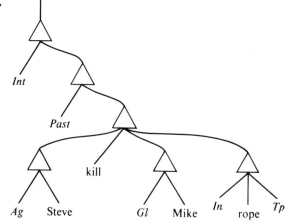

**e.**

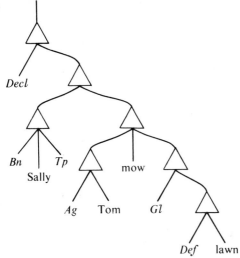

**f.**

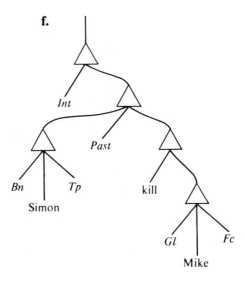

**g.**

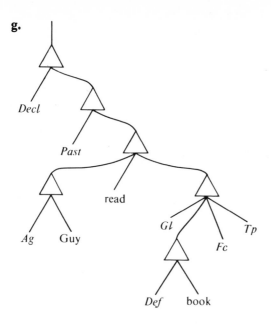

**h.**

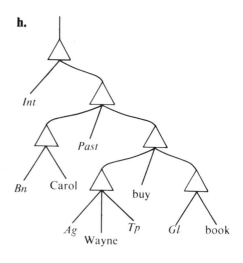

**i.**

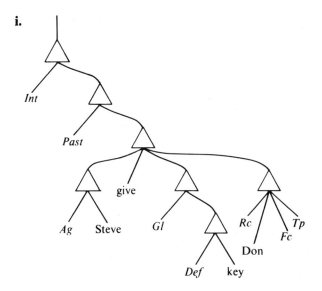

**j.**

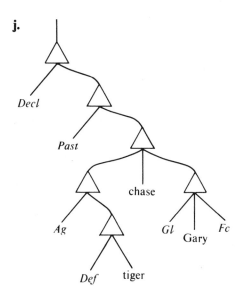

**2.** Draw the semotactic trace for each of the following English sentences.

    **a.** Steve washed the car for Elise with a hose.
    **b.** Was it Mike that gave Tim the magazine?
    **c.** Yesterday Wayne was scolded by Daphne.
    **d.** It was the mice that were caught by the cats.
    **e.** It was today that Tom gave Helen a coat.
    **f.** Was it Ken that was beaten by the thugs in the park?
    **g.** It is with a key that Stephanie opens the chest.
    **h.** Was it the wine that the guests drank?
    **i.** A friend wrote Steve a letter with a pencil.
    **j.** It is by friends that Carol is encouraged.

## Set 5B: Attribution and Subordination

**1.** Interpret the following semotactic traces as English sentences in accordance with the principles outlined in Section 5.4.

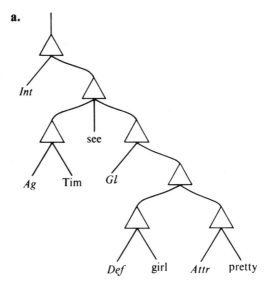

**b.**

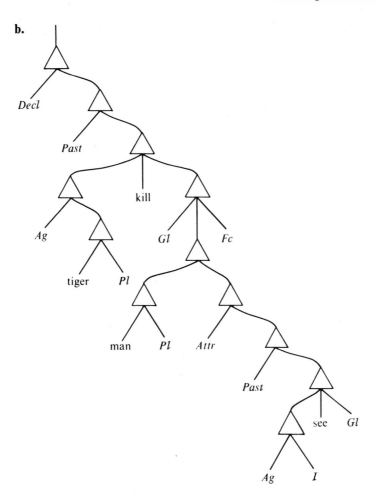

**c.**

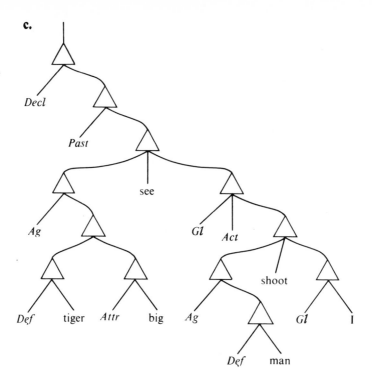

**d.**

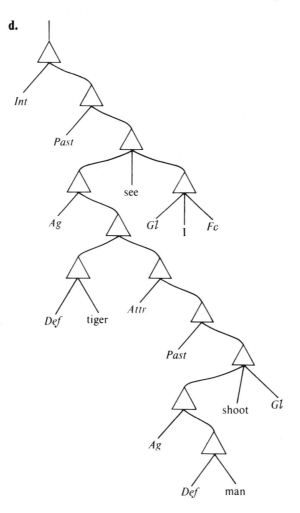

**e.**

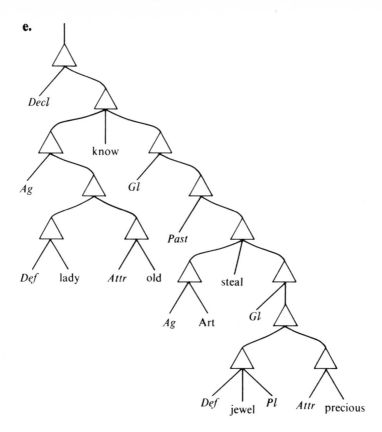

**f.**

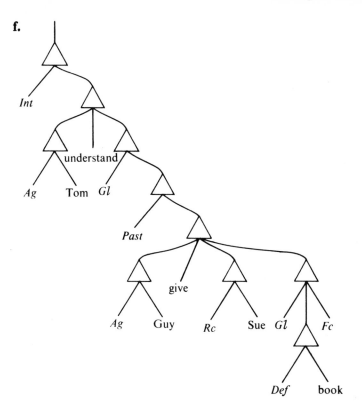

**g.**

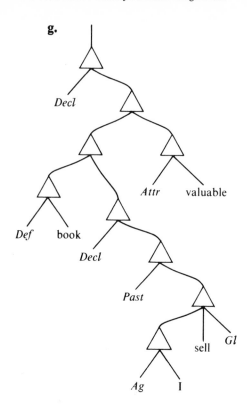

**h.**

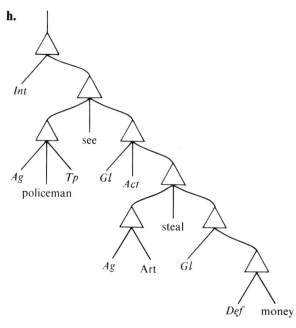

**i.**

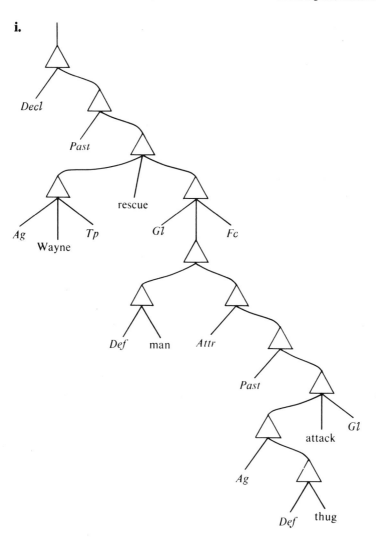

**j.**

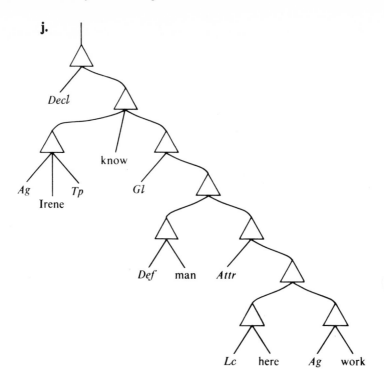

**2.** Draw the semotactic trace for each of the following English sentences.

    **a.** The pen that John sees is yellow.

    **b.** The young girls knew that the house was old.

    **c.** Was it Steve that was given the new desk?

    **d.** I saw the ferocious tiger that killed the man.

    **e.** Did Penelope see Steve shot by the thugs?

    **f.** Does Jim understand that Elise sold the old records?

    **g.** The women that I saw were attacked by the Indians.

    **h.** Is the girl that Tim met yesterday pretty?

    **i.** The young girl was given a book by the elderly lady.

    **j.** Was it yesterday that Helen bought the new dress?

# 6

# *Phonological Phenomena*

## 6.1 *Phonological Contrast and Distinctiveness*

The science of phonology, as distinct from phonetics, first arose as a result of the observation that a given language makes systematic use of only a relatively small number of the phonic distinctions which its speakers can and do make. At one time it was assumed that a phonetic description could provide an adequate characterization of the phonic side of a language, and that such a description would itself have to deal with only a limited number of distinctions. But as the acuteness of phonetic observations increased, it became apparent that no definite limit could be set on the number of discriminable sounds, even for a single speaker of a single language. Investigation of a wider variety of world languages by European and American scholars further increased their awareness of the infinite variety of sounds used in languages.

The rise of phonological analysis provided a basis for the quantification of an aspect of linguistic organization for which pure phonetics was unable to find a principled quantification. At the same time, phonology provided an explanation for the reactions of earlier, less phonetically sophisticated investigators who treated the sound system of a given language in terms of a finite inventory of distinct sounds, even from a phonetic point of view. Their intuitions had led them to practice an inexplicit and inconsistent version of phonological analysis.

The principled science of phonology (or phonemics) evolved in both the United States and Europe during the 1920's and 1930's. Its central idea was

190

that phonemes, the significant units of the phonic system of a given language, can subsume a variety of different actual sounds. The actual sounds subsumed by a single phoneme, however, had to be phonetically related and in such a distribution in the language as not to contrast. This **noncontrastive distribution** could include two types: complementation and free variation. **Complementation,** or **complementary distribution,** of course meant distribution in mutually exclusive environments in the language data. **Free variation** referred to occurrence in the same environment without signalling any significant difference. So the fronted [g̑] of English *geese* is in complementary distribution with the backed [g] of *goose* because the former occurs only before front vowels, while the latter never occurs there. Further, the unaspirated [k] and unreleased [k̚], which can occur in final position in varying pronunciations of such words as *sack, pick,* and *wreck,* are said to be in free variation, since the difference between them can never signal a different utterance. In practice, the principles of noncontrastive distribution and phonetic similarity have been combined with a third one known as **pattern congruity,** a requirement that the assignment of sounds to phonemes result in a system with as great a degree of symmetry as is compatible with the other principles and the data.

If any one of these principles is to be taken as the most important, it would have to be that of complementary distribution. Some critics, however, have seemed to take this principle as the *sole* basis of classical phonemic analysis and on this assumption have maligned the method unjustly. It is of course true that, viewed strictly, complementary distribution is neither a necessary nor a sufficient condition for the phonemic identity of sounds. It is not a necessary condition simply because sounds may be in free variation and still realize the same phoneme, as in the example cited above. Some linguists have simply used the term "complementary distribution" loosely to include free variation, when they might better have resorted to the more precise term "noncontrastive distribution." Nor is complementary distribution a sufficient condition for phonemic identity, because a given sound may be in complementary distribution with several sounds, not all of which are in complementary distribution with each other. English [g̑], for example, is in complementary distribution not only with [g] as cited above but also with the [kʰ] which occurs in *cool,* yet [kʰ] and [g] clearly contrast in *cool* and *ghoul.* To determine the correct analysis in such situations, we must resort to other principles, in this case degree of phonetic similarity.

These examples and others which have been cited by critics do not show that complementary distribution is a useless principle, but merely that it cannot stand alone without further supporting principles. Phonemicists who have used it in actual practice, of course, have always related it to such supporting principles. It has also been understood for a long time that free variation amounts to the same thing as complementary distribution for its most essential purpose: both are kinds of noncontrastive distribution. It has further been recognized that considerations of phonetic similarity and pattern congruity must be used together with the principle. Moreover, the complementary distribution of phones must be definable in terms of the environments of their phonemic realizates. If this should not be the case, the analysis would not allow the prediction of the phonetic representation, or set of freely variant representations, from the phonemic transcription.

This much has been fairly well understood by the practitioners of phonemic analysis for a long time. A further principle, which was not characteristic of much of the earlier phonemic practice, was enunciated in later years and eventually came to be one of the cornerstones of phonemic analysis, particularly in the United States. This is the principle of **distinctiveness,** which requires that the phonemic transcription represent all those phonic differences capable of distinguishing utterances and introduce no differences which lack that capability. A major consequence of this principle is a requirement that one should be able to predict the phonemic transcription of an utterance from the phonetic, and vice versa, given the completed analysis. This will be the case if there is no neutralization between the phonemic and phonetic levels resulting in the same sound representing different phonemes in the same environment. This requirement has become known as **biuniqueness,** and it is associated with the idea that the phonemic level should represent distinctive differences and only these. The connection between distinctiveness and biuniqueness is a straightforward one. In order for a difference to be distinctive, it must be audible. If two putative phonemes neutralize to a single sound in the same environment, there will be no audible, and therefore no distinctive, difference between them. If such spurious distinctions are eliminated from the phonemic representation, it will guarantee the predictability of this transcription from the corresponding phonetic transcription. The other side of the biuniqueness requirement—the predictability of the phonetic transcription from the phonemic—has already been enunciated as a property of all phonological transcriptions; it has never been called into question.

After becoming a well-established requirement for any phonemic analysis during the 1940's and 1950's, biuniqueness has more recently been the subject of considerable controversy. We have not yet viewed enough of the total picture to afford full discussion of the controversy at this point. As a preliminary to later discussion, however, let us distinguish biuniqueness in the sense we are using it here from some subsidiary notions with which it has sometimes been confused. We will see that these notions have been used by only some practitioners of phonemic analysis and are in fact unrelated to the basic principle of distinctiveness, from which biuniqueness derives.

The first of these subsidiary notions concerns the treatment of **phonemic overlap.** This phenomenon is definable as the situation in which a single sound serves as the realization sometimes of one, sometimes of another phoneme. It is a form of neutralization. In one possible situation, the allowance of overlap would clearly lead to a violation of biuniqueness, and consequently of distinctiveness as well. This will be true if overlap is posited in the same environment, resulting in the unpredictability of the phonemic form from the phonetic for any utterance containing such a neutralization.

Following Bloch (1941), however, another type of phonemic overlap came to be allowed in situations where recourse to it would result in simpler solutions. This was overlap always involving different environments. In other words, the same sound could be assigned now to one, now to another phoneme, provided that environmental differences would permit one to know which phoneme one was dealing with in a given case.

A particularly striking example of this kind of situation comes from Danish (Jakobson, Fant, and Halle 1952). In this language, two apical obstruents occur in initial position: [t] and [d]; and another two occur in final position (in monosyllables): [d] and [đ]. It has been argued that the optimal phonemic analysis of these will group initial [t] with final [d] into /t/, and initial [d] with final [đ] into /d/. This would mean that [d] would be a realization of /t/ in final position, but of /d/ in initial position. No violation of biuniqueness results, since the phonemic identification of the sound may be deduced from its environment.

If biuniqueness were to be defined in terms of the assignment of individual sounds to phonemes without recourse to their environment, such limited phonemic overlap would, of course, be ruled out. But such a strict requirement is not necessary in order for distinctiveness to be maintained. Furthermore, since phonemic environment must be considered in relating phonemes to their ultimate realizations, there is no reason to prohibit analogous consideration of phonetic environment in relating sounds to their realizates.

A greater number of linguists, however, have extended the biuniqueness requirement in an unmotivated way. They have required that once the evidence for the distinctiveness of two sounds is established on the basis of their distribution in one set of environments, the same two sounds cannot be viewed as alternate realizations of a single phonemic entity in some other set of environments in the same language, even if they are predictable as a result of noncontrastive distribution in this latter set. This principle was adopted by many Neo-Bloomfieldians and has often been summarized by the slogan "once a phoneme, always a phoneme." Since it prohibits an establishable contrast from being viewed as suspended in certain environments, it may be termed the principle of **nonsuspendability.**

On this point, Neo-Bloomfieldian practice differed significantly from that of most European linguists, particularly the phonologists of the Prague School. The Prague scholars considered that certain pairs of phonetically related phonemes could, in various languages, be subject to "neutralization"—the name which they gave to the suspension of an establishable contrast. (This term is not unrelated to that used for a type of discrepancy in stratificational linguistics, but it is less general.) In a widespread version of this view, the sound occurring in the position of suspension ("neutralization") was said to realize the "archiphoneme," an entity incorporating the common phonetic properties of both suspended phonemes, that is, all those properties which had not been suspended. To take a concrete example, Russian [t] and [d] contrast in such pairs as [tám] 'there' and [dám] 'I shall give,' or in medial position in [atóm] 'atom' and [adóm] 'against the house,' which establishes them as separate phonemes differentiated by the presence or absence of voicing. In final position, however, only voiceless [t] occurs in Russian, as in [gót] 'year' or [pót] 'sweat.' In the Prague view, the voicing distinguishing these phonemes (and other voiceless-voiced pairs) is suspended in final position, and the archiphoneme /T/, incorporating apicality and closure but with no indication of voicing, is realized in this position. According to the Neo-Bloomfieldian view, on the other hand, the sound in final position would be identified as a realization of /t/ on the basis of its voicelessness, and the lack of a contrasting /d/ in this position would be treated in terms of the defective distribution of the latter phoneme.

A still more pointed contrast in the results of these two approaches may be seen if we consider some further facts about Russian [t] and [d]: in the position before a voiced obstruent, such as [b] or [z], we do not get any contrast between [t] and [d], any more than in final position, but here [d] rather than [t] occurs, as in [adbór] 'selection' and [ódzif] 'reference.' To the Praguian using the archiphonemic principle, the [d] in these examples is a realization of the archiphoneme /T/, as is the [t] of [gót] or [pót]. The situation is the same with regard to contrast—there is none—and only the phonetic realization is different, this being predictable due to the difference of position. The Neo-Bloomfieldian, on the other hand, would assign all [d]'s to the /d/ phoneme and again cite a defective distribution, this one involving /t/, to account for the lack of a voicing contrast in this position.

Some have objected to the archiphonemic principle because it seems to have the effect of increasing the number of units in the inventory, since it adds a number of archiphonemes to the full phonemic inventory. If the question is viewed, however, in terms of the number of distinct properties needed to specify an utterance, with each phoneme and archiphoneme representing a particular set of these properties, we can get away with representing fewer properties with archiphonemes, since each of them corresponds to fewer specifications than the corresponding full phonemes. From this point of view, it seems desirable to specify /T/ instead of /t/ or /d/ whenever possible, for in doing so we leave the presence or absence of phonetic voicing to be predicted according to the environment.

Furthermore, the recognition of suspendability (neutralization in Praguian terminology) can be seen as a logical extension of the distinctiveness principle. As set forth so far, this principle requires us to represent all distinctions which are capable of signalling value in the language, allowing all other phonetic distinctions to be predicted. If we consider the segmental phones to be the ultimate items to which this principle is to be applied, we arrive at a view like that of the Neo-Bloomfieldians. On the other hand, if we extend this principle to the components of which sounds are composed, we are forced to abandon nonsuspendability as a principle and to recognize that in actual languages some properties of sounds are predictable in some environments but not in others.

Such a step represents only a slight extension of what is universal practice in the treatment of components of phonetically distinct segments. That is, no linguist has seriously proposed the adoption of a principle "once a phonemic component, always a phonemic component," requiring each general phonemic distinction which is ever distinctive for any set of phonemes to be given phonemic status in other segments where it does not turn out to be distinctive. The fact that the voiced-voiceless contrast is relevant for the stops of a language, for instance, does not necessarily imply that this will be true for the spirants as well. In Old English, we would be forced to recognize a voicing distinction for stops: note the contrasts *pinne* 'flask' / *binne* 'bin,' *cræft* 'skill' / *græft* 'graven,' *tūn* 'enclosure' / *dūn* 'hill.' For the spirants, however, we find voiced sounds in complementary distribution with their voiceless equivalents: voiced in positions between vowels or vowels and voiced consonants, and voiceless elsewhere. No competent phonemicist would recognize two distinct spirant phonemes /f/ and /v/ in an analysis of Old English [fæder] 'father' and [over] 'over' in view of this distribution. And there is no *a priori* requirement that would force a phonetic distinction to be regarded as phonemic in one pair of segments where it occurs just because it is phonemic in others.

All that the allowance of suspendability does, looked at in terms of components, is to extend this generally recognized principle from intrasegmental cases to intersegmental ones. That is, one has not traditionally recognized a distinction as phonemic if it is predictable on the basis of other phonemic components in the same segment. All that suspendability says is that distinctions which are predictable on the basis of phonemic components in neighboring segments will be treated in the same way.

We thus see that phonological contrast has been given somewhat different treatments in regard to the details discussed. All the practice of those whom we can call "classical phonemicists," however, revolves around a search to represent in terms of a level called the phonemic those phonic properties of a language which may serve within its system to distinguish utterances of different intended content.

## 6.2 *Morphophonemic Alternation*

One advantage which could be claimed for phonemic analysis over a purely phonetic treatment is that it reduces the amount of variation exhibited by different realizations of the same morpheme. Phonemicists found, that is, that many of the phonetic alternations which a prephonemic treatment of the morphology would have to mention could be treated as a matter of the allophones of different phonemes. In Spanish, for example, there is a phonetic difference between the vowel of the singular form [més] 'month' and that of its plural form [mésɛs] 'months.' Phonemically, however, we find that [ɛ] and [e] are allophones of a single phoneme /e/, so our morphology can deal with the phonemic forms /més/ and /méses/, leaving the general alternation between [ɛ] and [e] to an allophonic statement.

In the early days of phonemics, the limitations of this principle were not fully recognized, and it was applied to many situations where it was not justified in view of the distinctiveness principle. The Russian forms [górət] 'city,' [górədə] 'city's,' and [gəradá] 'cities' show, apart from differences of stress and suffixation, several alternations in the shape of the stem, only one of which is strictly subphonemic. The alternation in the second syllable, between [ə] and [a], turns out to be subphonemic, both of these sounds being allophones of /a/. But that in the first syllable, between [o] and [ə], is phonemically still an alternation between /o/ and /a/, and the consonantal alternation of [t] with [d] is also between separate phonemes. Some early phonemicists nevertheless tried to include one or the other of these alternations among the subphonemic ones. George Trager, for example, published a phonemic analysis of Russian (1934a) according to which this series of forms would be transcribed /górad/, /górada/, /garadá/. In other words, [t] and [d] were considered allophones of a single phoneme /d/ in such cases. Once the distinctiveness principle became established, however, this analysis was considered unacceptable, by Trager himself as well as others: it led to a form of phonemic overlap which violated the principle. It required the phonetic form [rót], for example, to be transcribed in two alternate ways: /rót/ if it were the nominative-accusative singular of the word for 'mouth,' and /ród/ if it were the same form of the word for 'gender, kind, species,' which has a [d] in other forms, such as the genitive [ródə]. This is, of course, overlap in the same position.

The same forms were analyzed in Bloomfield's *Language* (1933) in a different way, which led to another violation of the distinctiveness principle. His transcriptions would be /górot/, /góroda/, /gorodá/. It was the vocalic rather than the consonantal alternation which was treated as subphonemic. The analysis of the second vowel as /o/ was justified by comparison with other forms, such as [agarót] 'vegetable garden,' containing the same root with the stress on the second syllable. This treatment, however, would require us to distinguish such forms as /ródom/ and /ródam/, the instrumental singular and dative plural, respectively, of the word for 'gender, kind, species,' despite the fact that each has the same pronunciation, [ródəm]. This distinction would be made on the basis of the forms taken by the corresponding endings when they are stressed, as in the forms of 'table': [stalóm] and [stalám]. The fact that the supposed phonemic rendering of such forms is not automatically determinable from their phonetic shape means that the distinctiveness principle has been violated.

Bloch's 1941 article enunciated the distinctiveness principle fully enough to rule out these interpretations, but these examples are sufficient to show the somewhat confused state of phonemics in the United States prior to that time. The distinction which Trager and Bloomfield had not recognized when they proposed their analyses was that between subphonemic and morphophonemic alternation, as they have come to be termed. When such a distinction is recognized, it turns out that their transcriptions were neither phonemic nor morphophonemic. A properly morphophonemic transcription would incorporate both Trager's and Bloomfield's generalizations, making the form of this root a constant, **gorod**. The phonemic transcriptions of the forms cited would be /górat/, /górada/, and /garadá/. The difference between these types of transcription is tied to the distinctiveness of the phonemic level. An alternation is subphonemic if it can be so considered in the language without violating the distinctiveness principle. Other alternations, no matter how regular they may be, are alternations between the phonemes serving to realize the same morphophoneme. These include the alternations /o/ ∼ /a/ and /t/ ∼ /d/ in our Russian data.

There has been a wide divergence among linguists as to the treatment of such alternations, even among those who have kept them clearly apart from the subphonemic alternations. Perhaps the most simple-minded way of treating them is the classical allomorph approach. This approach insists that the only means of dealing with all alternations in the phonemic realizations of morphemes is by listing each phonemically distinct form as a separate allomorph. We have already considered this approach (Chapter 2) and found that while it is appropriate for suppletive alternations, it is not suitable for alternations of the type we have been examining, because it requires long series of allomorphs to be listed, for one morpheme after another, when a single general statement dealing with a morphophonemic alternation would do just as well, as in the case of our Russian alternations /o/ ∼ /a/ (conditioned by stress) and /d/ ∼ /t/ (conditioned by position).

A minimum requirement for the treatment of morphophonemic alternations, therefore, is that they be dealt with in terms of individual segments rather than whole morpheme-sized entities. But even within these confines, there has been a wide variance in the practice of linguists. One point of difference involves the basic way in which the alternation is characterized. One means is by a simple statement of alternation. For the above examples, for instance, we could say that /o/ alternates with /a/, the former occurring under stress, and the latter when unstressed. We could further say that /d/ alternates with /t/, the latter occurring finally, the other elsewhere. A second means of handling such alternations, which has received widespread acceptance, is to characterize each one by means of a process statement. This would involve setting up a basic shape of the morpheme, such as /gorod/. The discrepancies between this form and the actual realized phonemic forms would then be characterized by such statements as "/o/ becomes /a/ when unstressed" and "/d/ becomes /t/ when final."

The third means of statement, that which stratificationalists find most congenial, involves the recognition of a higher-level entity related to both the alternants in that it is realized by one or the other according to environment. For this example there would be a morphophoneme **o**, distinct from the phoneme /o/, which is realized phonemically as /o/ when stressed and as /a/ when not stressed. Similarly, there would be a morphophoneme **d**, distinct from the phoneme /d/, with the realization /t/ when final and /d/ elsewhere. This approach differs from the process format in its recognition that the morphophonemes are distinct from the phonemes in being on a different level from them. This distinction exists for segments showing no alternation as well as for those which do. The morphophoneme **r**, for example, shows no alternate realizations in our data, and perhaps none for the language as a whole. It is always realized as /r/. Nevertheless, the realizational approach recognizes a distinction between the phoneme /r/ and the corresponding morphophoneme, though the relationship between them is a simple one. In stratificational theory, of course, these stratal differences will be treated in terms of relationships rather than the units and relationships we are using in this preliminary statement. By contrast, a consistent process approach does not recognize different levels but only a set of items and a set of processes changing one item into another, deleting items, rearranging them, and so on, in appropriate environments.

In a sense, these three approaches to morphophonemic alternation conform to the more general types of linguistic approach which we earlier labelled descriptive, generative, and cognitive. The first approach *describes* the alternation, the second characterizes it by *rules*, while the third seeks to deal with it as a *relationship* which can ultimately take its place as a part of a larger system of relationships.

The process and realizational approaches share the fact that they posit what we may call "basic shapes" of morphemes, but there is some disagreement on the status of these shapes. There are considerable differences, particularly within the process view, as to the permissible degree of abstractness which these basic shapes may have from the actual data (phonemically or phonetically transcribed). The most stringent version would insist that basic shapes are chosen from among the actual phonemic forms of the morphemes which occur, taking the simplicity and generality of the total system into account. If we want a basic shape for our Russian stem for 'city,' without considering the related /agarót/ 'vegetable garden,' this version would lead us to choose /gorad/, which occurs in the genitive singular /górada/ as well as in some other forms not cited. We would be prohibited by this requirement, however, from relating this morpheme to the root of /agarót/ by setting up a single basic shape */gorod/ for the two. It is clear that this could not occur as an actual form, since phonemic /o/ can occur only under stress and there is only one stressed syllable in a word. Similar problems arise for other Russian forms, even a single stem. The word for 'lake,' for instance, has the nominative-accusative singular /óz,ira/ and the nominative-accusative plural /az,óra/.

To account for these actual forms, we need to be able to posit a basic shape *\*/oz,or/*, but this stringent requirement would prohibit us from using such a shape, because it never occurs.

In the face of this counterevidence, we may go on to a somewhat less stringent restriction on basic shapes. We could adopt a version which says that for each position where an alternation occurs, one attributes to the basic shape that alternate which allows the most general predictability of the actual shapes. This approach provides considerably greater leeway and would in fact allow the desirable basic shapes **gorod** and **oz,or** to be posited. But we are again faced with problems when we encounter further examples of alternation, such as those seen in English *leaf* versus *leaves* and *knife* versus *knives*. The alternation is between /f/ and /v/, yet it will not do to posit basic shapes ending in either of these, since there are other words which have a constant /f/ (*fife/fifes*) or a constant /v/ (*hive/hives*) and their basic shapes would have to end in the same consonants.

This kind of evidence seemingly forces us to allow the positing of elements in the basic shape which are not in any of the actual shapes. In some cases, these may nevertheless correspond to actual phonemes in the language, but in this case and many others, they will have to be special elements such as **F**, subsuming the alternation of /f/ and /v/, in contrast to constant **f** and **v**, which always have the same realization. It is, of course, desirable to limit the positing of such entities, often called "special morphophonemes," as much as possible. But in instances such as this one, they seem necessary if a fairly common alternation is to be treated with the degree of generality appropriate to it.

Sometimes, such abstract distinctions as that among **F**, **f**, and **v** are necessary to account for alternations involving the segment so represented. In other cases, they are needed to account for the behavior of adjacent segments. An example of the latter is provided by some further English forms. Compare the noun forms *knife* and *knives* with the related verb forms *knife* and *knifes*, as in *He always knifes his victims in the back*. The regular plural morpheme and the third-person singular ending have the same variety of forms with the same basic distribution: /əz/ after sibilants and affricates, /s/ after other voiceless consonants, and /z/ elsewhere. But the realization of **F** is shown by the above examples to be different before one of these endings than before the other (assuming, of course, a single basic shape for all these stems). Before the plural it is /v/, before the verbal ending, /f/. It will also be /f/ before the similar genitive ending, as we may see by comparing *wife's* and *wives*. This is evidence that these two endings must be different on the level of basic shapes, despite the identity of their realizations. We will thus posit a difference between **Z**, representing the plural, and **z**, for the verbal ending as well as the genitive. Looking at the picture in one way, we could say that these two entities are realized differently after **F**, **Z** being realized as /z/, **z** as /s/. These facts are actually *dependent* upon the realization of **F**, for they simply go along with its voicing characteristics. So we can say that the difference between **Z** and **z** is crucial for the realization of voicing in the case of a morphophonemic cluster beginning with **F**, since **FZ** is realized as /vz/ (as in *knives*) and **Fz** is realized as /fs/ (as in *wife's* or *knifes*).

On the basis of this and a host of similar evidence from a wide variety of languages, we arrive at the notion that the morphophonemic representation need not be tied to either the realized forms or the phonemic inventory. It will rather be that representation which fits best into the overall system to account for the alternations present. The economy of this system will be the overriding factor. We will set up as many morphophonemes and alternations as necessary to account for the facts, and no more. We will, of course, want to exclude such preposterous morphophonemic treatments as that suggested in Chapter 2 for the alternation of /gow/ and /wen/ (*go* and *went*) in the form **gʷœw̃**, a special series of morphophonemes to account for just this pair of forms. We need no special principles to exclude this analysis: it would surely be excluded by the simplicity principle once the analysis is translated into a network of relationships of the sort already considered on other strata.

### 6.3  *Morphonic Analysis and Description*

In stratificational theory, the equivalents of what we have been calling morphophonemes, following the more traditional terminology, are the morphons, the elementary units of the morphemic stratum. While morphons are in the morphemic stratal system, the account of their realizations belongs to the phonology. And since the determination of just what morphons exist in a linguistic system is intimately connected with the account of their realization, even this aspect is better handled together with the phonology, though the morphemic signs will figure in the determination as well.

In the preliminary stages of our account, we will deal with the relation of morphons to classical phonemes, expressed in realization formulas. After more aspects of the phonology have been considered, it will be shown how the relationships indirectly described by this means can be integrated into the total system expressed by a linguistic network.

Although the problem may surely be approached in other ways, perhaps the most convenient starting point for a discussion of morphonic analysis is a consideration of morphological data in classical phonemic transcription. We will thus begin by examining the Hungarian forms presented in Table 6.1.

Our task in examining this data is to come up with a hypothesis which will allow us to give a single morphonic form for each morpheme (or at least each morphemic sign). In connection with this, it will also be necessary to provide realization formulas for each morphon, assuming that the combinations of morphemes possible will be accounted for by the morphotactics.

### Table 6.1 Some Hungarian Data

| | Singular | Plural | my_____ | Gloss |
|---|---|---|---|---|
| 1. | padlo: | padlo:k | padlo:m | 'floor' |
| 2. | erdö: | erdö:k | erdö:m | 'forest' |
| 3. | fe:šü: | fe:šü:k | fe:šü:m | 'comb' |
| 4. | falu | faluk | falum | 'village' |
| 5. | fiu: | fiu:k | fiu:m | 'boy' |
| 6. | tok | tokok | tokom | 'sheath' |
| 7. | hu:g | hu:gok | hu:gom | 'younger sister' |
| 8. | bara:t | bara:tok | bara:tom | 'friend' |
| 9. | tök | tökök | tököm | 'squash' |
| 10. | fürt | fürtök | fürtöm | 'bunch' |
| 11. | köd | ködök | ködöm | 'fog' |
| 12. | hit | hitek | hitem | 'belief' |
| 13. | ke:p | ke:pek | ke:pem | 'picture' |
| 14. | kert | kertek | kertem | 'garden' |
| 15. | ing | ingek | ingem | 'shirt' |

The first five forms present a quite straightforward situation. The stem, ending in a vowel, takes the plural suffix /k/ and the first-person singular possessive suffix /m/. The rest of the examples show stems ending in consonants, like the simple forms of the first column, while the suffixed forms of these appear to have a kind of buffer vowel as the first element of the suffix. This vowel exhibits a form of vowel harmony with the vowel(s) of the stem. The harmony in this data operates as follows: the vowel is /ö/ if the last vowel of the stem is /ö/ or /ü/; /o/ if the vowel is /o/, /a/, or /u/; and /e/ if it is /i/ or /e/. It thus appears that the suffixes have the following alternate forms:

Plural:    -k, -ok, -ök, -ek

my_____:  -m, -om, -öm, -em

Since the variations seem to appear under identical conditions for each suffix, we can set up the morphonic forms of the suffixes beginning with a special morphon $^{MN}/V_x/$: $^{MN}/V_x k/$, $^{MN}/V_x m/$. The realizations of $^{MN}/V_x/$ may be accounted for by the following formula:

$$V_x \parallel V[:]\_\_ / \varnothing$$

$$, \parallel (ö,ü) [C] C\_\_ / ö$$

$$, \parallel (e, i) [C] C\_\_ / e$$

$$+ \parallel \text{---} / o$$

In this formula, V stands for any vowel and C for any consonant, and the brackets enclose optional parts of the environment. This accounts for all discrepancies, assuming that the stems will be assigned morphonic forms symbolized in the same way as the phonemic transcriptions of the first column, the symbols being reinterpreted as morphonic. A complete adherence to the realizational format would necessitate formulas for the morphons displaying no realizational discrepancies, of the form:

$$p \parallel --- / p$$

$$a \parallel --- / a, \text{ and so on}$$

We can avoid this, however, by assuming the convention that if the same symbols are used for corresponding morphons and phonemes (with appropriate differences of bracketing), the absence of a formula with a different effect means that a morphon will be realized by the correspondingly labelled phoneme. The ultimate form of a stratificational grammar, of course, will simply have lines connecting points on the different strata, with no actually significant symbols. Adopting this convention for our formulaic representation, we need no more formulas in our account of this data.

Now let us proceed to examine some more Hungarian data of a related sort to see how well the hypothesis based on the first set will hold up. This data is presented in Table 6.2.

A brief comparison of this data with the first set shows a number of things for which our original hypothesis provides no account. Among these are the vowel-length alternations in 18–26 and a different type of length alternation shown in the final syllable of 32–35. We note that all the forms in the 32–35 series have a short /a/ or /e/ in the simple form and a lengthening in the corresponding suffixed forms. All the forms in the first set of data whose simple forms ended in vowels involved rounded vowels such as /o, ö, u, ü/, and these were consistently long or short in all three forms. One hypothesis we could advance to account for this series is that $^{MN}/V_x/$ is realized as /:/ (the phoneme of length) after /$^{MN}$/e/ or $^{MN}$/a/. Another alternative is to recognize the forms ending in long vowels as the morphonic ones: $^{MN}$/fečke:, körte:, silva:, ta:bla:/. Then we would specify that : $\parallel$ __# / ∅ (where # symbolizes the end of a grammatical word). At present, it does not seem clear which of these alternatives would be preferable.

We will therefore proceed to the treatment of the other alternations. One is the other length alternation (18–26), but let us first consider the buffer vowels of the suffixed forms in 16–31. These vowels exhibit significant differences from what we were led to expect on the basis of the data previously considered. In the first place, we get a different vowel, /a/, in a number of forms (23–31). Most of these have stem vowels with which we would expect

### Table 6.2 Additional Hungarian Data

| | Singular | Plural | my_____ | Gloss |
|---|---|---|---|---|
| 16. | könv | könvek | könvem | 'book' |
| 17. | šült | šültek | šültem | 'roast' |
| 18. | fü:z | füzek | füzem | 'willow' |
| 19. | be:l | belek | belem | 'gut' |
| 20. | vi:z | vizek | vizem | 'water' |
| 21. | kere:k | kerekek | kerekem | 'wheel' |
| 22. | si:n | sinek | sinem | 'color' |
| 23. | ña:r | ñarak | ñaram | 'summer' |
| 24. | u:t | utak | utam | 'road' |
| 25. | hi:d | hidak | hidam | 'bridge' |
| 26. | dere:k | derekak | derekam | 'waist' |
| 27. | ha:z | ha:zak | ha:zam | 'house' |
| 28. | di:j | di:jak | di:jam | 'prize' |
| 29. | o:l | o:lak | o:lam | 'stable' |
| 30. | ta:r | ta:rak | ta:ram | 'warehouse' |
| 31. | na:d | na:dak | na:dam | 'reed' |
| 32. | fečke | fečke:k | fečke:m | 'swallow' |
| 33. | körte | körte:k | körte:m | 'pear' |
| 34. | silva | silva:k | silva:m | 'plum' |
| 35. | ta:bla | ta:bla:k | ta:bla:m | 'blackboard' |

/o/ by our previous principles, but there are also some examples of the stem vowel /e/ or /i/ (25, 26, 28), with which we would expect the buffer vowel /e/. We get /e/, furthermore, not only in places where we would have expected it (19–22) but also in 16–18, where we would expect /ö/. Such data might cause a traditional grammarian to throw up his hands and begin to compile lists of "exceptions." We must seek, however, to discover the system behind it.

One hypothesis which might be offered to deal with this problem is that we are faced with a long series of morphonically different vowels which have different effects on the harmonic agreement of $^{MN}/V_x/$. Thus we would recognize $^{MN}/ö_1/$ requiring /ö/ in 9 and 11, and $^{MN}/ö_2/$ requiring /e/ in 16; $^{MN}/ü_1/$ requiring /ö/ in 10, and $^{MN}/ü_2/$ requiring /e/ in 17 and 18; and similarly differing types of o (6 versus 29), u (7 versus 24), a (8 versus 23, 30, 31), i (12, 15, 22 versus 25, 28), and e (13, 14, 21 versus 26). This step, while accounting for the data, would require a considerable multiplication of the inventory of vowel morphons. Therefore another adequate hypothesis might prove more attractive.

One available alternative is this: all the morphonic forms of these stems end in a vocalic nucleus (vowel or vowel plus :). Forms 1–5 are unchanged from our original hypothesis, 6–15 end in $^{MN}$/œ/, 16–31 in $^{MN}$/æ/, and 32–35 in $^{MN}$/:/. The suffixes will then be simply $^{MN}$/k/ and $^{MN}$/m/, invariable for this data. The alternations present will be accounted for by the following realization formulas:

œ ‖ __# / ∅                    æ ‖ __# / ∅

+ ‖ (ö,ü) [C] C__ / ö          + ‖ (ö,ü,i,e) [C] C__ / e

, ‖ (e,i) [C] C__ / e          + ‖ --- / a

+ ‖ --- / o

The length alternations may then be taken care of by the following formulas:

: ‖ (a,e) __# / ∅              ∅ ‖ V__Cæ# / :

+ ‖ --- / :

The formula applying to $^{MN}$/:/ accounts adequately for the zero realization of morphonic length in final position after $^{MN}$/a e/, as in forms 32–35. The second formula defines an automatic length on just those stems which end morphonically in $^{MN}$/æ/, when not followed by a suffix. Since it applies only when a single consonant intervenes between the vowels concerned, it will not affect forms whose last vowel is morphonically long, such as 27–31, or those which end in a consonant cluster, such as 16 and 17.

The only phenomenon still unaccounted for is the distinction between the type of *i* or *e* determining front harmony for $^{MN}$/æ/ (19–22) and the type determining back harmony (25, 26, 28). This can be handled if we make a distinction between the morphons $^{MN}$/i/ and $^{MN}$/e/ (in the former stems) and $^{MN}$/ɪ/ and $^{MN}$/E/ (in the latter). The latter set will not satisfy the environmental specification in the subformula providing for the realization /e/ for $^{MN}$/æ/, leaving the realization as /a/ according to the following subformula. We need only add formulas for the realization of these two newly recognized morphons:

ɪ ‖ --- / i                    E ‖ --- / e

Thus we see that a small part of the rejected hypothesis is still needed, but its scope is greatly reduced by the zero realization of final short vowels which has been provided for. Also, without the final $^{MN}$/œ/-$^{MN}$/æ/ distinction, we could not have provided such a ready explanation of the length alternations of 18–26. As it is, this step even resolves an ambiguity concerning forms 19–22. Their last vowel would be either $^{MN}$/œ/ or $^{MN}$/æ/ by its own realization, but the fact that the stems concerned exhibit length alternations makes it desirable to consider them cases of $^{MN}$/æ/, there being no counterexamples with clear $^{MN}$/œ/ and length alternation. Furthermore, the distinction of $^{MN}$/i/ and $^{MN}$/ɪ/

as well as <sup>MN</sup>/e/ and <sup>MN</sup>/ɛ/ provides us with an example of morphons distinguished solely on the basis of their conditioning influence on other morphons, which is even clearer than the English example of <sup>MN</sup>/F/ presented in Section 6.2.

Note that all of these formulas are stated with environments in terms of morphons, so that all material to the left of the slash is morphonic, while that to the right is classical phonemic. So for the formula showing zero realized as /:/ we do not need to concern ourselves that <sup>MN</sup>/æ/ will itself be realized as zero in the same forms, as this will be dealt with in an independent formula. And, of course, it should be remembered that the formulas do not define operations on combinations of symbols; rather they define the phonemes which will realize each morphon on the next level. These formulas are applied in the order in which the realizates (morphons) occur. One can think of writing down the morphonic transcription on one line and determining, step by step, the corresponding phonemic transcription on the line below, not replacing one symbol with another but merely constructing an additional transcription following the formulas. If none of the formulas shown applies to the given case, we follow the convention mentioned, writing on the phonemic line the same symbol as is used for the morphon realized, understanding it as a phonemic rather than a morphonic symbol.

Using similar procedures, we can provide a preliminary account of a wide variety of morphophonemic alternations. To carry such an account to the cognitive level, the networks of relationships characteristic of stratificational linguistics, we need to consider the form of the phonotactics as well as the realizational relationships.

(The exercises of Set 6A at the end of this chapter may be done at this point.)

## 6.4 *Phonological Components*

We have spoken up to now only of the relation of morphons to phonemes, yet we know from our previous discussion (Chapter 2) that phonemes are not simple but have components. Different phonemes, that is, have patterned relations to each other based on properties of their articulation and audition. These patterned relations should be taken into account in a maximally general treatment of the realization of these phonemes.

Stratificational theory is by no means the only view of linguistic structure to recognize the relevance of components. It could be said, in fact, that the consensus of modern linguists recognizes the existence of components in one form or another. There is wide variation, however, in ideas about the place of these components in linguistic structure and the interpretation of particular phenomena. Some of these variations will now be taken up in some detail.

In the past, some linguists have questioned the linguistic relevance of components. Some Neo-Bloomfieldians, for instance, asserted that components were only phonetic properties and were therefore relevant only to phonetics and not to phonemics. Phonemes, they insisted, following a notion of Bloomfield himself, were to be distinguished purely on their distributional properties. Another position granted the place of components in the identification of phonemes but insisted that all matters relating to the distribution and alternation of phonemes had to be handled purely in terms of phonemic segments, and components were to be brought in only with reference to the realization of these segments. In many cases, no explicit recognition was given to components at all, but implicit recognition was given to them by the use of phonetic charts in summarizing the articulatory properties of the various phonemes in the system. The labels for the rows and columns of these charts, that is, corresponded to components. As an example, Table 6.3 charts a partial phonemic inventory from a hypothetical but typical language. Similar charts have accompanied many published phonemic analyses, and the various articulatory labels have commonly passed without comment.

### Table 6.3   Chart of a Consonant System

|          | Labial | Apical | Dorsal |           |
|----------|:------:|:------:|:------:|-----------|
| Stop     | p      | t      | k      | Voiceless |
|          | b      | d      | g      | Voiced    |
| Spirant  | f      | s      | x      | Voiceless |
|          | v      | z      | ɣ      | Voiced    |
| Nasal    | m      | n      | ŋ      |           |

Other linguists, however, have sought to provide a greater degree of systematization in the use of components and have therefore attempted to find an explicit place for them in the general theory of language. Some of those attempting to do this have focussed their prime attention on the dimensions of contrast among phonemes—for example, the articulator axis, the manner axis, and the voicing axis of Table 6.3. Others have emphasized the particular properties which serve as the poles of contrast, such as labiality, apicality, dorsality, and voicing. In view of these different emphases, we may divide attempts to give explicit recognition to phonological components into **feature theories** (those based on contrastive dimensions) and **component theories** (those based on individual properties).

The term "feature" is that used by some of the most prominent advocates of what we call feature theories. By a **feature**, we mean one of the dimensions of contrast; one of the significant points along this dimension will be termed a **feature value**. A direct feature interpretation of Table 6.3 would extract three features: articulator (A), manner (M), and voicing (V). The values of each of these could then be designated by numbers: A1 for labial, A2 for apical, A3 for dorsal, M1 for stop, M2 for spirant, M3 for nasal, V1 for voiceless, and V2 for voiced. This rather direct articulatory analysis leaves us with some features with two values, and others with more than two. Feature theories which allow a feature to have two or more values, up to as many as needed to account for the facts, may be termed **multinary feature theories.**

By contrast, the most prominent advocates of feature theories today insist that all apparent multinary features must be reduced to a binary system. Thus they favor a **binary feature theory,** in which each feature has two and only two values, symbolized conventionally as + or −. According to the well-known system of binary features established by Roman Jakobson, for example, the feature designated as A above would be divided into two, one opposing peripheral (labial and dorsal) to central and a second opposing front to back. The three-way M feature could similarly be broken down into continuant (spirant or nasal) versus noncontinuant and nasal versus nonnasal. Thus, leaving the voicing feature essentially unchanged, five two-valued features would be used by the advocates of a binary system in place of three multinary ones. This system would, of course, provide additional unused combinations of values, which might be usable in other languages with more contrasting phonemes.

Jakobson has attempted to set up a universal inventory of such binary features from which he sees all languages of the world selecting. His system has the further advantage that many of the same features are usable for both the vocalic and the consonantal system. If one adopts this binary system, a phonetic chart such as Table 6.3 can be replaced by a feature matrix such as that shown in Table 6.4. This array places the phoneme symbols across the top and the names of the features along the side. The value of each feature for each particular segment is shown at the intersection of the appropriate row and column. On the model of such a chart, we could prepare a larger representation covering all the phonemes of a language. Transcriptions of individual words, sentences, and texts can be prepared in a similar form.

Component theories focus on the individual properties taking part in a contrast rather than on the contrast as such (as do feature theories), though the latter is implicitly recognized. Component theories break each phonemic

### Table 6.4   A Jakobsonian Feature Matrix

|            | p | b | f | v | m | t | d | s | z | n | k | g | x | ɣ | ŋ |
|------------|---|---|---|---|---|---|---|---|---|---|---|---|---|---|---|
| Continuant | − | − | + | + | + | − | − | + | + | + | − | − | + | + | + |
| Nasal      | − | − | − | − | + | − | − | − | − | + | − | − | − | − | + |
| Grave      | + | + | + | + | + | − | − | − | − | − | + | + | + | + | + |
| Diffuse    | + | + | + | + | + | + | + | + | + | + | − | − | − | − | − |
| Voiced     | − | + | − | + | + | − | + | − | + | + | − | + | − | + | + |

NOTE: "Grave" is Jakobson's term for peripheral consonants, also applying to back vowels. "Diffuse" is his term for front (labial or apical) consonants, also applying to high vowels.

segment into various simultaneous components. A componential analysis of the material presented in Tables 6.3 and 6.4 is given in Table 6.5. A convenient label is chosen for each component; in this case, two-letter labels are used. The only one which does not have a mnemonic connection with those in Table 6.3 is /Cl/ (closed), which is used for the stops. For convenience of comparison, components in direct contrast have been placed in the same row of the table, corresponding to a single dimension of contrast. This is not absolutely necessary, however, since components are theoretically simultaneous within a segment and may be placed in any arbitrary order when they are written. The vertical arrangement is intended to suggest their simultaneity. It will also turn out that components which are mutually exclusive in the system or subsystem of one language may be capable of occurring in the same segment in another system or subsystem. In the vowel systems of many languages, for instance, the components /Lb/ (labial) and /Fr/ (frontal) are mutally exclusive. But in other languages, such as French, German, Turkish, or Finnish, some vowels are front (i, e), others are labial (u, o), and still others have both properties (ü, ö).

### Table 6.5   A Componential Analysis

| p | b | f | v | m | t | d | s | z | n | k | g | x | ɣ | ŋ |
|---|---|---|---|---|---|---|---|---|---|---|---|---|---|---|
| Lb | Lb | Lb | Lb | Lb | Ap | Ap | Ap | Ap | Ap | Do | Do | Do | Do | Do |
| Cl | Cl | Sp | Sp | Ns | Cl | Cl | Sp | Sp | Ns | Cl | Cl | Sp | Sp | Ns |
| Vl | Vd | Vl | Vd |   | Vl | Vd | Vl | Vd |   | Vl | Vd | Vl | Vd |   |

In Table 6.5, a component has been assumed for each contrast in a given dimension. Only where a contrast is not considered relevant for a given phoneme has no symbol been included, as for voicing with respect to nasals (though this is significant in a few languages). It is possible, however, to consider one contrasting property of a group to be unmarked, signalled by the absence of any component of the particular set. This is the phonological counterpart of the markedness property we have already considered in grammar. Instead of recognizing the two components /Vl/ and /Vd/, for example, we may mark voicing as /Vd/ and predict voicelessness for all other stops and spirants. We can follow a similar policy with articulators. In this case, the most likely candidate for the unmarked status is what we have been marking as /Do/. In many languages the so-called dorso-velar phonemes exhibit a considerable variability in their articulation, ranging all the way from fronto-palatal to glottal. Assuming that the language we are dealing with is typical in this way, we may regard /Do/ as the unmarked articulator. Applying the markedness concept we can replace the representation of Table 6.5 with that of Table 6.6, in which we use two fewer components and eleven fewer componential designations. This type of analysis, it must be emphasized, is not just a way to save symbols or relational specifications, though it does

### Table 6.6 Componential Analysis with Markedness

| p | b | f | v | m | t | d | s | z | n | k | g | x | ɣ | ŋ |
|---|---|---|---|---|---|---|---|---|---|---|---|---|---|---|
| Cl | Cl | Sp | Sp | Ns | Cl | Cl | Sp | Sp | Ns | Cl | Cl | Sp | Sp | Ns |
| Lb | Lb | Lb | Lb | Lb | Ap | Ap | Ap | Ap | Ap | | Vd | | Vd | |
| | Vd | | Vd | | | Vd | | Vd | | | | | | |

incontestably have this effect. More important is what it reflects about the particular language, and in some cases about language in general. Like the assignment of grammatical markedness, the assignment of markedness in phonology should ultimately be justifiable in terms of the simplicity and generality it imparts to the total system. Its assignment in a given language will demand a consideration of the sounds concerned in that language as well as in languages in general. Some aspects of markedness may apply universally; others seem to show variance from one language to another.

Though the dorsal position may be unmarked in many languages, it may not be desirable to regard it as such in languages which have a contrast between stops in the labial, dorsal, and labio-dorsal positions. Labio-dorsal stops are in some languages realized as labialized velars (as in a number of American Indian languages with /kʷ/) or as simultaneous labial and dorsal closure (as in the many African languages with /ᵏp/ and /ᵍb/). If dorsal were regarded as unmarked in such languages, there would be no way to distinguish labial from labio-dorsal. If labio-dorsal were regarded as a separate component to overcome this, its relationship to both labial and dorsal would be unexpressed. In such languages, therefore, we are forced to look elsewhere for an unmarked articulator.

In the case of manners of articulation, we have not posited one from among /Cl Sp Ns/ as unmarked for our hypothetical language. One reason is that the result would leave one of the dorsal phonemes with no components at all, and it is necessary for every phoneme to have at least one component. Suppose, however, that our language also has nonnasal resonants, such as /w/ and /l/. The dorsal position is commonly the one at which such a resonant is lacking, so if this manner were considered the unmarked one, such an assignment would make this absence a natural gap in the system.

Stratificational theory has generally favored a component theory with markedness, basically because of its great flexibility and its compatibility in terms of relationships expressed with the more general properties which it sees in the language. A component theory avoids the binary-multinary conflict among feature-theory advocates by positing a system that is essentially **singular**: a component is simply either present or absent in the makeup of a given phonemic segment. The flexibility of such a system will be exemplified by its application to some actual data below.

For purposes of componential analysis of this type, the following list of abbreviations (a revision of the list on page 57 of Lamb's *Outline*) provides a fairly flexible and useful inventory of possible components. The list may of course have to be augmented to deal with specific problems in particular languages.

| | | | |
|---|---|---|---|
| Lb | Labial | Vd | Voiced |
| Ap | Apical | Ts | Tense |
| Rz | Retracted (a component of English /r s z/) | As | Aspirated |
| | | Pz | Palatalized |
| Fr | Frontal | Vo | Vocalic |
| Do | Dorsal | Hi | High |
| Pd | Postdorsal | Mi | Mid |
| Ph | Pharyngeal | Lo | Low |
| Gl | Glottal | Cs | Close |
| Cl | Closed | Op | Open |
| Sp | Spirant | Lg | Long |
| Ns | Nasal | Ac | Accented (stressed) |
| Lt | Lateral | Tr | Treble (high tone) |
| Vb | Vibrant | Bs | Bass (low tone) |
| Vl | Voiceless | | |

To illustrate the applicability of this list, we will survey some tentative componential analyses of the phonemic systems of several languages. These analyses are tentative for several reasons. The most basic reason is that we have not considered their full integration into the system of the languages concerned, including the account of phonological distribution and alternation. Within the context provided so far, in fact, we would not even be prepared to do this, as we have not yet arrived at the full picture of the phonological section of a stratificational grammar. The analyses to be presented, therefore, are merely first approximations, which an analyst familiar with the language from a classical phonemic point of view might make as a working hypothesis prior to a detailed consideration of the systems involved.

We will first consider a componential interpretation of the well-known Trager-Smith phonemic inventory of English. This analysis, shown in Table 6.7, posits eleven components. It is presented in a form similar to the traditional phonetic chart, but some compromise in the groupings is made so that a single arrangement can accommodate both vowels and consonants. Each phonemic segment includes the components in the rows and columns in which it is located, with the relevance of a component to two or more rows or columns being indicated by the use of braces. Here the affricates /č ǰ/ are simply regarded as stops. The spirancy also present in their phonetic realization may be considered a determined element. The dorso-velar position is regarded as unmarked and is extended to include the glottal spirant /h/ as the unmarked spirant. The central vowels are considered unmarked, and the maximally unmarked vowel turns out to be /ə/. The use of this as a hesitation vowel may

### Table 6.7 Tentative Componential Analysis of (Trager-Smith) English

| | Fr | | Lb | Ap | Rz | |
|---|---|---|---|---|---|---|
| Cl | č | k | p | t | | |
| | ǰ | g | b | d | | Vd |
| Sp | š | h | f | θ | s | |
| | ž | | v | ð | z | Vd |
| Ns | | ŋ | m | n | | |
| | y | | w | l | r | |
| Vo | i | ɨ | u | | | Hi |
| | e | ə | o | | | |
| | æ | a | ɔ | | | Lo |

be cited as evidence for this interpretation. The nonnasal resonants are considered the unmarked manner, and there is one for each possible marked position.

We will next consider Czech, which has the somewhat different system presented in Table 6.8. In this language, affricates in two positions, /Fr/ and /Ap/, show a contrast with the corresponding stops as well as with the corresponding spirants. We are therefore led to recognize affricates as a separate category, identified by the presence of both /Cl/ and /Sp/ in the same segment. Czech /h/ is the voiced glottal which patterns with the dorsals in matters of distribution and alternation. There is no obstacle to placing the two together in the unmarked position. The nasal /n/ is considered to be unmarked rather than apical because some of its allophones are apical, while others may be dorsal. We can therefore consider it to be without a fixed articulator position.

### Table 6.8 Tentative Componential Analysis of Czech

| | Fr | | Lb | Ap | |
|---|---|---|---|---|---|
| Cl | ć | k | p | t | |
| | ȝ | g | b | d | Vd |
| Sp | č | | | c | |
| | š | x | f | s | |
| | ž | h | v | z | Vd |
| Ns | ń | n | m | | |
| Vb | ř | | | r | |
| | j | | | l | |
| Vo | i | | u | | Hi |
| | e | a | o | | |

Since there are two contrasting vibrants in Czech, the apical /r/ and the frontal /ř/, a separate component /Vb/ is set up. The other two nonnasal resonants (/j/ corresponding to English /y/) are considered unmarked as to manner. The Czech vowel system is of a common five-vowel variety with /a/ as the unmarked vowel. Vowel length may be regarded as a separate phoneme /:/ of one component, /Lg/.

For a third example of componential analysis, let us examine a common variety of Latin American Spanish. In this analysis, shown in Table 6.9, the greatest departure from previously considered languages comes in the obstruent system. The phonemes /g b d/, namely, have stop allophones in some positions and spirant allophones in others. Therefore none of them can be properly characterized as either a stop or a spirant. Each of them is always voiced, however, so we regard voicing as their constant property, there being no other obstruents of which the same can be said. The obstruents are thus divided into stops (/Cl/), spirants (/Sp/), and voiced (/Vd/).

**Table 6.9  Tentative Componential Analysis of Spanish (Latin American)**

|     | Fr | | Lb | Ap | |
| --- | --- | --- | --- | --- | --- |
| Cl | č | k | p | t | |
| Vd |   | g | b | d | |
| Sp |   | x | f | s | |
| Ns | ñ | n | m |   | |
| Vb |   | r |   |   | |
|    | y |   | w | l | |
| Vo | {i | | u | | Hi |
|    | e | a | o | | |

The situation concerning the Spanish nasals is similar to that of Czech. The postulation of a component /Vb/ (vibrant) rather than /Lt/ (lateral) is somewhat arbitrary at this point, so its tentativeness must be particularly recognized. The Spanish rolled vibrant, incidentally, may be interpreted phonemically as /rr/ in the intervocalic position, where it contrasts with the simple tapped /r/. In other positions such as initial, where it occurs without being in contrast, it can be treated as an allophone of /r/. The Spanish vowel system, finally, is basically the same as that of Czech.

As our last example, we will attempt a componential analysis of the phonemic inventory of standard German. Some linguists have postulated a somewhat larger inventory of phonemes for German than will be assumed here, particularly among the vowels. This analysis is presented in Table 6.10.

### Table 6.10   Tentative Componential Analysis of German

|      | Lb  | Ap  | Fr  |     |     |
|------|-----|-----|-----|-----|-----|
| Cl   | { p | t   |     | k   |     |
|      | { b | d   |     | g   | Vd  |
| Sp   | { f | s   | š   | x   |     |
|      | { v | z   |     |     | Vd  |
| Ns   | m   | n   |     | ŋ   |     |
|      |     | l   | j   |     |     |
| Vb   |     |     |     | r   |     |

|      | Fr ⌢ Lb |     |     |     |
|------|---------|-----|-----|-----|
|      | i       | ü   | u   | Hi  |
| Vo { | e       | ö   | o   |     |
|      |         | a   |     |     |

It is shown in a somewhat more traditional arrangement than the previous ones, since the vowel and consonant systems cannot be so easily integrated due to the occurrence of both /Fr/ and /Lb/ in the same segment among the vowels.

The horizontal braces at the top of the diagram of the vowel system indicate the overlapping applicability of /Fr/ and /Lb/. The lower horizontal brace within the vowel chart, however, indicates that none of the components above it will be part of the vowel below it—the unmarked /a/. The German consonant system as interpreted here presents no special peculiarities which are not self-explanatory from the chart.

As applied here, componential analysis of phonemic systems seeks to satisfy the following goals: (1) to permit each phoneme to be differentiated from every other phoneme by its componential interpretation; (2) to portray the structural interrelations of the phonemes in the system; and (3) to use as few total components and instances of components as will be consistent with the first two requirements. In addition, the analyses shown here are set up so that the phonetic property (or properties) associated with each component will actually be present in each occurrence of each phoneme of which the component is a part. On these grounds, for example, we rejected the identification of Spanish and Czech /n/ as an apical phoneme, though this is often done in traditional phonetic charts applying to these and other languages with similar properties. There are several reasons why this kind of interpretation seems to be possible within stratificational theory. First, we can use the unmarked category for phonemes showing extreme variation with regard to a particular property; second, failing this there is no theoretical objection to the use of specially defined components for a particular language. Such components could include those with alternate realizations on the phonetic level. It should also be emphasized that the analyses subject to this condition are those corresponding to classical phonemics. The condition is not expected to apply to any more abstract (semi-morphophonemic) componential analyses which may be used.

(The exercises of Set 6B at the end of this chapter may be done at this point.)

## 6.5   *Phonotactic Phenomena*

As on the higher strata, there are important tactic phenomena in the phonology. For purposes of surveying these phenomena, we may divide them into those which concern the arrangement of segments in syllables and those dealing with the arrangement of components in segments and clusters. We will first consider the various aspects of the syllable tactics.

An obvious function of a syllable tactics is to distinguish those segments which can occur in different positions within the syllable. Syllables in many languages may conveniently be divided into three parts: an onset, a nucleus, and a coda. The **nucleus** is the irreducible minimum of the syllable, manifested by a vowel or diphthong or by some consonant capable of being syllabic in the language. The **onset** is the element preceding the nucleus, usually manifested by a consonant or consonant cluster. In many cases, an onset may be optional. The **coda** is the element following the nucleus, again manifested by consonantal material. Codas are usually optional and are completely lacking in some languages. To see how such phenomena may be handled, let us consider a simple syllable tactic problem based on limited data from English.

A subset of the phonologically possible English monosyllables is defined by the following lists:

*Onsets*   /pl, bl, kl, gl, pr, br, tr, dr, kr, gr, sl, sm, sn, spl, skl, spr, str, skr, sp, st, sk/ and any single consonant of the above, namely, /p, t, k, b, d, g, s, l, r, m, n/

*Nuclei*   /i, iy, e, ey, u, uw, o, ow, æ, a, ə, ay, aw, oy/

*Codas*   /l, r, m, n/

These transcriptions are based on an adaptation of the Trager-Smith system to the author's idiolect. Since this idiolect lacks a contrast between Trager-Smith /o/ and /ɔ/, /o/ is used consistently; thus /o/ is the final sound in *law*, and /oy/ is the vowel nucleus in *boy*.

The following additional restrictions govern the combinability of these elements:

1. Onsets and codas are optional.
2. When there is no coda, the only nuclei permitted are /iy, ey, uw, ow, ay, aw, oy, o/.
3. When the coda is manifested by /r/, the only nuclei permitted are /i, e, u, o, a, ə, ay, aw/.

We must produce a tactic diagram which accounts for these facts. Basically we are faced with a syntactic problem of the same sort as we might have on the higher strata, dealing here with phonemic segments rather than morphemes or other entities.

There are important restrictions governing the juxtaposition of nuclei and codas (or the lack of same), but there are none governing the combinability of onsets with following nuclei. Let us begin our task, therefore, by trying to work out a diagram for the types of onsets. The simplest diagram which will account for all of these seems to be that shown in Figure 6.1.

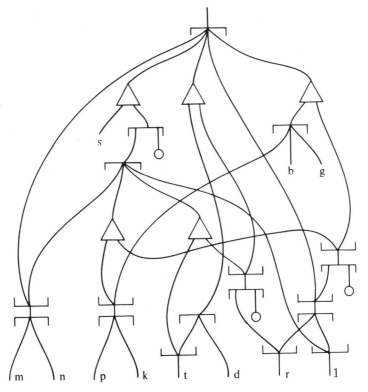

**Figure 6.1  Some English Onsets**

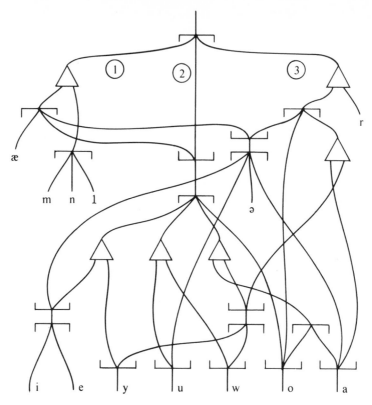

**Figure 6.2   Some English Nuclei with Codas**

Having this much in hand, we may attempt to work out the tactics for nuclei and codas and their combinations. The diagram of Figure 6.2 provides for these restrictions, dividing the set into the nucleus-coda combinations with coda /m n l/ at ①, those with no coda at ②, and those with coda /r/ at ③.

It is now a relatively simple task to integrate Figures 6.1 and 6.2 into a single representation, which is shown in Figure 6.3. This provides the phonotactic solution to our problem. Like a tactics on the higher strata, it provides for phonological constructions, represented by downward ANDs, and classes, represented by downward ORs.

Beyond these basic facts, another thing which the syllable tactics can account for is certain alternate realizations of morphons. In some cases, for example, the failure of the syllable tactics to provide a place for the normal realization of a given morphon will result in its zero realization. One example is seen in certain Polynesian languages, such as Fijian and Samoan. Consider the Samoan data shown in Table 6.11. The two verb forms labelled "Form A" and "Form B" differ in a way difficult to express in English translation,

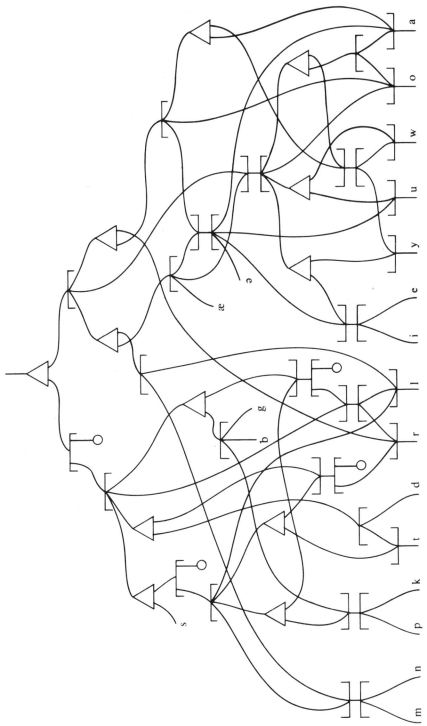

*Figure 6.3   Some English Onsets Combined with Nuclei and Codas*

### Table 6.11   Forms from Samoan

| Form A | Form B | Gloss |
|--------|--------|-------|
| 1.  alofa | alofagia | 'love' |
| 2.  ʔole | ʔolegia | 'cheat' |
| 3.  faʔaee | faʔaeetia | 'put' |
| 4.  fua | fuatia | 'weigh' |
| 5.  faʔafoi | faʔafoisia | 'send back' |
| 6.  gau | gausia | 'break' |
| 7.  faitau | faitaulia | 'read' |
| 8.  sila | silafia | 'see' |
| 9.  utu | utufia | 'fetch water' |
| 10. sio | siomia | 'surround' |
| 11. inu | inumia | 'drink' |
| 12. lilo | liloia | 'hide' |
| 13. sopo | sopoia | 'exceed' |

From Problem 7.G of H. A. Gleason, Jr., *Workbook in Descriptive Linguistics* (New York: Holt, Rinehart and Winston, 1955), p. 31.

and the distinction can be ignored as inessential for this problem. The alternations exhibited in all the pairs of verbs except the last two can be most simply accounted for by considering the suffix to be /ia/ and the stems to be morphonically representable as in the second column, minus the suffix. This means that most stems will end morphonically in a consonant. These consonantal morphons, however, will be subject to zero realization when they fall in word-final position due to the lack of a suffix, as in the "Form A" column. The basic reason for this zero realization can be sought in the syllable tactics. It is apparent that the syllable tactics of this language will have no provision for codas. Therefore the morpheme-final consonants must be realized as a part of an onset or not at all. They are realized in the second column because a vowel follows, but in the first column they are subject to zero realization.

When we discussed simulfixes in Section 4.3, we noted that these morphemes were divisible into different types on the basis of their connections to the phonology. We are now prepared to detail this differentiation. First we may deal with the preemptives, including both the traditional replacives and the infixes. Let us consider, for example, the preemptive $^{MN}/æ^{+}/$ and $^{MN}/ə^{+}/$ in *sang* and *sung*. As we informally described them in Chapter 4, they take precedence over any ordinary vowel in the syllable nucleus. This precedence will be indicated by a downward ordered OR whose precedence-taking branch will go to the preemptive vowels, and whose other branch will go to the ordinary vowels. Such a node is shown in the representation of Figure

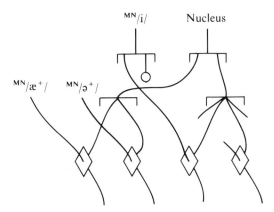

*Figure 6.4   Preemptives in Phonotactics*

6.4. At this point, the phonotactics will receive in the case of *sang* signals from the two vowels $^{MN}/æ^+/$ and $^{MN}/i/$. Since the former will have a connection to the precedence-taking branch, it will be realized rather than $^{MN}/i/$, and the latter will necessarily be realized as zero. A similar treatment would apply to the infixes, except that the result in the absence of a signal to the precedence-taking branch would be zero.

As for the interfixes, the morphology of a language having this organizing principle will put out, at least in part, consonant sequences simultaneous with vowel sequences. It will be the task of the phonotactics to provide for the properly interdigitated arrangement of these. For the imperative singular form $^P/wisəd/$, from the Amharic data in Table 4.9, for example, the morphology will provide the consonant sequence $^{MN}/wsd/$ simultaneous with the vowel sequence (simulfix) $^{MN}/iə/$. Apparently, the syllable tactics of such languages operates on the principle of a strict alternation of vowels and consonants, something of the form sketched in Figure 6.5. This provides for an indefinite number of CV sequences optionally followed by a final consonant. Further restrictions may, of course, need to be worked in for individual languages. For this sequence, the tactics will take the first consonant *w* and follow it by the first vowel *i*, then the second consonant *s* and the second vowel *ə*. The consonant left over, *d*, will come as the final coda. We provided, of course, for a zero vowel morphon to cover cases like the infinitive form /məwsəd/ 'to take' in the same data. Here we will have a prefix in the form *mə-*, followed by a simultaneous association of the root $^{MN}/wsd/$ with the simulfix $^{MN}/\varnothing ə/$. The tactics will operate as before, taking $\varnothing$ as the vowel following $^P/w/$. Since this vowel has no further realization, the realized form will actually contain the cluster *ws*.

In some cases, the phonotactics can provide for segments not realizing any morphon as determined elements. In the case of the English form $^P/wišəz/$

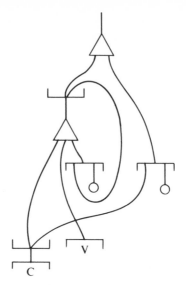

**Figure 6.5   Syllable Tactics for Interfixing**

(*wishes*), for example, the morphonic form will be <sup>MN</sup>/wišz/. The phoneme
<sup>P</sup>/ə/ will be provided as a determined element in the proper environment.
Other cases of so-called prothetic or epenthetic vowels or consonants in
phonological alternation can be provided for in a similar way.

Now we will proceed to illustrate a few matters which may be treated in
terms of the tactics of components, particularly matters involving the internal
structure of segments and clusters. The simplest kind of componential tactics
is one which provides for the various possible segments in a language. Such
a tactics may be called a **segment tactics.** As an example, let us consider a
segment tactics providing for the Czech phonemic inventory as componentially analyzed in Table 6.8 (in Section 6.4). This tactics, providing for only
these particular combinations of components, is shown in Figure 6.6. The
AND labelled Ⓐ in this diagram provides for the stops and spirants, that
labelled Ⓑ deals with the affricates and nonnasal resonants, Ⓒ with the
nasals, and Ⓓ with the vowels.

Many properties of consonant and vowel clustering may also be handled
by a componentially based tactic pattern. As an example, let us consider the
following facts about standard Russian. There are in Russian twelve apical,
consonants, the nonpalatalized /t d s z n l/ and the palatalized /t, d, s, z, n, l,/.
As a syllable onset, any one of these may occur, and we can also get the following clusters of them (this account is restricted to two-phoneme clusters
only): /st s,t, zd z,d, tl t,l, dl d,l, dn d,n,/. We can see that members of these

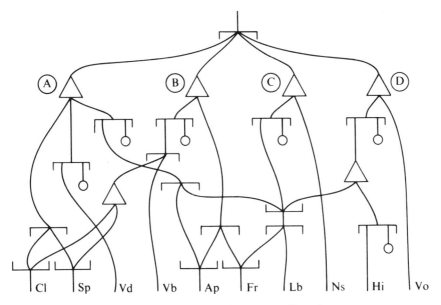

*Figure 6.6   Czech Segment Tactics*

clusters must agree with respect to the presence or absence of palatalization, and clusters of obstruents must show agreement with respect to the presence or absence of voicing. It is possible to describe this agreement phenomenon as a matter of reduplication. The voicing and palatalization characteristic selected for one member of the cluster, that is, will be reduplicated for the other. There are, however, two types of reduplication elements by means of which this reduplication may be described. We could use the anticipatory reduplication element, meaning the main selection of the characteristic is that signalled for the second consonant, while the first one reduplicates it. The repetitive reduplication element, on the other hand, would have the main selection for the first element, with the second element reduplicating this.

In order to be able to decide which of these possibilities is more appropriate, we need to examine the morphophonemic phenomena of the language to see if they provide any information which may be helpful. On examination, we indeed find relevant evidence. There are cases, for example, where a morphonic voiced obstruent and a morphonic voiceless obstruent come together. The voicing characteristic of the realized form of such a cluster is always determined by that of the second morphon. If we combine the prefix [MN]/iz/ with the root [MN]/tok/, the result is realized as [P]/istók/ 'source.' If we combine the prefix [MN]/s/ with the form [MN]/dam/ 'I shall give,' we get the realization [P]/zdám/

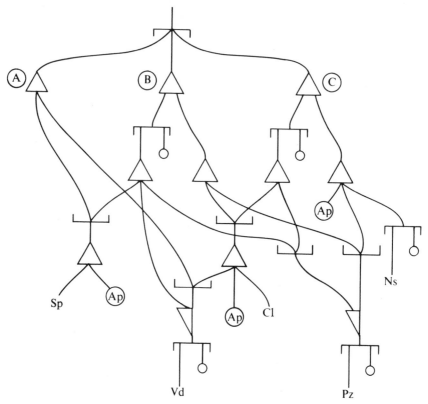

*Figure 6.7   Apical Onsets in Russian*

'I shall hand in.' In the case of palatalization, we get similar evidence of the influence of the following consonant on the preceding. Thus <sup>MN</sup>/roz/ plus <sup>MN</sup>/d,el/ is realized as <sup>P</sup>/raz,d,él/ 'division' and <sup>MN</sup>/s/ plus <sup>MN</sup>/l,it,/ is realized as <sup>P</sup>/s,l,ít,/ 'to pour out.' We can thus assume that it is appropriate to use anticipatory rather than repetitive reduplication in both cases of phonological agreement. A segment and cluster tactics providing for all the mentioned possibilities in this way is shown in Figure 6.7. The node marked Ⓐ in this diagram provides for the single spirants, that marked Ⓑ for the single stops and clusters of spirant plus stop, and that marked Ⓒ for single resonants and clusters of stop plus resonant. The three occurrences of /Ap/, circled in the diagram, should actually be joined at an upward OR, but this has been omitted to avoid unnecessary cluttering.

Phenomena such as these are frequently termed "assimilation." Actually, this term is better reserved for the historical processes which led to such a situation, but it is true that the voicing and palatalization characteristics of one consonant of a cluster, in this case the second, can determine those of the adjacent segments. Other kinds of components in adjacent segments can, of course, be affected in a similar way.

Now let us consider an example of the effect of stress on the realization of vowels, which produces an alternation in Belorussian. In stressed syllables, this language has five vowels, as illustrated by the examples /z,ími/ 'winters,' /l,és/ 'forest,' /brát/ 'brother,' /lós,/ 'elk,' and /rúki/ 'hands.' In unstressed syllables, however, only /i/, /a/, and /u/ may occur. Since there are many stress alternations in this language, a lexical item may have a stressed vowel in some of its forms and an unstressed vowel in others. This leads to two alternations, one between the stressed vowel /e/ and unstressed /a/, as in /l,así/ 'forests' (compare the data above), and one between stressed /o/ and unstressed /a/, as in /las,í/ 'elks.' The tactic aspects of this alternation may be characterized in terms of the combinability of various components, including /Ac/ (stress). Suppose the vowels are given the same interpretation as those of Czech and Spanish, shown in Tables 6.8 and 6.9. If this is the case, the nonhigh vowels are the ones involved in our alternation, and we need a tactics which provides for the unmarked /a/ = /Vo/ alone among these in the absence of stress. This provision is incorporated in the diagram of the Belorussian vowel tactics shown in Figure 6.8. In the presence of /Ac/, this

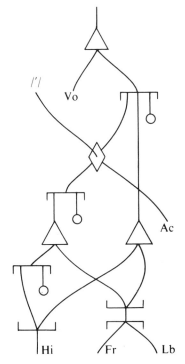

*Figure 6.8  Belorussian Vowels*

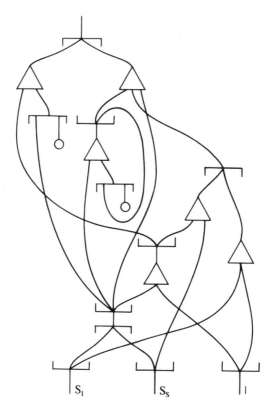

**Figure 6.9  Latin Stress**

diagram allows for any of the vowels, while in its absence only combinations equivalent to /i a u/ are permitted. The alternation involved is a separate matter, whose detailed diagrammatic treatment will be taken up in the next section. But note that this alternation can be componentially characterized as a matter of the zero realization of /Fr/ and /Lb/ under the circumstance that the tactics fails to permit their realization. The tactics thus makes its contribution to the explanation of the alternation concerned.

As a final example of tactic conditioning, let us consider the case of the predictability of stress in Classical Latin. This stress, as is well known, depends on the position of the syllable within a phonological word, and on the length of this syllable. Some syllables are long because they contain a long vowel, and others are considered long for this purpose because they have a coda. In phonological words of only one or two syllables, first of all, length is irrelevant. The stress will be on the only syllable of a monosyllable and on the first syllable of a disyllabic sequence. Representing stress as $^{|}$ and any long syllable as $S_l$ and any short one as $S_s$, we can represent these types formulaically as $^{|} \cdot (S_l, S_s) [(S_l, S_s)]$. For words of three or more syllables, the penultimate syllable will be stressed if long; otherwise the stress will fall on the antepenult. Words of three or more syllables with penultimate stress may be presented formulaically by $(S_1, S_s)^n \mid \cdot S_1 (S_1, S_s)$, where the superscript$^n$ indicates that the preceding element may occur an indefinitely large number of times. Those phonological words with antepenultimate stress, finally, may be represented by the formula $(S_1, S_s)^n \mid \cdot (S_1, S_s) S_s (S_1, S_s)$. By translating these three formulas into a tactic diagram, with appropriate simplifications, we can represent these facts about the occurrence of Latin stress as shown in Figure 6.9. This stress, unlike that of Belorussian, will be a purely determined element, not directly signalled from the morphology.

There are many other specific phonotactic phenomena which could have been surveyed in this section. It is hoped that the treatment of other phenomena can be readily generalized from the small sampling presented here. Some additional examples are given in the exercises.

(The exercises of Set 6C at the end of this chapter may be done at this point.)

## 6.6   *The Organization of the Phonological System*

In previous sections of this chapter, we have discussed four major types of phenomena for which the phonology may reasonably be expected to account. These phenomena are contrast, alternation, componency, and phonotactics. It is the purpose of this section to discuss the structure of an integrated phonology which can deal with all these phenomena.

In considering the treatment of these matters, we face the alternatives of building our model around two stratal systems with two separate tactic patterns or around one. The proposal for a phonology involving two tactic patterns appeared in Lamb's article "Prolegomena to a theory of phonology" (1966c). The upper tactic pattern of this system deals with syllable structures, and the lower one, termed the **hypophonotactics**, deals with the structure of segments and clusters. One of the major reasons cited in the paper for the separation of the two strata is the fact that segment and cluster phenomena can transcend syllable boundaries, and it seemed more desirable to Lamb to keep the syllable tactics fairly simple and account for deviations from the simple pattern with a separate hypophonotactics. Lamb concluded, furthermore, that the level of abstraction of the syllable tactics is neither that of the morphons nor that of the classical phonemes, but is intermediate between the two. This stratificational phonemic level, as it may be called, is partly morphophonemic in nature, and its -emes are whole segments. The -emes of the hypophonemic stratum, on the other hand, are component-sized and are on the level of abstraction of the classical phoneme. The equivalent of a classical phonemic transcription within this system, therefore, is a transcription in terms of hypophonemes, while the equivalent of the classical phoneme itself is a simultaneous bundle of hypophonemes, the typical realization of the (stratificational) phoneme on the stratum above.

The model proposed for phonology in Lamb's article has the structure represented in Figure 6.10. This figure may be profitably compared with Figure 4.23 in Section 4.7, to which it is basically analogous. The functions of the various patterns within it will now be surveyed.

The **morphonic alternation pattern** deals with alternations which are best treated in terms of whole segments, with environments statable in terms of syllable structure. It deals with various instances of diversification and neutralization between the morphons and stratificational phonemes.

The **phonotactics** describes the syllable structure in terms of units the size of the classical phoneme, but on a level of abstraction from the phonic correlations intermediate between the morphophonemic and the classical phonemic levels. It provides for determined segments in cases of epenthesis or prothesis and sometimes specifies arrangements of units which differ from those of their realizates.

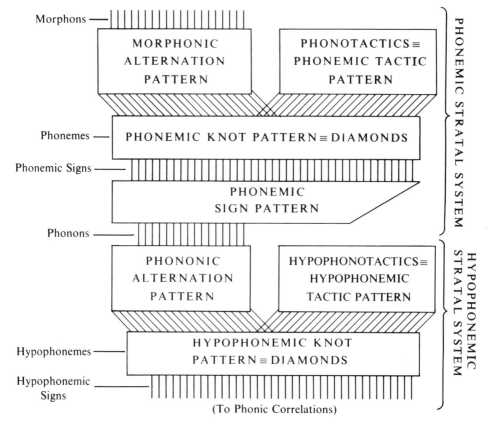

**Figure 6.10   Bistratal Model of Phonology**

The **phonemic diamonds** (originally the **phonemic knot pattern**) allow the morphons, through the morphonic alternation pattern, to control the operation of the phonotactics. At the same time, they allow the phonotactics to furnish environments for cases of morphonic diversification. Each diamond may be thought of as representing a phoneme as defined by this system.

The **phonemic sign pattern** spells out each phonemic sign in terms of phonons (quasi-morphophonemic components). Its downward ANDs, unlike those of higher strata, are unordered.

The **phononic alternation pattern**, a part of the hypophonemic stratal system, accounts for the remaining morphophonemic alternations, those better handled in terms of components with conditioning within the structure of segments and clusters, possibly across syllable boundaries. It thus handles various componential alternations involving diversification and neutralization.

The **hypophonotactics** specifies the structure of segments and clusters. It also provides for determined elements which have no realizates among the phonons. The difference between the entities of this stratum which realize elements from above and those which are determined corresponds to the traditional notion of distinctiveness, which explains why hypophonemic transcriptions (excluding determined elements) are analogous to classical phonemic transcriptions, having, among other things, a biunique relation to the phonetic transcription.

The **hypophonemic diamonds** (originally the **hypophonemic knot pattern**) allow the phonons to control the operation of the hypophonotactics in the normal use of language, while at the same time allowing the hypophonotactics to provide environments for the phononic alternations. Each of the diamonds with an upward connection toward phonons represents a hypophoneme. Diamonds without such a connection represent nondistinctive hypophonemic signs.

The hypophonemic stratal system lacks a sign pattern, since there are no "hypophonons." The hypophonemic signs connect to the phonic correlations. The possibility of a phonetic stratum intermediate between hypophonemic signs and the phonic correlations was briefly discussed by Lamb at the end of the article, but it was left open.

To get a better idea of what sorts of phenomena would be handled on the strata described here, we may go back to the examples discussed in Section 6.5 to see how each of them would fit into the phonological system.

The Samoan zero realization of consonants due to the absence of codas would belong to the phonotactics and the morphonic alternation pattern. The preemptives would also belong there. The interfixing of Semitic languages would belong to the phonotactics alone, as no alternate realizations of morphons are involved but only their positioning. Determined prothetic and epenthetic segments would also be provided for by the phonotactics alone.

The Russian consonant agreements, belonging to the phenomena which are conveniently handled componentially, would be treated in the hypophonotactics. The zero realization of certain phonons in the phononic alternation pattern would also be involved (that is, for cases of phononic voicing or palatalization which could not be realized due to their environment). The Belorussian vowel alternations would also be a matter of the interaction of the hypophonotactics and the phononic alternation pattern.

Stress in Classical Latin would apparently be a matter of hypophonotactically determined elements. This may seem strange, in that syllable length is one of the main determining factors for this stress. The apparent discrepancy is explained, however, by the fact that stress is a nondistinctive phonetic feature in Latin, for which reason we would not want to deal with it in the phonotactics but only in the hypophonotactics, where such nondistinctive properties are determined.

Since the time of the writing of the *Outline* and the "Prolegomena," as we have seen in previous chapters, Lamb's notion of the structure of a stratal system has been altered in a number of ways as the result of further empirical research. One of these previously described changes has been the addition of a lower or "-emic" alternation pattern below the tactics of each stratal system, accompanied by an explicit conditioning of all nonfree alternations via conditioning lines from the tactics to enablers. If we assume a similar change in the phonology, our first thought might be to add such a pattern to the phonemic and hypophonemic stratal systems. This step would produce, however, two additional levels of alternation, one in each stratal system. It may be questioned to what extent all these distinctions are necessary. It is conceivable that the two earlier stratal systems can be integrated into a single phonemic stratal system.

The more flexible use of diamonds is another development that may aid in the integration of the two phonological tactic patterns into a single one. Whereas the upward ANDs of the knot pattern used to relate tactics to alternation patterns in the 1966 works were all of a single type, and were gathered at a single point at the bottom of the tactics, diamonds can enter the tactics at various points.

In order to investigate these possibilities, let us take a phenomenon which would clearly be handled on the hypophonemic stratum in the 1966 model and see if we can develop an alternative working it into the syllable tactics. For this purpose, we will use the Belorussian vowel alternation discussed in Section 6.5. First, let us consider what the treatment of this phenomenon would be in a bistratal phonology of the 1966 form, modified only by the addition of diamonds.

Such a treatment is diagrammed in Figure 6.11. The alternation is provided for in the phononic alternation pattern, which connects to a hypophonotactics essentially the same in form as that previously represented in Figure 6.8 (Section 6.5). Above this is the relatively trivial treatment given to the vowels in the phonemic stratal system. They are shown by the phonotactics to belong to a single class capable of manifesting the nucleus. No alternations are indicated for them in the morphonic alternation pattern (which is, for this

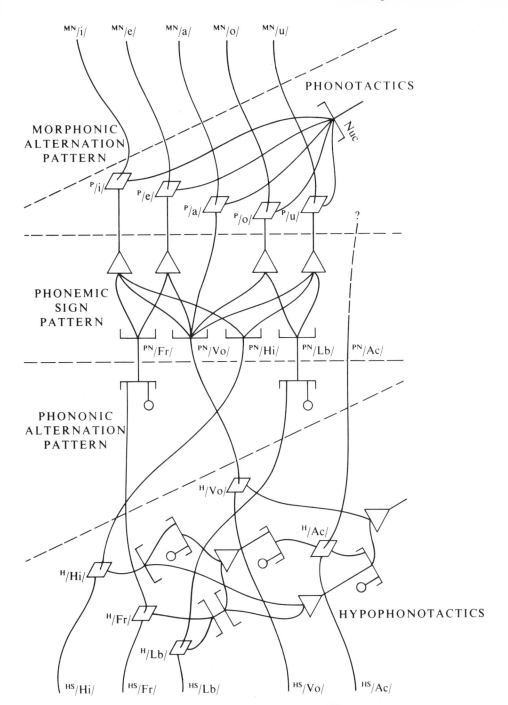

*Figure 6.11 Post-1966 Bistratal Treatment
of Belorussian Vowel Alternation*

data, vacuous). The phonemic sign pattern represents the breakdown of each phonemic sign into phonons. A phonon <sup>PN</sup>/Ac/ appears at the bottom of the phonemic sign pattern, but its upward connections are not fully specified. This is because there is a rather complex system of stress alternations in this and other East Slavic languages, whose details have not yet been worked out. It may be assumed that the phonotactics, operating with signals originating in the morphemic stratal system or above, will determine the location of the stress in every form. The stress-conditioned vowel alternation, in any case, must be handled at a point in the network at which it has been determined which syllables will be stressed and which unstressed. We are, of course, assuming here the 1966 treatment of conditioning, in which the highest-precedence alternative allowed by the tactics is chosen at any ordered OR in the alternation pattern. Thus <sup>PN</sup>/Fr/ and <sup>PN</sup>/Lb/ will be realized as <sup>H</sup>/Fr/ and <sup>H</sup>/Lb/, respectively, if they are part of a high or a stressed vowel but will be realized as zero in any other case, since the tactics will not allow the preferred alternate. The apparent unworkability of this conception in a model of performance has already been mentioned in Chapter 4.

An alternative monostratal treatment of the same data is presented in Figure 6.12. In this account, the alternations are treated in the phonemic alternation pattern. More striking than this, perhaps, is the way that the pattern seems to go from full segments—the morphons—to components in one step within the phonotactics. Actually, this example is somewhat deceptive in that a nonvacuous phonemic sign pattern would still be needed in some cases. Nevertheless, it is true that many of the lines leading down from the diamonds will connect to single components. This is possible because there is a great tendency in language for tactic classes to be definable componentially. Components which define classes can be worked into the system as determined elements.

Take the example of the vowels in this data. Each of these connects to a diamond of its own in the phonotactics. These diamonds can be thought of as representing the (stratificational) phonemes, which are in the case of this limited data in one-to-one correspondence with the morphons. The component <sup>PN</sup>/Vo/, however, is common to the whole class of vowels, which has to be recognized in the syllable tactics in any case. This component is therefore inserted as a determined element, a step which generalizes it over the individual treatment in the phonemic sign pattern shown in Figure 6.11. The determinations of stress (not shown here) specify whether or not the vowel will be accompanied by <sup>PN</sup>/Ac/. Since the vowel <sup>P</sup>/a/ involves no components in addition to <sup>PN</sup>/Vo/, there is no downward line from the diamond representing it. The realizations of <sup>MN</sup>/u/ and <sup>MN</sup>/i/, on the other hand, share the component <sup>PN</sup>/Hi/ in addition to the components which differentiate them. There is nothing in our tactics to prevent these from being grouped together to represent the generalization with a determined <sup>PN</sup>/Hi/, so this is done. The downward lines from <sup>MN</sup>/i/ and <sup>MN</sup>/e/ will thus both lead to <sup>PN</sup>/Fr/, and those from $^{MN}$/u/ and $^{MN}$/o/ will both lead to $^{PN}$/Lb/. In the case of $^P$/e/ and $^P$/o/, however, the alternative of zero realization is also open, so the neutralization must come below the point where these alternations are dealt with. The alternations come in the phonemic alternation pattern, controlled by enablers connected to the specification of $^{PN}$/Ac/ in the phonotactics. These phonemes are shown to be realized as $^{PN}$/Fr/ and $^{PN}$/Lb/, respectively, when stressed, and as zero elsewhere. These results neutralize with the differentiating realizations of $^P$/i/ and $^P$/u/, the additional differences being treated as determined elements. Thus an unstressed $^P$/e/ or $^P$/o/ will give the same result as $^P$/a/, a case of complete neutralization.

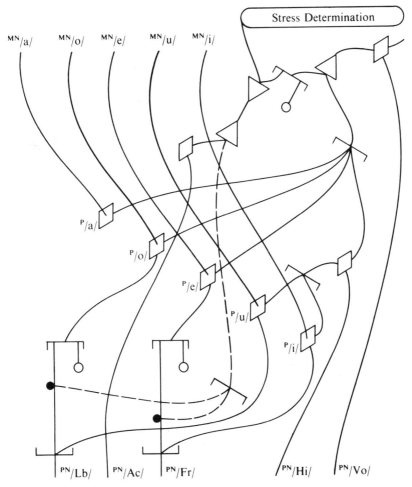

**Figure 6.12 Monostratal Treatment of Belorussian Vowel Alternation**

It now appears that this latter treatment of phonological phenomena, integrating the phonotactics and the hypophonotactics of 1966, will be preferable to the other alternative. For this particular problem, the bistratal treatment has an index of economy of $30 + 10 = 40$, while the monostratal version has $19 + 3 = 22$, a difference of 18 in favor of the monostratal version. To date this model has yet to see any extensive degree of application, but it seems that there will be no insuperable difficulties in adapting it to handle problems previously dealt with on two separate strata in the phonology.

Meanwhile, it does appear that a primitive phonetic tactics of segments and clusters, less complex than the former hypophonotactics, will also be needed to provide for phonetically determined elements. The exact shape of this tactics and the particular phenomena treated by it will have to be determined by further research.

We can now detail the structure of the single phonemic stratal system, which is diagrammed in Figure 6.13. The function of each of the designated patterns in this system may be outlined as follows.

The **morphonic alternation pattern** will handle the kinds of alternation which are better treated in terms of whole segments than in terms of components. Included within its scope would be such matters as zero realization of consonants in Samoan. This alternation will be conditioned by enablers connecting to the tactics. The alternations treated here will by and large correspond with those treated in the pattern of the same name in the bistratal version.

The **phonotactics** will handle the structure of syllables as well as that of the segments and clusters which make them up, and the phonological words and other higher ranks of the phonology as necessary. It will treat as determined elements those components which correspond to classes already needed in the tactics (for example, $^{PN}$/Vo/ in Figure 6.12) or capable of being worked into it without adding to the total complexity (for instance, $^{PN}$/Hi/ in Figure 6.12).

The **phonemic alternation pattern** will deal with the alternations better treated in terms of components, those which were handled in the hypophonology of the 1966 model. These alternations will have their conditioning environments shown by enablers connected to the phonotactics via conditioning lines. There will also be cases of unconditioned diversification, neutralization, and portmanteau realization handled in this pattern. The phonemic signs—the output elements of this pattern—will define a representation analogous to the classical phonemic in that only distinctive differences will be shown.

The **phonemic sign pattern** will break down complex phonemic signs into their constituent phonons. According to the current conception, a great deal of the phonemic-sign-to-phonon correspondence will be one-to-one, since the breakdown will be accomplished in the phonotactics where possible.

Below the phonemic stratal system will be the **phonetic stratal system**, which will provide for nondistinctive phonetic facts. These include nondistinctive determined elements as well as nondistinctive alternate realizations. The more

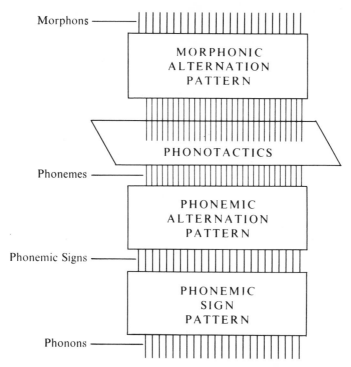

**Figure 6.13   Revised Phonemic Stratal System**

precise details of the organization of this stratal system remain to be worked out.

We may now conclude this section with a few remarks on the practical problems of arriving at an analysis of a particular set of data within the system described above.

In Section 6.3 we outlined a method of preliminary analysis arriving at a tentative set of morphons related by realization formulas to the classical phonemic representation. In the model outlined here, we will need to divide these alternations into two groups, one represented in the morphonic alternation pattern and the other in the phonemic alternation pattern. The latter group will doubtless include those which are componential in nature, while the former group is more likely to include alternations involving whole segments, such as zero or empty realization or alternations between componentially unrelated segments which sometimes occur.

The integration of these alternations into the system will also involve a full consideration of phonotactic phenomena, many of which will be intimately related to the alternations. We will expect the phonotactics to be statable, as we have said, in terms of a level of abstraction intermediate between the morphons and the phonemic signs (the latter being on the classical phonemic level). The final decision as to where a particular alternation will be treated, of course, will depend on the relative simplicity of the possibilities. A further important difference between morphonic and phonemic alternations is that the former are output-conditioned (in terms of the realizations), while the latter are input-conditioned (in terms of the realizates). This difference naturally results from the fact that conditioning lines for both will originate in the tactics.

The alternation patterns are most conveniently stated in realization formulas rather than graphic notation in a practical description. The realization formulas shown so far have been adapted for input-conditioned alternation such as that found in the phonemic alternation pattern. To provide for output-conditioned alternation such as that of the morphonic alternation pattern, a somewhat different type of formula is needed in order to represent the fact that the realizations will be on the same stratum as the conditioning elements. The easiest way to treat this is with a simple reversal of the order of symbols for environment and stratal difference within the formula. Thus while the formula

$$P \parallel \underline{\phantom{x}}t / s$$
$$+ \parallel \text{---} / p$$

would be appropriate for a phonemic alternation, where *P* and *t* are both on the same stratum (the phonemic), we could use

$$P / s \parallel \underline{\phantom{x}}t$$
$$+ / p \parallel \text{---}$$

if we meant for *s*, *t*, and *p* to be on the same stratum (again the phonemic). The first subformula of the former would be read "*P* in the environment of a following *t* is realized as *s*," while the corresponding line of the latter would be "*P* is realized as *s* in the environment of following *t*." In the spoken form the order of the environment with respect to the realization would signal the difference. The latter form would be appropriate if the *t* were itself the realization of several morphons, all of which affect the realization of *P* in the same way.

(The exercises of Set 6D at the end of this chapter may be done at this point. Further suggestions on the treatment of specific phenomena will be developed in the course of these exercises.)

## 6.7 *In Defense of Distinctiveness*

In the preceding sections of this chapter, we have proceeded on the assumption that it is desirable to recognize a level within the phonology conforming to the principle of distinctiveness, which has served as the cornerstone of classical phonemics. During the past decade, an influential group of linguists has sought to maintain, however, that this principle is valueless and that it should be ignored in phonological theory. In particular, linguists of this persuasion have maintained that the introduction of a level of representation which has a biunique relationship to a phonetic representation while still indicating only the distinctive information, will inevitably lead to a loss of generalization.

Nearly all attempts to demonstrate the latter point have been based on an argument originally advanced by Morris Halle in his 1959 work *The Sound Pattern of Russian*. In this argument, he used the example of voicing in Russian obstruent clusters. Although this example has been much discussed and repeated by both advocates and opponents of Halle's position, it will bear repeating again if it is to be confronted directly.

The relevant Russian data may be summarized as follows:

1. Any sequence of two obstruents within a phonological word or between phonological words in close transition will be either voiceless or voiced as a whole, unless the second obstruent in the sequence is /v/ or its palatalized equivalent /v,/.
2. In cases of alternation involving the members of such clusters, the influence with respect to voicing or voicelessness extends from the second obstruent to the first.
3. The alternations characterized in point 2 affect not only pairs of obstruents distinctively differing with respect to the presence or absence of voice but also the phonetic pairs [c/ʒ], [č,/ʒ,], and [x/ɣ], for which voicing is generally conceded to be nondistinctive.

Halle's criticism was based on the traditional analysis of these facts. This analysis regarded the alternation in [mók l,i] 'was (he) getting wet?' and [móg bɨ] 'were (he) getting wet' as a morphophonemic one, since /k/ and /g/ could be established as separate phonemes in Russian. At the same time, it treated the alternation in [žéč, l, i] 'should one burn' and [žéʒ, bɨ] 'were one to burn' as subphonemic (allophonic) in view of the lack of contrast between the two phones [č,] and [ʒ,] in any position. Halle pointed out that this traditional analysis failed to make a generalization, in that the conditions for voicing and voicelessness were the same for all obstruent clusters. He correctly showed that the traditional analysis would require a morphophonemic statement to handle the alternation of /k/ and /g/ and a necessarily separate allophonic statement to treat the alternation of [č,] and [ʒ,], despite the identity of conditioning. An alternative which allows one general state-ment applying to both instances and all similar ones would clearly have a greater generalizing power, and therefore it would be preferable.

Given the general principles of science, one cannot fail to agree with this much of Halle's argument. In attempting to draw general conclusions from this argument, however, Halle made a fatal error of reasoning which appears to have been overlooked by a great percentage of his readers. He concluded, namely, that what was responsible for the failure to capture this generalization was the biuniqueness principle (which, as we have seen, is a consequence of the distinctiveness principle). On this assumption, he further concluded that in view of such data from Russian and other languages, the recognition of a level of representation in conformity with the distinctiveness principle is in-compatible with the making of such generalizations and should therefore be scrapped in favor of the generalizations.

As a matter of fact, the traditional analysis conforms to a number of requirements, of which biuniqueness is only one. Halle never demonstrated that it was this particular property that was responsible for the shortcoming. Apparently, he and the many who have followed him and quoted him have never sorted out the properties sufficiently. If they had, it should have been clear that this line of reasoning cannot stand.

It should suffice to refute Halle's contention, therefore, if it can be shown that a representation in conformity with biuniqueness and distinctiveness will allow this generalization in the treatment of Russian. It turns out that the offending principle was not biuniqueness at all but the nonsuspendability principle ("once a phoneme, always a phoneme"), already discussed in Section 6.1. This requirement, as we have seen, was characteristic of Neo-Bloom-fieldian phonology, but not of the phonology of the Prague School, which rejected it in its theory of phonological suspension ("neutralization"). Incor-porating the suspension of phonological contrast in the treatment of this problem, we could recognize no distinctive occurrence of /Vd/ in an obstruent standing before another obstruent other than /v v,/. At the same time, we could recognize a nondistinctive occurrence of [Vd] as a determined element on the phonetic stratum for obstruents in this position, provided that the following obstruent is also voiced. By such an analysis, the phononic trans-criptions of the clusters in Halle's examples would be as follows:

|  | 1 |  | 2 |  | 3 |  | 4 |  |
|---|---|---|---|---|---|---|---|---|
| | [k | l, | g | b | č, | l, | ž, | b] |
| PN | Cl | Ap | Cl | Cl | Cl | Ap | Cl | Cl |
| | | Pz | | Lb | Sp | Pz | Sp | Lb |
| | | | | Vd | Fr | | Fr | Vd |

On the phonetic level, a tactically determined occurrence of voicing would be provided reduplicatively for the first segment in examples 2 and 4. By this means, the generalization which Halle sought to make is captured without abandonment of the distinctiveness principle. This transcription is fully bi-unique, because the occurrence of voicing is still predictable from the surrounding phonons. Far from abandoning the distinctiveness principle, this treatment carries it out on a wider scale than did the Neo-Bloomfieldian treatment, applying it to components as well as to whole segments.

Examples such as these also involve an alternation above the level of the phonons. We will find that the stratificational phonemic element $^P$/Vd/ will be realized as $^{PN}$/Vd/ only before a vowel or a resonant, including /v/. Elsewhere it will have zero realization (before another obstruent or the phonemic word boundary). Thus the morphonic clusters $^{MN}$/kb/ and $^{MN}$/gb/ in *rok by* 'were it fate' and *rog by* 'were it a horn' will both be realized phononically as

$$^{PN}\left|\begin{array}{cc} \text{Cl} & \text{Cl} \\ & \text{Lb} \\ & \text{Vd} \end{array}\right|$$

and phonetically as

$$\begin{bmatrix} \text{Cl} & \text{Cl} \\ \text{Do} & \text{Lb} \\ \text{Vd} & \text{Vd} \end{bmatrix}$$

And final $^{MN}$/k/ and $^{MN}$/g/, as in *rok* 'fate' and *rog* 'horn,' will both be realized phononically as $^{PN}$/Cl/ and phonetically as

$$\begin{bmatrix} \text{Cl} \\ \text{Do} \end{bmatrix}$$

The provision for the zero realization of $^P$/Vd/, however, does not add any complexity to the phonology, since it would be needed to account for the facts in any case. The suspension interpretation does extend it to the position before voiced obstruents, whereas without this principle it might be thought of as occurring only before voiceless obstruents or the phonological word boundary. If it were not for the provision of this suspension, however, the phononic transcriptions of *rok by* and *rog by* would not bear a biunique relationship to their identical phonetic representation. The former would be as above, while the latter would be the actually impossible

$$^{PN}\left|\begin{array}{cc} \text{Cl} & \text{Cl} \\ \text{Vd} & \text{Lb} \\ & \text{Vd} \end{array}\right|$$

The absence of $^{PN}$/Vd/ in the phononic representation of the first segment of these clusters despite the presence of [Vd] on the phonetic level is explained by the fact that the voicing present in that segment is not distinctive. This means, of course, that voiced obstruents before other voiced obstruents are assigned to the nonvoiced phoneme, but this is acceptable, since in a system with phonological markedness "nonvoiced" means simply "not distinctively voiced." This assignment is therefore a consequence of the distinctiveness principle.

Thus it turns out that distinctiveness is not incompatible with the principle of simplicity if it is carried out consistently on a componential level such as the phononic. This being the case, the major thrust of Halle's argument is vitiated. It would seem that the burden of proof should fall upon those who maintain that the distinctiveness principle is invalid. In the absence of such further proof, the usefulness of this principle seems to make it desirable that it be adhered to.

Postal (1968) has advanced two additional arguments against forms of phonology adhering to the distinctiveness principle. These arguments, however, are likewise invalid when considered in the light of stratificational phonology.

The first of these arguments points out that phonotactic restrictions are intimately related to morphophonemic alternations, and further that the phonotactics is not best stated in terms of biunique phonemes. Both of these points were in fact made by Lamb in his 1966 "Prolegomena," and they remain true in the revised system described here. Lamb made the first point by insisting on the integration of the phonotactics (and the then-recognized hypophonotactics as well) into the treatment of alternations. The second point was also recognized in Lamb's conclusion that the syllable tactics is best stated in terms of the non-biunique stratificational phonemes rather than classical phonemes. Neither of these points would refute the existence of a level answering to the distinctiveness principle, however. They merely point to the existence of additional phonological levels which must be recognized.

Postal's second argument is indeed a curious one. He shows evidence that two sounds in free variation with the same sound are not necessarily in free variation with each other. He gives the examples /edíšən/, /ædíšən/ and /ədíšən/ from American English, pointing out that in many dialects there may be a free variation between /e/ and /ə/ in the pronunciation of *edition*, and another between /æ/ and /ə/ in the pronunciation of *addition*. He then quite correctly points out that though both /e/ and /æ/ are in free variation with /ə/ in such dialects, they are not in free variation with each other. (In other words, free variation is in such cases a nontransitive relation.) He seems unaware, however, of the fact that such phenomena have been generally known to linguists for a number of years and presents them as a new discovery on his part. He also claims that such phenomena provide a further argument against the classical phonemic level, which he characterizes as one set up to account for the difference between free variation and contrast. These sorts of examples of nontransitive free variation, however, would quite clearly be set up by followers of classical, not to speak of stratificational, phonemics as morphophonemic in nature. This would be opposed to another type of free variation (subphonemic), which is a transitive relation.

The only other arguments against the distinctiveness principle are set forth in some of the writings of Chomsky. Some were included in his 1964 monograph *Current Issues in Linguistic Theory*, and these were partially repeated and augmented in his 1967 article "Some general properties of phonological rules." Far from being a genuine refutation of the essence of the distinctiveness principle, however, these arguments are only a criticism of certain statements of the principle and seem to be based on a misunderstanding of its intentions.

One of these arguments duplicates one credited to Jakobson (1931). It points out that [y] and [i] may be in complementary distribution in their *phonetic environment*, although the sequences [iy] and [yi] may contrast in the same environment. This apparent paradox is cited as evidence that the distinctiveness principle is invalid. The principle of complementary distribution, a consequence of the distinctiveness principle, has long been understood, however, as applying to environments in the phonemic transcription established. In order to be nondistinctive, that is, a phonetic property must be predictable from the immediate phonemic environment of its *phonemic* realizate. In this example, the nonvocalic nature of [y] can be predicted if we know about the vocalic nature of [i], and the vocalic nature of [i] can be predicted if we know about the nonvocalic nature of [y]. But if we symbolize both as /i/ we would not have either fact available for a phonemic transcription /ii/, and therefore this analysis does not meet the requirement. These criticisms seem to be evidence that the principle was not always stated with sufficient clarity and explicitness. It is one thing to show that a principle is not well stated but quite another to show that it is invalid.

Chomsky also cites examples of sounds which are in complementary distribution, although we would not want to identify them phonemically. This is evidence that complementary distribution alone, even if definable phonemically, is not a *sufficient* condition for phonemic identity (see the examples in Sections 6.1). These criticisms have no bearing on the most essential issue, which is that of biuniqueness.

We have thus disposed of the major arguments directed against the distinctiveness principle and its corollary, the biuniqueness principle. Unless more convincing arguments can be offered by those who advocate the abandonment of this principle, there seems to be no reason to abandon it. It remains to be seen, incidentally, whether the analyses presented here will fit readily into the system of rewrite rules advocated for phonology by Halle, Postal, Chomsky, and others. If they fail to fit, it may be evidence of the inappropriateness of that kind of formalization for human language rather than a basis for further attacks on the distinctiveness principle.

## EXERCISES FOR CHAPTER 6

### Set 6A: Morphonic Analysis

1. The spoken forms corresponding to the printed English words listed below give evidence of, among other things, a particular realization formula which is needed in a description of spoken English. Write this formula.

|  |  |
|---|---|
| hymn | hymnal |
| solemn | solemnize |
| condemn | condemnation |
| damn | damnation |
| autumn | autumnal |

2. The following data is from Monachi, a Utoaztecan language of California. The phoneme /'/, which is always followed by a consonant, is realized articulatorily as fortis articulation and long duration of that consonant. Assuming that all alternations in the data are matters of regular morphophonemics, account for them by writing (**a**) a morphonic representation for each morpheme shown, and (**b**) a list of realization formulas. Make your account as simple as possible.

|  | *my*_____ | *your*_____ | *like a*_____ | *Gloss* |
|---|---|---|---|---|
| 1. | ʔipu'ku | ʔy'pu'ku | pu'kuni'tu | 'dog' |
| 2. | ʔiwono | ʔy'kʷono | wononi'tu | 'basket' |
| 3. | ʔitawa | ʔy'tawa | tawani'tu | 'tooth' |
| 4. | ʔikʷiʔnaaʔa | ʔy'kʷiʔnaaʔa | kʷiʔnaaʔani'tu | 'eagle' |
| 5. | ʔiwupi | ʔy'mupi | mupini'tu | 'nose' |
| 6. | ʔi'sono | ʔy'sono | sononi'tu | 'lungs' |
| 7. | ʔiho'po'poʔo | ʔyho'po'poʔo | ho'po'poʔoni'tu | 'spider' |
| 8. | ʔiʔaa'paʔni | ʔyʔaa'paʔni | ʔaa'paʔnini'tu | 'apple' |
| 9. | ʔinopi | ʔy'nopi | nopini'tu | 'house' |
| 10. | ʔikuna | ʔy'kuna | kunani'tu | 'wood' |
| 11. | ʔi'xaa'nuʔu | ʔy'xaa'nuʔu | xaa'nuʔuni'tu | 'cup' |
| 12. | ʔijuhu | ʔy'tuhu | juhuni'tu | 'fat' |
| 13. | ʔicii'paʔa | ʔy'cii'paʔa | cii'paʔani'tu | 'bird' |

3. Account for the following Latvian data in the same manner as for the data of problem 2 above. The cedilla marks palatalization of consonants.

|  | *Masculine* | *Feminine* | *Gloss* |
|---|---|---|---|
| 1. | laps | laba | 'good' |
| 2. | ti:rs | ti:ra | 'clean' |
| 3. | yauks | yauka | 'nice' |
| 4. | vec | veca | 'old' |
| 5. | klus | klusa | 'silent' |
| 6. | ve:ls | ve:la | 'late' |

|     | *Masculine* | *Feminine* | *Gloss* |
|-----|-------------|------------|---------|
| 7.  | ka:c        | ka:da      | 'some'    |
| 8.  | rupš        | rupa       | 'rough'   |
| 9.  | mas         | maza       | 'small'   |
| 10. | lipi:ks     | lipi:ga    | 'sticky'  |
| 11. | zems        | zema       | 'low'     |
| 12. | garš        | gara       | 'long'    |
| 13. | gaiš        | gaiša      | 'pale'    |
| 14. | spoš        | spoža      | 'bright'  |
| 15. | su:rs       | su:ra      | 'bitter'  |
| 16. | yauns       | yauna      | 'new'     |
| 17. | liels       | liela      | 'big'     |
| 18. | zaļš        | zaļa       | 'green'   |
| 19. | slapš       | slapa      | 'wet'     |
| 20. | tumš        | tumša      | 'dark'    |
| 21. | balc        | balta      | 'white'   |
| 22. | mi:ļš       | mi:ļa      | 'dear'    |
| 23. | pilns       | pilna      | 'full'    |
| 24. | nabaks      | nabaga     | 'poor'    |
| 25. | pareis      | pareiza    | 'correct' |

**4.** In the following problem, morphonic and classical phonemic representations of some English verb forms are provided. Write the realization formulas needed to relate the morphonic representations to the phonemic ones.

|     | *Morphonic* |        | *Phonemic* |        |
|-----|-------------|--------|------------|--------|
| 1.  | sæg         | sægd   | sæg        | sægd   |
| 2.  | wɔk         | wɔkd   | wɔk        | wɔkt   |
| 3.  | sle·p       | sle·pd | sliyp      | slept  |
| 4.  | ke·p        | ke·pd  | kiyp       | kept   |
| 5.  | fe·d        | fe·dd  | fiyd       | fed    |
| 6.  | ste:p       | ste:pd | stiyp      | stiypt |
| 7.  | se:d        | se:dd  | siyd       | siydəd |
| 8.  | me·t        | me·td  | miyt       | met    |
| 9.  | rəb         | rəbd   | rəb        | rəbd   |
| 10. | šed         | šedd   | šed        | šed    |
| 11. | hi·d        | hi·dd  | hayd       | hid    |
| 12. | si:d        | si:dd  | sayd       | saydəd |
| 13. | set         | setd   | set        | set    |
| 14. | put         | putd   | put        | put    |
| 15. | pətt        | pəttd  | pət        | pətəd  |
| 16. | ækt         | æktd   | ækt        | æktəd  |
| 17. | se:t        | se:td  | siyt       | siytəd |

|  | *Morphonic* | | *Phonemic* | |
|---|---|---|---|---|
| 18. | blend | blendd | blend | blendəd |
| 19. | benD | benDd | bend | bent |
| 20. | senD | senDd | send | sent |
| 21. | rent | rentd | rent | rentəd |

**5.** In the following problem, the focus is on vowel and consonant alternations occurring when two words stand in juxtaposition in Sanskrit. The data is not adequate for the internal analysis of the words involved, so you are to **(a)** establish morphonic forms for each *word* and **(b)** state the appropriate realization formulas to account for the data. For purposes of this problem, do not recognize the word boundary ( # ) in formulas.

| | | |
|---|---|---|
| 1. | tatra tiṣṭhati | 'he stands there' |
| 2. | tatrecchati | 'he desires there' |
| 3. | tatropadiśati | 'he teaches there' |
| 4. | tatrāsyati | 'he throws there' |
| 5. | tatrānayati | 'he brings there' |
| 6. | nagare tiṣṭhati | 'he stands in the city' |
| 7. | nagara icchati | 'he desires in the city' |
| 8. | nagara upadiśati | 'he teaches in the city' |
| 9. | nagare syati | 'he throws in the city' |
| 10. | nagara ānayati | 'he brings in the city' |
| 11. | gr̥heṣu tiṣṭhati | 'he stands in houses' |
| 12. | gr̥heṣv icchati | 'he desires in houses' |
| 13. | gr̥heṣūpadiśati | 'he teaches in houses' |
| 14. | gr̥heṣv asyati | 'he throws in houses' |
| 15. | gr̥heṣv ānayati | 'he brings in houses' |
| 16. | agnāu tiṣṭhati | 'he stands in the fire' |
| 17. | agnāv icchati | 'he desires in the fire' |
| 18. | agnāv upadiśati | 'he teaches in the fire' |
| 19. | agnāv asyati | 'he throws in the fire' |
| 20. | agnāv ānayati | 'he brings in the fire' |
| 21. | vāriṇi tiṣṭhati | 'he stands in the water' |
| 22. | vāriṇicchati | 'he desires in the water' |
| 23. | vāriṇy upadiśati | 'he teaches in the water' |
| 24. | vāriṇy asyati | 'he throws in the water' |
| 25. | vāriṇy ānayati | 'he brings in the water' |

## Set 6B: Componential Analysis

**1.** Phonemic charts for three languages are presented opposite. Convert each of these into the form illustrated by Tables 6.7 through 6.10 to represent the componential analysis. Use the markedness principle where appropriate, and select symbols from the list presented in Section 6.4.

## a. Bulgarian

|  | LABIAL | APICAL | PALATAL | DORSAL |  |
|---|---|---|---|---|---|
| STOP | ⎧ p<br>⎨ b | t<br>d |  | k<br>g | VOICELESS<br>VOICED |
| AFFRICATE | ⎧<br>⎨ | c | č<br>ʒ |  | VOICELESS<br>VOICED |
| SPIRANT | ⎧ f<br>⎨ v | s<br>z | š<br>ž | x | VOICELESS<br>VOICED |
| LATERAL |  | l |  |  |  |
| VIBRANT |  | r |  |  |  |
| SEMIVOWEL |  |  | j |  |  |

|  | LABIAL | NONLABIAL |  |  |
|---|---|---|---|---|
|  | m | n |  |  |
|  | FRONT | CENTRAL | BACK-ROUNDED |  |
| VOWEL | ⎧ i<br>⎨ e | ə<br>a | u<br>o | NONLOW<br>LOW |

## b. Hawaiian

|  | LABIAL | APICAL | DORSAL | GLOTTAL |
|---|---|---|---|---|
| STOP | p |  | k | ʔ |
| NASAL | m | n |  |  |
| LATERAL |  | l |  |  |
| SEMIVOWEL | w |  |  | h |

|  | FRONT | CENTRAL | BACK-ROUNDED |  |
|---|---|---|---|---|
| VOWEL | ⎧ i<br>⎨ e |  a | u<br>o | HIGH<br>NONHIGH |

## c. Hungarian

|  | LABIAL | APICAL | PALATAL | DORSAL/GLOTTAL |  |
|---|---|---|---|---|---|
| STOP | ⎧ p<br>⎨ b | t<br>d | t′<br>d′ | k<br>g | VOICELESS<br>VOICED |
| AFFRICATE | ⎧<br>⎨ | c<br>ʒ | č<br>ž |  | VOICELESS<br>VOICED |
| SPIRANT | ⎧ f<br>⎨ v | s<br>z | š<br>ž | h | VOICELESS<br>VOICED |
| LATERAL |  | l |  |  |  |
| VIBRANT |  | r |  |  |  |

|  | LABIAL | NEITHER | PALATAL |
|---|---|---|---|
| SEMIVOWEL | w |  | j |
| NASAL | m | n | ñ |

|  | FRONT-UNROUNDED | FRONT-ROUNDED | BACK-ROUNDED |  |
|---|---|---|---|---|
| VOWEL | i<br>e | ü<br>ö | u<br>o | HIGH<br>MID |
|  |  | a |  | LOW |
| LENGTH | : |  |  |  |

**2.** Write a tentative componential analysis based on the classical phonemic interpretation of some language you have studied or worked on, or can find published material about. Present it in the same form as that used in Tables 6.7 through 6.10 and the solutions to problem 1 above. Suprasegmental material may be excluded from consideration if desired.

**3.** Components may also be utilized in the description of morphophonemic alternation. This may be illustrated by considering the Colloquial Bulgarian data presented below. Referring to the componential analysis established in your answer to problem 1a above, (**a**) establish a *componentially written* morphophonemic shape for each morpheme, and (**b**) state realization formulas accounting for all alternations in the realization of morphophonemic components in terms of phonemic components. If it should be necessary to refer to the absence of stress in any formula, this may be indicated by the symbol ᵕ. It may be taken for granted that stress is phonemic, and its position need not be accounted for in your treatment of this data, though reference to its position may be made in accounting for other phenomena.

Simultaneous environments are indicated by writing the environment elements below the blank line rather than to its right or left. The hypothetical formula listed below illustrates the use of this notational convention:

Lb ‖ __Cl / ∅<br>
      Vo<br>
      Fr

\+ ‖ __/ Fr<br>
      Vo<br>
      Lo

\+ ‖ --- / Lb

| | | | | | |
|---|---|---|---|---|---|
| 1. | glás | 'voice' | 1a. | gləsə́ | 'the voice' |
| 2. | mét | 'honey' | 2a. | midə́ | 'the honey' |
| 3. | mík | 'moment' | 3a. | migə́ | 'the moment' |
| 4. | móst | 'bridge' | 4a. | mustə́ | 'the bridge' |
| 5. | də́p | 'oak' | 5a. | dəbə́ | 'the oak' |
| 6. | kúm | 'godfather' | 6a. | kumə́ | 'the godfather' |
| 7. | və́lk | 'wolf' | 7a. | vəlkə́ | 'the wolf' |
| 8. | rók | 'horn' | 8a. | rugə́ | 'the horn' |
| 9. | mə́š | 'man' | 9a. | məžə́ | 'the man' |
| 10. | dróp | 'lung' | 10a. | drubə́ | 'the lung' |
| 11. | dól | 'ravine' | 11a. | dulə́ | 'the ravine' |
| 12. | lə́x | 'breeze' | 12a. | ləxə́ | 'the breeze' |
| 13. | kljúč | 'key' | 13a. | ključə́ | 'the key' |
| 14. | réf | 'roar' | 14a. | rivə | 'the roar' |
| 15. | kúp | 'heap' | 15a. | kupə́ | 'the heap' |

## Set 6C: Phonotactics

**1.** Consider a consonant system with the following componential analysis:

|     | Lb | Fr |   |    |
|-----|-----|-----|-----|-----|
| Cl  | ⎰p | t | k |    |
|     | ⎱b | d | g | Vd |
| Sp  | f | s | x |    |
| Ns  | m | n | ŋ |    |

   **a.** Draw, in as simple a form as possible, a tactic diagram allowing the combinations of components shown in the chart and no others.

   **b.** Draw a second tactic diagram accounting for everything in 1a above and also for the following relationships of possible consonants to the clause boundary ( # ). This account should likewise be as simple as possible.

     1. All twelve consonants may occur clause-initially (after #).

     2. Any nasal or spirant may occur clause-finally (before #).

     3. Any nasal, spirant, or voiced stop may occur clause-medially.

     4. A clause-medial spirant has determined voicing.

**2.** Consider a consonant system with the following componential analysis:

|     | Lb | Fr |   |    |
|-----|-----|-----|-----|-----|
| Cl  | ⎰p | t | k |    |
|     | ⎱b | d | g | Vd |
| Sp  | f | s | x |    |
| Ns  | m |   | n |    |
| Vb  |   |   | r |    |
| Lt  |   |   | l |    |
|     |   | j |   |    |

   In this language, all simple clusters (single consonants) and the following two- and three-phoneme consonant clusters occur either initially or medially:

pl, pr, pj, bl, br, bj, tl, tr, tj, dl, dr, dj, kl, kr, kj, gl, gr, gj, sp, spl, spr, spj, st, stl, str, stj, sk, skl, skr, skj, sb, sbl, sbr, sbj, sd, sdl, sdr, sdj, sg, sgl, sgr, sgj

The following clusters occur only in medial position:

fp, ft, fk, fb, fd, fg, xp, xt, xk, xb, xd, xg, pm, spm, pn, spn, bm, sbm, bn, sbn, tm, stm, tn, stn, dm, sdm, dn, sdn, km, skm, kn, skn, gm, sgm, gn, sgn

Draw two accounts of the above facts: (**a**) one representing the consonants as indivisible segments (segmental treatment), and (**b**) a second breaking down the consonants into components (componential treatment). Each diagram should have two starting points at the top, one labelled "I" for initial and the other labelled "M" for medial.

3. Consider the following data from Korean. In the notation used, ' and ʰ indicate tenseness and aspiration of the preceding consonants, respectively.

  The morphonic forms of the suffixes are *-ta*, *-ət'a*, *-ko*, and *-ci*, as in the forms given for items 1 and 2. The morphonic forms of the stems may be considered representable in the same form as the past-tense stems of column two, except for item 13, which should be regarded as ending in a special morphon, $^{MN}/T/$.

| | *to*____ | ____*(Past)* | ____*and whether one*____*s* | | *Gloss* |
|---|---|---|---|---|---|
| 1. | ipta | ipət'a | ipko | ipci | 'wear' |
| 2. | nopta | nopʰət'a | nopko | nopci | 'be high' |
| 3. | tat'a | tatət'a | tak'o | tac'i | 'close' |
| 4. | kat'a | katʰət'a | kak'o | kac'i | 'be alike' |
| 5. | wut'a | wusət'a | wuk'o | wuc'i | 'laugh' |
| 6. | it'a | is'ət'a | ik'o | ic'i | 'exist' |
| 7. | cʰat'a | cʰacət'a | cʰak'o | cʰac'i | 'find' |
| 8. | cot'a | cocʰət'a | cok'o | coc'i | 'follow' |
| 9. | mekta | mekət'a | mek'o | mekci | 'eat' |
| 10. | takta | tak'ət'a | tak'o | takci | 'polish' |
| 11. | iltʰa | ilhət'a | ilkʰo | ilcʰi | 'lose' |
| 12. | notʰa | nohət'a | nokʰo | nocʰi | 'put' |
| 13. | cĭt'a | cĭət'a | cĭk'o | cĭc'i | 'build' |
| 14. | təpta | təwət'a | təpko | təpci | 'be warm' |
| 15. | kət'a | kələt'a | kək'o | kəc'i | 'walk' |

a. Assuming the suggested morphonic analysis, write realization formulas to account for the realization of the various morphons.

b. The alternate realizations dealt with in 3a above all have relation to the permissible medial consonants and consonant clusters. Draw a componential tactics accounting for these possibilities and no others. Assume the following componential analysis:

| | | Lb | Ap | Fr | | |
|---|---|---|---|---|---|---|
| Cl | $\Big\{$ | p | t | c | k | |
| | | p' | t' | c' | k' | Ts |
| | | pʰ | tʰ | cʰ | kʰ | As |
| Sp | $\Big\{$ | | s | | | |
| | | | s' | | | Ts |
| | | | | | h | As |
| | | w | l | | | |

## Set 6D: Integrated Treatments

1. Consider each alternation in the following problems from Set 6A from the point of view of a treatment in a phonemic stratal system of the type outlined in Section 6.6. How would the conditioning of each one be handled? Is it better treated above the tactics or below it?

   a. Problem 1 (English)
   b. Problem 2 (Monachi)
   c. Problem 3 (Latvian)
   d. Problem 4 (English)

2. Draw a diagram which accounts for all the alternation phenomena in problem 3 of Set 6B (Bulgarian), using a phonotactics and alternation pattern(s). Omit details concerning consonants and consonant clusters.

3. The voiceless-voiced alternation exemplified by *life/lives*, *leaf/leaves*, and so on, is paralleled in some morphemes which end in other spirants, as in *house* /haws/ versus *houses* /hawzəz/, *wreath* /riyθ/ versus *wreaths* /riyðz/, *path* /pæθ/ versus *paths* /pæðz/, and *mouth* /mawθ/ versus *mouths* /mawðz/. What do these facts suggest about the treatment of these alternations in a stratificational phonology? Attempt to construct an account of them, bearing in mind that the voiced realization of the spirant occurs in the plural forms but not in the possessives, such as *house's* and *path's*. Also recall that there are nouns with constant /f/ (*fife*), constant /v/ (*hive*), constant /s/ (*pass*), constant /z/ (*cheese*), constant /θ/ (*myth*), and constant /ð/ (*lathe*).

   How might the verbal derivatives *house* /hawz/, *mouthe* /mawð/, and *wreathe* /riyð/ be treated in harmony with the above solution?

4. Vowel harmony, in its most usual form, is a situation in which the vowels within a stated domain, frequently coinciding with the phonological word, must agree with respect to one or more phonetic properties. The following hypothetical data gives an example of vowel harmony involving labiality (rounding):

| | | | | | |
|---|---|---|---|---|---|
| kutö | 'dog' | kutölɔ | 'dogs' | kutönü | 'my dog' |
| digɨ | 'cat' | digilæ | 'cats' | digini | 'my cat' |
| vopü | 'cow' | vopülɔ | 'cows' | vopünü | 'my cow' |
| bakə | 'horse' | bakəlæ | 'horses' | bakəni | 'my horse' |
| zɔdɔ | 'goat' | zɔdɔlɔ | 'goats' | zɔdɔnü | 'my goat' |
| gesæ | 'sheep' | gesælæ | 'sheep' | gesæni | 'my sheep' |

   If the whole language shows the phenomena exhibited in the above data, we can conclude that the property of vowel rounding or its absence is selected only once for the phonological word as a whole, so that it will be present on every vowel of such a word or absent on every vowel. This notion can be captured in a stratificational phonology by regarding the rounding as a property of the word as a whole. Its realization on each individual vowel would be specified in the phonetic system. Under such an interpretation, there would be only six distinct vowel segments instead of the twelve which would have to be recognized in a classical phonemic analysis, which is exemplified by the above transcription. Thus while 'sheep (plural)' would be phonemically /gesælæ/ as above, 'my dog' would be

$$\frac{R}{k\dot{i}teni,}$$

where R symbolizes the property of rounding. In terms of a trace from the phonotactics, the latter word can be represented as follows:

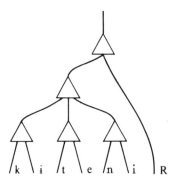

Some African languages exhibit a harmony involving the relative openness of vowels, as illustrated by the following data from the West African language Kasem:*

| | | | |
|---|---|---|---|
| fələ | 'white person' | fəli | 'white people' |
| kuə | 'bone' | kui | 'bones' |
| fana | 'knife' | fanɪ | 'knives' |
| tʊa | 'bee' | tʊɪ | 'bees' |
| lidə | 'medicine' | lidi | 'medicines' |
| tulə | 'granary' | tuli | 'granaries' |
| kala | 'type of pot' | kalɪ | 'pots' |
| bʊda | 'fishnet' | bʊdɪ | 'fishnets' |

This representation shows six distinct vowels, but if we abstract vowel openness as a property of the word, we can represent all the distinctions in terms of three vowels /i u ə/, with /ɪ ʊ a/ being these same three with the simultaneous property OP (openness). The traces from the phonotactics for 'type of pot' and 'fishnets' would therefore be

*Adapted from Problem 171 of Merrifield et al., *Laboratory Manual for Morphology and Syntax* (Santa Ana, Calif.: Summer Institute of Linguistics, 1967), p. 183.

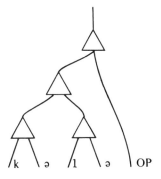 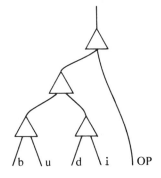

In the morphemic sign pattern, the abstracted harmonizing properties of such languages may be regarded as belonging with the root morpheme, with all affixes unmarked for them. Thus in the hypothetical language, the root meaning 'dog' would be represented as at the left, while the Kasem root meaning 'fishnet' would be represented as at right:

 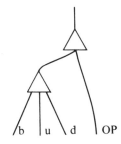

The phonotactics would then realize such properties as constituents of the phonological word as a whole, which means that they would apply to affixes as well as to roots. The phonetic system would then be called upon to specify that these phonetic properties are realized on each individual vowel. In many instances, the realizations of some or all consonants will likewise be affected by harmony. In the more traditional analyses, however, this effect is regarded as a subphonemic one, conditioned by the vowel qualities.

Consider the following Turkish data in the light of these general principles and answer the questions presented below.

| | | | |
|---|---|---|---|
| 1. | bildim 'I knew' | 3. | geldim 'I came' |
| 1a. | bildiler 'they knew' | 3a. | geldiler 'they came' |
| 1b. | bilmedim 'I did not know' | 3b. | gelmedim 'I did not come' |
| 1c. | bilmediler 'they did not know' | 3c. | gelmediler 'they did not come' |
| | | | |
| 2. | tašidim 'I carried' | 4. | kaldim 'I stayed' |
| 2a. | tašidilar 'they carried' | 4a. | kaldilar 'they stayed' |
| 2b. | tašimadim 'I did not carry' | 4b. | kalmadim 'I did not stay' |
| 2c. | tašimadilar 'they did not carry' | 4c. | kalmadilar 'they did not stay' |

| 5. | vürüdüm | 'I walked' | | 7. | gördüm | 'I saw' |
|---|---|---|---|---|---|---|
| 5a. | vürüdüler | 'they walked' | | 7a. | gördüler | 'they saw' |
| 5b. | vürümedim | 'I did not walk' | | 7b. | görmedim | 'I did not see' |
| 5c. | vürümediler | 'they did not walk' | | 7c. | görmediler | 'they did not see' |
| 6. | buldum | 'I found' | | 8. | sordum | 'I asked' |
| 6a. | buldular | 'they found' | | 8a. | sordular | 'they asked' |
| 6b. | bulmadim | 'I did not find' | | 8b. | sormadim | 'I did not ask' |
| 6c. | bulmadilar | 'they did not find' | | 8c. | sormadilar | 'they did not ask' |

**a.** Give an informal description of the harmony phenomena exhibited by the data, including both rounding and fronting harmony.

**b.** What special problem arises in treating the harmony in this data by the method outlined for the simpler cases illustrated above? How might this problem be solved in the specification of the realization of morphonic rounding and fronting on the phonemic stratum? Assume that the morphonic treatment will be the same as that suggested for the simpler data, but note that morpheme boundaries which are relevant in the phonology may be marked by junctures assigned in the morphology.

# 7

# *Stratificational Theory and Other Views of Language*

## 7.1  *American Structural Trends*

To the extent possible, the preceding chapters have presented stratificational theory on its own terms. Comparison with other contemporary and precontemporary views of linguistic structure has been only occasional and unsystematic. It is the purpose of this chapter to attempt a more detailed comparison of the stratificational view with the outlook of several other linguistic theories. Certain of these views have, in fact, made fundamental contributions to what is now considered to be the stratificational viewpoint.

The most prominent currents of what has become known as American structuralism may be grouped under the rubric of Bloomfieldian and Neo-Bloomfieldian linguistics. The latter term is now preferable to the frequently used "Post-Bloomfieldian," since "Post" implies simply after Bloomfield, which would properly include any view which came on the scene after Bloomfield's time. Neo-Bloomfieldian, on the other hand, refers more specifically to linguists who operated under the close influence of Bloomfield's work and sought to build upon it and improve it. In many ways stratificational linguistics can be seen as an outgrowth of the Neo-Bloomfieldian trend. At the very least, this view can be said to form one of the more essential ingredients of stratificationalism.

Of the Neo-Bloomfieldian ideas which have entered into stratificational thinking, perhaps the greatest number are to be found in the work of Charles Hockett. In several works, in fact, ranging from his *Manual of Phonology*  251

(1955) to his important 1961 article "Linguistic elements and their relations," Hockett maintained an explicitly stratified view of language, albeit with only two strata.

Hockett's view was far more stratificational in its essence than some earlier views, such as those of Bloomfield himself and his more immediate followers. Bloomfield's work, for example, showed a considerable degree of inconsistency regarding the relationships of the two most fundamental linguistic entities of his model: the phoneme and the morpheme. In his *Language* (1933), he at one point maintained that a morpheme consists of phonemes, while in another portion of the same chapter he asserted that a morpheme can have alternants, which are by definition phonemically different. Nowhere in the book did he attempt to resolve the conflict between these two statements. By the mid-1940's the situation had become clarified to an extent, in that the prevailing view saw the morpheme as a class of phonemic sequences, its allomorphs. This view still did not make a true stratal distinction between morphemes and phonemes, however.

Hockett, on the other hand, gave explicit recognition to the existence of two strata in asserting that the arrangements characteristic of the phonology are essentially independent of those of the grammar. This assertion had the effect of recognizing two tactic patterns. Hockett further realized that the relationship between phonemes and morphemes is neither one of composition nor of class membership, but a more complex relationship, which he termed "is programmed into." In his 1961 article, he considered evidence for recognizing what would amount to a morphophonemic stratum intermediate between the classical morphemic and phonemic, though he rejected it in favor of a bistratal view.

Before he wrote his monograph *Language, Mathematics, and Linguistics* (1966), Hockett became familiar with Lamb's more extensively stratificational views and was for a time attracted to them. The work referred to gives evidence of this interest in both the sections on phonology and those on semology. More recently, however, Hockett has reverted to what might be described as a Paleo-Bloomfieldian view, condemning both transformationalism and stratificationalism. This attitude is reflected in his monograph *The State of the Art* (1968b) and in his review of Lamb's *Outline of Stratificational Grammar* (1968a). In taking this stance, he rejected a great deal of his own earlier work, including in particular all reference to a system of more than one stratum. Despite this self-denunciation, however, stratificational theory owes a great deal to Hockett's thinking, as embodied in a number of significant works dating from 1947 ("Problems of morphemic analysis," which introduced the concepts of portmanteau and empty morphs and made explicit reference to considerations of tactic simplicity) to 1966.

Hockett went further than any of the other prominent Neo-Bloomfieldian linguists to dispel the essentially monostratal view held by Bloomfield himself. More than anything else, this monostratal view was a consequence of the strong insistence on the part of Bloomfield and his followers that linguistic structure is somehow contained in the actual speech signal. They tended to view language as a system in the speech itself rather than in the minds of the speakers. They saw language as the concrete behavior embodied in speech habits and sought to describe this. The result of this attitude was a tendency to mistrust abstraction and a concomitant tendency to seek every linguistic unit in speech itself. Bloomfield, writing before acoustic phonetics had advanced beyond its rather primitive beginnings, expressed a belief that the phoneme would eventually be discovered in the speech signal itself. Of course this discovery has never come to pass, and acoustic phoneticians have found the relation between their measurements of the speech signal and what speakers say and perceive to be a very complicated one indeed. The notions that the phoneme is contained in speech and that the morpheme is definable in terms of phonemes lent comfort to the idea that linguistic structure exists in speech.

Originally Bloomfield's attitude was a healthy reaction to certain extreme practices of more traditional grammarians, who frequently resorted to wildly speculative assertions about the likes and dislikes of speakers to explain linguistic facts. One might have heard, for example, that speakers of some language abhor certain types of consonant clusters as an explanation of the fact that the morphophonemics of the language filters out all potential occurrences of such clusters. Though Bloomfield was right in rejecting this speculative brand of "mentalism," his attitude had the unfortunate side effect of leading to a neglect of the distinction between language as an underlying system and speech as a concrete manifestation. The tendency to reject abstraction was one consequence of this neglect.

Another prominent Neo-Bloomfieldian who approached a stratificational interpretation of certain morphological phenomena was George Trager. In a 1955 article, "French verb inflection," he held that some morphemes had different allomorphs which were in turn composed of morphophonemes with their own phonemic realizations. These allomorphs were thus analogous to what we have termed morphemic signs, with the morphophonemes composing them corresponding to morphons. Trager's system was not fully stratified, however, since other morphemes were said to be composed directly of morphophonemes—this treatment was given to all morphemes whose alternants could be subsumed under a single morphophonemic shape. Trager and Henry Lee Smith eventually developed their own particular version of Neo-Bloomfieldian theory, which depended heavily on a system of levels showing considerable similarity to the stratificational view. Each of these levels was said to have its own specification of arrangements, similar to a stratificational tactics. An important difference between stratificational levels and those of Trager and Smith (as well as the often less explicit practice of many of the other Neo-Bloomfieldians) was that the levels were seen by them as stepping stones to the full description of the language. That is, these linguists insisted that in theory each lower level should be fully described before the one above it, and the treatment of any given level was based upon the description of the one immediately below it. No such procedural orientation is required by stratificational theory, of course, and the separation of levels or strata is required only in the description.

Perhaps the fullest use of a complete separation of levels is seen in the work of Archibald Hill, particularly his 1958 text *Introduction to Linguistic Structures*. This book set forth the view, for example, that every phonemic juncture must necessarily mark a morpheme boundary, regardless of countervening evidence in the morphology *per se*. It thus insisted that there was a morpheme boundary before the /t/ in *at all* when it was pronounced /ə+tɔ́l/, and that *winter* may be one morpheme for a speaker from Michigan but it is two morphemes for a speaker from New York who says /wín+tər/ with an open juncture. Hill's views showed considerable influence from those of Trager and Smith.

Most of the units posited on various levels by Neo-Bloomfieldian linguists have found their way into stratificational theory. In no case, however, are these units primitives in the theory. Rather they are treated as complexes of relationships. Stratificational theory also shares with the majority of Neo-Bloomfieldians the belief that process statements are inappropriate in synchronic linguistics. But stratificational linguistics has shown that significant generalizations do not have to be missed because of the disallowance of process description. Nor does a stratified system have to abandon the notion of the infinite generative power of a finite linguistic system as a consequence of its failure to employ process. In the usual Neo-Bloomfieldian framework it was much more difficult to come to grips with these problems.

In summary, the most important debt owed by stratificational linguists to the views of the Neo-Bloomfieldians was the theory of levels. Stratificationalists, however, have refined this view and clarified the relationships among the levels, and at the same time have abandoned the idea that linguistic analysis ought to proceed strictly from one level to another. Another important common point shared by the two groups is the dislike for synchronic process, if we keep in mind that stratificational theory has found a way to provide for both maximum generalization and infinite generative power without process.

A second American structural trend which shows important resemblances to stratificational theory is tagmemics. Like Neo-Bloomfieldianism, tagmemics owes a great deal of its foundation to the work of Bloomfield. It has developed in its own directions, however, and unlike the Neo-Bloomfieldian views proper, it has continued to develop and change to the present time and still has adherents in considerable numbers.

Though stratificational theory and tagmemics have a number of points in common, the coincidence of the two is due more to parallel development than to influence, since tagmemics did not exercise a great deal of influence on Lamb's thinking during the years of his initial development of the theory.

An essential feature of the tagmemic model of language is the positing of three hierarchically organized components of linguistic structure, which are roughly analogous to stratal systems. These are known as the *grammatical, phonological,* and *lexical* hierarchies. In Kenneth Pike's version of the theory, the *tagmeme,* from which the whole theory takes its name, is a correlation of grammatical function with class of "fillers" or manifestations; the tagmeme is the basic unit of the grammatical hierarchy. The other two hierarchies have the *phoneme* and *morpheme,* respectively, as their basic units. These units are generally defined in accordance with the Bloomfieldian tradition. The hierarchical organization of each of these components is manifested in a series of so-called levels. These correspond to what Lamb, following Halliday's terminology, has called ranks.

An alternate interpretation of tagmemic theory has been put forward by Robert Longacre. In his view, the morpheme is at the base of the grammatical hierarchy, while the lexical hierarchy has a *lexeme.* Tagmemes are then posited to provide for a tactics—in effect—for each of the hierarchies, though the grammatical tagmemes, corresponding to Pike's tagmemes, are said to be the most important. Longacre's view is more directly comparable with stratificational theory than is Pike's, the lexical hierarchy comparing with the sememic stratal system as outlined in this book, the grammatical hierarchy corresponding to the lexemic and morphemic stratal systems, and the phonological hierarchy corresponding, perhaps less exactly, to the phonemic stratal system. The interrelation of the hierarchies in tagmemics, however, is viewed in quite a different way than that of the stratificational stratal systems. Specifically, the structure defined by each hierarchy is taken to be simultaneously reflected in the data, and no realizational priority is given to any of the three. Units of the phonological hierarchy, for example, are not said to realize grammatical units, nor are the grammatical units said to realize units of the lexical hierarchy. All three types of organization are simply said to be simultaneously present as modes of language as a whole. If some such stratal priority were recognized, tagmemics would come much closer to stratificational theory.

Though tagmemics shares with stratificational theory the notion of multiple tactic patterns (particularly Longacre's version), it employs no formal means to relate the units of one hierarchy to those of another. As a result, statements about the relations pertaining across hierarchies are generally informal, incompletely integrated into the theory. Morphophonemics, for example, is considered a relationship between the phonological hierarchy and the lexical hierarchy (for Pike) or the grammatical hierarchy (for Longacre). Though morphophonemic facts are often described in tagmemic descriptions, no systematic framework has yet been provided within tagmemic theory itself for their description. No version of tagmemic theory, in fact, even provides an equivalent of the classical morphophoneme (the stratificational morphon).

A very important feature of tagmemics which is shared by stratificational theory is an insistence upon the linguistic relevance of suprasentence structures. Tagmemicists have been among the pioneers in the linguistic investigation of such phenomena, and many of their findings will undoubtedly prove to be accommodable in a stratificational framework as well.

On the issue of discovery procedures, tagmemicists have generally steered a middle course between those Neo-Bloomfieldians who equated linguistic theory with discovery procedure and the critics who have disdained all concern with discovery procedures. On the one hand, tagmemicists have in great part been either practicing field linguists or teachers of future field linguists, and in many cases both. With these interests, a concern with practical analysis seemed natural to them. At the same time, they were able to recognize from their own practical experience that the mechanical data-sorting procedures once proposed by Zellig Harris, among others, were not going to work. Nor could they have enthusiasm for the procedures advocated by such other Neo-Bloomfieldians as Trager and Hill, who maintained that each successive level had to be analyzed on the basis of an analysis of the level below it. They felt that the practical linguist must recognize that the various aspects of language —such as phonology, morphology, syntax, and vocabulary—are interrelated, and they sought to build this notion into their theory as well. The view they evolved is one which does not shy away from the description of discovery procedures. The procedures described are not mechanical operations, however; they are matters of hypothesis and verification on a trial-and-error basis. In these procedures, one is not confined to working within one hierarchy at a time, but may consider together aspects of as many of the different hierarchies as necessary. In short, tagmemics has sought to relate theory closely to analytical procedure, but the procedure involved has been practical rather than theoretical. In comparison, stratificationalists have not sought to build their theory around any analytical procedure, but have recognized that analytical procedure, though separate from theory, is nevertheless a legitimate concern of linguists.

Tagmemics has devoted less attention than stratificational linguistics to the relation of linguistic models to the process of communication, the role of language in relating conceptual correlations to phonic correlations. It does emphasize, however, the relation of expression ("form") to content ("meaning") in all aspects of language, concerning every one of the hierarchies.

In the overall view, the most significant difference between stratificational theory and tagmemics lies in their differing attitudes toward the interrelation of the major portions of linguistic structure. The stratificational view sees these portions as stratal systems, organized among themselves in a hierarchy intervening between phonic and conceptual correlations. The tagmemic view, in contrast, sees them as three aspects of linguistic structure each with a hierarchical structure (of ranks) within itself, but without hierarchical arrangement among themselves. Another fundamental difference, not unrelated to this one, has to do with the view of the two theories toward form and substance. Like the Neo-Bloomfieldians, tagmemicists have generally viewed language in terms of substance, though they have given greater attention to the content substance (meaning) than most Neo-Bloomfieldians. They have never given form the essential place it has in stratificational linguistics.

## 7.2  *European Schools*

Of the major European schools of linguistics which invite comparison with stratificational theory, perhaps the most closely related is the Glossematic or Copenhagen School, founded by Louis Hjelmslev. As was noted in Section 1.5, Hjelmslev clarified the relation of linguistic form, substance, and purport. He also emphasized the relational nature of language, which he viewed as a system connecting content to expression. His *content substance* corresponds essentially to the conceptual correlations of stratificational theory, while his *expression substance* corresponds to phonic correlations and graphic correlations.

Hjelmslev's notion that linguistic form consists solely of relationships was perhaps his most fundamental point in common with stratificational linguistics. At the same time, it has been one of the parts of his theory least understood by linguists of different persuasions. As should now be clear, to insist that linguistic form consists solely of relationships is not to completely divorce linguistic form from substance. Any theory of linguistic structure, being applied to language, must take both content substance and expression substance into account in determining the form of language. But the consideration of substance does not make it necessary to include substantive entities within the form, as has been done in both item-and-arrangement and item-and-process linguistics, to the extent that they recognized the form-substance distinction at all. The substance is only a reflection, or to use Hjelmslev's analogy quoted earlier, the shadow, of the unobservable form, which constitutes the linguistic knowledge of the speaker of each particular language.

Another of Hjelmslev's principles which may help to further clarify the above point is the notion of the arbitrariness and appropriateness of linguistic theory. By *arbitrariness*, Hjelmslev meant that such a theory as he proposed would have its own postulated form and would be independent of observed elements. By *appropriateness*, he meant that a linguistic theory must also be capable of providing a reasonable account of its data—in this case the substance of the language which it seeks to describe. It is important to remember that arbitrariness and appropriateness go together. The requirement of arbitrariness is essentially an attempt to guarantee that a linguistic theory will seek to deal with form rather than merely segmenting and classifying substance. The concomitant requirement of appropriateness assures that the theory will not be completely "arbitrary" in the conventional sense. That is, it will not be completely unrelatable to the linguistic data for which it is trying to account.

Another important requirement placed upon a linguistic description by Hjelmslev is that it provide an account of a given language which is "as simple as possible." By such a requirement, Hjelmslev meant that as little explicit specification as possible should be put into the account of a linguistic system. This simplicity is restricted, of course, by the concomitant requirements of exhaustiveness and self-consistency, which take precedence over simplicity. Any such simplicity principle demands that the theory provide a measure of the relative simplicity of accounts of the same data, which are equally exhaustive and self-consistent. Modern stratificational theory has, it should be clear, continually addressed itself to this question, striving to provide a general measure of simplicity which reflects notions of relative simplicity generally accepted by linguists and which can be extended to the more complicated cases in which intuition provides no clear guide. This measure is subject to further revision as research and theoretical advances make it necessary.

Hjelmslev also recognized the stratification of the linguistic system. Like other predecessors of the modern theory, however, he postulated less stratification than has been found necessary by more recent research. Hjelmslev's strata were basically the planes of content and of expression, viewed in their formal aspects. Thus expression form was a stratum encompassing phonological phenomena, while content form was a second stratum encompassing grammatical and semological phenomena. In more detailed treatments, Hjelmslev made it clear that it is necessary to postulate two distinct realizational levels within each of these planes. The two levels of each are termed "ideal" and "actualized." This means a total of four significant structural levels as shown in Figure 7.1.

While *actualized content form* can be compared to the morphemic stratum, *ideal content form* can be seen as a conflation of the phenomena of higher strata. The distinction may also be compared to the transformational dichotomy of "deep" and "surface" structure. Within the expression plane, *ideal expression form* is analogous to the classical morphophonemic or the stratificational morphonic level, while the level of *actualized expression form* corresponds to that of classical phonemics.

Like Lamb, Hjelmslev insisted that linguistic form consists entirely of

Ideal content form

CONTENT PLANE

Actualized content form

----------------------------------------------

Ideal expression form

EXPRESSION PLANE

Actualized expression form

**Figure 7.1   Strata in Hjelmslev's System**

relationships. The particular types of relationships which he postulated, how-ever, were different from those posited by Lamb. Hjelmslev's basic relation-ships were dependences, which within contemporary stratificational theory could be broken down into patterns of the more fundamental AND and OR relationships. Hjelmslev himself suggested part of this breakdown when he classified certain of his fundamental dependences into BOTH-AND (syntagmatic) and EITHER-OR (paradigmatic) types. But Lamb has extended this distinction from a classificatory dichotomy to a pair of fundamental linguistic relation-ships. He has in this way been able to significantly reduce the rather large inventory of basic relationships postulated by Hjelmslev.

Several of the most fundamental principles attributed here to Hjelmslev can be traced back further to Ferdinand de Saussure. These include the notion that the linguistic system is a form and not a substance, the notion of the planes of content and expression, and the relational nature of linguistic form. Saussure's ideas, in fact, contributed to several European schools which followed him, including the Copenhagen School of Hjelmslev, the Prague School, and the Geneva School, of which he himself is recognized as the founder. The Geneva School was a more or less direct continuation of the principles laid down by Saussure's famous *Cours de linguistique générale* (1916), while the other schools accepted some of Saussure's principles and rejected or modified others.

The Prague School, for example, emphatically rejected the Saussurian notion that the linguistic system is irrelevant to linguistic change, and that such change can therefore be treated only in an atomistic manner such as that of the Neo-Grammarians. Like the Copenhagen School, it also rejected the Saussur-ian notion that the sentence is not part of the linguistic system (*la langue*) but only part of speech (*la parole*). Both the Prague and Copenhagen schools, in common with contemporary stratificational theory, extended the purview of linguistic theory beyond the confines of the sentence, to encompass the paragraph and even the text as a whole.

The Prague School's most outstanding contributions lie in the realm of phonology. This is understandable, since the Prague School flourished in the 1930's, when phonology was the major concern of American as well as European linguists. In particular, the Praguians, under the leadership of N. S. Trubetzkoy and Roman Jakobson, did some of the earliest work in the area of phonological componency (albeit within a feature theory framework in the terms of Section 6.4). As part of a view which gives careful attention to componency, however, they developed the notion of phonological suspension ("neutralization"), as discussed in Sections 6.1 and 6.7. As was shown there, this principle may readily be incorporated into stratificational theory, leading to a more complete adherence to the distinctiveness principle.

Another important European linguistic view with significant affinities to stratificational theory is the theory developed by the British linguists J. R.

Firth and later M. A. K. Halliday. Although Firth had interests in all aspects of language, he and his immediate followers are best known for their work on phonology, particularly for the development of so-called *prosodic phonology*. As a follower of Firth, Halliday refined his view of language into a comprehensive theory. This view has become known as *systemic grammar*. It has also sometimes been termed "scale and category" grammar, but Halliday himself prefers the other designation. In phonology, Halliday has generally accepted Firth's prosodic view, and his most original work has come in the areas of grammar and semology.

A fundamental point of contact between systemic grammar and stratificational theory is the recognition by each of the autonomy of levels within the linguistic system. Basically, Halliday recognizes semantic, grammatical, and phonological levels equivalent to strata, though he uses different terms for them. It is of fundamental importance to both theories that each level (stratum) be set up so as to be autonomous in the description. The description of one level (stratum), that is, does not need to refer to the categories appropriate to other levels, though statements relating the categories of one level to those of the other are necessary. This **descriptive autonomy**, however, does not imply **analytical autonomy**, wherein the definition of a level and its categories is independent of the categories of adjacent levels. Many Neo-Bloomfieldians, for example, insisted on such analytical autonomy, so that morphological description could not begin until phonological description was completed, and so on. In contrast, stratificational and systemic grammar insist that the determination of the various levels and their appropriate categories are interdependent. The autonomy of the levels merely means that each will be ultimately describable on its own terms.

A further distinction which Halliday introduced in his treatment of grammatical phenomena has no exact correspondence in the stratificational system. This is the distinction between what he terms "system" and "structure." In the model which Halliday has used for the description of grammatical phenomena, the *system* is characterized as a series of available choices allowed by the language. Each language is characterized as having a number of such systems, which interlock to form a *system network*. This network thus corresponds to the paradigmatic relations of the language. The *structures*, on the other hand, deal with syntagmatic relations, and each available choice in the system network is characterized as being realized by a particular selection from among the structures. The structures are also organized along a scale of rank (size level). Lamb has borrowed the term "rank" from Halliday to distinguish it from other types of levels. Different systemic choices may be realized at different ranks.

This system-structure dichotomy partly corresponds to stratal differences within the stratificational model. The sememic stratum, for example, deals with abstract categories reminiscent of those found in systemic networks. The lexemic stratum, on the other hand, defines constructions more reminiscent of Halliday's structures. This correspondence is far from exact, since a stratificational system must have the equivalents of both systems and structures on each of its strata, though the systems of the lower strata are more rudimentary because of the control which the upper stratum exercises on those below. But to some extent both systems and structures must be interwoven as part of a single tactics.

Perhaps a closer translation of the systemic view into stratificational terms would use a model with two separate tactic patterns on a single stratum. One of these patterns would define the systemic choices, the other the available structures. These two tactic patterns would be arranged, however, so that the choices of structures would be controlled by corresponding systemic choices. But even short of such a complete modification of the structure of a stratal system, it may be possible to incorporate various aspects of the very penetrating analyses produced by Halliday (particularly with reference to English) into a stratificational framework.

Prosodic phonology differs from phonemic phonology in several ways. Perhaps the most fundamental of these is that instead of resolving phonological structures into one type of unit, the phoneme, the practitioners of prosodic phonology have recognized two fundamental types of phonological entities: phonematic units and prosodies. A *phonematic unit* is essentially a single segment, while a *prosody* is an abstracted property which has a potential domain larger than a single segment: a cluster, syllable, phonological word, or larger unit. Although the followers of prosodic phonology have tended to place great emphasis on this difference, it is perhaps of less fundamental significance than they have taken it to be. Prosodic practices, for example, were not completely unknown in Neo-Bloomfieldian phonology for the treatment of certain phenomena such as stress, tone, and intonation. It was a common practice to recognize that the distribution of these phenomena made it extremely desirable to recognize them as, in effect, prosodic units—that is, suprasegmental phonemes. What prosodic phonology does beyond this is to recognize that similarly distributed phenomena, whatever the nature of their phonetic realization, should be treated in the same way. In Neo-Bloomfieldian practice, in other words, there was an implicit requirement that only certain kinds of phenomena could be treated prosodically. Prosodic phonology, on the other hand, is free from such a constraint.

Prosodic treatments have been found extremely useful, for example, in the treatment of vowel harmony in various languages. The harmonic properties may be abstracted as prosodies of the phonological word (see exercise 4 of Set 6D). Similarly, in addition to stress and tone, certain phonological phenomena may be seen as having a domain of a single syllable. In a certain stage of Old Russian, for example, all syllables contained either a palatalized onset followed by a front vowel or a nonpalatalized onset followed by a nonfront vowel. A conventional phonemic analysis could recognize either a distinction of palatalized versus nonpalatalized consonants or one of front versus back vowels. It is clearly not necessary to recognize both distinctions, and either one could at this period be regarded as dependent on the other. Traditionally, the vocalic distinction has been taken to be phonemic, and the consonantal one has been regarded as a purely phonetic difference dependent on the following vowel. Such an interpretation has been preferred over one attributing the distinction to the consonants because it would add fewer phonemes to the inventory. A prosodic interpretation, however, would allow a still further reduction in the number of distinct entities by the recognition of a fronting prosody F on those syllables having fronted articulation. Table 7.1 shows the possibilities for such an interpretation with a few examples.

### Table 7.1   Prosodic Analysis of Old Russian Forms

| Phonetic Shape | Traditional Analysis | Prosodic Analysis | Gloss |
|---|---|---|---|
| lŭbŭ | lŭbŭ | lŭbŭ | 'forehead' |
| ɟĭṇĭ | dĭnĭ | $\overset{\text{F F}}{\underline{\text{dŭnŭ}}}$ | 'day' |
| dymŭ | dymŭ | dymŭ | 'smoke' |
| ļistŭ | listŭ | $\overset{\text{F}}{\underline{\text{lystŭ}}}$ | 'leaf' |
| puțĭ | putĭ | $\overset{\text{F}}{\underline{\text{putŭ}}}$ | 'road' |
| žŭkŭ | gükŭ | $\overset{\text{F}}{\underline{\text{gukŭ}}}$ | 'bug' |
| kŏşțĭ | kŏstĭ | $\overset{\text{F}}{\underline{\text{kŏstŭ}}}$ | 'bone' |
| ļĕsŭ | lĕsŭ | $\overset{\text{F}}{\underline{\text{lŏsŭ}}}$ | 'forest' |
| mostŭ | mostŭ | mostŭ | 'bridge' |
| şelo | selo | $\overset{\text{F}}{\underline{\text{solo}}}$ | 'village' |
| daṃĭ | damĭ | $\overset{\text{F}}{\underline{\text{damŭ}}}$ | 'I shall give' |
| ҏæțĭ | pætĭ | $\overset{\text{F F}}{\underline{\text{patŭ}}}$ | 'five' |

The step from allowing prosodic analyses for stress, tone, and intonation to permitting them for other similarly distributed phenomena is a small one within a theory which recognizes that it is dealing with form rather than substance. In such a theory, *a priori* substance-based constraints like the one implicit in the restricted use of suprasegmental phonemes in the practice of many Neo-Bloomfieldians clearly have no place. To the extent that they enhance the simplicity of the overall treatment, therefore, prosodic analyses may be appropriate in stratificational theory.

It can therefore be seen that in phonology as well as in grammar the views of Firth, Halliday, and their followers offer valuable insights which may be incorporated into stratificational theory. Certain fundamental similarities of outlook have further enhanced cooperation between practitioners of stratificational and systemic theories.

## 7.3   *Transformational Linguistics*

The number and significance of its practitioners alone would make a consideration of transformational linguistics imperative in any survey of contemporary linguistic theories. It also happens that transformational theory has made significant contributions to general linguistic theory, contributions which have been accepted by stratificationalists.

Some of the areas in which transformational linguistics has marked a distinct advance have been mentioned briefly in Section 1.5. These areas will be reviewed here and amplified. From the works of Zellig Harris it can be seen quite clearly that his goal for linguistic theory was the perfection of a set of procedures by which the linguist could *discover* the structure of a language. This orientation is evident from his book *Methods in Structural Linguistics* (1951), as well as from such articles as "From phoneme to morpheme" (1955). Many other Neo-Bloomfieldians advanced this goal far less explicitly than Harris, though their orientation was still procedural in nature. As a student of Harris, Noam Chomsky was strongly exposed to this orientation. He reacted in this context, maintaining that language is not of such a nature that its structure may be discovered by the mechanical processing of data alone. He further insisted that the goal of linguistic theory should not be the perfection of a *discovery procedure*. He considered the alternative goal of a *decision procedure*, by which a putative grammar of a language could be declared either right or wrong by confrontation with the data. He rejected this alternative also as unrealistic and concluded that the still weaker goal of an *evaluation procedure* was the strongest one that could reasonably be set for linguistic theory. Unlike the decision procedure, an evaluation procedure can only make a relative judgment, given the data and two different grammars, telling which grammar is better. The possibility of a still better alternative would not thereby be ruled out.

Chomsky's divorcement of linguistic theory from discovery procedure was a valuable contribution. Even such theorists as Hjelmslev had tended to phrase their theoretical discussion in procedural terms. Since linguistic form is an unobservable system, it seems a reasonable conclusion that its structure cannot be discovered by the classification and segmentation of data alone. In the beginning, there was a somewhat overzealous attitude on the part of several of Chomsky's followers, who considered analytical procedures unworthy of the attention of linguists at all. A more reasonable interpretation of Chomsky's contribution, however, is that the divorcement should not be to the detriment of either theory or analytical practice. Both are legitimate concerns of linguists. The most important aspect of the divorcement, furthermore, is that theory should not be based on or influenced by procedure, as it often was earlier. Procedure, on the other hand, can often benefit from the influence of theory. Such an influence in fact is virtually inevitable, since a linguist's theoretical bias determines the questions he will want to ask about linguistic data, and this in turn exercises a strong influence on the procedures he chooses to employ.

Stratificational linguistics has emphasized the importance of an evaluation measure for linguistic description, though Lamb would not regard the procedure of applying it as part of the theory. Rather he considers this process as much a practical matter as discovery procedure. The question of evaluation measures concerns the measurement of simplicity and generality. To be sure, simplicity was at times a concern of Neo-Bloomfieldian linguists as well, but they never systematized this concern. In phonology, for example, the most frequent consideration was the number of different phonemes in the inventory. Other factors, such as the simplicity of phonotactic statements or statements of alternation, might sometimes be taken into account, but no means of balancing simplicity in one area with that in another was ever worked out. Chomsky's call for an evaluation procedure would require the development of such an overall means of measuring the total simplicity of a grammar.

In practice, the followers of transformational theory have not been very successful in realizing the goal of an evaluation procedure. In their earlier work, many of them assumed that relative simplicity could be measured by counting the number of symbols used in their algebraic rules. Of two grammars accounting for the same data, therefore, the one employing the fewest symbol tokens would be considered the simpler. With further consideration of actual cases, it has become evident that such a simple count is not adequate to reflect the relative generality of alternate accounts within the rule framework which has characterized transformational grammars. One problem is that the types of rules used in the different components of a transformational grammar are rather different in nature, having in common only the fact that all are written in terms of algebraic symbols. For this reason, a measure which is successful for one component cannot necessarily be extended to other components. Even the development of a successful evaluation measure for each individual component of the grammar, furthermore, does not guarantee the possibility of comparing alternate solutions which simplify one component at the expense of a complication in another. An evaluation measure adequate to this task would have to be general enough to be applicable to all components. It could take the form of a single measure equally applicable to all components, or a series of special measures applicable to each component and a meta-measure for use across components. In addition to the inter-component difficulties, the simplistic symbol-count approach has been found to be inadequate even within a single component in a number of concrete instances where the symbolization does not correspond to clear notions of simplicity and generality.

Stratificationalists have sought to develop a system of grammatical description for which a simple procedure will achieve the desired results. This search has led to the development of a system by which the phenomena of various strata are describable with a relatively small inventory of basic relationships. The graphic notation was devised to represent these relationships in a more direct way than is possible within an algebraic system. With this approach, stratificationalists have been able to develop a general evaluation procedure which is both effective and easy to apply. It has thus given an answer to Chomsky's challenge.

The followers of transformational theory, on the other hand, have retreated from this goal when faced with adversity. In recent years the goal of accounting for linguistic universals has eclipsed that of the development of an evaluation procedure. From the stratificational point of view, the transformationalists' basic problem can be seen as residing in their notation system, which represents linguistic relationships in far too indirect and nonuniform a manner to be useful for the development of an effective evaluation measure.

Another positive contribution coming out of the rise of transformational linguistics is the revival of interest in various types of linguistic data which Neo-Bloomfieldian linguists tended to ignore. Agnation, for example, was generally taken by Neo-Bloomfieldians to be a purely semantic question and thus beyond the scope of linguistics. Chomsky rightly insisted that the relations pertaining between agnate structures ought to be accounted for by any adequate linguistic theory and thereby provided an impetus for renewed research in this neglected area. The situation with ambiguity is similar. Only a small percentage of the types of ambiguity found in language may be accounted for purely in terms of immediate constituency. Neo-Bloomfieldian linguists sought to account for only those types of ambiguity with which they could deal in this way. Other types were relegated to the domain of semantics and were thus considered to be beyond the confines of linguistic science, Chomsky correctly pointed out the relevance of other types of ambiguities, turning the attention of other linguists in this direction.

Originally, Chomsky's theory did not include a semantic component but endeavored to treat agnation and "structural" ambiguity as a matter of syntax. More recently, the attention of transformationalists has been turned to more purely semantic phenomena, and various followers of Chomsky, beginning with Jerrold Katz and Jerry Fodor in 1963, have sought to include semantics in an integrated theory of language. They have come to differ considerably among themselves as to how this task is best to be accomplished. Transformationalists thus provided part of the impetus for the greatly renewed interest in semantics which has come about in recent years. Other linguists, not the least among them Lamb himself, have provided part of this impetus as well.

While Chomsky is to be credited for posing new challenges to linguistic theory in general and pointing out inadequacies of earlier theories, his attempts to meet these challenges in terms of a new theory have raised new problems as serious as the ones they solved. It is one thing to challenge the adequacy of earlier theories, in other words, but quite another to provide a wholly adequate alternative.

The alternative proposed by Chomsky, transformational grammar, did provide a means to describe such phenomena as agnation and structural ambiguity. It accomplished these tasks, however, only at the expense of reintroducing item-and-process description in an elaborated form, incorporating a particularly complex type of process called a *grammatical transformation*. While a grammar including such transformations is clearly more nearly adequate for the treatment of phenomena such as agnation and structural ambiguity than a simple grammar of the type Chomsky dubbed "phrase structure," this does not prove that other alternatives may not be just as good for these purposes, and even better for other purposes.

It can never be asserted that Chomsky has proved any need for transformations. He showed only that a grammar with transformations is better than phrase structure for handling certain phenomena, but to actually prove that transformations are needed would involve demonstrating that no other conceivable alternative will do the same thing. That is, it would be necessary to show conclusively that *all possible alternatives* have been considered and found wanting. Short of this, Chomsky cannot really prove the need for transformations, nor can Lamb prove the need for strata. They can only show that their respective theories can handle various phenomena and must leave them to be judged on various grounds.

Psychological realism is one such ground, and from this point of view process grammars, including the transformational, can be questioned. On the basis of an initial comparison, it is understandable that one might be attracted to a process theory. Suppose, for example, that we compare the allomorph method of morphological description, which characterized much Neo-Bloomfieldian item-and-arrangement description, with the process method involving morphophonemes. Taking these as the only possible alternatives, we might be led to favor the process method, since it provides a greater degree of generalization than does the item-and-arrangement view based on allomorphs. But in actuality the use of morphophonemic description does not necessitate the use of process. It may just as well be used in an item-and-arrangement framework, not to speak of a system like stratificational grammar, which by virtue of not recognizing any essential items at all within linguistic structure is neither an item-and-arrangement nor an item-and-process grammar.

Any process view has a number of inherent drawbacks which make an equally adequate nonprocess view immediately preferable. A process view may be defined, first of all, as any model of language which produces quasi-substantive representations of language and derives an actual substantive representation from them by subjecting them to a series of processes. Among these processes may be replacements, deletions, additions, and rearrangements. The degree of sophistication with which process formulations have been applied by linguists has shown considerable variation. At the one extreme are those who think that all they can do is derive one substantive item from another, and who accordingly restrain the abstractness of their initial representations, and with it the generalizing power of their descriptions. At the other end of the spectrum is what Lamb (1966d) termed the "quasi-stratificational" degree of sophistication. In this view, the linguist recognizes that he is actually dealing with different levels of structure (strata) and that his rules are intended to define the relationships between these levels, but he continues to use the process form of description.

Even at this highest level of sophistication, the process conception has, first of all, the drawback that process rules must be intricately ordered if they are to be able to account for the data and be statable in the simplest possible form. Some of this rule ordering is structurally significant, corresponding in the stratificational formulation to the existence of different strata or levels within these (**stratificational ordering**), to the precedence built into a downward ordered OR (**precedence ordering**), or to the left-to-right generation of entities by a tactic pattern (**tactical ordering**). A great deal of the ordering necessary with process rules, however, corresponds to none of these structural features and is simply an artifice of the process formulation. This formulation not only has the weakness of requiring such artificial ordering; it also fails to distinguish the various types of structural ordering, which are by no means the same thing. Strong objection to this degree of ordering can be made from a psychological point of view, since many of the process formulations of language suggested by the transformationalists require a vast number of rewritings to produce even a simple sentence. This feature constitutes a major barrier toward the development of a plausible model of even ideal performance on the basis of transformational theory.

Another major objection to process formulations is based on the fact that they require the projection of substantive elements into the form. This is an inevitable result of the fact that process formulations are really adapted only to change items into other items of the same general sort. They are well adapted to diachronic linguistics, where they were originally used, but not to synchrony. In the course of processing, some items will turn out not to be affected by any process. For this reason the initial layer of structure must be expressed in quasi-substantive terms if the desired output is a transcription representing expression substance. In his 1965 book *Aspects of the Theory of Syntax*, Chomsky adopted a quasi-stratificational system involving a distinction between deep and surface structures. But because processes were still to be used to relate these quasi-strata, he found it necessary to place phonetically based distinctive features in the deep structure. The occurrences and arrangements of these features were not, to be sure, the same as those occurring in all the substantive realizations, but they were selected from the actually occurring phonetic features. A similar comment can be made about the syntactic relation of surface and deep structure as described in Chomsky's book. They were only quasi-strata because the deep structure was largely a rearrangement of surface elements, including noun phrases, verb phrases, subjects, and objects, arranged in a purely linear order. In a stratificational system, one can recognize that different sets of elements as well as basically different types of arrangements are involved.

Another criticism of transformational theory not completely unrelated to its use of the process description concerns its concept of the *lexicon*. This concept was not part of the earliest versions of transformational theory, but was introduced when the theory was reformed by Chomsky in 1964–65. The lexicon is conceived of as a listing of every lexical item ($\equiv$ lexeme?) of the language in terms of its underlying shape (in binary features) and all relevant morphological, syntactic, and semantic information pertaining to it. As it was originally conceived, the lexicon is referred to by the phrase-structure grammar of the base component to select compatible lexical items for underlying sentences, thus employing the syntactic information in the lexicon. The resulting phonological and syntactic information provided by the phrase-structure grammar and the lexicon then serve as input to the transformational component and the phonology. The semantic and syntactic information will be used by the interpretive semantic component.

From a stratificational viewpoint, such a lexicon conflates in one component of the grammar information relevant to various stratal systems, including (1) connections to the tactics (dealing with class membership), and (2) information in various sign patterns (pertaining to phonological shape). By examining the latter portion alone, one can see that no attempt at generalization is made in such a lexicon. The item *undergo*, for example, would be broken directly into distinctive features, occurring as a sequence of bundles of these features. Such a procedure will miss all sorts of generalizations, including the following: (1) the *under* in this lexical item recurs in other lexical items such as *undertake*, *understand*, and *under*; (2) the *go* portion (with the same suppletive alternate *wen* in the past) recurs in *forego*, *go through with*, and *go*; (3) the segments (bundles of features or components) all recur in many lexical items, for example, *n* in *need* and *van*, *d* in *dog* and *rod*, *g* in *girl* and *rag*. In short, the lexicon of a transformational grammar is set up in such a way that no consideration at all is given to its economic internal organization. If this factor were to be taken into consideration, the result would be the apportioning of the total information over several levels, as is done in stratificational theory.

Process thinking, however, constitutes one major barrier to the achievement of such a goal. Suppose it were proposed, for example, that lexical representation be in terms of whole segments rather than directly in terms of features, so that at least the generalizations referred to in (3) could be handled. Such a step, the transformationalist would point out, would require a series of rules to be added to the grammar to rewrite the arbitrary symbols for each segment in terms of its constituent features. If each segment consists of features anyway, why not state them directly rather than requiring extra rules? In actuality, this line of reasoning makes no more sense than saying that a grammar for a limited set of sentences is not worth writing, since all the constructions it would recognize consist of morphemes, so we might just as well list the sentences. Surely the fact that natural languages imply an infinite number of sentences is not the sole reason that makes it useful to write grammars. Each of these extra rules, if one wants to call them that, is able to express in a single statement a fact which a lexicon of the type transformationalists have discussed would have to repeat for each lexical item in which the segment is contained.

Paul Postal (1968) has criticized stratificational theory for being incompatible with a lexicon. To an extent this is true, since the information contained in a transformational lexicon would be spread out over several strata in a stratificational grammar. In view of the fact that the same information can be represented more economically in this way, however, this incompatibility seems to be more an advantage than a shortcoming. This says nothing, of course, about the use of dictionaries or lexicons for applied linguistic purposes. The usefulness of such compilations is not denied, and stratificational theory is by no means incompatible with their preparation. However, this practical matter should not carry any implications about the representation of such information in the speaker's knowledge, which is the only relevant consideration for a theoretical model of language.

Another shortcoming of the standard version of a transformational grammar is its failure to recognize more than one tactic pattern. All tactic facts must either be incorporated into a single tactic pattern in the base component of a transformational grammar or else be treated as a nontactic transformational or phonological rule. Some transformationalists, however, have recently begun to recognize the usefulness of separate tactic patterns. Part of this recognition has come in the form of discussion of "output constraints" in surface structure (Perlmutter 1970) and also in phonology. This development could result in the positing of full tactic patterns on each of several significant levels, thus bringing transformational theory a step closer to stratificationalism.

Another issue which should be mentioned is the question of the directionality of a grammar. It is the declared intention of transformationalists to have a model which is nondirectional, showing no bias for either speaker or hearer. There is a difference between declaring an intention, however, and having success in realizing that intention. The actual transformational model, with rules which are formally irreversible, has the inevitable effect of giving a bias to the model, however unintentional it may be. From deep structure down to expression a speaker bias is imparted, because the rules go irreversibly from deep structure downward. In the Katz-Fodor conception of interpretive semantics, on the other hand, there is a hearer bias, since the rules go irreversibly from deep structure to semantic interpretation. These features erect another barrier to the use of the transformational model of "competence" as the basis for a plausible model of performance. The stratificational competence model, by contrast, describes only static relationships, and the associated model of ideal performance can interpret its relations to account for both the speaker's activity (encoding) and the hearer's (decoding).

In summary, transformational grammar has made positive contributions in the area of the goals of linguistic theory and has stimulated valuable empirical research in formerly neglected areas. The model of language it has proposed, however, has fundamental defects which cannot be remedied by minor revisions alone. These shortcomings have served as a stimulus for the development of alternative models of language such as the stratificational.

# 8

# Extensions and
# Future Developments

## 8.1  Diachrony and Diatopy

It is to be expected that in the first stages of its development a new theory of language will concentrate on synchronic phenomena and their treatment. But any view of synchronic structure has implications for **diachrony** and **diatopy**, the studies relating to linguistic variation over time and space respectively. Partly similar to diatopy are other kinds of synchronic variation correlated with social class, occupation, or stylistic choice. These topics are related in two ways. First, they have in common the fact that each concerns the comparison of related systems. Second, they are united by the fact that situations of diatopic and other variation are the result of past diachronic change.

Traditional treatments of diachrony, such as those of the Neo-Grammarians, were centered almost entirely on substance and the changes undergone by it. Saussure believed that synchronic structure played no role in diachrony, which he continued to treat in the atomistic fashion of the Neo-Grammarians. Other twentieth-century linguistic schools, in contrast, have paid considerable attention to the relation of synchronic structure to diachronic change.

In any view which accepts the basic dichotomy of linguistic form and substance, it seems natural that just as synchronic substance reflects form, diachronic changes in substance will reflect changes in form. Within a form-oriented theory such as the stratificational, therefore, the study of diachronic phenomena will focus on changes in linguistic form. It will further attempt to

271

relate different types of substantive changes to different formal changes. The consideration of these aspects of stratificational theory is only in its beginning stages. No published works on this subject have yet appeared. What is said here, therefore, will be necessarily only a first approximation.

In stratificational theory, as we have seen, linguistic form is conceived of as a network of relationships, of which graphic diagrams provide a fairly direct representation. In considering the relation of such networks to diachronic facts, we must bear in mind that in a cognitive theory such as the stratificational the aim is to ultimately represent as closely as possible the knowledge of the speaker as he stores it in his brain. Changes in linguistic form, therefore, ultimately correspond to changes in the linguistic knowledge of speakers. These changes in knowledge in turn affect speech habits, and these in turn alter the substance.

Some consideration should be given to the types of changes which can occur in the linguistic knowledge of a speaker during his lifetime. Most such changes in knowledge involve what we term **learning**. Learning as a whole is, of course, a process which begins in early childhood and does not cease until complete senility or death. The learning of one's first or only language, however, is generally more confined than this. It is usually said that the normal child has mastered the essentials of his language by about the age of five or six years. There is evidence that the child retains a great deal of his language learning ability, however, until about the age of puberty. For example, the child can normally acquire other languages readily and naturally up to about that age. In the adult, the range of linguistic change is more limited. His vocabulary continues to change, but in the grammatical portion of his network such changes are confined to alterations in the membership of existing tactic classes and the addition of new lexemic and morphemic signs, usually made up of preexisting lexons and morphons. The semological portion of the adult's network, particularly the gnostemics, can continue to grow and develop in adulthood. Such an assumption is unavoidable in view of the fact that new concepts and new relations between established concepts are constantly learned in the course of one's daily life.

On the other hand, it is very difficult for an adult to accomplish any radical changes in his phonological system, such as the addition of new phonemes or components, or radically different patterns of syllable or segment structures. This difficulty shows up in the persistence of foreign accent in a second language learned later in life, despite the efforts one may make to eradicate it. Adults tend, to a greater or lesser extent, to reinterpret the phonological system of a foreign language in terms of that of their native language.

Despite the assertions made above, a person's pronunciation may undergo certain systematic changes in the course of his adulthood, after the establishment of his initial system. Evidence of dialectological investigation shows that such changes spread through a speech community with the aid of a natural tendency on the part of a speaker to adapt his own speech habits to those of his interlocutors.

Consider the following hypothesis about what happens when such a change occurs. For the purpose of this illustration, it will be assumed that we are dealing with the spread of a change *l* > *r* in all positions in a dialect, the *r* from this source merging with a previously existing *r* that occurred with a generally analogous distribution to former *l*. The former contrast between *l* and *r* is thus lost.

1. The redundancy of the linguistic system enables a great amount of variation to escape a listener's conscious attention. He will decode the message according to the expectations provided by the context. For the first few times he hears *r* in place of expected *l*, therefore, the speaker may treat it as a random error or unfamiliar accent feature and decode it as the expected *l*.
2. When a type of variation is encountered with a fair degree of frequency, alternatives may be provided in one's linguistic system to deal with its decoding. When a change first comes into a speaker's system, it is likely to be such an alternative used solely for decoding, and not for encoding. As a speaker increasingly hears *r* in place of an expected *l*, therefore, he will tend to build in a decoding option for the neutralization of his *l* and *r*.
3. If the change in question is spreading in a speech community, the speaker will find increasing occasion to use his decoding alternative. Barring a conscious effort to avoid its use, the decoding alternative apparently will tend to become at least an occasional encoding alternative as well. Ultimately, as the change similarly affects others in the speech community, it may become the favored alternative for encoding as well, the originally favored alternative existing only as a decoding option. Thus the speaker in question will come to pronounce *r* in place of his former *l* on a regular basis.

The above description accounts for the spread of phonetic changes among adults. It seems a reasonable hypothesis that such changes are superimposed on the preexisting phonological network, whose basic form became relatively frozen at puberty. This is true particularly of the phonetic as opposed to the phonemic stratal system. The changes which occurred were additions of new nodes and connecting lines to account for the new possibilities. It seems reasonable to hypothesize, furthermore, that these additions are made in such a way as to minimize the total number of additions needed, but not necessarily to create the simplest total network.

For the child, who retains considerable flexibility in his phonological network, the possibilities are different. All evidence indicates that children are still capable of building new phonological networks and discarding old ones. It is presumably just such a process, in fact, which occurs in the course of language learning, for grammar as well as phonology. Let us now consider the case of a child growing up in a speech community in which the change *l* to *r* has been accomplished. While the adults who have incorporated this change would have originally learned a system with a thoroughgoing *l/r* distinction, the child would have no motive for doing so. The actual adult system modified by such a change would likely retain the original distinction of *l* and *r* on the morphonic level and simply neutralize the two within the phonetic system.

The child learning the language on the basis of what he hears from adults, however, apparently has the ability to aim at the simplest overall system accounting for the data. His only preexisting "phonology" concerns the anatomical and physiological limitations imposed on his speech and hearing. If he learns the language on the basis of data reflecting only the changed system, he will have no basis for establishing a distinction between *l* and *r* on the morphonic or any other level. He will learn only one morphon, $^{MN}/r/$, and one set of phonological and phonetic realizations. Thus the adult system and that of the child will differ in such a case, even if both have identical outputs. The difference will reside in the fact that the adult system is the result of the superimposition of a change on a preexisting system, while that of the child has been built anew on the basis of the data to which that child has been exposed. This assumes that the child has the ability to aim for the simplest system possible. The linguistic networks used in stratificational descriptions, in other words, seek to represent the ultimate result of the child's ability to simplify and generalize in language learning. To the extent that they reflect superimposed changes, adult systems may be different and more complicated. It should also be understood that the maximally general network is an ideal which the child cannot be expected to achieve completely. It represents only the direction in which he is believed to aim.

Clearly, in the present case the child would never have a reason to posit a distinction *l/r* on the basis of the spoken language data to which he is exposed. More complex cases exist in language change, of course, but no complete survey of them can be undertaken here. In this instance, if a person who learned the language were to encounter other speakers from a different geographic region or social stratum who still retained the *l/r* distinction, it would be relatively easy for him to accommodate the decoding aspect of this difference. He would simply need to add a decoding option allowing either [r] or [l] to be the realization of his *r*. To completely learn the encoding of the other dialect, however, would be a much more formidable task. It would involve the apportioning of the entire vocabulary of morphemic signs containing his $^{MN}/r/$ into those with $^{MN}/r/$ in the second system, and those with $^{MN}/l/$. A child presumably does just this in the course of his language learning, but for the adult whose phonological system has matured, the task is very difficult. This fact explains, of course, the frequency of hyperurbanisms as well as the rarity of the spread of systems making more phonological (or grammatical) distinctions at the expense of those with fewer.

The origin, as opposed to the spread, of phonological and other linguistic changes is still another question. It has been suggested that language learning may be one source of such changes. The child's simplifications in the course of learning, that is, may sometimes lead to hypotheses that are only partly in conformity with the data. Ideally, such overgeneralizations are corrected before the period of language learning is completed. In some cases, however, this does not happen, and the pattern may spread to other children, thus giving rise to a linguistic change. More research into the application of stratificational theory to specific examples of linguistic change will be necessary to see what contributions it can make to the understanding of this phenomenon.

No examples of actual networks have been given in this brief consideration of the diachronic and diatopic implications of stratificational theory. It must be emphasized, however, that diachrony and diatopy will always involve the comparison of related networks. A single network cannot represent linguistic change. It can represent variation only within a single idiolect or dialect. This situation contrasts with that seen in a process type of theory, such as transformational grammar. In such theories an identical mode of description —the process rule—is used for linguistic relationships and linguistic changes. Depending on how one chooses to interpret the arrow, therefore, a single rule formulation can alternatively represent either a synchronic relationship or a diachronic change.

The intended differences of implication between the two systems may not actually be as great as this notational fact seems to suggest. The transformationalist still compares grammars in diatopic and diachronic studies, just as the stratificationalist compares networks. The grammar of rules, like the network, is intended to represent the linguistic system underlying the data. It is only a question of which format is more adequate to that task. Even if this is all that is intended by the users of process rules, the use of such rules for both purposes remains misleading, particularly to beginning students.

In this section, we have concerned ourselves primarily with the relation of the stratificational view of linguistic structure to diachronic and diatopic studies. Diachronic and diatopic studies, however, may also have implications for synchronic theory. A study of linguistic changes or of related dialects, for example, may provide evidence for the relatedness of certain phenomena in the synchronic sphere. This aspect of linguistic investigation is just beginning to receive attention but shows signs of being promising. As a result of studies aimed along this line, it may be possible to discover certain general facts about synchronic structure applying to all human languages.

## 8.2   *Language Universals*

American linguists through the Neo-Bloomfieldian period were generally suspicious of any consideration of "universals" in language. They tended, rather, to emphasize the diversity among languages. This attitude came about as a result of increased investigation of languages of different families, which exhibited much more diversity than the more familiar Indo-European languages of Europe, on which earlier investigators had tended to concentrate.

While it is true that generalizations applicable to European languages often turned out not to apply on a wider scope, it was doubtless an overreaction to state, as did one prominent Neo-Bloomfieldian, that languages may vary "unpredictably and without limit." Languages, after all, are built upon a common foundation encompassing several aspects. The organs of speech and hearing, to which phonic correlations pertain, are fundamentally the same in people of all races and nationalities. These common properties thereby impose limitations on the phonic end of the linguistic system. Human experience, as vast and varied as it may be in different cultures, is likewise restricted by the laws of nature. This restriction imposes limitations on the conceptual end of linguistic structure. Linguistic form itself is surely restricted by the anatomical and physiological properties of the brain, which are universal to human beings. All these factors serve to place limits on the variability of linguistic systems. The realization of such limits has led linguists to conclude that the discovery and statement of language universals is a legitimate activity of the scientific linguist, as well as an important goal for linguistic theory.

Transformational linguists have undoubtedly occupied the forefront in the concern for language universals. Though they have at times been somewhat overenthusiastic in proclaiming universals, as in the recently popular belief that the "base" syntax is a language universal, the legitimacy of their concern for language universals cannot be questioned. This concern has, among other things, been useful for the stimulation of valuable research in this hitherto neglected area.

Chomsky has set forth a distinction between formal and substantive universals, which will be useful for the discussion of the attitudes of stratificational linguists in this area. **Formal universals** are those concerned only with the form of grammars. Each theory of language has as one of its most essential parts a set of hypotheses about the nature of formal universals. In the stratificational view, formal universals include the inventory of different node types, the patterns by which nodes may be combined, the structure of stratal systems, the hypothesis concerning the existence of multiple stratal systems in a language, numbering no fewer than three or more than six, and the operation of the nodes in the model of performance. These hypotheses concerning formal universals, of course, differ from those that would be assumed by the advocates of transformationalism or other theories, and they will not in every case be interconvertible with them.

**Substantive universals,** on the other hand, concern the relation of formal patterns to substantive connections at the upper and lower interfaces of the linguistic system. They cannot be expressed strictly in terms of form, in other words, but must also refer to the connection of form to substance. This definition is specifically designed to account for the distinction between formal and substantive universals within stratificational theory. It has sometimes been asserted that statements concerning substantive universals are meaningless in the context of stratificational theory, or any theory which does not project quasi-substantive items into its form (Postal 1968). This assertion is completely erroneous. To show its error, let us interpret in stratificational terms several tentative substantive universals.

### Universal I

All languages have syllables of the form CV.

As stated, this universal could refer to the syllabification of the phonetic output of a grammar, or to syllables as they are defined by the phonotactics, or to both. In the first case, possible stratificational grammars would be constrained to include only those which allow at the phonic end a phonetically nonvocalic segment followed by a phonetically vocalic one, which is not necessarily in turn followed by another nonvowel. In the second case, the set of possible stratificational grammars would be constrained to include only those which have among the possible syllable types one consisting of CV, where C is a class of elements each having a nonvocalic phonetic segment as its most usual realization and V is a class of elements each having a vocalic phonetic segment as its most usual realization.

### Universal II

Nasalized high vowels occur only in languages that also have nasalized low vowels.

This universal is most likely a constraint on the combinations of phonetic components accounted for, and so will be interpreted as such. It excludes from the set of possible stratificational grammars those allowing combinations of phonetic Ns · Vo · Hi, but at the same time not allowing phonetic Ns · Vo · Lo.

### Universal III

All languages have nouns and verbs.

This universal presumably refers to the grammatical portion of a stratificational account, and would restrict the set of stratificational grammars to those making a lexotactic distinction between the classes N and V. N is a class of elements having an ultimate connection to the conceptual correlations which include the concept "objectified." V is a class of elements having a similar ultimate conceptual connection to "action" or "state." It could alternately be taken as a distinction between processes and things in the semology.

### *Universal IV*

Any language which has passive expressions has for each of these a corresponding active expression.

This universal would constrain the set of possible stratificational grammars so as to exclude those which allow focus to be combined with goal in the semotactics, but fail to allow an unmarked focus. The elements *focus, goal,* and *agent,* of course, imply certain connections to the conceptual correlations which will not be defined here.

These few illustrations demonstrate that substantive universals do after all have a significance in a stratificational framework. They differ from formal universals in that they concern in part the connection of the linguistic network to the phonic and/or conceptual correlations. All of the universals are in fact formal in the sense that they constrain the form of grammars in some manner. The substantive universals might more accurately be termed "formal-substantive," in that they constrain the form with reference to its external connections to substance. The more precise form of statement needed to provide a stratificational interpretation of such universals does not have to be used in practice, of course. It is only important that we understand what is actually meant by the less precise statements.

At least a basic hypothesis regarding the formal universals of language is inherent in any view of language which can purport to be a theory. A concern with substantive universals is not as inevitable, since the theory of formal universals may simply be applied to different languages. It seems desirable, however, for a theory to concern itself with the discovery of substantive universals as well, and to incorporate them as constraints on the form of grammars. Formal universals establish the basic framework of the theory, while substantive universals impose more particular constraints on this form. We can even think of the data of a particular language as imposing a still more particular constraint on this form. (In addition, certain cultures impose semological constraints on all languages of the cultural area, and certain geographic regions impose phonological constraints on all languages of their area.)

It is one thing to take note of substantive universals in the manner proposed and quite another to attempt to build them into the descriptive mechanism of the theory, in the manner that most formal universals are integrated. An example of a formal universal built into stratificational theory is that linguistic structure consists of relationships intervening between conceptual and phonic correlations. It is impossible within the theory to violate this universal by producing a description to which it does not apply. The substantive universal that all languages have CV syllables is not the same, however, since it would be perfectly possible to produce a stratificational description of an infinite number of languages which violate this universal. Such stratificational grammars can be ruled out only by the introduction of *ad hoc* provisions to prohibit them.

Followers of transformational grammar have attempted to account for substantive universals in a different way. They have proposed that certain universals be stated for languages in general. The grammars of particular languages would then contain only the additional, language-specific facts; these facts are not included in the universal grammar, which is part of linguistic theory. This separation of general and specific facts may be useful for certain purposes, but in other ways it is entirely unjustified and inappropriate.

Suppose, for example, that we tried to incorporate Universal I above, concerning CV syllable structure, into a stratificational grammar in such a way that the universal principle allowing such syllables is automatically distinguishable from principles allowing any other syllable types which may be possible in a given language. This step could be taken only at the expense of failing to integrate the information concerning the existence of CV structures with that concerning other syllable types, such as CVC, V, or VC. In general, the separation of the universal facts from the particular ones will be an artificial one. It is not only *ad hoc* but also incompatible with the more basic aims of stratificational grammar. Such aims include the representation of the knowledge of the native speaker about the language in the way he stores and uses it in encoding and decoding, and the representation of generalizations within this system.

The separation of such universal facts may seem a bit more natural in a theory such as the transformational, in which the facts of the linguistic system are broken into separate "rules" rather than being integrated into a network of relationships. Stratificational theory recognizes "rules" only to the extent that they correspond to nodes, which is by no means always the case if transformational rules are translated into stratificational terms. Whichever theory one uses, it is possible to distinguish the substantive universals from particular facts only in an *ad hoc* manner. The task can be accomplished in one of two ways: by the separation of the universal facts from the particular in the description, or by the representation of universals as constraints on the form of grammars. The first approach can result in a failure to integrate the total facts of the language, all of which are equally a part of the linguistic knowledge of the adult speaker. The second approach has no similar drawbacks, however, and therefore seems to be superior. Such a "constraints" approach would seem to be adaptable to transformational as well as stratificational grammar.

Still another important question concerns the reasons for language universals. In transformational theory there has commonly been an assumption that language universals reflect innate properties of the human brain, sometimes termed "innate ideas." It is clear that innate properties of the brain must provide *some* of the basis for language universals, but the total picture surely involves the interaction of other factors as well. Properties of the brain alone would seem to provide the basic explanation for the formal universals, however close or distant our current hypotheses may be from the actual truth about them. The matter of substantive universals is quite different. Universals relating to phonetic substance are based on our common human equipment for articulation and audition. This equipment includes various organs other than the brain—the tongue, lips, velum, larynx, ear, and so on—as well as the parts of the brain which control their operation. Also playing a role in the basis for these universals are certain physical facts concerning the transmission of sounds, which are studied by the science of acoustics.

Universals relating to the connection of form to the conceptual correlations are based in part on the common equipment human beings have for perceiving the universe. This includes all the senses, encompassing both the organs involved and the portion of the brain controlling them. In the case of conceptual correlations, the factors external to the human body, not to speak of the brain, play a much more important role in conditioning universals than is the case with the phonic correlations and universals relating to them. Conceptually based universals, in other words, depend on the universals of the world in which we live, mediated by our abilities to perceive this world. In the case of substantive universals, therefore, the properties of the brain are only a part of their basis. A full explanation of such universals would take us far afield from the subject of language *per se*.

Even for those aspects of the total basis for language universals which do concern inherent properties of the brain, the term "innate ideas" is a very unfortunate choice. That such properties are innate is not questioned. The term "idea," however, suggests something that may be consciously articulated by the persons in whom it resides. It does not seem reasonable to assume that the properties in question are of such a nature. Rather they are physical and physiological properties of the brain which enable it to react and develop in certain ways and not in others, in response to stimuli. To call such properties "ideas" seems a misleading distortion of the normally understood meaning of the term.

The following statements summarize the stratificational position on language universals as outlined in this section.

1. The discovery and articulation of formal and substantive universals of linguistic structure is a legitimate goal for linguistic theory.
2. Formal universals will be accounted for principally by the form of the theory itself.

3. Substantive universals are most reasonably accounted for by constraints on the form of grammars over and above those provided by the formal universals. Such constraints will involve reference to the connection between form and substance, as well as to purely formal properties. (A similar approach may be adapted to quasi-universals, that is, properties more likely to be present than not.)

4. The explanation of language universals involves a wide number of factors. Anatomical and physiological properties of the brain form one of these foundations, perhaps the sole one in the case of formal universals. For the explanation of substantive universals, however, reference must also be made to the properties of the organs of speech and perception, and to the properties of the universe in which the speakers live. The latter factor plays a particularly important role in the explanation of universals relating to the conceptual correlations.

## 8.3  *Extralinguistic Extensions*

As has been stated elsewhere, stratificational linguists did not originally aspire to the development of a cognitive theory of language. They simply sought an abstract model of the relationships between expression and content. Lamb's development of the theory beyond its initial conception came during the period 1958–64, when he was directing the Machine Translation Project at the University of California, Berkeley. The process of translation involves the decoding of a message in one language and its encoding in another. Since Lamb was then concerned with developing the model for this purpose, it was imperative that it be adapted to processing in both directions —from expression to content as well as from content to expression. A practical concern therefore provided an initial motivation for one of the central properties of the theory.

Later, Lamb began to devise the graphic notation and to adopt the purely relational view of linguistic structure. It was only following these developments, which were based on consideration of purely linguistic data, that Lamb began to explore the degree of correspondence between his model of linguistic structure and what is known, or at least believed, about the function of the human brain.

In one sense, the advance to such a concern is natural. It is self-evident that a speaker's knowledge of his language must be stored in the brain, if by language we understand the system which humans use in vocal communication. Therefore the ultimate test of the veracity of a linguistic theory would be its degree of correspondence to the facts concerning the brain.

At the same time, such a concern involves risks which may seem needless. This difficulty stems most of all from the fact that neurophysiologists themselves are in agreement on only a few fundamentals about the workings of the brain. On such an important matter as the manner in which information is stored, there is serious disagreement among experts. This state of affairs may lead the cautious linguist to refrain from any reference to neurophysiological information in setting up his theories in order to protect himself from needless attack. Peter Reich has answered this kind of objection in his article "Competence, performance, and relational networks" (1968a), in which he points out that every theory involves some fundamental assumptions, even if they are unconscious and inexplicit. It seems reasonable to conclude that linguistic behavior must have a close relationship to the brain in the real world, so the possibility of incorporating some properties compatible with neurophysiological notions of the brain into linguistic theory seems worthy of consideration.

In the same article Reich points out some of the properties which can be incorporated in this way. Perhaps the most important of these properties which have a neurophysiological correspondence is the network form, which the theory takes to be basic for linguistic structure. That is, the theory models linguistic structure by building networks out of a few types of formal elements. Further, the related model of performance will allow these formal elements to communicate with each other using a few different types of signals. These properties correspond to the generally acknowledged fact that the brain consists of a network of neurons which communicate with each other by means of discrete impulses.

Neurophysiologists are less in agreement about the way knowledge is stored in the neural network. As was mentioned previously, stratificationalists consider the hypothesis that information (specifically, long-term information) is stored in the connectivity of the network to be the most reasonable one. In the stratificational model, permanent information is stored in the connectivity of the linguistic network rather than within the logical elements which make it up. A model storing the information within these elements would be compatible with the alternate neurophysiological hypothesis that information is stored within individual neurons.

Reich concludes his paper by emphasizing that the network approach of stratificational theory is not to be viewed as a neurological theory of language. Rather it is a formal system within which certain neurologically motivated restrictions can be incorporated. The correspondence of the stratificational model of language to the neurophysiologists' model of the brain should be an ultimate goal for cognitive linguistics. The above restrictions are a step toward that goal, but the theory is not yet in a position to claim to have achieved it completely. It can claim, however, to have approached this goal more closely than any competing theory of language now on the scene. How truly close this "more closely" will turn out to be can be determined only by further experimentation and application of the theory to a wider range of linguistic and psycholinguistic data.

A further step in relating stratificational theory to the brain is growing out of current research by Lamb in devising a refined form of the network notation. The results of this experimentation are not yet sufficiently complete to be reported upon in detail, but some of the preliminary results can be enumerated. The notation involved is intended not to replace the form of notation currently used but to supplement it. Fundamentally, it involves breaking down each node of the current notation into further component parts, which will recur in different configurations corresponding to different nodes of the earlier system. For convenience of discussion, the nodes of the system we have been using will be termed **macronodes**, while those of the refined system will be termed **micronodes**. It is the goal of the refined notation system to define each macronode in terms of micronodes.

One of the basic facts about the brain which is clearly not represented in the macronode notation is that neurons can send impulses in only one direction. In any reasonable model of performance based on macronodes, in contrast, each macronode is capable of transmitting signals in either direction. In the micronode system, this further property is incorporated, for each macronode capable of bidirectional transmission corresponds to a configuration of micronodes governing transmission in one direction, and a second governing transmission in the other direction. All micronodes and the lines associated with them are thus unidirectional. This step means, of course, that the number of micronodes in the representation of a given structure will generally be greater than the number of macronodes. At the same time, the number of types of micronodes is significantly less than the number of types of macronodes. The current hypothesis reduces this number to just four. This small inventory of basic relationships makes the micronode system considerably simpler conceptually than the macronode system. In the course of this ongoing research, it has been found necessary to recognize a greater number of macronode types, but the micronode interpretation of these still involves the same basic inventory of four elements. It is also apparent that the refined notation will have implications for the simplicity measure. The internal micronode structure of various macronodes may sometimes need to be considered in measuring simplicity.

It should be clear why the micronode notation cannot be expected to be a practical replacement for the current notation based on macronodes in actual linguistic analysis and description. The greater number of lines and nodes necessary makes it too cumbersome for these purposes. Its major use, therefore, will be in providing precise definitions for the macronodes. In addition, from what has been observed to date, the micronode notation shows promise of being relatable in a fairly direct way to actual neurological structure.

In either form, the stratificational notation appears to be readily adaptable to the representation of nonlinguistic information which must be stored in the brain. Its adaptability in this area may offer further evidence of its relation to brain structure. One of the more obvious applications is in the area of nonlinguistic communication. The essentials of a description of one such system were offered by Magnus Ljung in his article "Principles of a stratificational analysis of the Plains Indian sign language" (1965). A more complete and up-to-date stratificational analysis of Classical East Indian dance gestures is contained in Ikegami (1971).

Due to the generality of the basic relationships of stratificational theory, the stratificational notation also appears to be adaptable to the representation of cultural knowledge which relates to nonlinguistic behavior as well as to linguistic behavior. At the very least, it can provide a convenient display of information about cultural systems. But beyond this it is possible that the adaptability of the notation may be evidence of the basic correspondence of the stratificational relationships to the structures which reside in the brain. The fact that a single system appears to be adaptable to the representation of linguistic as well as nonlinguistic information seems to be a point in its favor. One example of the adaptability of the stratificational notation to a cultural structure is provided by Lamb's diagram of the structure of a baseball game, which appears in his paper "Linguistic and cognitive networks" (1971). This diagram is reproduced in Figure 8.1.

Among the other nonlinguistic systems in the brain are those dealing with motor functions and with perception. These are also related, directly or indirectly, to language. Certain motor functions are, of course, related to articulation—the encoding output of the linguistic system. Others are related to the encoding output of the written language system, which in languages with written manifestations partly or fully overlaps with the system for the spoken language on the upper strata but is distinct on the lower due to the diverse means of expression involved. Other motor functions are not so directly relatable to language, but it is interesting to note that many of them may serve as part of an alternative to linguistic responses in a given situation and are thus integrated with language as a part of the total culture. Bloomfield in his *Language* cited the now-famous example of the girl Jill who feels hunger and sees an apple on a tree. In this situation she has the alternatives of reaching for the apple herself (a direct motor reaction) or asking her friend Jack to get it for her (a linguistic motor reaction). Still other motor reactions, such as gestures, may be related to language by virtue of their frequent use as an accompaniment to linguistic behavior. From this brief consideration, it becomes evident that motor functions exhibit a high degree of interrelation and integration with language.

Perception is, of course, similarly related to language. Most obvious perhaps is the fact that hearing perception provides the input for linguistic decoding. All the senses serve in an important relation to the conceptual correlations, since it is only through them that we may receive our experience of the world in which we live. In the case of written language, of course, the sense of sight plays a special role, providing the decoding input.

Further experimentation will be necessary to determine the extent to which

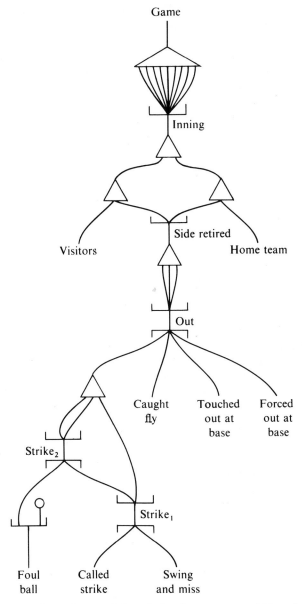

*Figure 8.1  Essentials of the Structure of Baseball*

the stratificational notation will be adaptable to the description of motor and perceptual abilities.

All the above considerations indicate that language is a part of a much broader system encompassing the brain as a whole. A system of linguistic description which is readily relatable to the brain, therefore, can be expected to be applicable to the nonlinguistic parts of this total system as well as to the linguistic ones. If stratificational theory is indeed on the right track in pursuing the goal of cognitive linguistics, it is conceivable that it will be able to provide as a by-product of its linguistic studies an important breakthrough in the understanding of the structure and function of the brain.

For the present, this must remain a hope, not a claim. There have been a number of encouraging results from the preliminary application of the theory to nonlinguistic data. To date, however, this application has scarcely scratched the surface of the existing possibilities and challenges. Much more complete research in all these areas will be necessary before even tentative claims can be advanced.

It is encouraging, however, that stratificational theory seems by its very nature to be much more adaptable to the representation of the nonlinguistic aspects of the total system of information than other theories of language, particularly those which are centered upon items. We can still not rule out, of course, the possibility of a theory as yet unknown which will be even more adaptable to these purposes. Whatever the structure of such an ultimately correct theory, it seems likely that it will have more in common with present-day stratificational theory than with any of the item-based views.

### 8.4   *Unity and Diversity in Stratificational Theory*

Linguists attempting to find out about stratificational theory by reading the existing literature have sometimes been discouraged by the lack of correspondence in terminology and concepts among the various works. Even the works of Lamb show a considerable variability over the past decade. The works of other stratificationalists show still further variation.

One reason for this state of affairs is that stratificational theory, considering all its practitioners, came about as the result of a convergence in the thought of its principal founders, Sydney Lamb and H. A. Gleason, Jr. This convergence has at no point been complete. As a result, stratificational theory never went through a period in which it was homogeneous and monolithic. It has exhibited diversity throughout the period during which it has been known to the linguistic community.

Transformational theory, in contrast, was relatively homogeneous during its early period of development, when it was building the base of support it has come to enjoy. This homogeneity made the task of learning about transformational theory in those years relatively simpler than that of learning about stratificational theory today. Now that it has become relatively well known and established, of course, transformational theory has also begun to show considerable diversity, and there is increasing controversy among its various practitioners.

Even if we confine ourselves to the works of Lamb, who has written by far the most concerning the theory, we still see diversity. This is a result of the development of Lamb's thought over the years. It is evidence that the theory is living and growing.

This section is intended to help smooth the way for readers of the literature of stratificational theory by pointing out some of the major points of diversity, while at the same time emphasizing the common points of belief which unite the various versions of the theory.

The most important change affecting Lamb's conception of the theory was the adoption of the notion that language consists entirely of relationships. This development was accompanied by the introduction of the graphic notation, which first reached print in two publications of 1966, "Prolegomena to a theory of phonology" and *Outline of Stratificational Grammar.*

Previous stages of the theory were based on items, just as item-and-arrangement and item-and-process theories are. Its items, however, were *within* linguistic structure, and their relations included not only matters of arrangement but also matters of realization. This early stratificational theory, therefore, might be termed an "item and relationship" theory.

The notion of the primacy of relationships over items began to be reflected in some of Lamb's works even during this earlier period. In his paper "Linguistic structure and the production and decoding of discourse" (1966a), for example, he suggested that the items within linguistic structure are not "objects" but only points in a series of connections. No definite choice between this and alternate conceptions was made at that time, however. A primitive "wiring diagram" notation was also suggested in that paper, which was originally written in 1963.

The changes which have occurred since the publication of the *Outline* in 1966 have concerned details rather than fundamentals. The basic principles which have remained constant since that time include the following:

1. Language is a code relating concepts to articulation and audition. It is traversed in one direction in the encoding of messages, and in the opposite direction in decoding.
2. Linguistic structure consists entirely of relationships, which connect to objects only at the outer periphery of the structure.
3. The most fundamental relationships are ANDs and ORs, which may be either ordered or unordered and may have either an upward or a downward orientation.
4. Linguistic structure is organized into a number of stratal systems. In the period since 1966 the number posited has varied from four to six.

The possibility of typological variation among languages of the world as to the number of stratal systems has also been allowed for.

5. Each stratal system contains a tactic pattern, defining the arrangement of its elements or -emes, and a realizational portion, broken into sign and alternation patterns.

6. The tactics provides the environments for alternate realizations within each stratal system, though the precise means of implementing this provision have varied.

Developments altering details within this basic framework have come about as a result of the increased application of the theory to linguistic data. Different hypotheses have been tried to allow the theory to handle data in an increasingly satisfying way. This development has of necessity followed the kind of procedures characteristic of scientific investigation, involving the formulation, testing, and reformulation of hypotheses. Due to the integrated nature of the linguistic system, a hypothesis which handles one set of phenomena may have less felicitous repercussions for the treatment of others, so still newer hypotheses for the treatment of both have been attempted.

Among the developments since 1966 that are reflected in the present work are the following:

1. Each stratal system now contains two alternation patterns instead of the one posited in the *Outline*. One of these is situated above the tactic pattern, the other below it.

2. The conditioning of alternation in both alternation patterns is now provided by enablers connected to the tactics of the same stratal system by conditioning lines. This contrasts with the position expressed in the *Outline*, according to which all conditioning was handled by the tactics directly.

3. Most of the phenomena formerly handled by the hypophonemic and phonemic stratal systems together are now treated in a single stratal system, called phonemic. A phonetic stratal system has been postulated to handle phonetic segment and cluster structure and allophonic variation.

4. Diamond nodes have been introduced to represent points of intersection between tactic and realizational portions of a stratal system. Various types of diamonds allow greater flexibility than the former system.

This version of the theory represents what Lamb considers the best available hypothesis today, based on a consideration of the data and the basic principles of the theory. Additional refinements can be expected in the future as a result of further investigation.

The ideas of two other important stratificationalists differ in a number of significant ways from those of Lamb, while still adhering to most of the same basic principles.

Gleason arrived at stratificational ideas about linguistic structure independently of Lamb. The two men later began to influence each other's thinking and came to some basic agreements with regard to terminology. Gleason's emphasis has continued, however, to differ from that of Lamb. He has not employed the graphic notation as thoroughly as Lamb, for example, and has made much greater use of less completely formalized descriptive statements, particularly for interstratal relationships. Gleason has generally recognized fewer stratal systems than Lamb, never recognizing as many as six. His most significant work within the theory has been in the area of semological structure, particularly the structure of texts. Only a small part of his work in this area has reached print, though his influence is apparent in the work of his students, such as Charles Taber.

Peter Reich became interested in stratificational theory in his search for a framework which could allow him to relate linguistic structure to the psychologist's view of language behavior. His version of the theory has come to differ from that of Lamb in a number of ways. Unlike Gleason, he makes a thorough use of the graphic notation system. He has departed from Lamb's use of this system, however, in a number of ways. He also differs from Lamb in the way he defines the workings of the nodes in a model of performance. He interprets each node as a kind of process system known as a finite-state machine. This contrasts with the micronode definitions now being attempted by Lamb, which break down each macronode into more fundamental relationships. Reich also differs from both Lamb and Gleason on the nature of the strata, in that he does not posit a separate tactic pattern for each one. Rather he has an initial tactic pattern and attempts to account for additional variation entirely in the realizational portion. For this reason, Reich feels that the term "relational network theory" is more appropriate to his ideas than "stratificational."

The persistence of these variations gives evidence that the final answer has not been reached by any of the investigators concerned. But in view of the complexity of the subject matter and the short time it has been investigated, it is unrealistic to expect the ultimate model to have been achieved yet, or indeed to expect it in the near future. There is still far too much relevant data about which we know far too little.

This book has tried to provide evidence that the general stratificational point of view, which is shared by linguists like Lamb, Gleason, and Reich as well as others, provides a worthwhile approach to the structure of language and a whole range of related phenomena. If it serves its purpose, it will encourage the broader application of the theory. Such a development will doubtless lead to further changes in the theory, and alternate versions of it. In so doing, it may bring us at least a few steps closer to the ultimate truth about the nature of language and its place in the universe. This is surely what all linguists are seeking.

# APPENDIX I

# *Multistratal Description*
# *of a Sample Sentence*

This appendix is designed to illustrate the principles of stratificational linguistics discussed in the text by showing their application to the structure of a single sentence over several strata. Because gnostemic structure is a relatively unexplored area, the discussion will begin with the semology and work downward. The sample sentence, chosen for the number of points on various strata which it illustrates, is *The best woodpeckers have been shot by Lance's friends.*

## I.1 *Semological Structure*

The semological structure associated with the sample sentence is shown in Figure I.1 in terms of sememes. This structure (a trace from the semotactics) shows the agent—realized as *Lance's friends*—and the focussed goal—realized as *the best woodpeckers*—associated in a predication with the event sememe $^S$/shoot/. The perfect aspect element $^S$/Pf/ is shown to dominate the entire predication. It occurs in a position apparently similar to that of the past tense element $^S$/Pt/, but these two are not actually members of the same semotactic class, since they may co-occur, as illustrated by the phrase *had been shot*. We must therefore assume that aspect is a separate option from tense. Here zero tense, equivalent to "present," has been selected. The only feature within the agent portion of the predication which has not been illustrated in Chapter 5 is the association of $^S$/Lance/ with the possessive element $^S$/Poss/. This combination is shown here to be subordinated to the combination $^S$/friend/ $\cdot$ $^S$/Pl/, since it modifies the latter. In other instances, $^S$/Poss/

290

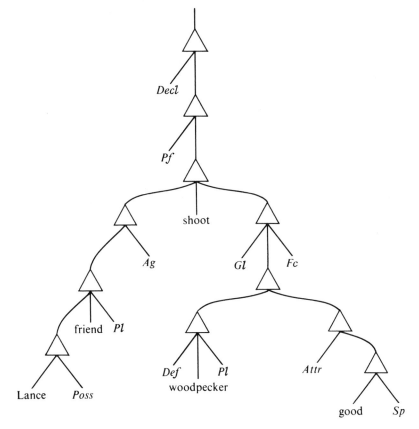

**Figure I.1   Sememic Structure of Sample Sentence**

will be realized as a verb *have*, but here it is realized as the possessive suffix-*'s*. It may also be realized as the preposition *of*, as in *the president of the university*.

The general predication structure illustrated here is discussed in Section 5.2. As also discussed in that section, the goal is shown to be in focus. This goal is further shown to have an attributive element, in accordance with principles discussed in Section 5.4. This attribution is composed of an association of $^S$/good/ with the superlative element $^S$/Sp/.

Most of the sememes shown here will turn out to be in one-to-one correspondence with semons. For the following examples, however, certain discrepancies between these two levels must be noted.

1. $^S$/Decl/ will be realized as zero in the sememic alternation pattern in this case. When the same element occurs with a subordinate predication, it will presumably have an overt semonic realization, leading in the lexotactics to the selection of relative markers, as in *the pencil* THAT *is green*.

2. Likewise, in the sememic alternation pattern $^S$/Attr/ will be realized as zero here. In other cases, it may be ultimately realized as a form of the verb *to be* on the lower strata.

3. $^S$/Gl/ and $^S$/Fc/ are realized portmanteau as $^{SS}$/Ps/ in the sememic alternation pattern. This semic sign is in turn composed of the semons $^{SN}$/S/ (subject selection), $^{SN}$/be/, and $^{SN}$/PP/, as discussed in Section 5.3. The latter breakdown will be shown in the sememic sign pattern.

4. $^S$/Pf/ is realized as a single sememic sign, $^{SS}$/Pf/, but the sememic sign pattern will show this element to be composed of the semons $^{SN}$/have/ and $^{SN}$/PP/. This matter is also treated in Section 5.3.

Figure I.2 shows the fuller treatment of semological structure implied by the above remarks. Those sememes which have discrepant semonic realizations are given an internal label corresponding to that of Figure I.1. The further realizations are shown below this label.

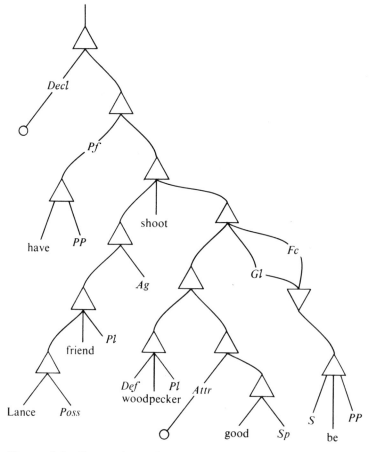

**Figure I.2  Extension of Figure I.1 to the Semonic Level**

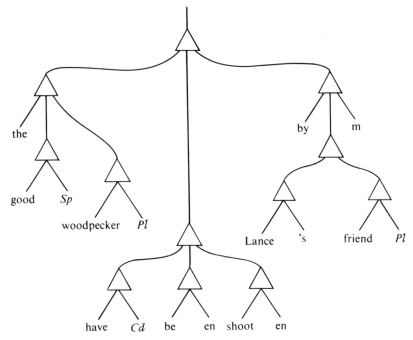

**Figure I.3  Lexemic Structure of Sample Sentence**

## I.2  Lexological Structure

The lexemic structure associated with the sample sentence is shown in Figure I.3. In this structure, the goal has been selected as subject as a consequence of the occurrence of $^{SN}$/S/ as a component of $^{SS}$/Ps/. Further instances in which the lexemes occurring do not have a label corresponding to that of their sememic realizate are shown in Table I.1. The first two differences

**Table I.1  Discrepancies and Label Differences Between Semons and Lexemes**

| Semon | Lexeme |
|-------|--------|
| *Def* | the |
| *PP* | en |
| *Ag* | by |
| *Poss* | 's |
| ∅ | m |
| ∅ | *Cd* |

listed in the table are merely a matter of labelling, while the last two differences are cases of empty realization, the details of which will be explained below.

A significant portion of the discrepancy between the sememic and lexemic structures lies in the amount of sequential ordering imposed on the elements by the lexotactics. The AND at the top of Figure I.3 orders three major constituents, which may be termed "subject noun phrase," "verb phrase," and "agent phrase," respectively. Within the subject noun phrase, the article and adjective are now placed before the noun and ordered with respect to each other.

Three major elements of the verb phrase are now ordered and distinguished. The first of these elements consists of $^{L}$/have/ with its concord affix $^{L}$/Cd/. The $^{L}$/have/ is a part of the realization of $^{SS}$/Pf/, while $^{L}$/Cd/ will be a determined lexeme placed by the lexotactics on the first element of the verb phrase (it will have a zero realization in this case). The second element of the verb phrase consists of $^{L}$/be/ with its affix $^{L}$/en/. The former is the second part of the realization of $^{SS}$/Ps/, while the latter is the last part of the realization of $^{SS}$/Pf/. The final element is the main verb $^{L}$/shoot/ with its affix $^{L}$/en/, which in this instance is the third and last part of the realization of $^{SS}$/Ps/. All affixes are still shown as simultaneous with their associated words, since the morphotactics will provide for their necessary orderings. The general procedure reflected by this analysis involves refraining from assigning an order to elements until the final order can be determined, all other things being equal. The interaction of the semology with the lexotactics needed to produce verb phrases of this type is discussed in Section 5.3.

In the agent phrase, the preposition $^{L}$/by/ is a realization of $^{S}$/Ag/. In this case, it is followed by a noun phrase and the objective marker $^{L}$/m/. The major elements of the noun phrase are also ordered.

The following cases of discrepancy between lexemes and lexons may be noted.

1. $^{L}$/woodpecker/ is realized as a complex lexemic sign, which the lexemic sign pattern will show to consist of $^{LN}$/wood/ followed by $^{LN}$/peck/ followed by $^{LN}$/er/. This example is referred to in Section 5.1.
2. $^{L}$/Cd/ is realized as zero in the lexemic alternation pattern, since the subject is plural. With a singular subject it would be overtly realized as $^{LS}$/s/. Compare the discussion in Section 4.6.
3. $^{L}$/m/ is realized as zero in the lexemic alternation pattern, since it will have an overt realization only with certain pronouns, as mentioned in Section 5.3.

Figure I.4 incorporates these discrepancies in a lexonic extension of Figure I.3 similar to the semonic extension shown in Figure I.2.

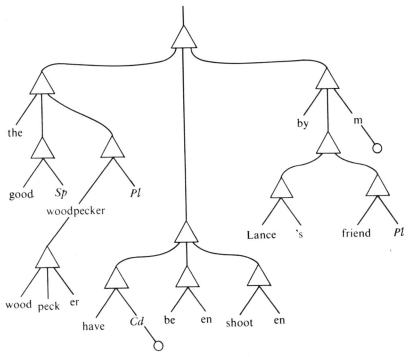

**Figure I.4   Extension of Figure I.3 to the Lexonic Level**

## I.3   *Morphological Structure*

The structure assigned by the morphemic stratal system is primarily concerned with the internal structure of morphological words. The basic cycle of the morphotactics is word-sized, and the structure assigned by this tactics to combinations of morphological words is not really significant. Bearing this point in mind, we will deal on this level with the traces from the tactics for individual morphological words.

The morphological words in the sample sentence are *the, best, woodpeckers, have, been, shot, by, Lance's,* and *friends.* Of these, *the* and *by* have exceedingly simple traces from the morphotactics, since they are not even potentially complex morphologically, while *have* is just as simple in this case, despite the potential occurrence of a suffix, as in *has* and *had.* The remaining morphological words consist of two or more morphemes. The traces from the

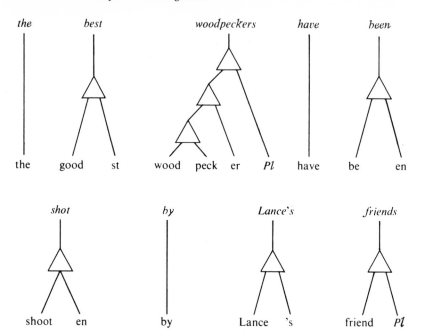

**Figure I.5   Morphemic Structures of Words in Sample Sentence**

morphotactics for each of these morphological words are displayed in Figure I.5. The major difference between these morphological structures and their lexonic realizates lies in the greater amount of sequential ordering which the morphotactics has assigned. The only simultaneous morphemes are ᴹ/shoot/ and ᴹ/en/, so represented because a simulfix is actually involved. All other inflectional affixes, treated as simultaneous in the lexology, are now shown to be suffixes. We may assume that the morphotactics will assign a juncture to the beginning of each morphological word as a determined element. For convenience, these junctures have not been shown in the traces, but they will become significant when we consider phonological structure.

Table I.2 outlines several cases of discrepancy between these morphemes

**Table I.2   Discrepancies Between Morphemes and Morphemic Signs**

| Morpheme | Morphemic Sign Selected | Alternate Morphemic Signs |
|----------|------------------------|---------------------------|
| good | beᴛ | gud |
| *Pl* | z | i⁺ (mice), en (oxen), ∅ (sheep), and so on |
| en | n (been), a⁺ (shot) | d (filled), ə⁺ (sung), and so on |

and the morphemic signs which will realize them, which will be handled in the morphemic alternation pattern. Each morphemic sign will have been assigned a morphonic "spelling" by the morphemic sign pattern. Table I.3 summarizes the appropriate representations for the various morphemic signs in the sample sentence.

### Table I.3 Morphonic Composition of Morphemic Signs

| Morphemic Sign | Morphonic Composition |
|---|---|
| the | ð ē |
| beT | b e T |
| st | s t |
| wood | w u d |
| peck | p e k |
| er | r |
| Z | Z |
| have | h æ v |
| be | b i |
| n | n |
| shoot | š ū t |
| a⁺ | a⁺ |
| by | b ī |
| Lance | l æ n s |
| 's | z |
| friend | f r e n d |
| Z | Z |

The representations of the vowels employed here are somewhat different from those of the system used in exercise 4 of Set 6A, which involved less abstraction from the classical phonemic level. Here the vowel nuclei regularly pronounced [ay], [iy], [uw] have been represented by the single morphons $^{MN}$/ī, ē, ū/. This step has been taken to provide for an easier treatment of such alternations as those illustrated by the words *derive* versus *derivative*, *serene* versus *serenity*, and so on.

## I.4 Phonological Structure

Our account of the phonological structure associated with the sample sentence will of necessity be more sketchy and incomplete than those of the higher strata, because much work remains to be done on English phonology from a stratificational point of view. Particularly obvious is the omission of all reference to stress and intonation. We do know that some elements ultimately realized in terms of stress and intonation will be assigned on strata much higher than the phonemic. The ultimate realization of the sememe $^S$/Int/, for example, is sometimes a rising intonation contour. Various sememes of emphasis and contrast may also be realized in terms of stress and intonation characteristics. Moreover, many morphemes have inherent stress as a part of their representations in the morphemic sign pattern. The phonology will have to take account of the various bits of information fed to it by the upper strata and assign stress and intonation features to the various syllables in accordance with its own principles for their realization. Our detailed account here, however, will be confined to the segmental phonemes, and even this will be tentative.

We will take phonological word and syllable to be the most significant ranks in the phonotactics for the present investigation. We can tentatively define a phonological word as a sequence of one or more syllables bounded by open junctures and containing one major stress (despite our failure to explicitly deal with stress). Figure I.6 presents the phonemic structures for the phonological words in the sample sentence. In all examples the first row of downward ANDs below the single one representing the phonological word as a whole stands for the syllable rank. The row of ANDs below this one, when it occurs, stands for the syllable elements: onsets, nuclei, and codas. Where these elements are phonemically simple rather than complex, of course, no AND will be represented in the traces.

These structures exhibit a number of discrepancies from the morphonic structures which they realize. One discrepancy involves the realization of the single morphons $^{MN}$/ē ī/ as the combinations of phonemes $^P$/e:/ and $^P$/i:/, respectively. Another involves the resolution of the conflict between $^{MN}$/ū/ and $^{MN}$/a$^+$/ in the main verb in favor of the latter. Thus $^{MN}$/ū/ will be realized as zero in the morphonic alternation pattern. It should further be noted that while $^{MN}$/a$^+$/ will be simultaneous with the whole morpheme $^{MN}$/š ū t/, in the phonology it will be localized in the syllable nucleus. A further discrepancy involving vowels is the empty occurrence of $^P$/ə/ in $^P$/wudpekərZ/ and $^P$/lænsəz/. In both instances there is an occurrence of this maximally unmarked vowel to fill out the syllable structure. Finally, there is a discrepancy involving consonants which will be handled in the morphonic alternation pattern: $^{MN}$/T/ will be realized as zero before $^P$/s/.

The realization of the various phonemes in terms of phonemic signs are shown in the middle column of Table I.4. The phonemic sign transcription, it should be remembered, is the one most closely corresponding to classical phonemic representation. The discrepancies between phonemes and phonemic signs may be explained as follows.

1. In certain unstressed environments, certain vowel nuclei, among them the $^P$/e:/ of $^P$/ðe:/ and the $^P$/æ/ of $^P$/hæv/, will be realized as the unmarked vowel $^{PS}$/ə/.

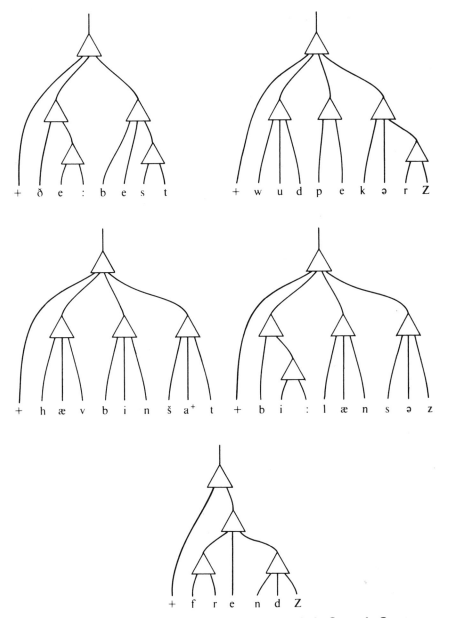

**Figure I.6 Structures of Phonological Words in Sample Sentence**

### Table I.4  Phonological Representations of
### Words in Sample Sentence

| *Phonemic* | *Phonemic Sign* | *Phononic* |
|---|---|---|
| +ðe:best | +ðəbest | +SpVoCl VoSpCl<br>Ap    LbFrRzAp<br>Vd    Vd |
| +wudpekərZ | +wudpekərz | +LbVoCl Cl VoClVoRzSp<br>LbApLbFr          Rz<br>Hi Vd               Vd |
| +hævbinša⁺t | +əvbinšat | +VoSp Cl VoNs SpVoCl<br>LbLbFr ApFrLoAp<br>VdVdHi |
| +bi:lænsəz | +baylænsəz | +Cl VoFrApVoNs Sp VoSp<br>LbLo       Fr ApRz   Rz<br>Vd         Lo        Vd |
| +frendZ | +frends | +Sp RzVoNs Cl Sp<br>Lb    Fr ApApRz<br>Vd |

2. Under similar unstressed conditions, initial $^P$/h/ will be realized as zero, as in the realization of $^P$/hæv/ as $^{PS}$/əv/.

3. Before $^P$/:/, $^P$/i/ is realized as $^{PS}$/a/, but after the front vowels $^P$/i, e, æ/, $^P$/:/ will be realized as $^{PS}$/y/. Thus the sequence $^P$/i:/ is realized as $^{PS}$/ay/.

4. Two phonemic distinctions are needed to provide conditioning environments in the phonotactics, but they are neutralized unconditionally in the phonemic alternation pattern. These are the distinction of $^P$/a/ and $^P$/a⁺/, part of a series of contrasts needed to distinguish preemptive vowels from the nonpreemptive counterparts, and the distinction of $^P$/z/ and $^P$/Z/, needed to deal with the different effects of the possessive and plural suffixes in such examples as *wife's* versus *wives*. The former pair is neutralized to $^{PS}$/a/. In the latter case, the neutralization results in $^{PS}$/z/ in some environments, among them that exhibited in $^{PS}$/wudpekərz/, and $^{PS}$/s/ in those environments where the realization is either voiceless or with environmentally predictable voicing, as in $^{PS}$/frends/.

The last column of Table I.4 shows the phononic representation corresponding to each of the phonemic sign representations of the middle column in accordance with the equivalences shown in Table 6.7.

## I.5  *A Remark on Phonetic Representations*

Since not even a general outline of the structure of the phonetic stratal system has been developed to date, we cannot expect to present the treatment of the sample sentence on this stratum in any detail at all. A few remarks on phenomena for which this stratal system will be called upon to account do seem in order, however. First, it will surely be called upon to provide a specification of phonetic components whose presence can be predicted in terms of other components. Two examples of this situation from our data involve the presence of phonetic voicing ([Vd]) in the segment $^{PS}$/l/ $=$ $^{PN}$/Ap/ (*Lance's*), and also in the segment $^{PS}$/s/ $=$ $^{PN}$/Sp $\cdot$ Rz/ (*friends*). In the first case, only components in the same segment need be considered to allow the prediction, while in the second, we must also consider an adjacent segment —namely, $^{PS}$/d/ $=$ $^{PN}$/Cl $\cdot$ Ap $\cdot$ Vd/—to allow voicing to be predicted.

There are also cases of diversification for particular components, in environments statable in terms of the components of the same or adjacent segments. English $^{PN}$/Lb/, for example, will be realized as "labiodental" when it occurs in the same segment with $^{PN}$/Sp/ (the initial consonant of *friends*) but as "bilabial" in the same segment with $^{PN}$/Cl/ (the initial consonant of *best*).

Finally, there may be cases in which two components considered sequential on the phononic level are realized simultaneously phonetically. So $^{PS}$/ər/ $=$ $^{PN}$/VoRz/ will be realized as a single phonetic segment: [Vo $\cdot$ Rz], a retracted vowel.

These are just a few examples of the phenomena for which the phonetic stratal system will be called upon to account.

# APPENDIX II

# *Answers to Exercises*

## CHAPTER 2

**1.** Diversification

**2.** Composite realization

**3.** Neutralization with composite realization

**4.** Portmanteau realization

**5.** Composite realization

**6.** Composite realization

**7.** Portmanteau realization

**8.** Diversification with composite realization

**9.** Neutralization with composite realization

**10.** Portmanteau realization

## CHAPTER 3

### Set 3A

**1.** 32    **3.** 10    **5.** 36

**2.** 19    **4.** 576    **6.** 28

**Set 3B**

**1.**

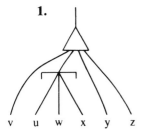

**2.**

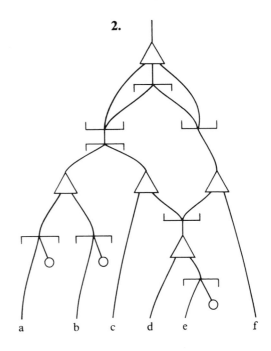

**3.**

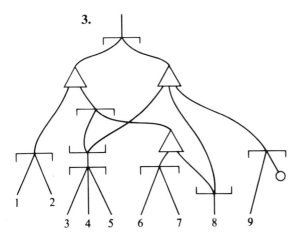

**Set 3C**

**1.** Any five of
 a, b, at, av, bt, bv, ti, tj, tk, vi, vj, vk, ia, ib, ja, jb, ka, kb

**2.** Any five of
 ZAX, ZAXD, ZAXCD, ZBX, ZBXD, ZBXCD, YX, YXD, YXCD

3. Any five of
   EVJ, EWH, FVJ, FWH, GVJ, GWH, SE, SF, SG, TE, TF, TG

4. Any five of
   RN, QN, RM, QM, PKM, PKN, PKMN, RLMN, QLMN

5. **a.** +      **f.** −      **k.** −
   **b.** −      **g.** +      **l.** −
   **c.** +      **h.** −      **m.** −
   **d.** −      **i.** +      **n.** −
   **e.** −      **j.** −      **o.** +

**Set 3D**

**1.**  a

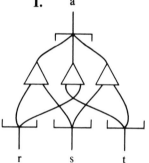

r    s    t

**2.**  b

p

**3.**  c

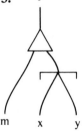

m    x    y

**4.**  d

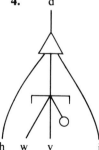

h   w   v        j

**5.**  e

t    m   a   r   1

**6.**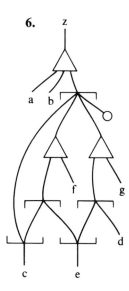

**7.**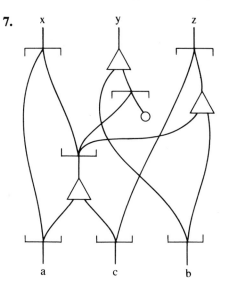

**8.**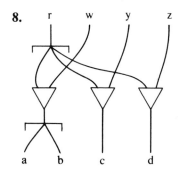

## Set 3E

**1.** S / Sb Pr

Pr / Vb Ob

Sb, Ob / NP

NP / D N

D / the, a

N / man, janitor, woman

Vb / V E

V / see, kill, take

E / -s, -ed

**2.** X / $X_1$, $X_2$

    $X_1$ / Y D W

    W / $Z_1$, $V_1$

    $X_2$ / U &

    & / e, f

    e / E $Z_2$

    f / F $V_2$

    $Z_1$, $Z_2$ / Z

    $V_1$, $V_2$ / V

    Y / A, B, C

    U / M, N

    Z / S, T

    V / P, Q, R

**3.** S / (John, Bill, June, Mary, Tom, Art) (see, kill, take) (-s, -ed) (John, Bill, June, Mary, Tom, Art)

**4.** X / (A, B, C) D (P, Q, R, S, T)), ((M, N) ((E(P, Q, R)), (F(S, T))))

NOTE: The use of a single formula in problems 3 and 4 is less than ideal because it fails to represent the generalizations shown by the upward ORS in the graphic form, thereby requiring a multiple listing of the members of some classes. Also the many parenthesizations required make the account confusing. Multiple parentheses are used for multiple bracketings because the brackets and braces of conventional algebra have distinctive applications in linguistics (for instance, the stratificational use of brackets to show optionality).

**5.**

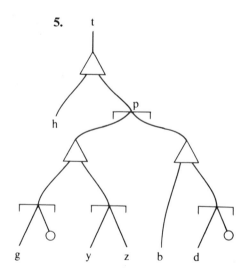

**6.**

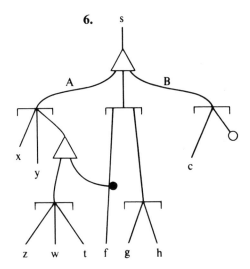

**7.**

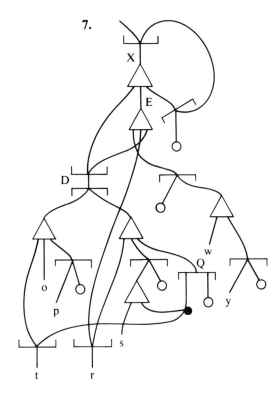

## CHAPTER 4

NOTE: In these and other tactic diagrams, the zero element is used as the origin part of the tactics.

### Set 4A

**1.**

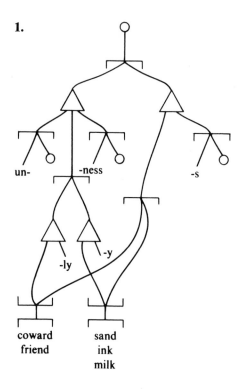

**2.**

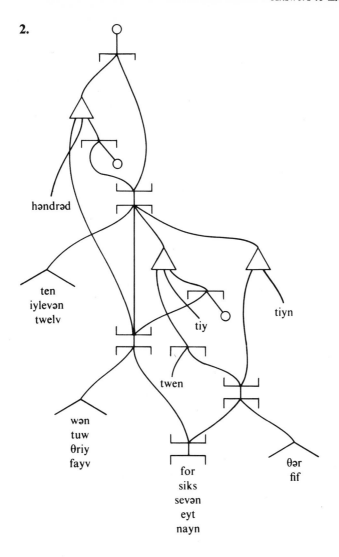

**3.**

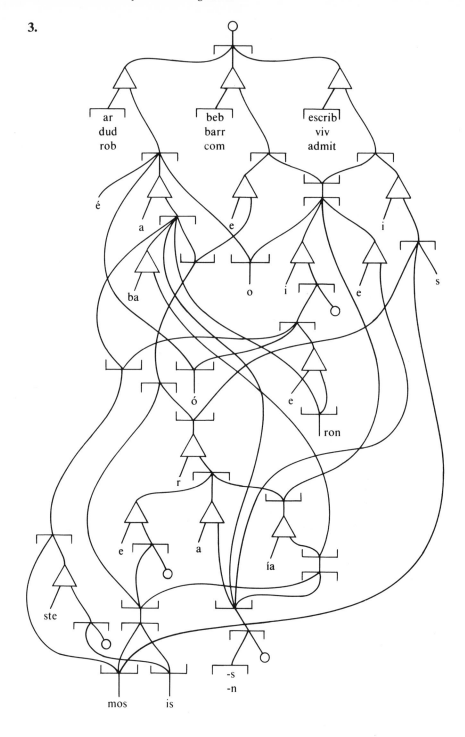

## Set 4B

**1.** If we consider the alternations /tuw/ ~ /twen/, /θriy/ ~ /θər/, and /fayv/ ~ /fif/ to be alternate realizations of the same morpheme, the following tactics and alternation pattern would be produced:

**a.**

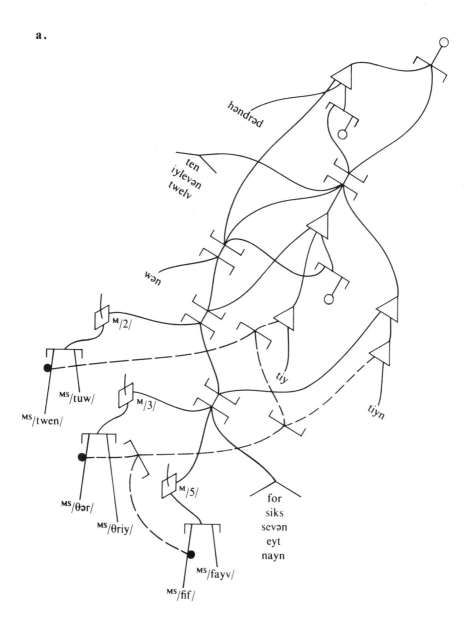

Still greater simplification of the tactics could be achieved by considering /iylevən/ and·/twelv/ portmanteaus of 1+*teen* and 2+*teen*, respectively. This analysis would produce the following account:

**b.**

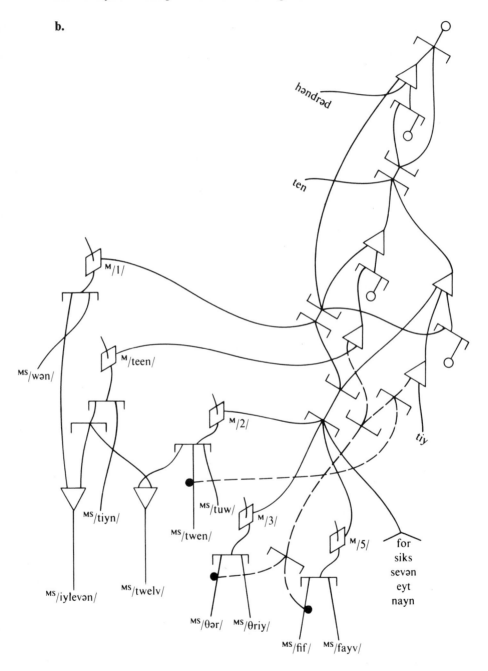

2.

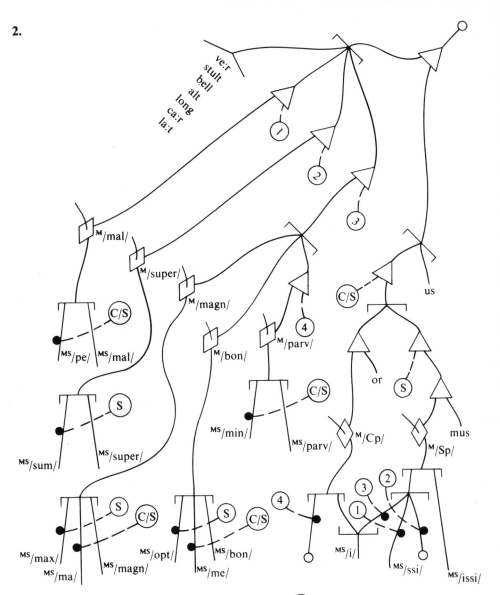

NOTE: Ⓢ is mnemonic for "superlative," C/S for "comparative or superlative."

**Set 4C**

**1.**

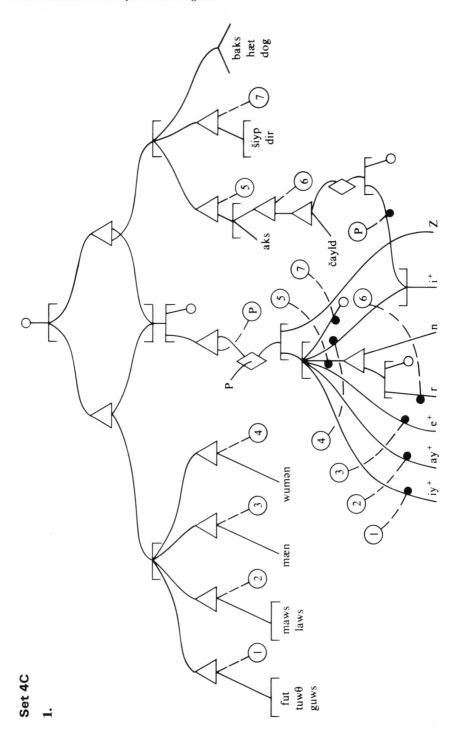

NOTE: In view of the limited amount of preemption in the English plural formation (virtually all such forms in common use are represented in this problem), it seems likely that the variants $e^+$, $i^+$, $ay^+$, $iy^+$ can be considered phonologically conditioned. (There may be a problem, however, in the case of *feet* versus *women*, as the vowels preempted are *u* in both cases.) In such an analysis, all four would be alternate phonological realizations of an umlaut morphon $^{MN}/\dot{V}/$. Such an analysis would reduce the complexity of the morphology. This principle could also be applied to at least some extent to the preemptive verb forms, reducing the number of distinct preemptive morphons.

**2.**

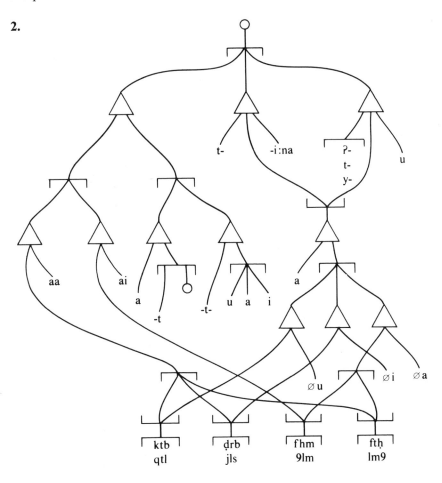

**3.**

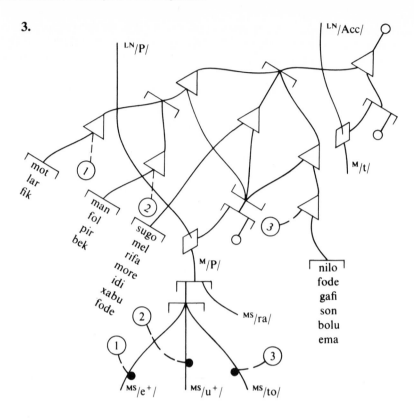

**Set 4D**

1.

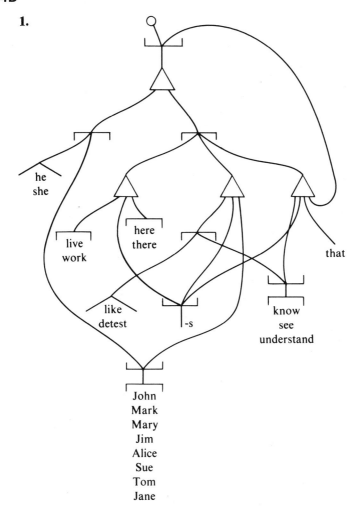

**2.**

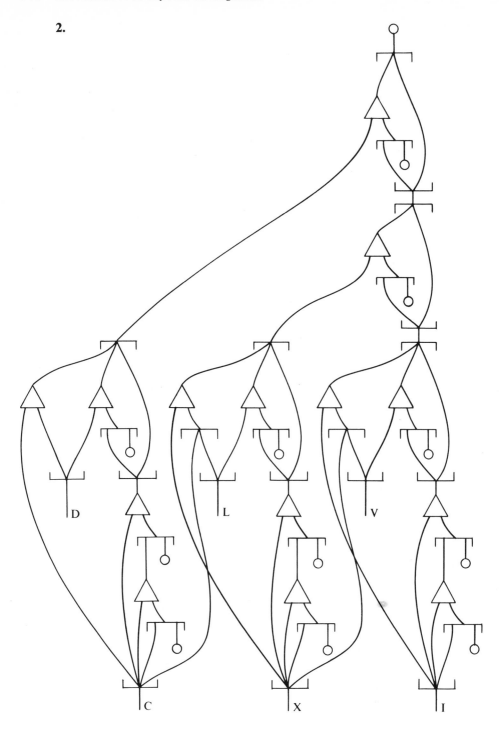

**3.**

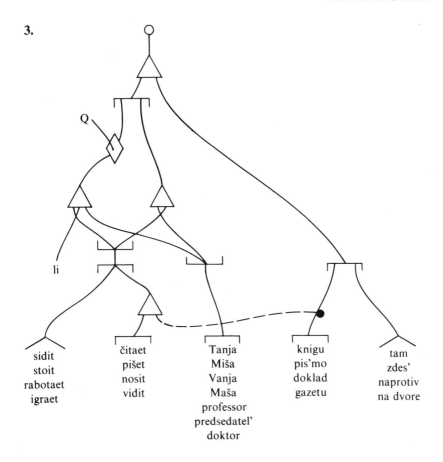

Q

li

sidit
stoit
rabotaet
igraet

čitaet
pišet
nosit
vidit

Tanja
Miša
Vanja
Maša
professor
predsedatel'
doktor

knigu
pis'mo
doklad
gazetu

tam
zdes'
naprotiv
na dvore

**Set 4E**

1.

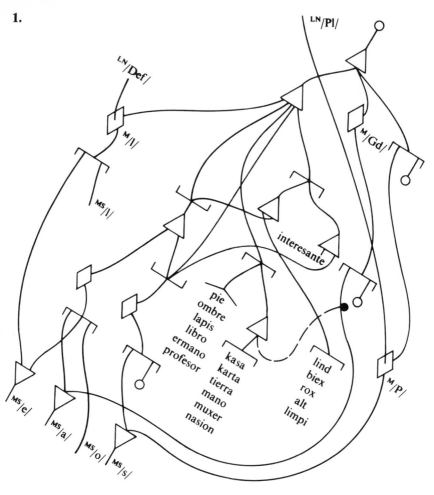

**2.**

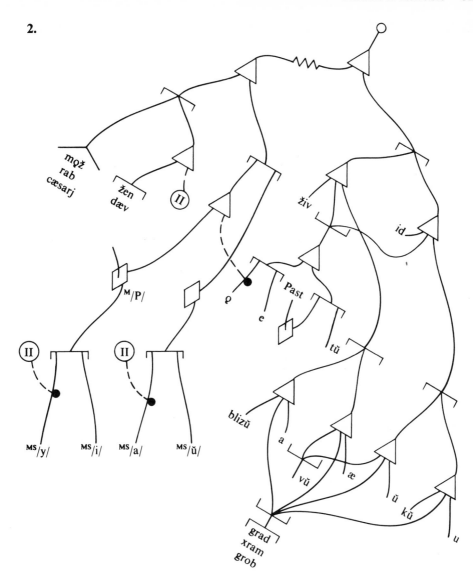

**Set 4F**

**1.   a.**

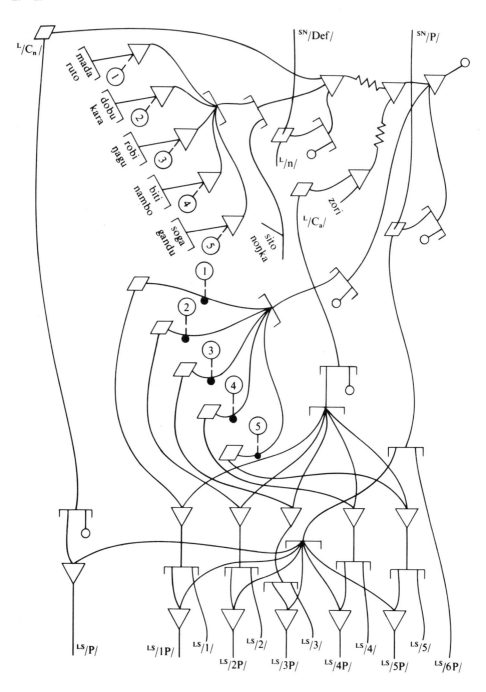

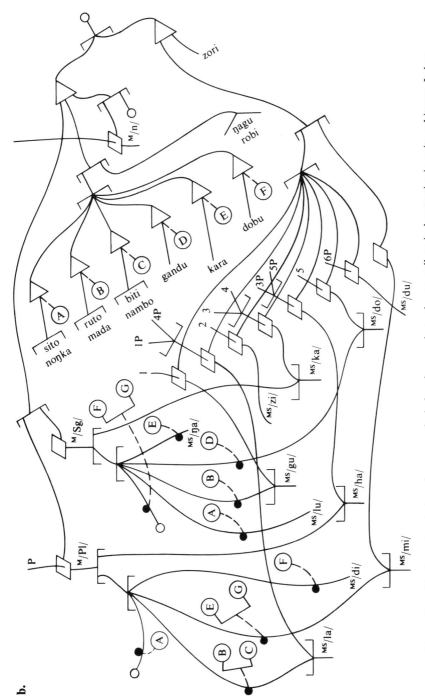

b.

NOTE: For this data, the choice of an unmarked class in morphotactics as well as in lexotactics is quite arbitrary. It has been done here simply to illustrate one of the possibilities. Since concord and noun-inflection classes are partly coincident, it might be worth considering an alternative which allows some of the concord class information to be used in the morphological treatment of nouns.

**2.**

Lexotactics

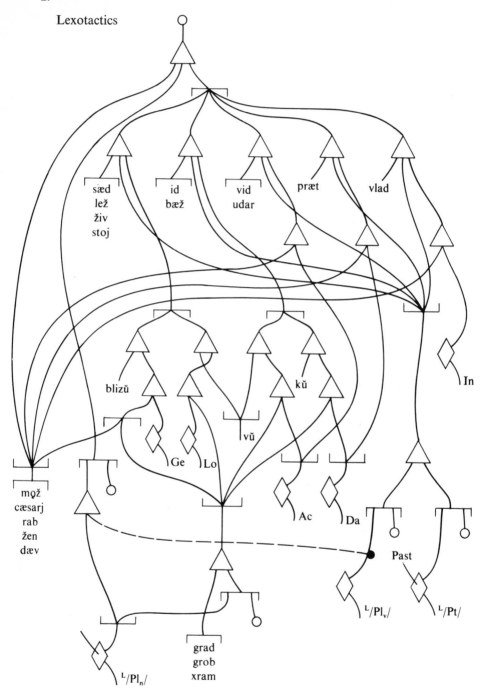

Morphotactics: Nouns

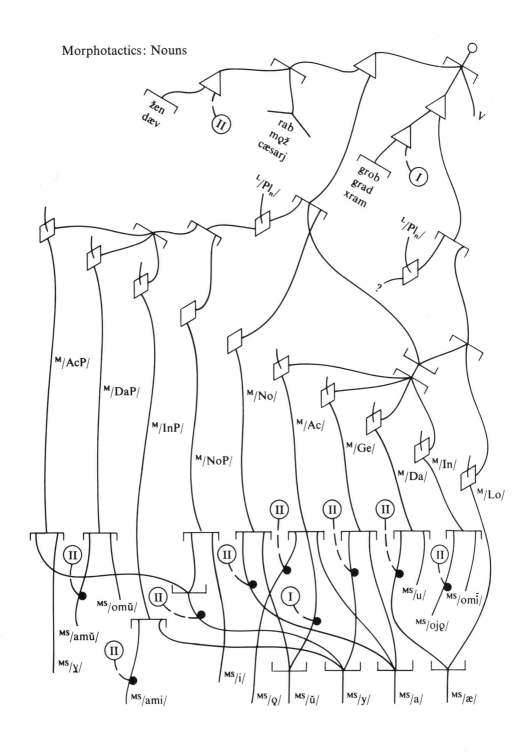

Morphotactics: Verbs

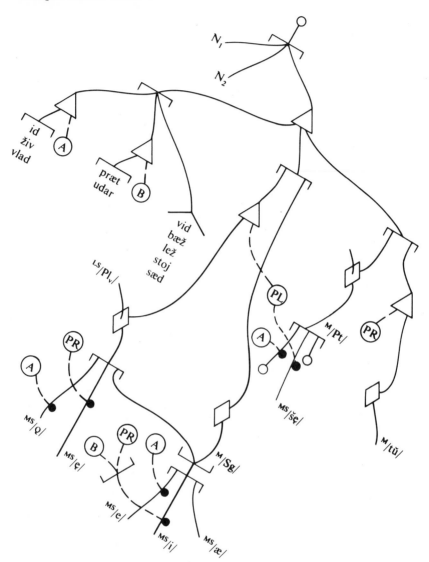

## CHAPTER 5

### Set 5A

**1.**

    **a.** Does John wash the windows with a brush?
    **b.** Were the tigers seen by the man?
    **c.** It was Tim that shot the lion with a gun.
    **d.** Was it with a rope that Steve killed Mike?
    **e.** It is for Sally that Tom mows the lawn.
    **f.** Was it for Simon that Mike was killed?
    **g.** It was the book that was read by Guy.
    **h.** Was it Wayne that bought a book for Carol?
    **i.** Was it Don that was given the key by Steve?
    **j.** Gary was chased by the tiger.

**2.**

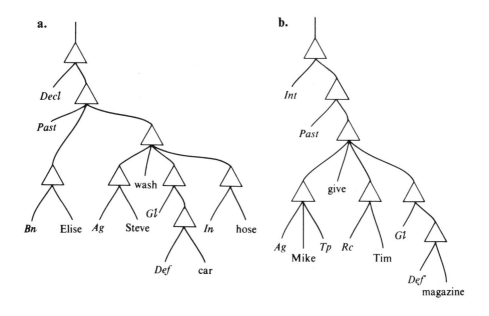

**c.**

**d.**

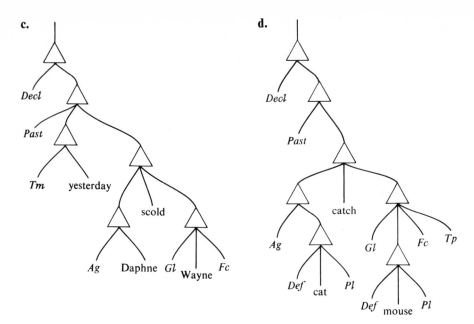

**e.**

**f.**

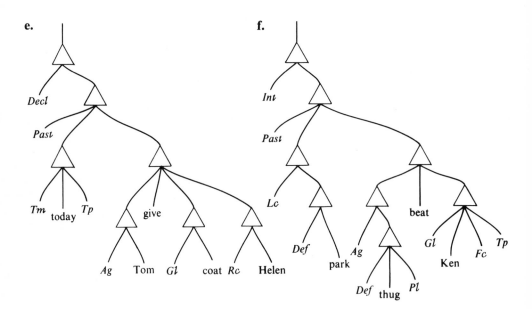

**g.**

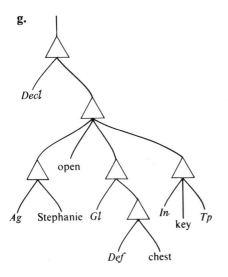

**h.**

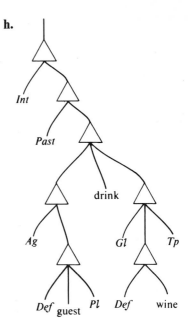

**i.**

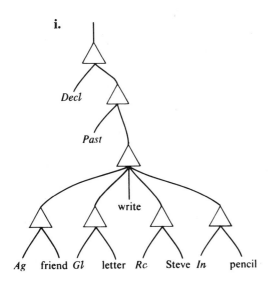

**j.**

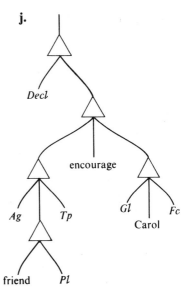

**Set 5B**

**1.**

    **a.** Does Tim see the pretty girl?
    **b.** Men that I saw were killed by tigers.
    **c.** The big tiger saw the man shoot me.
    **d.** Was I seen by the tiger that the man shot?
    **e.** The old lady knows that Art stole the precious jewels.
    **f.** Does Tom understand that the book was given to Sue by Guy?
    **g.** The book that I sold is valuable.
    **h.** Is it a policeman that sees Art steal the money?
    **i.** It was by Wayne that the man that the thug attacked was rescued.
    **j.** It is Irene that knows the man that works here.

**2.**

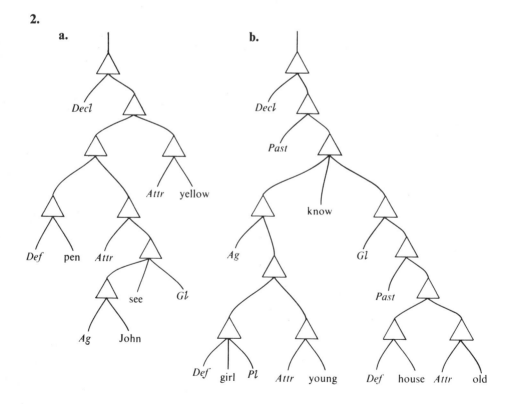

**c.**

**d.**

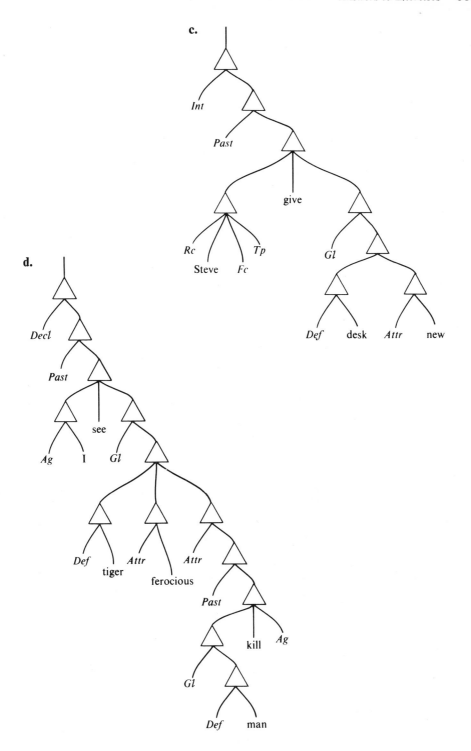

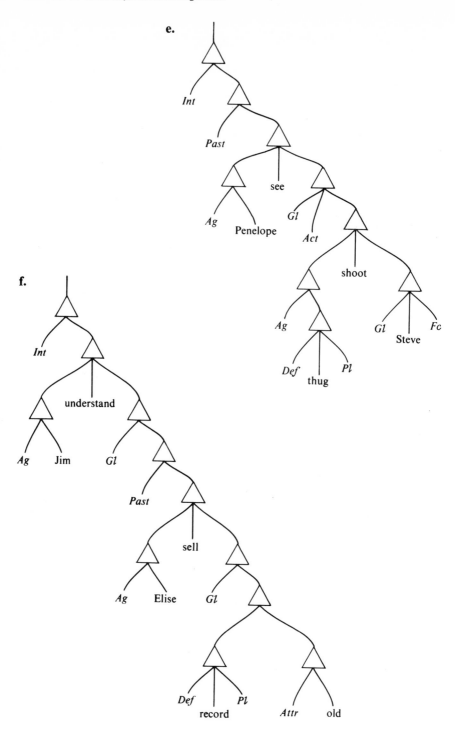

**g.**

**h.**

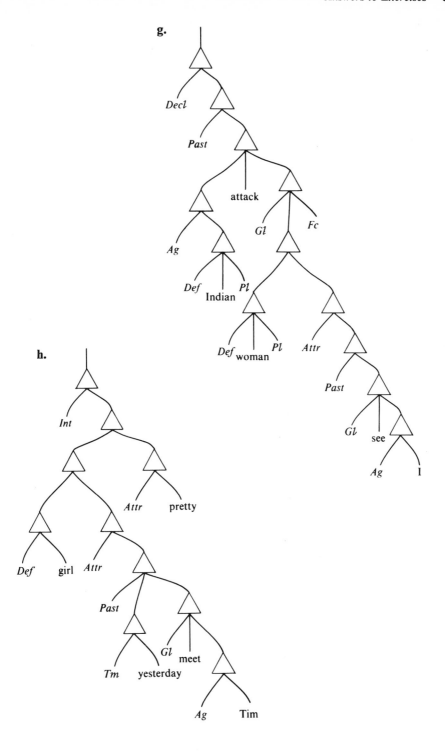

**i.**

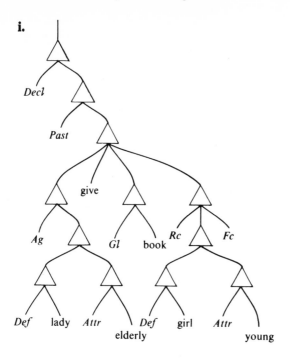

**j.**

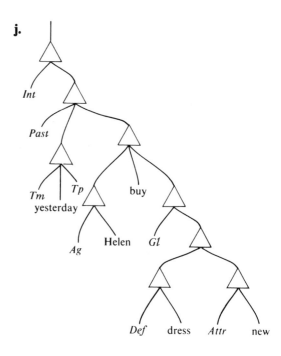

## CHAPTER 6

### Set 6A

**1.** n ‖ m__# / ∅

   + ‖ --- / n

**2.**

  **a.** Morphemes

    $^{MN}$/pu'ku/ 'dog'     $^{MN}$/'sono/ 'lungs'     $^{MN}$/'xaa'nuʔu/ 'cup'

    $^{MN}$/wono/ 'basket'     $^{MN}$/ho'po'poʔo/ 'spider'     $^{MN}$/kuna/ 'wood'

    $^{MN}$/tawa/ 'tooth'     $^{MN}$/ʔaa'paʔni/ 'apple'     $^{MN}$/juhu/ 'fat'

    $^{MN}$/kʷiʔnaaʔa/ 'eagle'     $^{MN}$/nopi/ 'house'     $^{MN}$/cii'paʔa/ 'bird'

    $^{MN}$/mupi/ 'nose'

    $^{MN}$/ʔi/- 'my'     $^{MN}$/ʔy'/- 'your'     $^{MN}$/ni'tu/ 'like'

  **b.** Formulas

    ' ‖ __(', h, ʔ), #__ / ∅     w ‖ '__ / kʷ

     + ‖ --- / '     + ‖ --- / w

    j ‖ '__ / t     m ‖ V__ / w

     + ‖ --- / j     + ‖ --- / m

NOTE: On the basis of the data given, it is not clear whether the solution to the alternation exhibited in the forms of the words meaning 'lungs' and 'cup' should be as stated above or should be stated in terms of the following morphonic forms and formulas to the extent that they would be different from those above: $^{MN}$/sono/ 'lungs,' $^{MN}$/xaa'nuʔu/ 'cup'

    ' ‖ __(', h, ʔ) / ∅     s ‖ V__ / 's     x ‖ V__ / 'x

     + ‖ --- / '     + ‖ --- / s     + ‖ --- / x

**3.**

  **a.** Morphemes

    $^{MN}$/lab/- 'good'     $^{MN}$/klus/- 'silent'     $^{MN}$/maz/- 'small'

    $^{MN}$/ti:r/- 'clean'     $^{MN}$/ve:l/- 'late'     $^{MN}$/lipi:g/- 'sticky'

    $^{MN}$/yauk/- 'nice'     $^{MN}$/ka:d/- 'some'     $^{MN}$/zem/- 'low'

    $^{MN}$/vec/- 'old'     $^{MN}$/rup̦/- 'rough'     $^{MN}$/gaɽ/- 'long'

$^{MN}$/gaiš/- 'pale'     $^{MN}$/zaḷ/- 'green'     $^{MN}$/mi:ḷ/- 'dear'

$^{MN}$/spož/- 'bright'     $^{MN}$/slaṗ/- 'wet'     $^{MN}$/piln/- 'full'

$^{MN}$/su:r/- 'bitter'     $^{MN}$/tumš/- 'dark'     $^{MN}$/nabag/- 'poor'

$^{MN}$/yaun/- 'new'     $^{MN}$/balt/- 'white'     $^{MN}$/pareiz/- 'correct'

$^{MN}$/liel/- 'big'

$^{MN}$/s/ 'masculine suffix'     $^{MN}$/a/ 'feminine suffix'

**b.** Formulas

s ‖ ɾ, ḷ, ṗ— / š

, ‖ c, t, d, s, z, š, ž— / ∅

+ ‖ --- / s

g ‖ —s / k         d ‖ —s / c         z ‖ —s / s
+ ‖ --- / g         + ‖ --- / d         + ‖ --- / z

b ‖ —s / p         t ‖ —s / c         ž ‖ —s / š
+ ‖ --- / b         + ‖ --- / t         + ‖ --- / ž

**4.**

d ‖ (:, C) (t, d)— / əd         D ‖ —d / ∅
+ ‖ (t, d)— / ∅         + ‖ --- / d

+ ‖ C$_{vl}$, D— / t         t ‖ —t / ∅
+ ‖ --- / d         + ‖ --- / t

i ‖ —· Cd / i         e ‖ —· Cd / e
+ ‖ —(:, ·) / a         + ‖ —(:, ·) / i
+ ‖ --- / i         + ‖ --- / e

· ‖ —Cd / ∅         : ‖ i, e— / y
‖ --- ‖ :

(The symbol ‖ means 'is realized the same as,' indicating the need for reference to another formula to determine the appropriate realization.)

(For this data alone, no environment statement is needed, but in a broader context the restriction is needed.)

**5.**

**a.** Morphonic forms of words

| | |
|---|---|
| $^{MN}$/tatra/ 'there' | $^{MN}$/tiṣṭhati/ 'he stands' |
| $^{MN}$/nagare/ 'in the city' | $^{MN}$/icchati/ 'he desires' |
| $^{MN}$/gṛheṣu/ 'in houses' | $^{MN}$/upadiśati/ 'he teaches' |
| $^{MN}$/agnāu/ 'in the fire' | $^{MN}$/asyati/ 'he throws' |
| $^{MN}$/vāriṇi/ 'in the water' | $^{MN}$/ānayati/ 'he brings' |

**b.** Formulas

| | |
|---|---|
| a ‖ a, e__ / ∅ | i ‖ __i / ī |
| , ‖ __i / e | , ‖ i, a__ / ∅ |
| , ‖ __u / o | + ‖ __V / y |
| , ‖ __(a, ā) / ā | + ‖ --- / i |
| + ‖ --- / a | |
| e ‖ __i, u, ā / a | u ‖ C__u / ū |
| ‖ --- / e | + ‖ __V / v |
| ā ‖ a__ / ∅ | , ‖ u__ / ∅ |
| + ‖ --- / a | + ‖ --- / u |

## Set 6B

**1.**

**a.**

| | Ap | Fr | | Lb | |
|---|---|---|---|---|---|
| Cl | t | č | k | p | |
| Cl | d | ǯ | g | b | Vd |
| Cl, Sp | c | | | | |
| Sp | s | š | x | f | |
| Sp | z | ž | | v | Vd |
| Ns | | | n | m | |
| Vb | r | | | | |
| | l | j | | | |
| Vo | | i | ə | u | |
| Vo | | e | a | o | Lo |

NOTES:

1. /č/ and /ǯ/ have the phonetic property of spirancy as well as closure but have been treated as shown in view of the lack of contrasting true stops in the same position.
2. The apicality of /c/ and /r/ may be considered unmarked.
3. /r/ could just as well have been considered to be componentially /Ap/ with /l/ as /Lt/ (or /$\frac{\text{Lt}}{\text{Ap}}$/).

**b.**

| | Fr | | Lb | Gl | |
|---|---|---|---|---|---|
| Cl | | k | p | ʔ | |
| Ns | n | | m | | |
| | l | | w | h | |
| Vo | i | | u | | Hi |
| Vo | e | a | o | | |

NOTE: Due to the lack of contrast between apical and frontal position in this language, it is possible to subsume both phonetic varieties under a single phonemic component, which has been labelled /Fr/. The more specific stipulation of the phonetic value of this component will be predictable from the other components accompanying it in the segment, and will be given in the phonetic system.

**c.**

| | Lb | Ap | Fr | |
|---|---|---|---|---|
| Cl | p | t | t′ | k |
| Cl | b | d | d′ | g |
| Cl | | c | č | |
| Cl, Sp | | ʒ | ǯ | |
| Sp | f | s | š | h |
| Sp | v | z | ž | |
| Ns | m | | ñ | n |
| Vb | | r | | |
| | w | l | j | |

| | Fr | Fr, Lb | Lb |
|---|---|---|---|
| Vo | i | ü | u |
| Vo | e | ö | o |
| Vo | | a | |

Lg :

(See note 3 to the solution to problem 1a above.)

**2.** No solution can be provided, since the result will depend on data selected by the student.

**3.**

    **a.** Componential morphophonemic shapes

| ClApVoSp | | ClVoNs | | Cl VoAp | |
|---|---|---|---|---|---|
| Vd   LoAp 'voice' | |   LbLb | 'godfather' | ApLb | |
| | | | | VdLo | 'ravine' |

| NsVoCl | | SpVoApCl | | ApVoSp | 'breeze' |
|---|---|---|---|---|---|
| LbFrAp | | Lb | | | |
|   LoVd | 'honey' | Vd | 'wolf' | | |

| NsVoCl | | VbVoCl | | ClApFrVoCl | |
|---|---|---|---|---|---|
| LbFrVd | 'moment' |   LbVd | |     LbFr | 'key' |
| | |   Lo | 'horn' | | |

| NsVoSp Cl | | NsVoSp | | VbVoSp | |
|---|---|---|---|---|---|
| LbLbApAp | | Lb   Fr | |   Fr Lb | |
|    Lo | 'bridge' |    Vd | 'man' |   LoVd | 'roar' |

| Cl VoCl | | Cl VbVoCl | | ClVoCl | |
|---|---|---|---|---|---|
| Ap   Lb | | Ap   LbLb | |   LbLb | 'heap' |
| Vd   Vd | 'oak' | Vd   LoVd | 'lung' | | |
| | | | | Vo | 'the' |

    **b.** Formulas

$$\text{Vd} \parallel \_\!\_\# \,/\, \varnothing \qquad \text{Lo} \parallel \overset{\smile}{\_\!\_} \,/\, \varnothing$$
$$+ \parallel \text{---} \,/\, \text{Vd} \qquad + \parallel \text{---} \,/\, \text{Lo}$$

**Set 6C**

**1.**

   **a.**

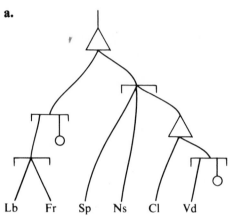

   **b.**

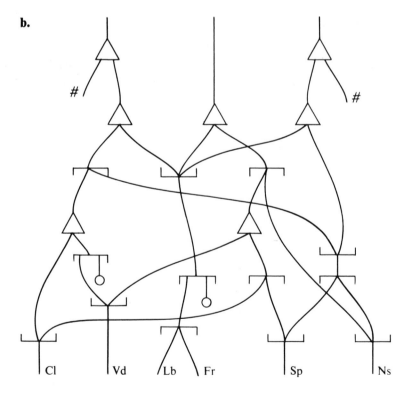

**2.**

   **a.** Segmental treatment

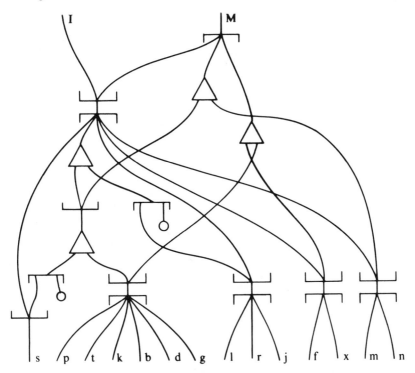

**b.** Componential treatment

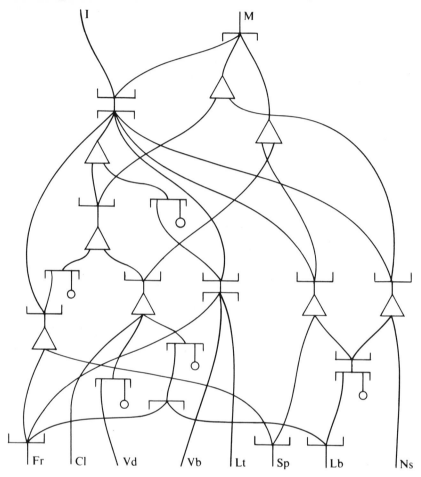

**3.**

    **a.** $(t, t^h, \text{\textsc{t}}, s, s', c, c^h, l)\ C_{x_1} \parallel --- /\ C_{x_1}'$

        $(k, k')\ k \parallel --- /\ k'$

        $w, p^h \parallel \_C_x /\ p$

        $h\ C_{x_1} \parallel --- /\ C_{x_1}^{\ h}$     ($C_x$ is any one of the consonants t, c, or k)

        $\text{\textsc{t}} \parallel \_V /\ \varnothing$

**b.**

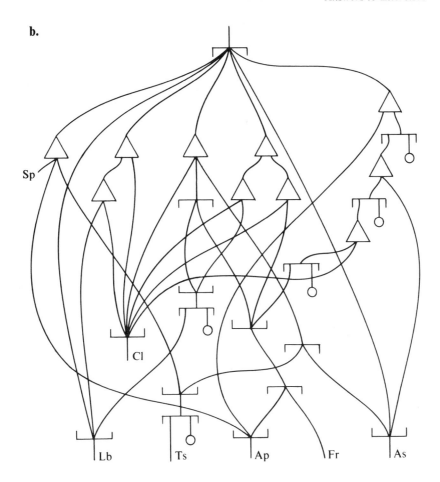

## Set 6D

**1.**

   **a.** This alternation would be handled in the morphonic alternation pattern as the zero realization of $^{\text{MN}}$/n/ in the environment m__#, conditioned by enablers from the appropriate points in the phonotactics.

   **b.** The zero realization of ' could be treated in the morphonic alternation pattern, conditioned by enablers from preceding or following ', h, ʔ (a tactic class). The actual realization of ' as a component /Lf/ (long fortis) could be handled as a matter of its occurrence simultaneously with the realization of the consonant it precedes morphonically, provided it is not itself realized as zero. Two segments in sequence on the morphonic level, therefore, could be realized simultaneously on the phonemic stratum. The realization of *j* as *t* and *w* as $k^w$ in the accompaniment of ', however, can be treated in the phonemic alternation pattern, in terms of the occurrence of different or additional components in the same segment with '.

The alternation of *m* and *w* as realizations of $^{MN}$/m/ may also be treated in the phonemic alternation pattern, in terms of the zero realization of the nasality of $^{P}$/m/ in postvocalic environment.

**c.** If voicing is treated as a phonotactically determined element accompanying the realization of the appropriate consonants, its zero realization can be handled in the phonemic alternation pattern. It would be conditioned by the occurrence of following $^{P}$/s/.

The realization of $^{MN}$/t/ or $^{MN}$/d/ as /c/ before /s/ can actually be treated as a portmanteau, such that (t, d) s/c. It is probably best handled in the phonemic alternation pattern.

The zero realization of $^{MN}$/s/ will have to be handled in the phonemic alternation pattern, since the *s* will be needed as a phoneme to condition other alternations. If /c/ is given the portmanteau treatment suggested above, the conditioning factor for the realization of $^{P}$/s/ as zero will be preceding $^{P}$/c, s, z, š, ž/.

The palatalization of /s/ can be treated as an alternate realization of a component in the phonemic alternation pattern.

**d.** The realization of $^{MN}$/d/ as /əd/ can readily be treated as the occurrence of a determined $^{P}$/ə/ supplied by the phonotactics under the appropriate conditions. The other realizations of $^{MN}$/d/ can be treated in the phonemic alternation pattern as alternate realizations of $^{P}$/d/ under the appropriate conditions.

The zero realizations of $^{MN}$/t/ and $^{MN}$/D/ must be treated in the phonemic alternation pattern, since the distinctions they represent are needed in the output of the phonotactics to condition other alternations.

The alternate realizations of $^{MN}$/·/ are appropriately treated in the morphonic alternation pattern. This step will simplify the treatment of the realizations of $^{MN}$/i/ and $^{MN}$/e/, which may be handled in the phonemic alternation pattern. In the morphonic alternation pattern, that is, we would have the equivalent of the realization formula:

$$· \; / \; \varnothing \; \| \; \_Cd$$
$$/ :$$

and in the phonemic alternation pattern we would have

$$i \; \| \; \_: / a \qquad e \; \| \; \_: / i \qquad : \| \; i, e\_ / y, \text{ and so on}$$
$$\| \; --- / i \qquad \| \; --- / e$$

**2.**

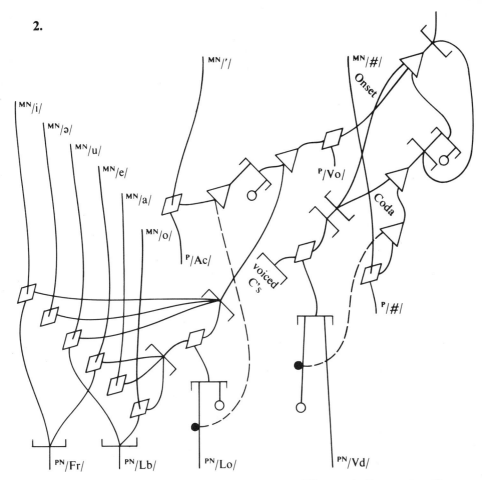

**3.** In addition to the morphonic distinction of <sup>MN</sup>/f v F/, discussed earlier, we must postulate <sup>MN</sup>/S/ with the realization /z/ before <sup>MN</sup>/Z/ (of the plural) and /s/ elsewhere. It will be in contrast with <sup>MN</sup>/s z/. Similarly <sup>MN</sup>/Ð/, subsuming /ð/ and /θ/ as its realizations, will be in contrast with <sup>MN</sup>/θ ð/. In view of the recurrence of this voicing alternation, it should be treated componentially. We can characterize the phonemic realizations of these "special" morphons as being realized as <sup>PS</sup>/f s θ/, respectively; the phonemes <sup>P</sup>/F S Ð/, however, condition the occurrence of a phonotactically determined element <sup>P</sup>/Va/, which is realized as <sup>PN</sup>/Vo/ when <sup>P</sup>/Z/ follows and otherwise as zero.

The verbal derivatives could be handled by positing a morphon <sup>MN</sup>/V/ realized as an obligatory voicing of the spirant which morphonically precedes it. Since all the examples of this voicing in our data involve <sup>P</sup>/F S Ð/, we can consider the realization of <sup>MN</sup>/V/ to take precedence over the determined <sup>P</sup>/Va/ as an accompaniment of these three. The following diagram shows this integrated treatment.

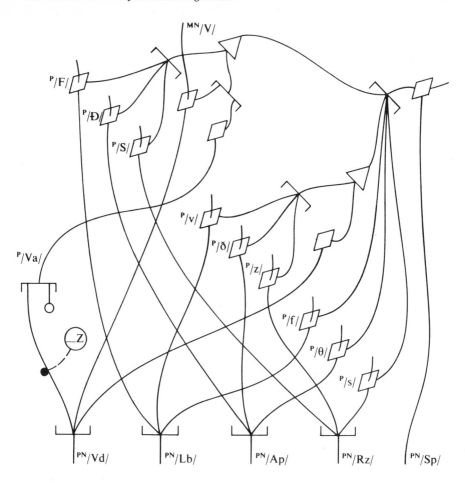

**4.**

**a.** Harmony may be characterized as involving agreement with regard to the presence or absence of fronting and the presence or absence of rounding. For high vowels, it conditions an alternation /i ~ ü ~ ɨ ~ u/ in affixes; as such high vowels follow the voicing and rounding characteristics of preceding vowels. For low vowels, it conditions an alternation /a ~ e/ according to the fronting characteristics of preceding vowels. Fronting harmony is absolute: vowels in the word must be either all front or all nonfront. Rounding harmony, however, applies only up to the first suffix containing a low vowel. All vowels of subsequent suffixes are unrounded. Thus we get /buldum/ but /bulmadim/, /gördüm/ but /görmedim/, and so on.

**b.** There is a special problem with rounding harmony, in that it applies only up to the first suffixal low vowel, this and subsequent suffixes being necessarily unrounded. If we were to posit a special juncture, inserted by the morphotactics between stem and affix, we could easily provide for the phonotactics realizing <sup>MN</sup>/R/ (rounding) as an element simultaneous with the stem and any high vowel affixes next to it, but ending its domain at the first nonhigh suffixal vowel, specified as <sup>P</sup>/a/. This solution would give us two vowel morphons <sup>MN</sup>/i a/ and the elements <sup>MN</sup>/R/ and <sup>MN</sup>/F/ (fronting). If the domain of the former is defined by the phonotactics as suggested, that of the latter may be defined as the whole phonological word. The realization of these elements individually on the vowels can then be handled on the phonetic stratum, in the same manner as the simpler cases discussed in the introduction to the problem.

# APPENDIX III

# Suggested Readings

This selection of additional readings for further information on the various topics discussed in this book is keyed to the Bibliography which follows. It is arranged by chapters and, where pertinent, by section within the chapter.

**Chapter 1**

**1.1**
Lamb 1966a.

**1.2**
Hockett 1961.
Lamb 1971.

**1.3**
Gleason 1964.
Lamb 1964b.
Makkai, A. 1969b.

**1.4**
Chomsky 1965, Ch. 1.
Herrick 1966, 1969c.
Pike 1964.
Reich 1968a.

**1.5**
Bloch 1947.
Chomsky 1957, 1968.

Hjelmslev 1961.
Hockett 1947, 1954.
Nida 1948.

**Chapter 2**

**2.1**
Hockett 1961.
Lamb 1964a, 1969a.

**2.2**
Lamb 1966d.

**2.3**
Lamb 1964a, b.

**Chapter 3**

Lamb 1964b (algebraic notation for realization), 1966a (first suggestion on graphic notation), 1966d, 1971.
Reich 1968b, 1969a, 1970b.

348

## Chapter 4

Lamb 1964b (especially for Section 4.2),
1965b, 1966d.
Lockwood FORTHCOMING a, b.
Longacre 1960.
Makkai, V. B. 1969.
Newell 1966.
Nida 1949, Ch. 4; 1966.
Reich 1969a, 1970a, b.
Rogers 1967.
Sampson 1970a.
Sullivan 1969.
Wells 1947.

## Chapter 5

### 5.1
Bennett 1968, 1969, 1970.
Bloomfield 1933, Ch. 10.
Ikegami 1970.
Lamb 1964a, 1965b, 1971.
Makkai, A. 1969a, 1971.

### 5.2
Chafe 1970.
Fillmore 1968.
Halliday 1967–68.
Leech 1970.

### 5.3
Reich 1969b.

### 5.5
Gleason 1968
Lockwood 1969a.
Stennes 1968.
Taber 1966.

## Chapter 6

### 6.1
Bloch 1941, 1947.
Chomsky 1964, Ch. 4 (critique of classi-
cal phonemics based largely on mis-
interpretation).
Hockett 1942.
Jakobson, Fant, and Halle 1952.
Lamb 1966c.
Pike 1947.
Sapir 1925.

Swadesh 1934.
Trubetzkoy 1969.
Twaddell 1935.

### 6.2
Lamb 1964b, 1966c.
Trager 1934.

### 6.3
Lamb 1964b, IN PRESS.

### 6.4
Hockett 1955; 1966, Chs. 3, 4.
Jakobson, Fant, and Halle 1952.
Lamb 1966c.
Lockwood 1969b.
Rogers 1967.
Sullivan 1969.
Trubetzkoy 1969.

### 6.5, 6.6
Lamb 1966c.
Lockwood 1969c.
Rogers 1967.
Sullivan 1969.

### 6.7
Chomsky 1964, 1967.
Halle 1959.
Lamb 1966c.
Postal 1968.

## Chapter 7

### 7.1
Bloomfield 1933.
Hill, A. 1958.
Hockett 1955, 1961.
Longacre 1964a, b.
Pike 1967.
Trager 1955.
Trager and Smith 1951.

### 7.2
Firth 1948.
Halliday 1961, 1967–68.
Hill, T. 1966.
Hjelmslev 1961, 1970.
Lamb 1966b.
Saussure 1916.
Trubetzkoy 1969.

Uldall 1957.
Vachek 1964, 1966.

**7.3**
Chomsky 1957, 1964, 1965.
Fodor and Garrett 1966.
Katz and Fodor 1963.
Katz and Postal 1964.
Lamb 1967, IN PRESS.
Perlmutter 1970.
Postal 1968.
Reich 1970a, b.

**Chapter 8**

**8.1**
King 1969.
Kiparsky 1968.

Saussure 1916.
Weinreich, Labov, and Herzog 1968.

**8.2**
Chomsky 1968.
Greenberg 1960, 1966.

**8.3**
Bloomfield 1933.
Ikegami 1971.
Lamb 1965a, 1971, FORTHCOMING.
Ljung 1965.
Reich 1968a.

**8.4**
Fleming 1969.
Gleason 1964.
Reich 1969a, 1970a, b, c.

# *Bibliography*

Works belonging to the literature of stratificational linguistics are indicated by *italic* type for the date or other publication designation. All works referred to in the text are included, whether stratificational or not. Many stratificational works annotated in Fleming 1969 are not listed, however, though an effort has been made to include all works which appeared too late to be treated there. The reader is referred to that more detailed bibliography for further information.

BACH, EMMON, AND HARMS, ROBERT T.
   1968       *Universals in Linguistic Theory*. New York: Holt, Rinehart and Winston.

BEACHAM, CHARLES G., JR.
   *1968*       "The phonology and morphology of Yom." Unpublished doctoral dissertation. Hartford Seminary Foundation.

BENNETT, DAVID C.
   *1968*       "English prepositions: a stratificational approach." *Journal of Linguistics* 4.153–72.
   *1969*       *A Stratificational View of Polysemy*. Linguistic Automation Project Report, February 1969. Yale University.
   *1970*       "Spatial and temporal uses of English prepositions." Unpublished doctoral dissertation. Yale University.

BLOCH, BERNARD
   1941       "Phonemic overlapping." *American Speech* 16.278–84.
   1947       "English verb inflection." *Language* 23.399–418.
   1948       "A set of postulates for phonemic analysis." *Language* 24.3–46.

BLOOMFIELD, LEONARD
1933          *Language.* New York: Holt, Rinehart and Winston.

BOAS, FRANZ
1963          *Introduction to the Handbook of American Indian Languages.*
              Washington, D.C.: Georgetown University Press.

CHAFE, WALLACE
1968          Review of Lamb 1966d. *Language* 44.593–603.
1970          *Meaning and the Structure of Language.* Chicago: University of
              Chicago Press.

CHOMSKY, NOAM
1957          *Syntactic Structures.* The Hague: Mouton.
1964          *Current Issues in Lingusitic Theory.* The Hague: Mouton. Re-
              printed in Fodor and Katz 1964, pp. 50–118.
1965          *Aspects of the Theory of Syntax.* Cambridge, Mass.: MIT Press.
1967          "Some general properties of phonological rules." *Language*
              43.102–28.
1968          *Language and Mind.* New York: Harcourt Brace Jovanovich.

FILLMORE, CHARLES J.
1968          "The case for case." In Bach and Harms 1968, pp. 1–88.

FIRTH, J. R.
1948          "Sounds and prosodies. "*Transactions of the Philological Society*
              127–52. Reprinted in *Papers in Linguistics 1934–1951* (London:
              Oxford University Press, 1957), pp. 121–38.

FLEMING, ILAH
*1969*        "Stratificational theory: an annotated bibliography." *Journal of
              English Linguistics* 3.37–65.

FODOR, JERRY A., AND GARRETT, MERRILL
1966          "Some reflections on competence and performance." In John
              Lyons and R. J. Wales, eds., *Psycholinguistic Papers* (Chicago:
              Aldine), pp. 135–79.

FODOR, JERRY A., AND KATZ, JERROLD J., EDS.
1964          *The Structure of Language: Readings in the Philosophy of Language.*
              Englewood Cliffs, N.J.: Prentice-Hall.

GLEASON, HENRY A., JR.
*1964*        "The organization of language: a stratificational view." *Mono-
              graph Series on Languages and Linguistics* 17.75–95. Georgetown
              University Institute of Languages and Linguistics.
1965          *Linguistics and English Grammar.* New York: Holt, Rinehart and
              Winston.
*1968*        "Contrastive analysis in discourse structures." *Monograph Series
              on Languages and Linguistics* 21.39–63. Georgetown University
              Institute of Languages and Linguistics.

GREENBERG, JOSEPH
1960          *Universals of Language.* Second edition. Cambridge, Mass.:
              MIT Press.
1966          "Language universals." In Thomas A. Sebeok, ed., *Current
              Trends in Linguistics, III* (The Hague: Mouton), pp. 61–112.
              Also published as Janua Linguarum, Series Minor 59.

HAJIČOVÁ, E., AND PIŤHA, P.
1968  Review of Lamb 1966d. *Prague Bulletin of Mathematical Linguistics* 8.71–76.

HALLE, MORRIS
1959  *The Sound Pattern of Russian*. The Hague: Mouton.

HALLIDAY, M. A. K.
1961  "Categories of the theory of grammar." *Word* 17.241–92.
1967–68  "Notes on transitivity and theme in English." *Journal of Linguistics* 3.37–81, 199–244; 4.179–215.

HARRIS, ZELLIG
1951  *Methods in Structural Linguistics*. Chicago: University of Chicago Press.
1955  "From phoneme to morpheme." *Language* 31.190–222.
1957  "Co-occurrence and transformation in linguistic structure." *Language* 33.283–340. Reprinted in Fodor and Katz 1964, pp. 155–210.

HERRICK, EARL M.
1966  *A Linguistic Description of Roman Alphabets*. Hartford Studies in Linguistics, No. 19. Hartford Seminary Foundation.
1969a  "A stratificational restatement of a problem in Manyika phonology." In *Papers from the Fourth Regional Meeting of the Chicago Linguistics Society*, pp. 11–19.
1969b  "Orderedness and stratificational 'and' nodes." Paper delivered at the Annual Meeting of the Michigan Linguistic Society, October 1969.
1969c  *The Graphonomy of English*. Preliminary edition. Mimeographed.

HILL, ARCHIBALD A.
1958  *Introduction to Linguistic Structures: From Sound to Sentence in English*. New York: Harcourt Brace Jovanovich.

HILL, T.
1966  "The technique of prosodic analysis." In C. E. Bazell et al., eds., *In Memory of J. R. Firth* (London: Longmans), pp. 198–226.

HJELMSLEV, LOUIS
1961  *Prolegomena to a Theory of Language*. Translated by Francis J. Whitfield. Madison: University of Wisconsin Press.
1970  *Language: An Introduction*. Translated by Francis J. Whitfield. Madison: University of Wisconsin Press.

HOCKETT, CHARLES F.
1942  "A system of descriptive phonology." *Language* 18.3–21.
1947  "Problems of morphemic analysis." *Language* 23.321–43.
1954  "Two models of grammatical description." *Word* 10.210–34.
1955  *A Manual of Phonology*. International Journal of American Linguistics, Memoir 11.
1961  "Linguistic elements and their relations." *Language* 37.29–53.
1966  "Language, mathematics, and linguistics." In Thomas A. Sebeok, ed., *Current Trends in Linguistics, III* (The Hague: Mouton), pp. 155–304. Also published as Janua Linguarum, Series Minor 60.

| | |
|---|---|
| 1968a | Review of Lamb 1966d. *International Journal of American Linguistics* 34.145–53. |
| 1968b | *The State of the Art.* The Hague: Mouton. |

HUDDLESTON, RODNEY

| | |
|---|---|
| 1969 | Review of Lamb 1966d. *Lingua* 22.362–73. |

IKEGAMI, YOSHIHIKO

| | |
|---|---|
| 1970 | *The Semological Structure of the English Verbs of Motion: A Statificational Approach.* Tokyo: Sanseido. Seletions published as Linguistic Automation Project Report, April 1969. Yale University. |
| 1971 | "A stratificational analysis of the hand gestures in Indian classical dancing." *Semiotica* 4.365–91. |

JAKOBSON, ROMAN

| | |
|---|---|
| 1931 | "Phonemic notes on standard Slovak." In *Selected Writings, I* (The Hague: Mouton, 1962), pp. 221–30. |

JAKOBSON, ROMAN, FANT, GUNNAR, AND HALLE, MORRIS

| | |
|---|---|
| 1952 | *Preliminaries to Speech Analysis: The Distinctive Features and Their Correlates.* Cambridge, Mass.: MIT Press. |

KATZ, JERROLD J., AND FODOR, JERRY A.

| | |
|---|---|
| 1963 | "The structure of a semantic theory." *Language* 39.170–210. |

KATZ, JERROLD J., AND POSTAL, PAUL

| | |
|---|---|
| 1964 | *An Integrated Theory of Linguistic Descriptions.* Research Monograph No. 26. Cambridge, Mass.: MIT Press. |

KING, ROBERT D.

| | |
|---|---|
| 1969 | *Historical Linguistics and Generative Grammar.* Englewood Cliffs, N.J.: Prentice-Hall. |

KIPARSKY, PAUL

| | |
|---|---|
| 1968 | "Linguistic universals and linguistic change." In Bach and Harms 1968, pp. 171–202. |

LAMB, SYDNEY M.

| | |
|---|---|
| 1964a | "The sememic approach to structural semantics." *American Anthropologist* 66:3 (Pt. 2). 57–78. |
| 1964b | "On alternation, transformation, realization and stratification." *Monograph Series on Languages and Linguistics* 17.105–22. Georgetown University Institute of Languages and Linguistics. |
| 1965a | "The nature of the machine translation problem." *Journal of Verbal Learning and Verbal Behavior* 4.196–210. |
| 1965b | "Kinship terminology and linguistic structure." *American Anthropologist* 67:5 (Pt. 2). 37–64. |
| 1966a | "Linguistic structure and the production and decoding of discourse." In Edward C. Carterette, ed., *Brain Function III: Speech, Language, and Communication*, UCLA Forum in Medical Sciences, No. 4 (Berkeley: University of California Press), pp. 173–99. |
| 1966b | "Epilegomena to a theory of language." *Romance Philology* 19.531–73. |
| 1966c | "Prolegomena to a theory of phonology." *Language* 42.536–73. |
| 1966d | *Outline of Stratificational Grammar.* Revised edition. Washington, D.C.: Georgetown University Press. |
| 1967 | Review of Chomsky 1964 and 1965. *American Anthropologist* 69.411–15. |

| | |
|---|---|
| *1969a* | "Lexicology and semantics." In 'Archibald A. Hill, ed., *Linguistics Today* (New York: Basic Books), pp. 40–49. |
| *1969b* | "The stratificational treatment of *have...en* and other discontinuous morphemic realizations." Paper presented at the Annual Meeting of the Linguistic Society of America, December 1969. Abstract and handout in the meeting handbook, pp. 120–23. |
| *1971* | "Linguistic and cognitive networks." In Paul Garvin, ed., *Cognition: A Multiple View* (New York: Spartan Books), pp. 195–222. |
| IN PRESS | "Some types of ordering." In V. B. Makkai IN PRESS. |
| FORTH-COMING | "Stratificational linguistics as a basis for machine translation." In Makkai and Lockwood FORTHCOMING. |

LEECH, GEOFFREY

| | |
|---|---|
| 1970 | *Towards a Semantic Description of English.* Bloomington: Indiana University Press. |

LJUNG, MAGNUS

| | |
|---|---|
| *1965* | "Principles of a stratificational analysis of the Plains Indian sign language." *International Journal of American Linguistics* 31.119–27. |

LOCKWOOD, DAVID G.

| | |
|---|---|
| *1968* | "Two species of concord in the Czech noun phrase." Paper delivered at the Annual Meeting of the Linguistic Society of America, December 1968. |
| *1969a* | "Pronoun concord domains in English." *Linguistics* 54.70–85. |
| *1969b* | "Markedness in stratificational phonology." *Language* 45.300–08. |
| *1969c* | "Russian vowel hypophonology." Unpublished manuscript. |
| IN PRESS | "Neutralization, biuniqueness, and stratificational phonology." In V. B. Makkai IN PRESS. |
| FORTH-COMING *a* | "The problem of inflectional morphemes: a stratificational view." In Makkai and Lockwood FORTHCOMING. |
| FORTH-COMING *b* | "Replacives without process." In Makkai and Lockwood FORTHCOMING. |

LONGACRE, ROBERT E.

| | |
|---|---|
| 1960 | "String constituent analysis." *Language* 36.63–88. |
| 1964a | "Prolegomena to lexical structure." *Linguistics* 5.5–24. |
| 1964b | *Grammar Discovery Procedures: A Field Manual.* Janua Linguarum, Series Minor 33. The Hague: Mouton. |

MAKKAI, ADAM

| | |
|---|---|
| *1969a* | "The two idiomaticity areas in English and their membership." *Linguistics* 50.44-58. |
| *1969b* | "Why language is stratified." *KIVUNG, Journal of the Linguistic Society of the University of Papua and New Guinea* 2:3.16–51. |
| *1971* | *Idiom Structure in English.* The Hague: Mouton. |

MAKKAI, ADAM, AND LOCKWOOD, DAVID G., EDS.

| | |
|---|---|
| FORTH-COMING | *Readings in Stratificational Linguistics.* University: University of Alabama Press. |

MAKKAI, VALERIE BECKER

| | |
|---|---|
| *1969* | "On the correlation of morphemes and lexemes." In *Papers from* |

*the Fifth Regional Meeting of the Chicago Linguistic Society*, pp. 159–66.

IN PRESS   *Phonological Theory: Evolution and Current Practice*. New York: Holt, Rinehart and Winston.

NEWELL, LEONARD E.

*1966*   "Stratificational analysis of an English text." Appendix to Lamb 1966d, pp. 71–106.

NIDA, EUGENE

1948   "The identification of morphemes." *Language* 24.414–41.

1949   *Morphology: The Descriptive Analysis of Words*. Ann Arbor: University of Michigan Press.

1966   *A Synopsis of English Syntax*. Janua Linguarum, Series Practica 19. The Hague: Mouton.

PALMER, F. R.

1968   Review of Lamb 1966d. *Journal of Linguistics* 4.287–95.

PERLMUTTER, DAVID M.

1970   "Surface structure constraints in syntax." *Linguistic Inquiry* 2.187–250.

PIKE, KENNETH L.

1947   *Phonemics*. Ann Arbor: University of Michigan Press.

1964   "Beyond the sentence." *College Communication and Composition* 15.129–35.

1967   *Language in Relation to a Unified Theory of the Structure of Human Behavior*. Janua Linguarum, Series Maior 24. The Hague: Mouton.

POSTAL, PAUL

1968   *Aspects of Phonological Theory*. New York: Harper & Row.

REICH, PETER

*1968a*   *Competence, Performance, and Relational Networks*. Linguistic Automation Project Report, March 1968, Yale University.

*1968b*   *Symbols, Relations, and Structural Complexity*. Linguistic Automation Project Report, May 1968, Yale University.

*1969a*   "The finiteness of natural language." *Language* 45.831–43.

*1969b*   "Order in deep structure." Paper presented at the Annual Meeting of the Linguistic Society of America, December 1969.

*1970a*   "Relational networks." *Canadian Journal of Linguistics* 15.95–110.

*1970b*   "The English auxiliaries: a relational network description." *Canadian Journal of Linguistics* 16.18–50. Originally published as Linguistic Automation Project Report, November 1968. Yale University.

*1970c*   "A relational network model of language behavior." Unpublished doctoral dissertation. University of Michigan.

ROBERTS, THOMAS H.

*1968*   "Noun phrase substitutes and zero anaphora in Mandarin Chinese." Unpublished doctoral dissertation. University of Hawaii.

*1969*   "A critique of Lamb's 1966 stratified model." *Working Papers in*

*Linguistics* 1:3.29–100. Department of Linguistics, University of Hawaii.

1970    "Morphophonemics in a stratificational grammar." *Working Papers in Linguistics* 2:2.93–134. Department of Linguistics, University of Hawaii.

ROGERS, HENRY E.

1967    "The phonology and morphology of Sherbro." Unpublished doctoral dissertation. Yale University.

SAMPSON, GEOFFREY

1968    "Noun phrase indexing, pronouns, and the 'definite article.'" Paper presented at the Annual Meeting of the Linguistic Society of America, December 1968.

1970a   "On the necessity for a phonological base component." *Language* 46.586–626.

1970b   *Stratificational Grammar: A Definition and an Example.* Janua Linguarum, Series Minor 88. The Hague: Mouton.

SAPIR, EDWARD

1921    *Language: An Introduction to the Study of Speech.* New York: Harcourt Brace Jovanovich.

1925    "Sound patterns in language." *Language* 1.37–51.

SAUSSURE, FERDINAND DE

1916    *Cours de linguistique générale* (Fifth edition, Paris: Payot, 1955). Translated by Wade Baskin as *Course in General Linguistics* (New York: Philosophical Library, 1959).

STENNES, LESLIE H.

1968    "The identification of participants in Adamawa Fulani." Unpublished doctoral dissertation. Hartford Seminary Foundation.

SULLIVAN, WILLIAM J., III

1969    "A stratificational description of the phonology and inflectional morphology of Russian." Unpublished doctoral dissertation. Yale University.

1970    "Russian stress: specification and realization." Unpublished manuscript.

SWADESH, MORRIS

1934    "The phonemic principle." *Language* 10.117–29.

TABER, CHARLES R.

1966    *The Structure of Sango Narrative.* Hartford Studies in Linguistics, No. 17. Hartford Seminary Foundation.

TRAGER, G. L.

1934    "The phonemes of Russian." *Language* 10.334–44.

1955    "French verb inflection." *Language* 31.511–29.

TRAGER, G. L., AND SMITH, H. L., JR.

1951    *Outline of English Structure.* Studies in Linguistics, Occasional Paper 3.

TRUBETZKOY, N. S.

1969    *Principles of Phonology.* Translated by Christiane A. M. Baltaxe. Berkeley: University of California Press.

TWADDELL, W. F.

1935　　　　　*On Defining the Phoneme.* Language Monograph No. 16. Baltimore: Waverly Press.

ULDALL, H. J.

1957　　　　　"Outline of glossematics. Part I: General Theory." *Travaux du cercle linguistique de Copenhague* 10.1–89.

VACHEK, JOSEF

1964　　　　　*A Prague School Reader in Linguistics.* Bloomington: Indiana University Press.

1966　　　　　*The Linguistic School of Prague: An Introduction to Its Theory and Practice.* Bloomington: Indiana University Press.

WEINREICH, URIEL, LABOV, WILLIAM, AND HERZOG, MARVIN

1968　　　　　"Empirical foundations for a theory of language change." In W. P. Lehmann and Yakov Malkiel, eds., *Directions for Historical Linguistics* (Austin: University of Texas Press), pp. 95–188.

WELLS, RULON S.

1947　　　　　"Immediate constituents." *Language* 23.81–117.

WHITE, JOHN

1969a　　　　"Stratificational grammar: a new theory of language." *College Communication and Composition* 20.191–97.

1969b　　　　"Language and the brain." *Yale Alumni Magazine* December. 47–51.

*Index*

# Index

Terms proper to stratificational theory are indicated by **bold italic** type, as are terms used in a special sense by the author. Page numbers refer to the pages on which the term is defined or discussed, the linguist or his work is mentioned, or data from a given language is presented or analyzed.